21世纪国际经济与贸易专业系列教材

# International Business Contract Translation Course

# 国际商务合同翻译教程

（第四版）

兰天 屈晓鹏 编著

flight class

return date

departure date

4528

东北财经大学出版社
Dongbei University of Finance & Economics Press

大连

**图书在版编目（CIP）数据**

国际商务合同翻译教程/兰天，屈晓鹏编著．—4版．—大连：东北
财经大学出版社，2019.1（2020.12重印）
（21世纪国际经济与贸易专业系列教材）
ISBN 978-7-5654-3405-1

Ⅰ.国…　Ⅱ.①兰…②屈…　Ⅲ.国际贸易-贸易合同-英语-翻译-高
等学校-教材　Ⅳ.①F740.4②D996.1

中国版本图书馆CIP数据核字（2019）第002624号

东北财经大学出版社出版

（大连市黑石礁尖山街217号　邮政编码　116025）

网　　址：http：//www.dufep.cn

读者信箱：dufep@dufe.edu.cn

大连永盛印业有限公司印刷　　　　东北财经大学出版社发行

幅面尺寸：170mm×240mm　字数：434千字　印张：20.25　插页：1

2019年1月第4版　　　　　　　2020年12月第7次印刷

责任编辑：李　彬　刘东威　　　　　　责任校对：孟佳威

封面设计：冀贵收　　　　　　　　　　版式设计：钟福建

定价：42.00元

# 21世纪国际经济与贸易专业系列教材编委会

**主 任**

李东阳　教授，博士生导师

阙澄宇　教授，博士生导师

郭连成　教授，博士生导师

**副主任**

王绍媛　姜文学

**委员（以姓氏笔画为序）**

邓立立　王国红　兰　天　孙玉红

田玉红　叶富国　李　虹　李艳丽

李勤昌　杜晓郁　苏　杭　范　超

施锦芳　党　伟　黄海东　鄂立彬

# 总　　序

国际经贸活动是在原始社会末期和奴隶社会初期随着阶级和国家的出现而产生的，但直至资本主义生产方式确立后才获得了广泛的发展，才真正具有了世界性。对国际经贸活动的系统研究始于15世纪的重商主义学派，至今已形成涉及领域广泛、结构完整的学科知识体系。

与一国国内经济不同，国际经贸活动要涉及两个或两个以上国家（或地区）的当事人，而全球范围内又不存在一个超国家的权力机构对这些活动进行规范和管理，因此，国际经贸活动的习惯做法及各种规则往往是先发国家国内做法和规则的延伸，由此决定了先发国家和后发国家在国际经贸人才培养方面的差异：先发国家由于国内外经贸活动的做法和规则差异不大，因此很少专门设立国际经贸类专业，而是将其内容分散在相关专业的课程中进行介绍；后发国家由于国内外经贸活动的做法和规则差异很大，因此往往专门设立国际经贸类专业。

中华人民共和国成立后，在计划经济体制下，国际经贸本科层次人才的培养主要集中在少数几个财经类院校。改革开放以后，国内各类高校在本科层次纷纷设立了名称各异的外经贸相关专业或方向，包括对外贸易、国际贸易、国际经济、世界经济、国际经济合作、工业外贸等。1993年，国家教委印发了《普通高等学校本科专业目录》，将国际经贸本科层次专业规范为3个，即经济学学科门类下的"国际经济"专业和"国际贸易"专业、工学学科门类下的"工业外贸"专业。2012年《普通高等学校本科专业目录》中，"国际经济与贸易"专业没有调整，是经济学学科门类下的"经济与贸易类"专业之一。

最先在国家（或地区）之间发生的经贸活动是货物贸易，它至今仍是国际经贸领域的重要内容。关于国际货物贸易的教学与研究起步早，成果多，课程体系完整，主要包括理论、实务与惯例、专业外语三类课程。随着国际经贸活动领域的不断拓展，国际经贸类专业的课程体系也随之完善，增加了诸如"国际技术贸易""国际经济合作""国际投资""国际服务贸易""国际物流"等课程，国内部分院校还基于这些领域设立了专业方向，细化了课程体系。

21世纪是一个催人奋进的时代，科技革命迅猛发展，知识更替日新月异，国际竞争日趋激烈。

从国际经济环境看，跨国投资飞速发展，世界各国和地区间的经济依赖程度不断加深，经济全球化和区域经济一体化趋势不断加强，国际经济协调日显重要，经济集团内部以及经济集团之间的合作与竞争日益成为关注的焦点。

从国内经济环境看，社会主义市场经济体制的建立与不断完善改善了我国企业参与国际竞争的条件，加入世界贸易组织承诺的逐步履行、我国产业结构和贸易结构的调整也为我国企业参与国际竞争提供了机遇和挑战。

为了培养熟悉国际经济运行规则、符合社会主义市场经济建设需要的人才，优化人才的知识结构，我们组织东北财经大学国际经济贸易学院的专业骨干教师编写了"21世纪国际经济与贸易专业系列教材"。这套教材在保留原有教材体系优点的同时，结合教师多年教学的经验，尽可能地反映本学科领域最新的研究成果和发展趋势。

我们深知，教材从编写出来的那一天起就已经"过时"了，这就需要教师在讲授过程中不断充实、调整有关授课内容，我们也将根据国内外经济环境的变化适时修订本系列教材。为了便于读者深入理解相关知识和在教材更新期间及时更新信息，我们在部分教材（尤其是理论类教材）中设计了"延伸阅读"栏目，提供相关章节的主要数据来源和建议阅读的书目。

本系列教材是专门为国际经济与贸易专业本科生课程编写的，同时也适合于其他经济类专业和有兴趣学习、更新国际经济与贸易知识的人士使用。

由于作者学识和资料所限，本系列教材难免有不足之处，敬请广大读者批评指正。

21世纪国际经济与贸易专业系列教材编委会

# 第四版前言

　　《国际商务合同翻译教程》第四版是在第三版的基础上，由作者兰天、屈晓鹏又一次成功合作的结果。第四版历时五年完成，吸取了作者在各自教学和国际商务合同实践工作中的宝贵经验。感谢广大读者和同学们十几年来对这本书的喜爱和支持，我们一直在努力，就是为了能编写出更成熟、更实用的国际商务英语合同翻译的教材。

　　第四版沿用了第三版的整体架构，即第一部分基础篇和第二部分实践篇。在基础篇中，作者补充了一些基础知识点，包括对特殊法律条文的讲解，法律专用词汇的添加，法律词汇的辨析和应用例句等。在实践篇中，删除了几份相对过时的商务合同，增加了从业务角度来看条款设计得细致和全面的包销合同，还有参考性较强的实习合同等。

　　本教材主要适用于外经、外贸以及法学专业高校师生、涉外企业管理人员、涉外律师及司法人员、涉外合同的谈判人员、翻译工作者以及其他从事国际商务交流的人士；同时，教材的编写和设计还针对在校的具有英语四级水平以上的各专业本科或硕士学生或具有相当英语水平的其他专业人员，旨在提高他们英语合同及其法律文件起草与翻译的基本技能和业务水平。

　　由于作者水平有限，书中难免出现纰漏，敬请读者批评指正。

编著者

2018年岁末

# 第三版前言

　　《国际商务合同翻译教程》（第三版）的问世，要感谢广大读者多年来不弃不离的支持和鼓励，要感谢我的学生们给予我丰富和精炼合同翻译教学经验的热情，更要感谢的一个人是屈晓鹏。作为我多年前的硕士研究生，他以勤奋、好学的研究精神和认真、严谨的敬业态度在其跨国国际商务合约的工作领域取得了令人欣慰的成绩。由于有了他的支持和帮助，才有了读者看到的第三版。

　　第三版仍然沿袭了第二版两大部分的构架，即第一部分基础篇和第二部分实践篇。第三版在保留了前两版精华的基础上，在实践篇中更是吸纳了屈晓鹏从事国际商务合同谈判和制定的宝贵经验，添加了六份操作性强、实效性高的国际商务合同，其中包括三方合作协议、第三方监管账户协议、保密协议、目前比较通用的雇佣合同和广为各进出口公司采用的货物买卖合同等。相比前两版，第三版的基础篇内容更加充实和完整，其中包括对合同结构的更为精细的剖析和归纳，并添加了对Incoterms 2010国际贸易术语的介绍。书中还补充和完善了原有的一些注释，并添加了一些词汇。为了便于读者的记忆和查询，书后还配置了索引。

　　本教材主要适用于高校外经外贸及法学专业师生、涉外企业管理人员及司法人员、涉外合同的谈判人员、翻译工作者以及其他从事国际商务交流的人士；同时，教材的编写和设计还针对在校的具有英语四级水平以上的各专业本科或研究生学生或具有相当英语水平的其他专业人员，旨在提高英语合同及其法律文件的起草与翻译的基本技能，以及专业写作和翻译水平。

　　由于编著者水平有限，书中难免出现纰漏，敬请业内人士和读者朋友批评指正。

编著者

2013年岁末

# 目　　录

## Part One　基础篇　Learning Basics

# Part One

# 基础篇

# Learning Basics

# Unit One /国际商务合同的基础知识

# Basic Knowledge of International Business Contracts

## 1.1    合同的基本概念 Basic Concept of Contracts

合同和契约都是指自愿订立的共同遵守的条件。《中华人民共和国合同法》第2条规定"合同是平等主体的自然人、法人、其他组织之间设立、变更、终止民事权利义务关系的协议"（Contracts referred to in this Law the agreements between equal natural persons, legal persons and other organizations for the purpose of establishing, altering and terminating mutual civil rights and obligations）。

根据这个定义，我们可以了解一般合同的法律特征：

（1）合同是一种法律行为。这是指当事人之间为实现一定的目的，而产生的一定的权利义务关系，而且这种权利义务关系受国家强制力的保护，任何一方不履行合同或不完全履行合同，都要承担法律责任。

（2）合同是合法的法律行为。双方当事人按照法律规范的要求达成的协议，产生双方所预期的法律后果，它是一种合法行为，因而为国家所承认和保护。

（3）合同是双方或多方当事人之间的协议。这并不是讲当事人之间的任何协议都是合同，它只是当事人之间关于设立、变更、终止民事权利义务关系的协议。

（4）合同是当事人在平等、自愿的基础上所进行的民事法律行为。这是合同法律关系同建立在领导与被领导、命令与服从基础上的行政关系的根本区别。

## 1.2    合同的分类 Classifications of Contracts

狭义的合同包括合同（contract）和协议（agreement）。

广义的合同包括合同、协议，以及订立正式合同、协议之前当事人之间已经达成的有约束力的法律文件，包括但不限于谅解备忘录（memorandum of understanding, MOU）、合作备忘录（memorandum of cooperation）或者框架性协议（framework agreement）、意向性协议（agreement of intent）或合作意向书（letter of agreement for cooperation）、意向书（letter of intent, LOI）、初步协议（preliminary agreement）、君子协议（gentlemen's agreement）、订单（order）和章程（articles of association/incorporation）等。

## 1.3　国际商务合同的特征
## Main Features of International Business Contracts

国际商务合同是我国和外国平等主体的自然人、法人、其他经济组织之间设立、变更、终止民事权利义务关系的协议。它依法成立，受国家法律保护和管辖，对签约各方均有法律约束力。合同一经签订，各方必须严格执行。对于一国而言，国际商务合同也常称为涉外合同。中国的涉外合同具有以下特点：

（1）合同的主体一方或双方不具有中国国籍，如中国某公司与外国某公司订立买卖合同，进口外国的货物。

（2）合同的客体位于中国境外或者超过中国国境，如中国某进出口公司与境外某公司签订买卖合同，其标的物从国外进口。

（3）合同的某种法律事实发生于中国境外，如中国某公司与外国某企业在国外签订合资经营合同。

涉外合同的当事人可以选择合同适用的法律，这是"意思自治原则"在涉外合同的法律适用上的体现。

## 1.4　国际商务合同的种类
## Categories of International Business Contracts

我国国际商务合同的种类，根据当事人之间权利和义务关系的不同，主要可作如下分类：

（1）国际货物买卖合同，即售货确认书/售货合同（Sales Confirmation/Sales Contract）和购货确认书/购货合同（Purchase Confirmation/ Contract for Purchase）。

（2）代理合同，主要有独家代理协议（Sole Agency Agreement）、独家经销协议（Sole Distributorship Agreement）、包销协议（Exclusive Sales Agreement）以及货运代理合同（Forwarding Agency Agreement）。

（3）形象代言协议（Endorsement Agreement）。

（4）融资租赁协议（Finance Lease Agreement）、经营租赁合同（Contract of Operating Lease），租赁协议（Tenancy Agreement）和国际租赁合同（Contract for International Leasing）。

（5）合资经营企业合同（Joint Venture Contract），合作经营企业合同（Cooperative Joint Venture Contract）和合作协议（Co-operation Agreement）。

（6）劳务合同（Labor Service Contract）。

（7）国际技术咨询服务合同（International Technical Consultancy Service Contract）、技术转让和设备材料进口合同（Contract for Technology Transfer and

Importation of Equipment and Materials）、技术转让和技术援助合同（Technology Transfer and Technical Assistance Agreement）以及咨询协议（Consulting Agreement）。

（8）国际借贷协议（International Loan Agreement）。

（9）土木建筑工程承包合同（Contract for International Works or Civil Engineering Construction）。

（10）外包协议（Outsourcing Agreement）。

（11）服务协议（Service Agreement）。

（12）协作协议/合作协议（Collaboration Agreement）、三方合作协议（Tripartite Cooperation Agreement）.

（13）商标特许（许可）协议（Trademark License Agreement）。

（14）风险资本管理协议（Venture Capital Management Agreement）。

（15）股权转让协议（Share Transfer Agreement）。

（16）第三方支付协议/第三方监管账户协议（Escrow Agreement）。

（17）保密协议（Nondisclosure Agreement / Secrecy Agreement / Agreement of Confidentiality）。

# Unit Two /国际商务合同的语言特征

# Language Features in the International Business Contracts

---

## 2.1 　　　　使用正式的法律用词 Big Words Used

---

重要的国际商务合同，由于是依法成立的具有法律约束力的文件，所以合同的草拟者要习惯采用书面的形式，使用法律词汇，以显示合同的正规、庄严、准确、规范以及威严的语言特色。

In convening a general meeting of shareholders, notice shall be dispatched to shareholders.

要召开一次股东大会，须将通知发给各股东。

句中的 convene（召开）和 dispatch（分发）为大字眼，即合同的正式用词。convene 比 hold 和 assemble 要正式，dispatch 比 spread out 和 hand out 要正式。

The work shall be performed in accordance with the provisions of the Contract.

工程须按照合同条款规定进行。

in accordance with 在合同等法律文件中常用，比 according to 要正式。

The accounting principles employed shall be the same as those applied in preceding years.

所使用的会计原则要与以往各年的会计原则相一致。

employ 在合同中是个大字眼，比 use 要正式得多。

It hereby covenants that the Consignee guarantees the payment of all bills and accounts for goods.

兹订立契约，代销人保证付清货物的一切票据及账款。

covenant 是法律用词，表示签订有法律约束力的正式合约。

Except AAA's prior written consent, no party shall enter in or assume any mortgage.

除非经甲方事先书面同意，任何一方不得参加或承担任何抵押。

consent 作名词，在合同中表示"同意"替代常用词 agreement。

This Agreement shall supersede all previous commitments.

本协议将取代以前的一切承诺。

在这个句子中，有两个大字眼，supersede 和 commitments。supersede（替代）

比 take the place of 要正式，commitments 表示"承诺"，比 promise 要正式。

The Licensee shall not dispute or object to the validity of said Letters Patent.

许可证受证人不应对所述专利证书的有效性提出争议或异议。

object 在合同中应翻译成"反对"或"异议"。在普通文书中"反对"可以用 disagree 表示。

The Principal shall be obliged to pay the commissions to the Sales Agent.

委托人应对经销代理商负有支付手续费的义务。

oblige（迫使、责成）是个典型的法律用词，替代 have the responsibility to do sth.或 be compelled to do sth.

If any of the terms or conditions of this Agreement is substantially breached by either Party, the other Party shall have the right to terminate this Agreement.

如果当事人任何一方实质上破坏了本协议中所签订的条款或条件，那么另一方有权终止该协议。

terminate（终止）在法律文书中替代 stop。

The first annual royalty period shall commence with the date of execution hereof.

第一年租赁期应从本协议签署之日开始。

Party A shall repatriate the patient to China and bear the cost of his passage to Beijing.

甲方应将病人遣返中国，负担他返回北京的旅费。

与 send back 相比，repatriate 是正式的书面用语。

## 2.2　同义词使用 Synonyms Used

### 2.2.1　同义词连用 Series Synonyms Used

在写作法律文件时，对一些关键性的词常常采用同义词连用。这主要是为了克服由于许多英语单词具有一词多义的特点，而在句子中可能发生意思不明，合同双方可能按自己的意图来理解。为了确保所用词不被曲解，采用同义词连用，如双词式（doublets）、对句（couplets）和三词并列（triplets）等形式，以保证内容准确，使合同具有周密、严谨的特色，以减少漏洞和争议，维护法律文件的独解性尊严。这种用法在法律文书上通常被称为赘述（tautology）。

This agreement is made and entered into by and between Party A and Party B.

在句中 made and entered into 是一组同义词，表示"签订协议"。by and between 是另一对同义词，表示由甲方和乙方签署。

Nothing contained in this Agreement shall be deemed to obligate Seller to permit Buyer to examine any patent application of Seller otherwise than upon a secret and confidential basis and upon the written request of Buyer.

除了在保守机密的情况下和买方书面要求以外，本协议并未谈到责成卖方允许买方对卖方的专利申请书加以检查。

Change in the Work shall mean any modification of, amendment of/to, or alteration in the Work.

工程的改变应指在工程的任何变更、修订或更换。

modifcation of、amendment of/to 和 alteration in 在句中是三个同义短语。

The Contractor shall always have the sole responsibility for the due and proper execution and performance of all of its rights and obligations under the Contract.

根据该合同规定，承包商的唯一职责就是要如期严格地执行和履行其全部的权利和义务。

在句中，execution 和 performance 是同义词。

Any such consent shall not relieve the Contractor from any liability and obligation under this Contract.

任何此类同意均不应解除合同规定的承包人的责任与义务。

liability 和 obligation 在句中是同义词。

This Agreement, and all rights vested in the Second Party, shall forthwith become null and void, if the Second Party shall violate, or omit to perform, any of the following terms and conditions.

如乙方违反或忘记执行以下条款及条件，则本协议及赋予乙方之所有权利，将立即失效。

在句中，null 和 void 是一对同义词，terms 和 conditions 是另一组同义词。

常见的合同中法律配对词或三联词即我们所理解的同义词和短语有：

1.acknowledge and agree 确认并同意

The Parties acknowledge and agree that Joint Venture Company shall be formed forthwith upon satisfaction of the following condition.

各方确认并同意在下列条件得到满足时立即创办合资公司。

2.authorise and grant 授权与授予

You are authorized and granted exclusive authority to conduct an absolute auction sale.

兹授权于你，并授予你完全的拍卖独家经营之权。

3.cease and terminate 取消与终止

Any and all obligations of the Company to the Operator under this Agreement shall immediately cease and terminate upon payment of the Company's dues.

公司对经营者的一切合同义务在公司付款后，应立即予以取消与终止。

4.each or any 各自的

The Guarantor hereby coverants that the Creditors, and each or any of them, may extend the time of payment.

保证人特此放弃约定，债权人中的每个人或任何人都可以延期支付。

5.each and every 每一个

The Borrowers agree to repay the loan to the Lender by paying（amount）on the first day of each and every following month，after the date hereof.

借款人同意在本文规定的日期以后的每月第一日付款（总额），以偿还贷款人的贷款。

6.fair and equitable 公平和公正

Fair and equitable treatment has become one of the most controversial clauses in international investment agreements.

国际投资协定中的公平和公正待遇目前已成为最具争议性的条款之一。

7.final and conclusive 决定性的和结论性的

Acceptance of the Work by the Owner shall be final and conclusive except as regards latent defects.

除了关于潜在的缺陷以外，业主验收的工程应是决定性的与结论性的。

8.force and effect 生效

This Agreement shall commence on（date）and shall continue in full force and effect until（date）.

本协议应从（……）日开始，而且直到（……）日为止，都应继续生效。

9.fraud and deception 欺骗

If a sale has been made through fraud or deception，the Sales Company shall retain an amount equal to the commission paid out to the salesman.

假如交易是由于欺骗成交的，则销售公司应保留一笔款项，这笔款项相当于已支付给推销员的佣金。

10.free and clear 免除……

The Consignee shall keep the consigned goods free and clear of all taxes.

承销人应使所承销的货物免除一切税金。

11.keep，observe and perform 坚持、遵守并执行

The Second Party shall keep，observe and perform all of the terms，provisions，covenants and conditions of this Agreement.

乙方应该忠实地坚持、遵守并执行本协议的各项条款、规定、契约及条件。

12.remise，release and quitclaim 出让、让与并放弃

The First Party remised，released，and forever quitclaimed to the Second Party all the right，claim and demand of the First Party in and to the following described property.

对下述财产，甲方愿立契出让，让与并永远放弃对乙方的一切权利和要求。

13.right，interest and title 权利、利益和权益

AAA represents that it is the owner of the entire right，title and interest in and to（country）Letters Patent No.（…）.

甲方表示，它是（某国）（……）号专利证书的全部权利、利益与权益的所有者。

14.save and except 除……之外

No share in the capital stock of the Joint Venture Company can in any way be assigned save and except for directors' qualifying shares.

除董事的资格股外，合资公司的资本股概不能转让。

15.sole and exclusive 独家的

The Author hereby grants and assigns to the Publisher the sole and exclusive right to publish in book from a work now entitled….

为此，作者指定并授予该出版商以唯一的独家权利，用书籍的形式出版现名为……的这本书。

同义词在英语中为数不少，在合同英语中也时常出现，但翻译时必须作出正确选择。否则，如果同义词选用不当，轻者会影响双方的权利义务，重者可能造成履约争议。

除了上述列举的词语外，还有以下常见的组合：

acknowledgement and acceptance 承认

affect or prejudice 影响

agree and covenant 同意，约定

agree and undertake 同意，承担

aid and abet 同谋

annul and set aside 废止，取消

any and all 如何，所有

assign and transfer 转让

authorize and empower 授权

bind and obligate 约束

cease and desist 制止

construe and interpret 解释

duties，obligations or liabilities 义务和责任

each and all 每一个

entered into and concluded 订立

entirely and completely 完全地

examine and certify 检验

fair and equitable 公允

false and untrue 虚假和不真实

fit and proper 适当地

for and in consideration of…作为……对价，考虑到……

force and effect 效力

full faith and credit 完全诚信

give，devise and bequeath 遗赠

give and grant 授予

hold and have 拥有并持有

in lieu of and in place of 替代

in relation to or in connection with 与……有关

in truth and fact 真实

knowledge and belief 获悉，了解

legal and valid 合法有效

ownership and title 所有权

part and parcel 部分

pay，meet and discharge 偿还，支付

represent and warrant 声明并保证

set forth and prescribe 规定

supersede and replace 替代

release and discharge 解除

theirs heirs，successors，and assigns 继承人

rest，residue and remainder 剩余

vague，nonspecific and indefinite 模糊，不确定

will and testament 书面遗嘱

withdraw and rescind 取消

### 2.2.2　考虑单词的内涵 Considering the Connotation

在进行汉译英合同翻译时，如遇到具有同义词特征的关键词现象，要了解同义词在表现出共性的同时，还会体现出它们的个性。因此，就要求译者深入细致地研究其本质的区别，选出最恰当的单词。

改进和开发的技术，其所有权属于改进和开发一方。

"属于"是该句的关键词，可选择的同义词有 own，possess 和 belong。

The improved and developed technology shall be owned by the party who has improved and developed the technology.

The ownership of any improved and developed technology shall belong to the party who has improved and developed the technology.

合同在有效期内，任一方对合同产品涉及的技术如有改进和发展，都应免费将改进和发展的技术提供给对方使用。技术所有权归改建和发展技术的一方所有。

"提供"是该句的关键词，可选择的同义词有 supply，offer 和 provide。这几个词都有"提供"的意思。supply 和 offer 较为随意，不太适合法律文书的严肃表达；

而 provide 表示 to give sb. sth. free of charge，非常贴近例句的用意。

Within the validity term of the Contract，both parties shall provide each other with the improvement and development of the technology related to the Contract Products free of charge.

A deduction of … per day will be made for every calendar day after the above completion date if the Contract is not completed in every detail.

如果没有在每个细节上完成合同，那么，就应按上述完工日期期满后的每一日历日计算，每天扣除……美元。

在句中，"完成"是关键词，与 completion 相关的同义词有 finish，但 completion 是合同用词。

## 2.2.3 考虑语法要求 Considering the Grammar

有些英语同义词的选择，是由句子的结构和搭配所要求的，这时译者应认真研究这些同义词的搭配关系，避免出现句法搭配上的错误。

承包商必须遵守和服从与该工程有关的一切适当的法律、规章和条例。

上述句子中的"遵守"一词，英语中有 observe，obey，abide by 和 comply with 等，在选择表示"遵守"的词汇时，应根据句子的搭配关系进行选择。由于句子中的主语是合同的当事方，因此选择 observe 和 abide by，全句可译为：

The Contractor shall observe and abide by all applicable laws，rules and regulations in connection with the Work.

合资经营企业的一切活动应遵守中华人民共和国法律。由于句子的主语是 activities，在翻译成汉语时就要选择 comply with，表示 to act in accordance with a provision，rule 或 demand。全句可译为：

All the activities of a joint venture shall comply with the provision of laws，decree and pertinent regulations of the People's Republic of China.

再如，合同经常出现的"由于"，在英语中，常用 due to，owing to，in view of，because of，considering，in consideration 一组短语来表示。请比较下列句子：

a. The Landlord shall not be liable for any failure to supply such heat，water，or electricity，not due to gross negligence on its part.

如果不是因为房主方面的重大疏忽，房主对于不能供应暖气、水、电不负责任。

b. His failure is due to causes beyond the control of Area Franchisee such as strike，weather，etc.

他的失误是由于地域加盟商所无法控制的原因，例如罢工、天气骤变等等所造成的。

在句子 a 和 b 中，由 due to 引出的短语均属形容词性质，分别在句中作定语和表语，一般不引出状语。引出状语的，表示"由于"的短语往往选用 because of 和

owing to。

A tender price offered by a tender shall remain unchanged during the performance of the Contract，and shall not be modified because of any reasons. According to Clause 24 of the Notice，tender documents containing any adjustable prices will be rejected as non-responsive tenders.

投标人所报的投标价在合同执行过程中是固定不变的，不得以任何理由予以变更。根据本须知第24条的规定，以可调整的价格提交的投标文件将作为非响应性投标而予以拒绝。

Neither the Seller nor the Buyer shall be held responsible for late delivery or non-delivery owing to generally recognized "Force Majeure" causes.

由于一般公认的"人力不可抗拒"原因而延迟交货或不能交货，卖方或买方都不负责任。

### 2.2.4  考虑合同的文体 Considering the Writing Style

合同英语属于条法英语，其文件的基本要求是用词规范、正式，符合约定俗成的含义。

在选择同义词时，译者应充分考虑合同文本的特点，选择符合合同文体的正式和规范的词汇，避免在文字选择上的随意性。

例如：

如果我们认为有此必要，那么，我们对建议的任何部分保留修改的权利。

译文：

We reserve the right to revise any part of this proposal，if we deem it necessary to do so.

条款中的"有权"，英文合同中大多选用 to have the right to 或 keep the right，但该句选用 reserve the right to do sth. 比前两种表达更正式，因为 reserve 本身就属条法英语中的专用词汇，表示 to have a specified power of right in law。比如，我们经常看到的"版权所有"，用英语表达就是 All Rights Reserved.

不管什么情况都不能要求销售代理商维修陈列室。

原译文：

The Sales Agent shall，under no circumstances，be asked to maintain a showroom.

在译文中的 ask 应换为 require 或 request，ask 和 require 还有 request 的意思虽然都是"要求"，但 require 和 request 更正式。

卖方应立刻支付这些余额的全部。

原译文：

Seller shall immediately make full payment of the balance.

在句中，"马上"应该选择 forthwith，因为 forthwith 是公文体，比 immediately 或 at once 要正规、严谨。

未经委托人事先书面许可，本协议不允许经销代理人转让。

句中的"转让"一词，一般情况下多数译者会选用 transfer，但 assign /
assignment 是正式的法律文体词，表示 to transfer property，rights to sb. in accordance
with laws；而 transfer/transference 仅表示 to hand over the possession of property，etc.
因此，本句可译为：

This Agreement shall not be assigned by the Sales Agent without the Principal's prior
written consent.

## 2.3　选词准确 Picking up the Right Words

### 2.3.1　一词多义的处理 Words with Multi-interpretations

在合同英语中，一词多义或一义多词的现象较为普遍，要透彻理解这些词义，
必须结合上下文，仔细推敲。合同文体具有很强的逻辑性，词与词之间、段与段之
间、条款与条款之间总是相互依存、相互制约的。在翻译时，绝对不能孤立地、片
面地和静止地去理解条款中的词义，应全面地、客观地去理解和选择词义。

1.根据词性确定词义 Considering the Part of Speech

英语中有许多书写形式相同的词，却有着不同的词性，而词性不同，意义也有
所差异，因此，在翻译时首先要判定这个词在原文中的词性，根据词性再进一步确
定其词义。

Unless the claims are fully paid，ZZZ shall not be discharged from the liabilities.

除非这笔债款全部清偿，否则，乙方不能免除承担该债务。

Subject as hereinafter provided，the Lay time allowed to Buyer for discharging a
Cargo shall be seventy - two （72） running hours after the arrival of the vessel at the
discharge port including Sundays and holidays.

在下列所列条件下，每船卸货时间为船舶抵港后72小时，含星期日和节假日。

The invalidation，cancellation or discharge of a contract does not impair the validity
of the contract provision concerning the method of dispute resolution，which exists
independently in the contract.

合同无效、被撤销或解除，不影响合同中独立存在的有关解决争议方法的条款
的效力。

Routine duties of the Joint Venture Company are to be discharged by the general
manager appointed by the Board of Directors.

董事会任命的总经理，负责履行合资公司的日常职权。

以上四个句子都含有 discharge，在不同的合同条款中，其词义也有很大的不
同。第一个句子的 discharge 是动词，词义为"免除"；第二个句子的 discharge 也是
动词，表示"卸货"；第三个句子的 discharge 是名词，意思为"合约的解除"；第

四个句子的 discharge 是动词，意思为"履行"。

2.根据行业来确定词义 Considering the Profession

合同英语中会涉及各类不同的行业，行业不同，某些词语的词义也就需要相应地调整。因此，根据不同的行业来确定词义也是重要的选词手段。

All the rights and interests of the Salesman shall cease and/or terminate upon his breach of any of the preceding Articles.

在违反上述任何条款时，应停止和/或终止推销员的所有权利与利益。

句中的 interest 在商务中有"利益"的含义。

Should either Joint Venture fail to pay the contribution on schedule according to Clause 5, the default party should pay the other 10% interest one month after the deadline.

如果合资一方未能按本合同第5条规定按期付款，违约方应在逾期1个月后付给另一方10%的利息。

句中的 interest 在银行业务中表示"利息"。

Loss of or damage to any fixed or movable object or property or other thing or interest whichever, other than the Vessel, arising from any cause whichsoever in so far as such loss or damage is not covered by Clause 17.

除了船舶以外的任何固定或可移动物体或财产或其他物品或无论何种被保险标的物的灭失或损害，此种灭失或损害是由于除第17条承保之外的任何其他原因所致。

句中的 interest 在保险业务中指"保险标的物"。

3.根据词的搭配关系确定词义 Considering the Collocation

搭配关系，是指一个词与另一个词连用而产生意义上的联系。一个词单独存在时是一个意思，但与其他词搭配使用就可能产生不同的词义，因此，在确定和选择词义时，还必须考虑词与词的搭配关系。

In case of late delivery or non-delivery due to Force Majeure, the time of shipment might be duly extended, or alternatively a part or whole of this contract might be cancelled, but the Seller shall advise the Buyer of the occurrence mentioned above and send to the Buyer for its acceptance a certificate issued by the surveying institute where the accident occurs as evidence thereof within 14 days.

一旦发生不可抗力造成迟延交货或不能交货，卖方可延长交货时间或者解除合同的部分或全部，但卖方必须在14天内通知买方并提交买方可接受的公证机构出具的不可抗力事件的证明。

句中含有 case 的介词短语 in case of，其含义为"假使""如果"，引出状语。

This Clause 9 shall in no case extend or be deemed to extend to any sum which the Assured may become liable to pay or shall pay for or in respect of。

在任何情况下，本第9条皆不扩展或视为扩展承保被保险人可能有责任或应支付的任何金额。

　　句子含有 case 的介词短语 in no case，意思是"决不"，具有副词性质，用作状语。

No claim under this Clause 11 shall in any case be allowed where the loss was not incurred to avoid or in connection with the avoidance of a peril insured against.

　　如果损失不是为避免承保风险而发生或与之有关，根据本第11条提出的索赔在任何情况下均不予认可。

　　句子含有 case 的介词短语 in any case，意思是"无论如何"，具有副词性质，在句中作状语。

In the case of dangerous and/or poisonous cargo（es），the Seller shall be obliged to take care to ensure that the nature and the generally adopted symbol shall be marked conspicuously on each package.

　　如系危险及/或有毒货物，卖方负责保证在每件货物包装上明显地标明货物的性质说明及习惯上被接受的标记。

　　句子中含有 case 的介词短语 in the case of 表示"假使""如果"。

The method of payment shall in all cases be determined by the sales company.

　　在所有情况下，付款方式应由销售公司决定。

　　句中含有 case 的介词短语 in all cases，意思是"在所有情况下"。

### 2.3.2　易混淆的词 Easily-confused Words

　　国际商务合同中还有一些易混淆的词，这些词中有的书写虽基本相同，内容却有很大区别；有的可以表达同一概念，但使用场合有区别；还有的词语由于发生变形，产生了权利、义务的改变等。

　　1.注意书写基本近似，但意义不同的词 Attention to Meaning

　　在英语合同中，有许多词书写上基本相同，但在内容上却存在较大差异，特别是一些短语，更换一个介词或添加一个冠词，其内容就会有很大的不同。

The buyers are requested always to quote the number of this sales confirmation in the Letter of Credit to be opened in favor of the Sellers.

　　买方开给卖方的信用证上请填注本确认书号码。

　　句中的短语 in favor of sb.意思是"以……为受益人"或"有利于……"。

The quality of the goods in the previous contract was much in favor on the European Continent.

　　上次合同中的货物质量在欧洲大陆颇受好评。

　　短语 in favor 在这个句子中表示"受欢迎""受好评"。

In the event we are not favored with the award of the Contract，this proposal shall be returned to us forthwith.

　　如果我们不接受合同的仲裁裁决，要立即将申请书归还我们。

在句中短语 be favored with 表示"支持"或"赞同"。

在英语合同中，还有一种现象，就是有些名词的词形变化也是容易被混淆的。比如，名词 damage 表示"损失，破坏"的时候，是不可数名词；而 damages 作为复数名词却具有了法律含义，表示"赔偿金"。

另外，damage 作为名词，与 injure 的区别是：damage 用在财产受损方面，而 injury 是指人格权受损方面。

The heavy rain didn't do much damage to the crops.

这次暴风雨没有对农作物造成很大的损失。

The great damage to property has been caused by the force majeure.

不可抗力已造成财产损失。

The court ordered Party A to pay $10,020 damages to Party B for the loss sustained.

法院裁令甲方对乙方所遭受的损失支付 10,200 美元的赔偿金。

**2.注意同一概念但表达不同权利、义务关系的词 Attention to the Relation**

英语合同中的某些单词，单独看，其概念是一致的，但在条款的具体应用中，其表现的权利、义务关系和用词的规范与否是不同的。

The prices quoted above do not include any taxes, duties, impost and any other charges of any kind which may be levied in (countries).

以上所报的价格并不包括（在某国）所征收的各种税款、关税、进口税以及其他各种费用。

该句中除了 taxes 外，还有两个单词都表示"税"，即 duty 和 impost。其中 duty 主要强调 the tax imposed by a government on merchandise imported from another country，可理解为"关税"；impost 纯粹表示"进口税"，但不一定是通过海关征收的税。

The Contract Price set forth in this Contract shall not include any withholding tariff and any charges imposed on the Contractor by the government in (countries).

本合同中规定的合同价格，不应包括（某国）政府向承包商征收的扣缴关税和任何费用。

前句中的 duty 和本句中的 tariff 有本质的区别。duty 表示 tax to be paid for importing；而 tariff 除表示 tax to be paid for importing 外，还可以表示 tax to be paid for exporting。所以，在翻译 tariff 时，一般应结合上下文。

The China Corporation shall bear all relevant taxes and levies imposed upon the personnel by the Chinese Government, whereas the Employer shall bear the same imposed upon the personnel by the Government of the Project-host Country.

中国公司应负责缴纳中国政府对人员所征收的一切税金，雇主应负责缴纳项目所在国政府对人员所征缴的一切税金。

句中有两个有关"税金"的单词，即 taxes 和 levies。其中 tax 在表示"税"时，主要强调 money taken compulsorily by the government or by an official body to pay for government services；levy 作为名词，主要表示一种"征税"的行为，即 money which is demanded and collected by the government or by an agency or by an official body。因此，句中的 taxes and levies 被统译为中国政府和项目所在国政府所征收的"一切税金"。

3.注意表达不同法律关系但意义近似的词 Attention to the Legal Expressions

某些表达当事人法律关系的汉语词或其近义词在不同的上下文中，其内涵不尽相同。把这些词译成英语时，必须认真研究分析，必要时应对合同中当事人约定的权利、义务条件进行比较，选出最恰当的英语词汇。

当事人方有另一方不能履行合同的确切证据时，可以中止履行合同，但是应当通知另一方。

原译文：

The Party shall terminate its performance of the Contract if it has conclusive evidence that the other party is unable to perform the contract.However，it shall immediately inform the other Party of such termination.

原句中的翻译有个原则性的错误，即译者误将"中止"理解成了"终止"，译成了 to terminate its performance of the Contract。"中止"和"终止"在法律上均有"停止"的意思，但前者表示，因故暂停正在履行的合同，待造成中止的原因消除后，再恢复合同的履行，其英译应该是 to suspend its performance of the Contract；后者表示完全结束正在履行的合同，其英译应该为 to terminate the Contract。

4.注意避免出现拼写错误 Attention to the Wrongly-spelt Words

有些单词拼写极为相似，但不是一个词，而且也不表达同一个意思。

在合同的翻译或起草过程中，要留意 lien 和 lieu 的拼写，以免造成对合同条款的曲解。

lien 和 lieu 都是名词，但词义不同。lien（留置权），是指债务未偿还前债权人可扣押担保品的权利；lieu 则表示场所和取代之意。

The Borrower agrees to transfer to the lender the right to accept and substitute other assigned accounts subsequent to this date，in lieu of accounts this day assigned.

借款人同意向出借人转让收取和兑取自即日起的以后各项应付账款的权利，用以取代今天的各项应收账款。

Machinery shall become the sole property of the Joint Venture Company，free and clear of all liens，charges and claims of any kind whatsoever.

这些设备应成为合资公司的独有资产，不存在任何留置权，不存在任何费用、索赔等情况。

The court granted me a lien on my debtor's property.

法庭授予我对我债务人财产的留置权。

## Notes

1.forthwith adv. 立刻

The Company shall forthwith notify the Operator of such fact.

公司应该立刻把事实通知经营者。

The parties acknowledge and agree that Joint Venture Company shall be formed forthwith upon satisfaction of the conditions.

当事各方承认并同意，当这些条件得到满足以后，就立刻组建合资公司。

2.convene vt./vi. 召集，召开（会议）

The next shareholders meeting will convene on the coming Sunday at the same place.

下届的股东大会下星期日在同一地点举行。

3.employ vt. 雇用，用，使用；v. 使用

The Distributor shall no use or employ any colorable imitations of the trademarks or anything similar thereto.

批发商不应使用任何具有欺骗性、伪造性的商标，或其他类似的东西。

The Sales Company shall employ the salesman to act as its salesman for the sale of land.

推销公司应雇用推销员担任它的土地销售推销员。

employer 雇主，老板

employee 职工，雇员，店员

employment n. 雇用，使用，利用，工作，职业

Seller shall, prior to the closing, enter into an employment agreement with AAA satisfactory to Buyer.

在结算以前，卖方应与甲方达成符合买方要求的雇用协议。

unemployment n. 失业，失业人数

4.covenant n. 契约，盟约；v. 缔结（盟约），立约

All of the terms, conditions, provisions and covenants contained in the lease are made a part of this Agreement.

包括在租约里的所有条款、条件、规定和契约都是构成本协议的组成部分。

The Mortgagor covenants with the Mortgage that it shall keep the building on the premises insured against loss by fire.

抵押者与受押人签订协议，即抵押者要继续为房产地上的建筑物保火险。

5.consent vi. 同意，赞成，答应；n. 同意，赞成，允诺

Except AAA's prior written consent, no party shall enter in or assume any mortgage.

除甲方事先书面同意者外，任何一方均不得接受或承担抵押。

The consent in writing is necessary in proceeding the suit.

书面同意在起诉中是必不可少的。

Notice may be waived by the unanimous consent of all directors.

通知可以经全体董事的一致同意予以取消。

Distributor shall consent to resell the product only at not less than the minimum retail price established by the Producer.

经销商只同意转售那些不低于生产者所订的最低零售价的产品。

6.supersede vt.代替，取代，废除

This Agreement supersedes any and all other agreements，either oral or written，between the parties.

本协议可以代替当事人双方间签订的任何的和所有其他的口头或书面协议。

Nothing contained in exhibit shall supersede or annul the terms and provisions aforesaid.

附表中所列事项均不应该替代或取消上述条款和规定。

We are sending you herewith Amended Invoice No.88，which is to supersede the Invoice No.84 sent previously.

随函寄去第88号更正发票以取代先前寄去的第84号发票。

The old methods have been superseded.

旧办法已被废弃。

This Agreement，when effective，shall supersede any previous existing Agreement between the parties.

本协议一经生效，即应替代双方之间原有的协议。

7.commitment n.委托事项，许诺，承担义务

The Buyer shall designate representatives for the purpose of Contracts or commitments for purchases.

为履行合同或购买承诺，买方应指派代表。

Purchase Orders shall be approved by the Owner before a commitment is made.

在作出承诺之前，业主应该核定采购单。

The work under all sales contracts and commitments assumed by the Buyer will be performed by the Buyer for its account.

按照所有销售合同和买方承担义务的规定，该项工程应由买方完成。

commit v.委托，承担，作

One Party shall not at any time commit any breach of any covenant.

单方在任何时候都不得违约。

The Contractor shall not commit or permit any act which will interfere with the work by other Contractor.

该承包商不应该或容许干预其他承包商工作的任何行动。

This report will compare the budget with actual committed and forecast expenditures.

这份报表应将预算和实际承担的与预计支出作一比较。

8.liability n.责任，义务，债务，作负债时与assets相对，表示资产与负债

We expressly disclaim any liabilities arising in connection with the sale of products.

我们特别声明不承认因销售产品而引起的任何法律义务。

When property is encumbered by mortgage or other liabilities，the Seller may require the Buyer to assume them upon the sale of the property.

如果财产作了抵押或有其他负债，卖方可以要求买方于财产出售时承担偿付债务的责任。

AAA further agrees that it shall assume and agree to perform and pay when due all of the debts，liabilities，obligations and charges on AAA of any kind.

甲方再进一步答应它应承担并同意履行与支付一切到期的欠债、债务、义务以及属于甲方的任何合同费用。

assets and liabilities accounts 资产负债账户

9.under no circumstances 无论如何不，绝不

还有一些否定短语如in no way，in no case，at no time，by no means，in no sense，on no account都可译为"绝不"。这些否定短语常放在句首，但句子要倒装。

Under no circumstances，shall the Buyer be required to register with the Securities and Exchange Commission.

无论如何不能允许买方在证券交易委员会注册。

You may be assured that under no circumstances will we delay the shipment of the goods.

你方可放心，我方绝不耽误发货。

10.case n.事，病例，案例，情形，场合，讼案

在商务英语中，它与许多介词连用，构成一些重要的短语。

（1）in case

a.如果，假若

Please tell us in case you are interested in this article.

你方如对此商品感兴趣，请告知我方。

b.以备（万一），以防（万一）

We would suggest placing an order at present in case the new crop may fail.

建议你们现在订购，以防新庄稼歉收。

（2）in any case 无论如何

In any case we are unable to effect shipment in this month.

这个月我们无论如何无法发运。

（3）in case of 假若，如果，万一

In case of offer，please quote your best price.

如能报盘，请开最惠价。

（4）in no case 绝不

You may be assured that in no case will the L/C be delayed.

你方可放心，信用证绝不会迟开。

（5）in the case of 就……而言，至于

In the case of payment terms，we are unable to accept D/P at 60 day's sight.

至于付款条件，我方无法接受远期60天的付款交单。

（6）in this case 假使这样，既然这样

In this case，we will not fail to fax you an offer.

如果这样，定去传真给你报盘。

（7）such being the case 情况既然如此

Such being the case，we regret being unable to make you an offer at present.

情况既然如此，抱歉我们目前无法报盘。

11.null n.无效，作废

null 和 void 在合同中往往连用，表示失效。

It is agreed that if the Second Party shall breach any of the terms contained in the now existing lease between the First Party and the Second Party，then this Agreement shall immediately become null and void in all respects.

双方同意，如乙方违反甲、乙双方现行租约的任何条款，则本协议在各方均将立即失效。

nullify vt.使无效

This Guarantee shall be valid up to the date of the provisional acceptance of the Plant at which date this Guarantee will be nullified.

本保证书直至工厂临时验收之日一直有效，从验收之日起失效。

The Architect may withhold or，nullify the whole or a part of any certificate to such extent as may be necessary in his reasonable opinion to protect the Owner from loss.

建筑师按照他的合理意见认为必要时，可以保留或取消整个证明书或证明书中某部分，以保护业主免受损失。

12.request v./n.请求，要求，恳求

request sb. to do sth.请求某人做某事

We will fax you if additional is requested.

如需追加，我们将传真你们。

It is requested that the two orders be shipped in one lot.

两笔订货请一次发运。

Visitors are requested not to touch these exhibits.

来宾请勿触摸展品。

As requested，we are sending you herewith our commercial invoice in duplicate.

按你方要求，随函寄去商业发票一式两份。

at…request（at the request of…）应……的请求

At your request，we give you an estimate of approximate requirements for next year.

应你们的请求，我们给你一个明年大概需求量的估计数。

We are sending you the enclosed at the request of your representative.

应你方代表的请求，现将所需文件随函寄去。

by request 依照请求

We gave your representative，by request，a list of our current availabilities.

如所请，我们给你们代表一张我方现在可供货清单。

on request 一经要求就……

Catalogues will be sent on request.

目录承索即寄。

in request 需要

This commodity is now in enormous（great，popular，small）request.

要此货者甚多（很多，甚普遍，不多）。

13.require v.需求，需要

Buyers require 50 tons additional.

买主还需要追加50吨。

后接宾语加动词不定式可接that引起从句。

The import licence requires the goods to arrive on/before September 15.

进口许可证规定货物应在9月15日或以前到达。

Our contract with the buyers requires that we（should）ship the goods not later than April.

我们和买方所订合同规定我们不得晚于4月装船。

require后接动名词。这个动名词含有被动意义，与后接被动语态的动词不定式相同。

As the question is an important one，it requires careful thinking over./ As the question is an important one，it requires to be carefully thought over.

由于这是一个重要问题，需要慎重考虑。

14.due adj.适当的，正当的，应有的，应得的；（票据等）到付款日期的，到期的；当付的，所欠的；（预定）应到的，预期的。n.（复数）应付款

After due consideration，we have decided to grant your request.

经过适当考虑，我们决定答应你方的要求。

We trust the shipment will reach you in due course.

我们相信这批货将按期到达你处。

The draft will fall due on May 20.

汇票于5月20日到期。

The remittance is in payment of all commissions due（to）you up to date.

这笔汇款是付迄今为止欠你方的各项佣金。

The steamer is due at 20：00.

轮船应在20点到。

Fresh supplies are due to arrive early next month.

这批货应于下月初到达。

ZZZ shall have the right to reimburse itself from future royalties becoming due hereunder.

乙方将有权从下述的、将来到期的租金中扣款偿还给本人。

harbour dues 码头费

overdue/pastdue adj.逾期的

The shipment of 10 tons Hemp is rapidly becoming overdue（pastdue）.

10吨大麻的装船期很快就要过期了。

ZZZ shall pay interest to AAA upon any and all amounts of royalties that are overdue.

对于过期未交的一切专利使用费，乙方应按金额向甲方支付利息。

15.interest n.兴趣，感兴趣的事物，利益（复数较普通），权利，所得的货物，利息（保险用语），股份，同业者……界（以专有名词作定语，用复数），财团，财界；v.引起兴趣

We have（feel，take）no interest in cotton piece goods.

我们对棉匹头不感兴趣。

This article is of special（particular）interest to us.

我们对这种商品特别有兴趣。

Some of our customers who profess interest for your porcelain ware have approached us for offers on the following：

我们有些对你方瓷器表示兴趣的客户向我们联系下列货物的报盘：

This suggestion is made in the interest of all parties concerned.

这个建议是照顾各有关方面的利益而提出的。

We agree to 60 days time L/C provided you pay interest for the period intervening.

我们同意60天远期的信用证，但此期间的利息须由你方负担。

The interest insured is valued at £19,500.

此货按19,500英镑投保。

The group has a large interest in this department store.

该集团在这家百货公司有大量股份。

| | |
|---|---|
| annual interest | 年利息 |
| compound interest | 复利 |
| credit interest | 存款利息 |
| interest bill | 有息票据，计息票据 |
| shipping interests | 航运界，航运业者 |

banking interests            银行界

The offer（price，shipment，quality）does not interest us.

这个报盘（价格、船期、质量）提不起我们的兴趣。

Your price is too high to even interest buyers in counter-offer.

你的价格太高，买方连还盘都没有兴趣。

16.favor n.欢迎，赞许；v.有利于，赞成，支持

Chinese commodities have enjoyed growing favor among buyers abroad.

中国商品在国外受到越来越多的欢迎。

They looked with favor on your sample shipment.

你发来的样货得到他们的称赞。

The opportunity does not favor our making a binding arrangement.

这一机会不便于我们作出一项有约束性的安排。

He said he favored development of permanent trade relations with China.

他说他赞成同中国发展永久性的贸易关系。

in favor of 支持；赞同；有利于；以……为受款人；以……为受益人

We are in favor of her promotion to president.

我们赞成她升为总裁。

The court decided in favor of the plaintiff.

法庭的判决有利于原告。

The letter of credit has been opened in your favour.

信用证已开到你方名下。

17. damage n.损坏，损害，（复数）（法律用语）损害赔偿费；vt.损坏，残损；vi.受损坏

damage in transit    运途中受损

damage report   残损单

ZZZ shall hold harmless AAA from any damages and/or claims.

乙方认为甲方不应受到任何损失和/或不予索赔。

AAA is entitled to file a claim against ZZZ for his property damage.

甲方有权为其财产蒙受损失向乙方提出索赔要求。

The force majeure accident caused great damage to property and loss of life.

不可抗力事件造成财产损坏和生命损失。

说大的损坏，形容词常用great，much，serious，material，heavy，considerable等；说小的损坏，形容词常用slight，immaterial，trifling等。

The shipment was found seriously damaged upon arrival.

货到时发现受损严重。

The Dealer shall pay to the distributor as liquidated damages the sum of（amount）for each sale.

经纪人须付给经销商一笔……的金额，作为每次销售的清偿损失额。

This cloth damages easily.

这件衣服易受损坏。

辨析：damage，injury，harm

这组词均含有使人或某物遭受损失的行为或结果之意。

damage 含有损失的伤害（如财产、价值或有用性）。

injury 其词义广泛，指损害或破坏权利、健康、自由和身心健全的行为或其后果，或表示导致某个具有使用价值的事物的部分的或全部的损失。

harm（通常不加冠词）指导致（或会导致）伤害的坏事，经常表示所遭受的后果（如悲伤或羞耻等）。

The typhoon caused much damage to the crops.

台风对农作物造成极大的损害。

It is mutually agreed that if, prior to the transfer of the property, any part of it shall be destroyed or injured by fire or other casualty, then the purchase price specified above shall be abated to the extent and amount of such loss.

双方同意，如果在财产转移前，财产的任何部分由于失火或其他事故而遭到毁坏或损害，则须视该项损失的程度和数额，在前文所述的买价中予以扣除。

Did the storm do any harm to the corn?

风暴损害庄稼没有？

18.tax n. 税，税额

| | |
|---|---|
| tax avoidance | 避税 |
| tax abatement | 减税 |
| tax dodger | 偷税人 |
| tax evasion | 逃税 |
| tax haven | 避税天堂 |
| tax holidays | 免税期 |
| to levy a tax on sth. | 对某物征税 |

If they levy taxes on capital, they could come on the trustees.

如果他们要征收资本税的话，他们可以找那些受托人。

taxing adj.难以负担的，使人感到压力的

Such an amount is taxing for a firm of moderate means.

这样一笔数额对一个中等资力的商号是有压力的。

taxable adj.应纳税的，可征税的

taxable earnings 应纳税的收入

taxation n.征税、课税、税制、税金

the taxation bureau 税务局

double taxation 双重课税

19. 辨析 lien，mortgage，pledge，hypothecate，encumbrance（incumbrance）

除了 lien 之外，mortgage，pledge，hypothecate 和 encumbrance 这几个词在合同英语中也经常出现，区分其准确的法律含义尤为重要。

mortgage 为"按揭"，指房地产按揭人将其房地产的产权（业权）移转给债权人，作为偿还债务的担保，但实际占有权却仍然为债务人所有。在按揭期间，债权人即成为按揭房地产的产权所有人，如债务人不履行债务或有其他违约行为，债权人可以按揭房地产所有权人的名义起诉，取消按揭人的回赎权，从而取得按揭房地产包括占有权在内的绝对产权（title）。

pledge 为"质押"或"质权"，指动产（包括代表无形财产产权的证券等）的占有权而非所有权因债务担保的转移。

hypothecate 特指为担保债务清偿和义务履行，以特定财产作为抵押，但债权人通常不实际占有抵押物或其产权。

encumbrance 为"不动产产权"，指附加于土地等财产上、使财产价值降低的请求权及其他义务负担，如留置权或抵押权；也可指任何非所有权的财产权利。财产负担不能对抗财产占有的转移，但在财产或财产权利转让之后，财产负担仍继续存在。该词又可拼作 incumbrance。

Neither this Agreement nor any rights hereunder shall be assigned，mortgaged，pledged，hypothecated or otherwise alienated by the Lender.

不论是本协议本身还是本协议中的任何权利，出借人都不得转让、抵押、抵借、典让或以其他方式转让之。

The share of capital stock of the Corporation shall not be sold，pledged，hypothecated，or transferred.

公司的股票不得予以出售、典当、抵押或转让。

The assets are free from all security interests，mortgages，liens，claims，and encumbrance.

此资产不受一切物权担保、抵押、留置权、索赔及不动产债权的影响。

Party A further represents and warrants that the Premise is free and clear of any and all claims，charges，easement，encumbrances，lease，covenants，security interest，liens，options，pledge，rights of others，or restrictions，whether imposed by agreement，understanding，law，equity or otherwise.

甲方进一步陈述并保证，上述房产不存在任何权利主张、抵押、地役权、权利负担、租约、契约、担保权益、留置权、购买权、质押、他人权利或限制，无论是以协议、谅解、普通法、平衡法还是其他方式设定。

● Exercises

I.Translate the following sentences into English：

1.第一次董事会应在公司营业执照签发后 1 个月内召开。

2.此证书所涉及的股票均系按照本协议条款规定发行的。

3.业主特此立约保证向承包人支付合同总价，以作为本工程施工、竣工及修补工程中的缺陷的报酬。

4.未经甲方同意，乙方不得出售该种特许装置。

5.本条款同样适用于财务方面的承诺。

6.本协议一经生效，即应替代双方之间原有的协议。

7.商业的性质以及计划中的交易、推销与实现利润的目标与目的，就是做好契约中所提及的任何或者全部事情。

8.裁决或商妥的方案是，买方要完成支付，不然就放弃某些资产。

9.本协议应从本日开始，到（……）日为止。

10.对于甲方如何运用其销售所得的收入问题，银行在任何情况下概不负责。

II.Translate the following sentences into Chinese：

1.The property rights and interests of each member in the Association shall be always equal.

2. The Voting Trustees shall possess the rights of every kind to exercise at stockholders meetings.

3.The Company shall forthwith notify the Operator of such fact.

4.The Sales Agent shall be required to maintain a showroom.

5.The question of law shall be submitted to arbitration by the parties， or either of them， at the request of the expert.

6.Any taxes， duties or imposts shall be borne by the Foreign Party.

7.The Seller agrees to sell， assign and transfer such assets as mentioned below.

8.AAA grants the right to use trademark upon the authorized products which comply with the relative standards.

9.The operation of the former Agreement shall be suspended.

10. AAA agrees to execute， seal and deliver this Agreement without a exception when the said amount of money is paid in full.

# Unit Three /国际商务合同的结构

## Contract Structures

国际商务合同的前言部分，在合同上被称为"合同的效力条款"（Validity Clauses of Contracts），是合同生效的基本条件，在法律上具有重要的意义。通常，前言部分由这几个要点组成，即开场部分（Premises/Commencement）、鉴于条款（Whereas）、过渡条款（Transitional Clause）。

### 3.1.1　合同的名称

主要写明合同的准确名称，如"售货确认书"（Sales Confirmation）、"中外合资经营企业合同"（Contract for Sino-foreign Joint Ventures）等。

### 3.1.2　合同各方名称及法定地址

合同各方的名称第一次在合同中出现时一定要写全名，不能缩写，只有在后面重复出现时才能用简称，简称甲方或乙方、买方或卖方、许可方或被许可方（hereinafter referred to as / hereinafter called Party A or Party B; the Buyer or the Seller; the Licensor or Licensee）等；法定地址，主要指营业地、住所地或居所所在地，即载明合同当事人的名称或者姓名、国籍、主营业务或者住所（the corporate or personal names of the parties to the contract and their nationalities, principal places of business or residential addresses, etc.）。但是，"registered office"是指一个公司的"注册所在地"，它与"principal office"即"主营业地"并不一定是同一地点。

法人组织的国籍一般用 organized（incorporated）and existing under the laws of；自然人的国籍一般用 a national of 或 an individual with the nationality of。

### 3.1.3　订约日期及地点

订约日期和地点是关系到合同发生纠纷时适用法律的问题，必须写明。

### 3.1.4　合同双方法律关系

合同双方法律关系主要是在明确了当事人全称后，指明谁是买方谁是卖方，或出让方、受让方，贷款人、借款人等等。

### 3.1.5　签约的背景

每份合同都要在合同的前言中对签约背景和/或目的进行事实描述（the background and or purpose or the reason for signing the contract）。

其中的一个关键词是 whereas。whereas 的意义相当于 considering / in consideration of，that being the case 等。鉴于条款（whereas clause），因其主要部分由 whereas 条款引导而得名。有时，为了使合同简单明了，合同背景部分直接用"背景（Background）"这个词。

The government of the People's Republic of China and the Government of the United States of America（hereinafter referred to as the Parties）；

Considering the offenses against Customs laws are prejudicial to the economic，fiscal and commercial interests of their respective countries；

Considering the importance of assuring the accurate assessment of Customs duties and other taxes；

HAVE AGREED as follows：

中华人民共和国政府和美利坚合众国政府（以下简称各方）在下面背景下，背景一是考虑违反海关法的行为有损于两国的经济、财政和贸易利益；背景二是考虑到正确计征关税及其他税的重要性，达成协议如下：

WHAREAS，this Agreement is supplemental to an agreement dated 5 December 2018 between the parties to this Agreement（the Principal Agreement）under which the Purchaser agreed to buy certain assets of the Vendor for an aggregate sum of $3 million.

本合同系为补充双方当事人此前于 2018 年 12 月 5 日业已缔结之合同（以下称"主合同"）所立，买方于主合同中同意从卖方购买总价值 300 万美元的资产。

BACKGROUND

（A）Party A wishes to obtain some professional legal support in the Project.

（B）Party B is an international law firm，quite experienced and professional in such project and is willing to provide such professional legal service to Party A，subject to and on the terms and conditions of this agreement.

背景

（A）甲方希望就该项目获得一些专业的法律服务。

（B）乙方是一家国际律师事务所，在这种项目上有丰富的经验和专业知识，愿意根据本协议条件为甲方提供专业的法律服务。

### 3.1.6　同意订约的词句

同意订约的词句如"双方同意按以下条款及条件买卖下列货物"（Both parties agree to buy and sell the following commodities according to the terms and conditions stipulated below）。

This Agreement is made and concluded in duplicate in Beijing, China by and between XYZ Company, a Corporation incorporated under the law of USA having its Head Office and a place of business in the city of New York, USA, （hereinafter called XYZ）as the First Party and China Dalian Corporation （hereinafter called Party B）as the Second Party.

In consideration of the mutual convenants and agreements herein contained, the XYZ and the Purchaser agree on the following terms, conditions and provisions hereof:

协议书由按美国法律成立的并在美国纽约设有总部和营业地的XYZ有限公司（以下简称XYZ）为甲方和中国大连公司（以下简称买方）为乙方在北京签订，一式两份。

鉴于相互契约及约定，XYZ与买方同意以下条款：

This Agreement was made this 12th date of October 2018 in Beijing China by and between ABC Company, a company registed in People's Republic of China （hereinafter referred to as the Company）and the Seiji Bank Ltd. Hong Kong Branch, a bank incorporated in Japan but registered in Hong Kong （hereinafter referred to as the Bank）. Whereas the Bank has agreed to extend a Short‐term Credit Facility for the purpose of providing general working capital to the Company, it was hereby mutually agreed as follows:

本合同由在中华人民共和国注册的ABC公司（以下简称公司）和在日本成立而在中国香港注册的"和田"银行（以下简称银行）于2018年10月12日在北京签订。鉴于上述银行同意向上述公司提供短期贷款作为周转资金之用，合同双方特此达成协议如下：

## 3.2　合同的正文 Main Body of a Contract

合同的正文是合同的主干部分，是合同的实质性条款，包括除了合同前言和合同的结尾的所有合同条款部分。具体细则如下：

### 3.2.1　合同的种类与合同的范围 Type of Contract and Scope of the Object in the Contract

合同的种类包括各类对外经济贸易合同，如合资企业合同、涉外劳务合同、国际买卖合同、国际工程承包合同等。各类合同都有自己的合同范围的条款，其中包括公司的建立、业务范围、生产经营目的、范围和规模、技术条件、质量、标准、规格、数量等条款，以及履行合同的期限、地点和方式等条款。

### 3.2.2　合同价格、支付金额、支付方式和各种附带的费用 The Contract Price，Amount，Method of Payment，Other Various Incidental Charges

这项内容实质上由两部分组成，即价格条款和支付条款。价格条款（terms of payment）往往涉及许多复杂的内容。有时它不仅是价格问题，而且涉及合同各方应承担的责任、风险和费用等问题，如国际货物销售合同中常用的两个价格术语 FOB 和 CIF，当事人选择不同的价格术语，其承担的责任是截然不同的，因此，价格条款往往是双方当事人商谈的重点。支付条款也是合同中较敏感的条款，它不仅涉及不同国家的货币、外汇制度，还涉及结算方式等一系列复杂的问题。因此，在起草这部分条款时，应详细规定支付金额（amount of payment）、支付工具（instrument of payment）、支付时间（time of payment）、支付地点（place of payment）和支付方式（method of payment）。

有关合同价格、合同款的支付以及其他有关支付条款是涉外经贸合同中极为重要的条款，事关重大，所以，在草拟这部分合同时，一定要做到用词准确、达意。除了当心语言上的问题外，还要把各种其他因素考虑在内，以避免日后发生这方面的争议。

The registered capital of the Joint Venture Company shall be the same as the total amount of the investment，i.e.4.5 million U.S.Dollars（four million and five hundred thousand U.S.Dollars）.

合资公司的注册资本和投资总额相同，即为450万美元。

在书写合同金额时一定要把大写金额（amount in words）和小写金额（amount in figure）一并写明。

Party A shall，in accordance with the provisions of this Contract，pay to Party B the Technical Documentation Fee of USD 2,400,000（two million and four hundred thousand U.S.Dollars only）.The above price shall be firm including all expenses for sending the technical Documentation CIF Beijing Airport，Party B's technical personnel and training of Party A's personnel（excluding Sub-clause 4.8 of Annex 3 and Sub-clause 5.3 of Annex 4）.

根据本合同的规定，甲方应付给乙方技术资料费贰佰肆拾万美元整。上述报价为实盘，包括技术资料托运至北京机场交货价（CIF北京机场）、乙方技术人员服务费和甲方人员的培训费（不包括附件3的第4.8款和附件4的第5.3款）。

Price of the Contract

Price of the contract shall be calculated on Royalty in accordance with the content and scope stipulated in Section 2 to the contract and the currency shall be in U.S.Dollars.

Royalty under the contract shall be paid from the month after the date of coming into force of the Contract in terms of Calendar Year. The date of settling accounts shall be December 31 of each year.

Royalty at the rate of··· % （say percent） shall be calculated in terms of net selling price after the Contract Products are sold in the year, the Contract products which have not been sold shall not count.

The report of the selling quantity, net selling amount of the Contract Products and Royalty which should be paid for the past year shall be submitted to Licensor in written form by Licensee within 10 （ten） days after the date of settling accounts to Royalty. The specific methods for calculating net selling amount and Royalty are detailed in Appendix 3 to the Contract.

If Licensor demands to audit the accounts of Licensee, he shall notice Licensee within 10 （ten） days after receiving the written notice from Licensee in accordance with Section 3.4 of the Contract.

The specific content and procedure of auditing accounts are detailed in Appendix 4 to the Contract.

合同价格

按照第二条规定的内容和范围，本合同采用提成方式计算价格，计价的货币为美元。

本合同提成费的计算时间从合同生效之日后的第1个月开始，按日历年度计算，每年的12月31日为提成费的结算日。

提成费按当年度合同产品销售后的净销售价格计算，提成率为……%，合同产品未销售出去的不应计算提成费。

在提成费结算日后10天之内，被许可方应以书面通知的形式向许可方提交上一年度合同产品的销售数量、净销售额和应支付的提成费。净销售额和提成费的具体计算方法详见本合同附件三。

许可方如需查核接受方的账目，应在接到被许可方根据第3.4条规定开出的书面通知后10天之内通知被许可方，具体的查账内容和程序详见本合同附件四。

### 3.2.3　合同的转让条件 The Conditions for the Assignment of Contract

合同转让实质上是一种特殊的合同变更，即合同条款一方将合同中的权利或义务的全部或部分转让给合同另一方或合同以外的第三方，是主体的变更。有一类合同如中外合资企业、合作企业及外资企业合同，还有如"交钥匙合同"等都必须有转让条款。在起草这部分内容时，可以明确约定合同可以转让以及转让合同的条件和程序，但这些约定必须依法进行。

If one party to the Joint Venture intends to assign all or part of its investment subscribed to a third party, consent shall be obtained from the other party to the Joint Venture and approval from the examining and approving authorities is required. When one party assigns all or part of its investment subscribed to a third party, the other party has pre-emptive right. When one party assigns its investment subscribed to a third party, the terms of assignment shall not be more favorable than those to the other party to the Joint Venture. No assignment shall be effective should there be any violation of the above stipulations.

中外合资企业合同中可以规定："合营一方如向第三方转让其全部或部分出资额，须经合营他方同意，并经审批机构批准。合营一方转让其全部或部分出资额时，合营他方有优先购买权。合营一方向第三方转让出资额的条件，不得比向合营他方转让的条件优惠。违反上述规定的，其转让无效。"

Party B shall, in accordance with the provisions of the Contract, guarantee that he is the legitimate owner of such Know-how and such Technical Documentation as are supplied to Party A and that he is lawfully in a position to transfer the Know-how to Party A.

乙方保证他是向甲方提供的专有技术和技术资料的合法所有者，符合合同条款，依法能够向甲方转让专有技术。

The Contractor shall not assign the Contract or any part thereof without the written consent of the Chief Engineer.

未经总工程师书面同意，承包商不得转让本合同或其中任何部分。

### 3.2.4 违反合同的赔偿及责任 Liability to Pay Compensation and Other Liabilities for Breach of Contract

违反涉外合同的责任是指涉外合同的当事人不履行合同、不完全履行合同、不符合双方在合同中约定的条件时，依有关法律的规定或合同的约定应当承担的赔偿责任或其他经济责任。

关于违约责任条款，几乎所有的涉外合同都有，一般遵循过失原则和损害赔偿原则，违约要承担责任，要赔偿。在涉外合同中明确约定违反涉外合同承担的经济责任，对于保证合同的履行，促使合同当事人全面履行合同中约定的义务有着重要的意义。

至于当事人，若一方违反涉外合同应承担的责任和承担责任的方式，当事人可以在合同中约定违约金（penalty），也可以约定赔偿损失（compensation for losses），也可以约定支付利息（payment of interest）、中止履行合同（suspension of the contract performance）或解除合同（cancellation of the contract）。

The Purchaser agrees to pay Corporation the Total Purchase Price, as follow：

买方同意向公司支付买价，总金额为：

The Purchaser shall, upon receipt of Corporation's respective invoices therefore, pay to Corporation all amounts which become due by the Purchaser to Corporation hereunder, including without limitation an amount equal to the taxes and duties.

收到公司的各种发票后，买方必须即刻付给公司业已到期应付的所有款项，包括各种税收费用在内，不得有例外。

If by reason of delay on the part of the Purchaser or Purchaser's agent or representative, any payments due to Corporation are not made in accordance with the agreed payment schedule, Corporation reserves the right to apply a late payment charge of one and one-half（1.5%）percent per month（19.56% per annum）on all overdue amounts and Purchaser agrees to promptly pay any such late payment charges which are properly due hereunder.In the event that one or more payments are delayed for sixty（60）days or more, Corporation shall have the right to stop all work under this Agreement and shall also have the right to claim such period of work stoppage and the effects thereof as excusable delay pursuant to Article 7 hereof（Excusable Delay）.Purchaser agrees to reimburse Corporation for those additional reasonable costs incurred by Corporation resulting from such work stoppage（s）and restart（s）.Should one or more payments be delayed for one hundred and twenty（120）days or more, this Agreement may, at Corporation's option, be deemed to be cancelled under the provisions of paragraphs（b）through（e）of Article 23 hereof（Termination for Insolvency & Cancellation）.

如果由于买方或买方代理商或代理人的延迟，不能按议定的付款时间支付公司业已到期的款项，公司保留收取延付款的权利，延付款月率为到期未付款的1.5%（年率为19.56%），买方也同意即刻交付本协议所规定的此种费用。如一次或数次延迟付款达60天或以上，公司有权停止本协议所规定的工作，并有权根据本协议第7条（可谅解的延迟）称此段工作停顿及其产生的后果为可谅解的。买方同意对公司因停工和重新开工的额外费用作合理补偿。如一次或数次延迟付款达120天或以上，根据本合同第23条（因无力清偿债务而终止和撤销）第2~5款规定，按公司的意愿，本协议可视为被撤销。

Liabilities for Breach of Contract:

Should either Party A or Party B fail to pay on schedule the contributions in accordance with Clause 5 of this Contract, the breaching Party shall pay the other Party 10% of interest of the contribution from the month after exceeding the time limit.Should breaching Party fail to pay the contributions after 3 months exceeding the time limit, the other Party shall, in accordance with the Clause 53 hereof, have the right to terminate the Contract and to claim damages to the breaching Party.

违约责任：

如果合资一方未能按照本合同第5条规定按时入资，违约方应在逾期后1个月付给合同另一方10%利息。如果违约方逾期后3个月仍未入资，合同另一方应根据合同第53条款的规定有权终止合同，并向违约方索赔损失。

In the event that Party B fails to complete the Works in time owing to such reasons as Party B shall be liable for, Party B shall pay a penalty for the default based on 0.1% of the total price for work per day, i.e., Party B shall pay one thousand two hundred and sixty (1,260) U.S.Dollars only for day of such default.

如果乙方因自身的原因而未准时完工，乙方应付违约罚款，每天按总价的1‰计算，即1,260美元整。

If, under the Contract, the Purchaser requests to cancel the Contract, ABC Company shall, upon written request by the Purchaser, advise Purchaser of the estimated cancellation costs for which Purchaser would be liable.

如果买方根据合同要求撤销合同，ABC公司应根据买方书面要求，告知买方应承担的撤销费用。

### 3.2.5　合同发生争议时的解决方法 The Ways for Settling Contract Disputes

在合同的执行过程中发生争议是正常的。涉外合同一旦发生争议，解决的方法有和解（conciliation）、调解（mediation）、仲裁（arbitration）和诉讼（litigation/lawsuit）。在起草合同时，应明确约定争议的解决方法，而不同的解决方法将导致不同的法律后果。为解决重大争议，涉外商务合同都有仲裁条款，一般包括仲裁地点、仲裁机构、仲裁程序、仲裁员的组成、仲裁费的负担和仲裁裁决的权威性等细则规定。

Any disputes arising from the execution of or in connection with the Contract shall be settled through mutual consultations between the Parties thereto.In case no settlement can be reached through consultations, the disputes shall be submitted for arbitration. The arbitration shall take place in Beijing, China, and shall, in accordance with its rules of procedures, be conducted by the Foreign Economic and Trade Arbitration Commission of the China Council for the Promotion of International Trade.The arbitration award shall be final and binding on the parties thereto.

在履行合同时合同双方如发生争议，双方应通过相互协商解决。如经过协商解决无效，则应提请仲裁部门解决。仲裁应在中国北京进行，由中国国际贸易促进会对外经济贸易仲裁委员会根据其仲裁程序进行仲裁。仲裁裁决是终局性的，对双方都有约束力。

Any disputes arising out of this Contract shall first be settled by the Parties hereto through consultation with their higher authorities in accordance with the spirit of mutual trust. Should such consultation fail to settle the dispute within thirty (30) days of notification to such higher authorities, mediation may be conducted by a third party selected by the Parties hereto.

合同双方对本合同发生的任何争议应首先通过各方主管部门本着相互信赖的精神予以解决。如在30天内本合同双方不能解决，双方可推荐第三方予以调解。

The arbitration shall take place in Stockholm, Sweden, and shall be conducted by the Arbitration Institute of Stockholm Chamber of Commerce in accordance with the statutes of the institute in question.

仲裁在斯德哥尔摩由瑞典斯德哥尔摩商会仲裁院依据该院的仲裁规则实施。

Arbitration：All disputes in connection with this Contract or in the execution thereof shall be settled by negotiation between two parties. If no settlement can be reached, the case in dispute shall then be submitted for arbitration in the country of defendant in accordance with the arbitration regulations of the arbitration organization of the defendant country. The decision made by the arbitration organization shall be taken as final and binding upon both parties. The arbitration expenses shall be borne by the losing party unless otherwise awarded by the arbitration organization.

仲裁：凡与本合同有关事项或因执行本合同所发生的一切争执，应由双方通过友好的方式协商解决。如果不能解决，则在被告国家根据被告仲裁机构的仲裁程序规则进行仲裁。仲裁决定是终局的，对双方具有同等约束力。仲裁费用除非仲裁机构另有决定外，均由败诉一方负担。

The arbitration tribunal shall consist of three arbitrators, one appointed by each Party and, if either of the Parties fails to appoint an arbitrator within the time specified in the Arbitration Rules, the Chairman of CCPIT shall make such appointment, taking into consideration the criteria set out in this Article 18.2.

仲裁庭应由三名仲裁员组成，其中双方各指定一名，如果任何一方不能在仲裁规则具体规定的时间内指定一名仲裁员，中国国际贸易促进委员会主席将参考本合同第18.2条载明的标准指定仲裁员。

### 3.2.6 保险条款 Insurance Clause

国际商务合同的履行，大多数时间长、路途远，可能受到各种因素的干扰，产生各种不测的事件，如洪水、火灾、盗窃、海难、经营不善等。这类风险一旦发生，就会造成不同程度的损失，从而产生承担风险损失的责任问题。在国际经贸活动中，风险往往和保险连在一起。为了使风险造成的损失及时得到经济上的补偿，就需要办理保险。因此，在合同中明确风险责任，约定风险范围（the limits of the risks to be borne by the parties in performing the object and the coverage of insurance of the object），对于确定当事人的投保责任、避免风险发生后产生保险责任纠纷，都有着重要的法律意义。

Marine insurance policies or certificates in negotiable form, for 110% full CIF invoice value covering the risks of War & W.A.as per the People's Insurance Co.of China dated 01/01/1976.with extended cover up to Kuala Lumpur with claims payable in（at）Kuala Lumpur in the currency of draft（irrespective of percentage）.

作为可议付格式的海运保险单或保险凭证按照到岸价的发票金额110%投保中国人民保险公司1976年1月1日的战争险和基本险，负责到吉隆坡为止。按照汇票所使用的货币在吉隆坡赔付（不计免赔率）。

Insurance policy or certificate settling agent's name is to be indicated，any additional premium to cover uplift between 10% and 17% may be drawn in excess of the credit value.

保险单或保险凭证须表明理赔代理人的名称，保险费如增加 10%~17% 可在本证金额以外支付。

This insurance must be valid for a period of 60 days after arrival of merchandise at inland destination.

本保险扩展到货物到达内地目的地后 60 天有效。

Insurance to be covered against all risks including war risks as per ocean marine cargo clauses and air transportation cargo insurance clauses and ocean marine cargo war risk clauses and air transportation cargo war risk clauses of the People's Insurance Company of China dated⋯

按照中国人民保险公司××××年××月××日海洋运输货物保险条款和航空运输货物保险条款以及海洋运输货物战争险条款和航空运输货物战争险条款投保海空联运一切险和战争险。

### 3.2.7　不可抗力条款 Force Majeure

不可抗力条款，也称意外条款，是国际商务合同中普遍采用的一项除外条款，或称免责条款。条款一般规定合同一方遇到不可预见或无法预防的天灾、人祸或意外事故，以致不能履行合同时，可以免除责任，另一方无权要求其赔偿损失。

不可抗力条款通常包括两部分：一是确定不可抗力事故的范围，对此合同双方应在合同中有明确、具体的规定。二是在草拟合同时对不可抗力的结果要有两种安排：合同无法继续执行时，要终止合同；合同仍可继续执行，但需要延长履行合同的期限。对于两种情况，即终止合同和延长履行合同期限，都需要在合同中明确规定。

The Sellers shall not be held liable for failure or delay in delivery of the entire lot or a portion of the goods under this Sales Confirmation on consequence of any Force Majeure incidents.

本确认书所述全部或部分商品，如因人力不可抗拒的原因，以致不能履约或延迟交货，售方概不负责。

Force Majeure：The sellers shall not be held responsible for the delay in shipment or non-delivery of the goods due to Force Majeure，which might occur during the process of manufacturing or in the course of loading or transit. The sellers shall advise the Buyers immediately of the occurrence mentioned above within fourteen days thereafter. The Sellers shall send by airmail to the Buyers for their acceptance a certificate of the accident. Under such circumstances the Sellers，however，are still under the obligation to take all necessary measures to hasten the delivery of the goods.

不可抗力：由于不可抗力的原因发生在制造、装载或运输的过程中导致卖方延期交货或不能交货者，卖方可免除责任。在不可抗力发生后，卖方须立即通知买方及在14天内以空邮方式向买方提供事故发生的证明文件。在上述情况下，卖方仍要负责采取必要措施尽快发货。

Should either of the Parties to the Contract be prevented from executing the Contract by Force Majeure, such as earthquake, typhoon, flood, fire and war and other unforeseen events, and their happening and consequences are unpreventable and unavoidable, the prevented Party shall, by fax, notify the other Party without any delay, and shall, within 15 days thereafter, provide the detailed information of the events and a valid document for evidence issued by the relevant public notary organization for explaining the reason of its inability to execute or delay the execution of all or part of the Contract. The Parties to the Contract shall, through consultations, decide whether to terminate the Contract or to exempt the part of obligations for implementation of the Contract or whether to delay the execution of the Contract in accordance with the effects of the events on the performance of the Contract.

如果合同一方由于不可抗力因素而不能履行合同，比如地震、台风、洪水、火灾、战争及其他无法预见的事件，其发生和后果均无法预见并无法避免，该方应立刻以传真通知对方，并在其后的15天内提交有关公证机关出具的详细的事件描述及有效文件，用以解释其无法履行合同或迟延履行全部或部分条款的缘由。双方应通过协商，根据事件对履行合同的影响程度，确定是终止合同，或是免除履行合同的责任，或是延缓合同的执行。

### 3.2.8　合同的有效期限 A Period of Validity for the Contract

对于需要较长时间连续履行的合同（a contract which needs to be performed continuously over a long period），如合资经营合同、合作经营合同、成套设备技术引进合同以及国际承包工程合同等，当事人可以约定合同的有效期限，并在合同中规定有效期届满时，延长合同的条件或提前终止合同有效期的条件（the conditions for contractual extension and contractual termination before its expiration）。

This Contract shall come into force after it has been approved by the examination and approval authority of China.

本合同经中国审批机关批准后即生效。

This Contract shall be valid for two years after its effective date, and shall be renewable for further two years thereafter.

本合同从生效之日起有效期2年，期满后可延长2年。

This Contract shall be effective as of the date of signature by the last-to-sign of Parties hereto and shall remain in force for 365 days.

本协议将在协议各方中最后一方签署后生效，有效期365天。

This Contract comes into effect on the first day of the engaged party's arrival at the AA University and ceases to be effective at its expiration. If either party wishes to renew the

Contract，the other party shall be notified in writing one month before it expires.Upon agreement by both parties through consultation，a new contract may be signed between two parties.

本合同自受聘方到 AA 大学第一天之日起生效，到聘期届满时失效。如一方要求延长聘期，必须在合同期满前 1 个月以书面形式向对方提出，经双方协商同意后另签延聘合同。

The provisions of this paragraph shall survive termination of this Agreement.

本段各条款的有效期在本协议结束后仍然有效。

## 3.3　　　　　　　合同的结尾 Final Clauses

合同的结尾，也称为合同最后条款，写在合同的结尾部分。结尾条款（witness clause）主要应明确的内容有合同使用的文字及其效力（languages in which the contract is to be written and its validity）。除了明确使用的文字及其效力外，有时还应订立对合同进行修改或补充的内容。

### 3.3.1　合同使用的文字及其效力 The Language Used in the Contract & Its Validity

This Contract is made out in two originals，each copy written in Chinese and English languages，both texts being equally valid.In case of any divergence of interpretation，the Chinese text shall prevail.

本合同正文一式两份，分别以中文和英文书写，两种文本具有同等效力。若对其解释产生异议，则以中文文本为准。

Any amendment and / or supplement to this contract shall be valid only after the authorized representatives of both parties have signed written document（s），forming integral part（s）of this Contract.

本合同的任何修改和/或补充，只有在双方授权的代表在书面文件上签字才能生效，并为本合同不可分割的组成部分。

This Contract shall come into force after the signatures by the authorized representatives of both parties.

本合同将在双方授权的代表签字后正式生效。

This Agreement is written in Chinese and English languages and is signed in triplicate by Party A and Party B as follows：

In case of difference of interpretation，the English version shall be valid for the Parties hereto.

本合同用中英文两种语言书写，一式三份，经甲乙双方签字如下：

如因翻译而出现解释上的差异时，双方应以英文文本为准。

### 3.3.2　约尾条款 IN WITNESS WHEREOF/THEREOF

"IN WITNESS WHEREOF/THEREOF" 条款也称为约尾条款，常见于主条款之后，附件之前。

IN WITNESS WHEREOF, this Agreement has been signed and delivered as of the date and the year first above written by their duly representatives of Party A and Party B.

甲乙双方各自的合法授权代表于上述第一次所提到日期签署本协议，以兹为证。

IN WITNESS WHEREOF, this Agreement has been signed and delivered as of the···date···month, and ···year by the duly authorized representatives of the Parties.

双方授权各自代表于……年……月……日签署本协议，以兹为证。

In witness thereof, this contract is signed by both Parties in two original copies; each Party shall keep one copy.

本合同一式两份，双方签字，各执一份，特此证明。

### 3.3.3　附件 Appendices

在内容繁多的合同中，为了避免合同文本过于冗长和内容表述不够详尽，往往使用附录（addendum, attachment, appendix, annex, exhibit, schedule）来详述某些项目的细节。如果合同中订有附件，应在合同中另立一章列出附件的具体内容，并明确在合同的结尾部分规定附件为本合同不可分割的组成部分。

All other terms and conditions of the Agreement shall remain in full force and effect, except to the extent that any such terms and conditions is inconsistent with the terms of this Addendum of this Agreement.

所有的其他条款，该协议将留有完整的力量和影响，除了在某种程度上，任何这样的条款和条件不符合本协议的附录条款。

Party A grants to Party B a nonexclusive license to sell said products to Dealers as attachments.

甲方授予乙方一份可出售附件所述的产品给销售商的非独家经营执照。

Actual names and specifications of Products are shown in Appendix 1.

产品的名称、规格详见附录1。

Details of the information offered by Party B to Party A are shown in Appendix 2.

乙方向甲方提供的资料详见附录2。

The Appendices attached hereto are made an integral part of this Contract and are equally binding on both parties.

本合同所有附件作为本合同不可分割的组成部分，对双方具有同等约束力。

The annexes as listed in Articles 19 of this Contract shall form an integral part of this Contract.

本合同第19章列出的附件为本合同不可分割的组成部分。

## 3.4  合同结构概述 Conclusion of the Contract Structures

通常一份完整的合同在格式上除了前言、正文和约尾条款外，还要有标题。多数合同还会有一个封页，上面注明合同的名称、签约各方、签约的日期和地点。如果合同很长，条款又多，就需要在封页之后做一个目录，以便查询和阅读。这样的目录排列也有利于整理谈判的思路并研究谈判的要点。

| Part 1    Name | Name of the Contract | 第一部分 | 合同名称 |
|---|---|---|---|
| Part 2    Preamble | Background of the Contract, <br> Signature Place of the Contract <br> Signing Date of the Contract | 第二部分 <br> 前言 | 签约背景 <br> 签约地点 <br> 签约时间 |
| Part 3    Main Body of the Contract | 1.Definition | 第 三 部 分 <br> 主 要 条 款 和 条件 | 1  定义 |
| | 1.1    Definition | | 1.1  定义 |
| | 1.2    Interpretation Principles | | 1.2  解释原则 |
| | 2.Representation and Warrants | | 2.陈述与保证 |
| | 2.1    Representation and Warrants | | 2.1  陈述与保证 |
| | 2.2    Consequences of Misrepresentation | | 2.2  不实陈述的后果 |
| | 3.Operative Terms and Conditions | | 3.具体权利义务条款 |
| | 4.Term of Contract | | 4.有效期 |
| | 4.1    Term | | 4.1  有效期 |
| | 4.2    Extension | | 4.2  延期 |
| | 5.Termination | | 5.终止 |
| | 5.1    Termination | | 5.1  终止 |
| | 5.2    Continuing Obligations | | 5.2  合同方持续的义务 |
| | 6.Confientiality | | 6.保密 |
| | 6.1    Scope of Confidentiality | | 6.1  保密义务的范围 |
| | 6.2    Exceptions | | 6.2  保密义务不适用的情形 |
| | 6.3    Confidentiality Rules and Regulations | | 6.3  保密规则和法规 |
| | 6.4    Return of Confidential Information | | 6.4  保密资料信息的返还 |
| | 7.Breach of Contract | | 7.违约 |
| | 7.1    Remedies for Breach of Contract | | 7.1  违约救济措施 |
| | 7.2    Limitation on Liability | | 7.2  责任限制 |
| | 8.Force Majeure | | 8.不可抗力 |
| | 8.1    Definition of Force Majeure | | 8.1  不可抗力的定义 |
| | 8.2    Consequences of Force Majeure | | 8.2  不可抗力的后果 |
| | 9.Settlement of Disputes | | 9.争议的解决 |
| | 9.1    Friendly Consultation | | 9.1  友好协商 |
| | 9.2    Arbitration | | 9.2  仲裁 |

| | | | |
|---|---|---|---|
| | 9.3 Continuing Rights and Obligations | | 9.3 持续的权利和义务 |
| | 9.4 Enforcement of Award | | 9.4 仲裁的执行 |
| | 9.5 Injunctive Relief | | 9.5 禁令救济 |
| | 10.Applicable Law | | 10.适用的法律 |
| | 11.Miscellaneous Provisions | | 11.其他规定 |
| | 11.1 Independent Contractor Relationship | | 11.1 合同方之间的独立关系 |
| | 11.2 Binding Effect | | 11.2 合同约束力范围 |
| | 11.3 Party Entitled to Enforcement | | 11.3 合同权利人范围 |
| Part 3 Main Body of the Contract | 11.4 Amendment | 第三部分 主要条款和条件 | 11.4 变更 |
| | 11.5 No Publicity/Announcement | | 11.5 禁止对外发布 |
| | 11.6 No Solicitation | | 11.6 禁止招揽对方雇员 |
| | 11.7 Notices | | 11.7 通知 |
| | 11.8 Waive | | 11.8 是否放弃权利 |
| | 11.9 Assignability | | 11.9 转让 |
| | 11.10 Severally | | 11.10 可分割性 |
| | 11.11 Entire Agreement | | 11.11 全部协议 |
| | 11.12 Counterparts | | 11.12 合同签约份数 |
| | 11.13 Schedules and Annexes | | 11.13 附录及附件 |
| | 11.14 Language | | 11.14 语言文本 |
| Part 4 Final Clause | Execution | 第四部分 签署（约尾） | 实施 |

合同的正文条款是合同的主干，是合同各方权利义务的集中体现。按照制式结构的条款顺序，合同的正文条款一般包含以下各项各条款：

条款一，定义 Definition

条款二，陈述与保证 Representation and Warrants

条款三，具体权利和义务条款 Operative Terms and Conditions

条款四，有效期 Term of Contract

条款五，终止 Termination

条款六，保密 Confidentiality

条款七，违约 Breach of Contract

条款八，不可抗力 Force Majeure

条款九，争议的解决 Settlement of Disputes

条款十，适用的法律 Applicable Law

条款十一，其他规定 Miscellaneous Provisions

（1）合同方之间的独立关系/不构成代理关系/合伙关系 Independent Contractor Relationship/No Agency/No Partnership

（2）合同约束力 Binding Effect

（3）合同权利人范围 Party Entitled to Enforcement

（4）变更 Amendment

（5）禁止对外发布 No Publicity/Announcement

（6）禁止招揽对方雇员 No Solicitation

（7）竞业禁止 Non-competition

（8）通知 Notices

（9）弃权 Waivers

（10）转让和分包 Assignability

（11）知识产权 Intellectual Property Rights

（12）条款的独立性 Severability/Severance

（13）平衡救济 Equitable Relief

（14）标题与副本 Headings and Counterparts

（15）全部协议 Entire Agreement/Understanding

（16）合同签约份数 Counterparts

（17）合同附录及附件 Schedules and Annexes

（18）合同语言 Language

为了更好地理解合同的结构，我们可以把合同中的条款分成三大类：第一类，通用条款（General Provisions），也就是我们在几乎所有的合同中都可以见到的条款，如定义（Definition）、合同变更（Modification）、人力不可抗拒（Force Majeure）、陈述与保证（Representation and Warranties），纠纷解决（Settlement of Disputes）以及违约条款（Breach of Contract）等。第二类，常用条款（Common Provisions），它出现的频率很高，如我们常见到的税收条款（Taxation Provision）和保险条款（Insurance Clause）等。"通用条款"和"常用条款"是我们学习掌握合同结构的重点。第三类，操作性条款（Operation Provisions），是根据合同本身具有的不同特性而设计出来的一些特定条款。如工程承包合同中才会出现的工程建造的时间表，即计划时间表（Project Schedule）。

## Notes

1.preamble n.导言，前言，序言

AAA agrees to dismiss without prejudice the lawsuit referred to in the preamble to this Agreement.

甲方同意不抱偏见地撤销本协议导言中提到的讼诉。

2.principal n.本金，主要负责人，委托人；adj.主要的，首要的

principal trading partners　　　　主要贸易伙伴

principal subsidiary　　　　主要子公司（或子行）

principal office　　　　总店，总部，总社

principal 与 interest 并用时，意思是"本金"，构成了本金和利息的概念。

principal 与 agent 并用时，意思是"委托人"，构成了委托人和代理人的关系。

The whole of said principal sum and interest shall become due at the option of the Mortgagee, after default in the payment of any installment of principal or of interest for (…) days.

在拖欠支付分期付款本金或利息的（……）天以后，全部该项本金与利息应由受押人决定支付期限。

Seller is a corporation organized and existing under the laws of（country）with its principal office in（place）.

卖方就是遵循（某国）法律建立起来的并在（某地）设有总店的股份公司。

The term of this agency may, at the election of the Principal, be terminated by the principal serving upon the Agent a written notice to that effect.

代理期限可以根据委托人的抉择，在委托人就此事以书面形式通知代理人时，予以终止。

This Agreement shall be governed by the law of the principal place of business.

本协议应受主要商业区法律的管辖。

辨析 principal 和 principle

这是很容易搞混的两个单词，发音一样，但是词性和词义都有不同。

principle n. 原理，原则

The parties shall abide by the principle of good faith in exercising their rights and performing their obligations.

当事人行使权利、履行义务应当遵循诚实信用原则。

3. 在美式英语中，习惯把公司和机构名称当作单数，所以会见到 State Farm Insurance trains its agents well。而英式英语把公司和机构名称当成复数，如 Lloyds of London train their agents well

4. in duplicate 一式两份，在合同中，常常出现一式若干份的写法

in triplicate 一式三份

in quadruplicate 一式四份

in quintuplicate 一式五份

in sextuplicate 一式六份

in septuplicate 一式七份

in octuplicate 一式八份

in nonuplicate 一式九份

in decuplicate 一式十份

除了上述的写法外，一式几份还可以用 fold 和 copy 表示。用 fold 时就不需要有名词的复数形式了，如 in 5 fold。但是 copy 要有复数形式，如，in 5 copies。

5. sublet v. 转租，分租，转包；n. 转租的房屋

Neither the Owner nor the Architect shall assign or sublet his interest in this

Agreement.

业主和建筑师都不应把他在本协议中的股权转让或转租出去。

AAA shall not assign this lease or sublet any part of the premises without written consent of the Landlord.

未经房东同意，甲方不应转让租借权或转租房产的任何部分。

英文合同中常见的"租赁"有以下几个动词：sublet，lease，rent，hire，let，charter。

sublet 主要用于转租或分租业务；

lease 根据租赁合同进行租赁，并且对象为大型机器、设备、土地，同时租赁期限较长；

rent 指房屋租赁，时间可长可短，且不一定存在租约；

hire 用于杂物及劳务租用，时间短；

let 一词是英式英语的用法，用于房屋租赁，时间可长可短；

charter 一般用于大型交通工具如飞机、轮船的租赁，必须签订租约。

AAA shall lease to Joint Venture Company facilities suitable for the manufacture of the products.

甲方将把适合用于生产的设备租借给合资公司。

She rents office space from a letting agency.

她从一家房屋中介租用办公场地。

The rooms are hired out for corporate meetings.

这些房屋已经对外租给公司召开会议。

They decided to let out the smaller offices at low rents.

他们决定以低廉的租金将这些较小的办公室租出去。

The company has chartered two carrying vessels to ship the cargo.

公司包租了两条运输船运送货物。

6.reimburse v.偿还；补偿

辨析动词 reimburse，indemnify 与 compensate

reimburse 指付还自己为盈利而花的钱或付还别人（如代理人或律师）为自己做事而花的钱。

action for reimbursement 申请赔偿的诉讼

claim reimbursement 索赔

demand for reimbursement 索赔

indemnify：（1）指一种允诺或实际的对损失（如火灾造成）或伤害（如事故）、损害（如战争或灾害造成）所做出的赔偿。（2）其词义有时接近于 compensate，多指抵消。

indemnifying subject 赔偿主体

indemnifying measure 补偿方法，赔偿措施

compensate：（1）有时不指按法律规定偿付债款，也不指无偿服务，而强调付钱回报，这里钱被看作是所付出的服务、风险或花费时间的等值物。（2）用于上述意义时，该词不意味着对他人负有义务或进行付钱，而常指进行平衡，如以好抵坏，以得补失这种平衡。

make compensation 予以赔偿

claim for compensation 索赔

We must reimburse him the costs of the journey.

AAA shall have the right to reimburse itself from future royalties.

甲方有权从将来的使用费中得到补偿。

In addition to the reimbursements provided for herein，AAA shall pay ZZZ technical assistance fees.

除这里所提供的补偿外，甲方应向乙方支付技术援助费。

He promised to indemnify me for my losses.

他答应赔偿我的损失。

We will indemnify you for any expenses you may incur on our behalf.

我方会补偿你方为我方所花的一切费用。

The applicant for the credit shall be bound by and liable to indemnify the banks against all obligations and responsibilities imposed by foreign laws and usages.

凡由外国法律和习惯赋予银行的一切义务和责任，应由开证申请人承担，他且应对银行负补偿之责。

You have to compensate us for the short shipment of 600 kilos.

你方须为短装600千克给予赔偿。

In order to compensate your purchases，we are allowed by our government to buy your handicrafts as much as 40% of the total value of your purchases.

为了补偿你方购货，我国政府允许我公司购买高达你方购货总值40%的手工艺品。

Our users insist that you have to compensate for the inferior quality.

我方用户坚持认为，你方须为劣质给予赔偿。

7.violation n.违反，违背

Violation of any term of this Agreement shall cause the termination of the Agreement.

一旦违反协议的任何条款，必然导致协议终止。

The Buyer hereby represents that the price charged by the Seller hereto is not in violation of the price controls imposed by any said executive orders.

为此，买方提出，卖方索价并未违反有关行政命令所制定的物价管理办法。

violate v.违反，侵犯

Should any Employees，or agents of the Contractor violate the laws of（country），the Employer may，at his own and sole discretion，terminate the Agreement immediately.

如果承包商的雇员或代理人违反（某国）法令，雇主可以随意单方终止协议。

8.conduct v.管理，引导，处理；n.行为

The Architect shall conduct inspections to determine the date of completion.

建筑师应检查工作以确定完工日期。

Seller has the corporate power to carry on its business as now being conducted.

销售商具有法人权利按现行方式继续开展经营。

Any expenses, including reasonable attorney's fees in connection with the conduct of any suit or claim shall not be borne by Buyer.

任何费用，包括因诉讼或债权而用于辩护律师的合理费用，都不应由买方承担。

9.breach n.违背，破坏，不履行

Any disagreement arising out of this Contract or from the breach of it shall be submitted for arbitration.

本合同所产生的意义不一致或由于违反合同而造成的争执，均须提交仲裁（处理）。

A breach of any of terms and conditions shall be entitled to a termination.

任何条款、规定和条件的违反（破坏），将赋予（协议）终止的权利。

10.compensation n.赔偿，补偿；补偿金，赔款

compensation business/transaction/deal    补偿交易

compensation trade 补偿贸易

unemployment compensation  失业救济金

Buyers claim a compensation of ￡120.

买方要求赔偿120英镑。

You will get ample compensation for your efforts.

您的努力将得到足够的补偿。

The bargain price may be taxed either as compensation or dividend.

交易价格既可按报酬征税，也可按股利征税。

Nothing contained in this Agreement shall authorize the Optionor to demand compensation for any money expended subsequent to the date of this Agreement.

本协议没有任何条款授权优先购买者，要求对本协议日期以后的任何花费进行补偿。

11.authority n.权力（后接动词不定式或介词for），当局（复数）

competent authorities                 主管当局

customs authorities                   海关当局

exchange control authorities          外汇管制当局

government authorities                政府当局

licensing authorities                 签发许可证当局

| money authorities | 金融当局 |
| port authorities | 港务当局 |

The Contractor shall notify the contracting officer of the taxing authorities' refusal to recognize such a tax exemption.

承包商应将税务当局拒绝认定该项免税的情况通知立约官员。

He has the authority of his home office for immediate（on the spot）decision.

他的国内公司授权给他可以立即（当场）决定。

The Buyer has already applied to the authorities concerned for import licence.

买方已向有关当局申请进口许可证。

No agent or salesman of the Company has authority to change any of the conditions or provisions or covenants of this Agreement.

任何代理人和公司的推销员都无权变更本协议的任何条件、条款。

authorize v. 授权，认可，批准，正式承认

authorized stock 授权资本，注册资本

The Finance Committee authorized the spending of USD500,000 on this project.

财政委员会批准用50万美元建设这一工程项目。

authorization n. 授权，认可，委任，批准

12. appendices n. 附录的复数形式，单数是 appendix

All licensed machines shall incorporate as a part thereof, such parts as are listed in Appendix A.

所有获得许可的机器将作为部件之一收编入列有各种部件的附录 A 中。

The Contractor shall render all services of the plant in accordance with this Contract, appendices thereto and the technical specifications and data, drawings, plans and specifications referred to therein.

承包商将按照本合同、合同附录及其中所提到的各种技术规格、数据、图纸、计划等规定提供建筑厂房所需的一切服务（项目）。

在合同中表示附件的词还有 annex，schedule，exhibit，attachment 和 addendum。

The "Manufacturer's Price Schedule", which is annexed, shall make an integral part of this Agreement.

所附的"制造商价目表"将构成本协议整体的一部分。

The Employee shall execute an assignment in the same form as per attached exhibit, marked "Exhibit A".

雇员必须执行一项与所附的标有"附件 A"的相同形式的任务。

"Licensed Products" are any and all the products as listed in Schedule A attached hereto and all improvements in such products which may be developed by the Licensor during the Effective Period.

"特许产品"的含义是指合同附表 A 中所列的所有产品和许可方在合同有效期

内可能对这些产品做的全部改进。

Project Document means Project Specification as issued by Engineer, and any attachment thereto and Contractor's Tender.

项目文件是指由工程师发布的设计说明书以及其他任何附件和承包商的投标书。

The contract documents consist of this Agreement, drawings and all addenda issued prior to execution of this Agreement.

合同文件包括协议本身、施工图样以及在本协议执行前所签订的各附录。

13. insurance n. 保险

部分常用词组

| | |
|---|---|
| insurance agent | 保险代理人 |
| insurance amount | 保（险）额 |
| insurance certificate | 保险凭证 |
| insurance claim | 保险索赔 |
| insurance company | 保险公司 |
| insurance cover | 保险 |
| insurance coverage | 保险范围 |
| insurance endorsement=insurance rider | 保险批单 |
| insurance policy | 保（险）单 |
| insurance premium | 保（险）费 |
| insurance declaration | 保险声明书，保险通知书 |
| air transportation insurance | 航空运输保险 |
| marine insurance | 水险，海上保险，海运险 |
| ocean marine cargo insurance | 海洋运输货物保险 |
| overland transportation insurance | 陆上运输保险 |
| parcel post insurance | 邮包保险 |
| to arrange insurance | 投保，洽办保险 |
| to cover insurance | 投保，洽办保险 |
| to effect insurance | 投保，洽办保险 |
| to provide insurance | 投保，洽办保险 |
| to take out insurance | 投保，洽办保险 |

说明保险情况时，insurance 后接介词的一般用法：

表示所保的货物，后接 on，如 insurance on the 100 tons of wool；

表示投保的险别，后接 against，如 insurance against all risks；

表示保额，后接 for，如 insurance for 110% of the invoice value；

表示保险费或保险费率，后接 at，如 insurance at a slightly higher premium，insurance at the rate of 5‰；

表示向某保险公司投保，后接 with，如 insurance with the People's Insurance Company of China.

We have covered insurance on the 100 metric tons of wool for 110% of the invoice value against all risks.

我们已将100公吨羊毛按发票金额的110%投保一切险。

insure v. 保险，投保

通常用作及物动词，宾语一般为所保的货物，如：

Please insure the goods against all risks and war risk.

请将此货投保一切险及战争险。

宾语有时也可为投保的险别，如：

The insurance company here insures this risk with 5% franchise.

此保险公司保此种险有5%的免赔限度。

有时也用作不及物动词，如：

Please insure against breakage.

请投保破碎险。

过去分词 insured 作定语构成的部分常用词组：

insured amount（insurance amount）　　保（险）额

insured cargo 或 insured goods　　　投保的货物

insured 还可作名词用，前面加定冠词，即 the insured，作"被保险人"解。

In international trade, by transportation insurance we mean that the insured, who is usually the importer or the exporter, covers insurance on one or several lots of goods against certain risks for a certain insured amount with the insurer, i. e. the insurance company, at an agreed premium.

在国际贸易中，我们所说的货物运输险，是指被保险人，通常是进口商或出口商，对一批或若干批货物向保险人，即保险公司，按一定的保额和约定的保费投保一定的险别。

14.合同的生效有几种表示法

come into force/effect, enter into force, become effective/valid, be in effect, be in force 以及 validate。

enter into force 生效，开始实行

come into force 同样表示"生效"和"开始实行"。

The present rules shall come into force from the date of their adoption by the China Council for the Promotion of International Trade.

本规则自中国国际贸易促进委员会通过之日起施行。

The Contract shall become effective on the date when the Contract executed by the parties hereto heas received the approval from the appropriate governmental authorities of both（one country）and（another country）.

这里各方所签署的合同被（某国）与（另一国）有关政府当局批准之日，即为该项合同生效之时。

in force（法律、规章等的）有效力，有约束力

These regulations are still in force.

这些规章仍然有效。

to put …in/into force 实施……；使……生效

● Exercises

I.Translate the following sentences into English：

1.所有按固定费用不能收回的成本，应由你方按实际情况予以补偿。

2. "外方"应采取一切必要措施，以保证商标的注册。

3.根据本协议规定，当事人任一方不履行或延期履行其所承担的义务，应以违约论处。

4.如果承包商聘请或拟聘请某人担任他的合同代理人、律师或调解人，那么，承包商与该人在各方面应遵守（某国）法律中关于聘用人员及其活动的各项规定条款。

5.兹约定，如果按照现存的保险单的现价，预付了乙方工厂财产保险费，那么，各方之间应最后调整该项保险金额。

6.本协议自即日起生效，为期（……）年。

7.代理人在代理期间有义务展出产品的最佳样品。

8.如果比甲方固定的价格低的话，则许可证持有方不同意出售特许设备。

9.甲方宣布，它有资格同（某国）签署一项建设公路的总价格为（……）美元的合同。

10.如果存在任何争议，任何一方可以要求仲裁。

II.Translate the following sentences into Chinese：

1. No compensation will be allowed or paid by the Landlord, by reason of inconvenience to business arising from the necessity of repairing.

2.Whereas，the Principal requires the employment of agent，and Agent is willing to represent the Principal…

3. Neither the Owner nor the Architect shall assign or sublet his interest in this Agreement to any other person.

4.The Second Party shall keep such costs fully insured against loss by fire and theft for the benefit of the First Party.

5.A third arbitrator（the "Presiding Arbitrator"）shall be appointed by agreement between the Parties，and，if the Parties fail to jointly appoint the Presiding Arbitrator within the time specified in the Arbitration Rules，the Chairman of CIETAC shall make such appointment，taking into consideration the criteria set out in this Article 18.2.

6.The Leasee shall have the right to renew this Sublease for a further period of（…）years.

7.In case of doubt as to interpretation of any of the provisions of this Agreement， the local language version shall be controlling.

8.Any event or circumstance beyond the control of the Parties to the Contract shall be deemed an event of Force Majeure and shall include， but not restricted to， fire， storm， flood， earthquake， explosion， war， rebellion， insurrection， epidemic and quarantine restriction. If， due to an event of Force Majeure， either Party is prevented from performing any of its obligations under this Contract， the time for performance under this Contract shall be extended by a period equal to the period of delay caused by such Force Majeure.

9. No submissions will be accepted without quoting the price for the project in question.

10. In consideration of mutual covenants hereinafter set forth， the parties hereto agree as follows.

# Unit Four /符合合同文体的规范用词及用语

## Words & Expressions Following Contractual Norms

---

### 4.1　　　　　　　　特殊副词 Special Adverbs

---

在合同中迄今为止仍然使用一些古体词语，最突出的形式是仍然使用如 hereto，thereafter，whereby 这些在现代英语中已很少使用的词。这些古体词语多为副词，由 here，there，where 加上介词，作为正式法律文书中的词汇，在句中作定语或状语。其作用主要是为了避免重复，使行文显得正式、准确、简洁，同时也起着承接合同条款的作用。here 表示 this，there 表示 that，where 代表 which 并引出从句。

#### 4.1.1　特此，在此 hereby

相当于 by this，或 by reason of this，表示"特此""在此"。

The Seller hereby warrants that the goods meet the quality standard and are free from all defects.

卖方在此保证：货物符合质量标准无瑕疵。

The parties mutually agree that the said Agreement shall be and is hereby cancelled.

缔约双方彼此同意，特此取消该协议。

We hereby employ you as our Broker to bring about the sale of our Company.

我们特此雇用你为我们的经纪人，以促进公司的销售业务。

#### 4.1.2　此中，于此 herein

相当于 in this，译成"此中""于此"。

The license herein granted is conditioned on ZZZ selling Licensed Devices at prices no more favorable than those followed by AAA.

在这里授予的许可证是以乙方出售特许装置的价格不得优于甲方所遵循的价格为条件的。

The minimum royalty herein specified shall be paid by ZZZ to AAA.

于此规定的最低使用费（租费）应由乙方付给甲方。

### 4.1.3 以下，在下文 hereinafter

相当于 later in this Contract，译成"以下""在下文"等。

Any complaint which either party does not wish to refer to a Conciliation Committee may then be submitted by the First Party to arbitration as hereinafter provided.

如果任何一方不愿意把申诉提交给调解委员会，就可由甲方将其提交给下文所提出的机构以便仲裁。

This Contract is made on 20th day of May, 2006 by ABC Corporation（hereinafter referred to as "Seller"）and XYZ Corporation（hereinafter referred to as "Buyer"）.

本合同由 ABC 公司（以下简称"卖方"）与 XYZ 公司（以下简称"买方"）于 2006 年 5 月 20 日订立。

Party A agrees to pay to Party B an amount hereinafter called royalty equal to 5% of the gross sales.

甲方同意向乙方支付以下称为特许权使用费的费用，该费用等于售货总额的5%。

### 4.1.4 在上文中 hereinbefore

相当于 in a preceding part of this Contract，译成"在上文中"。

The Debtor may deem compromise with any other Creditor, in such manner as the Debtor may consider advisable, anything hereinbefore to the contrary notwithstanding.

尽管有上述相反的情况，只要债务人认为是适宜的，他可以与任何其他债权人达成妥协。

If the Offeree does not advise the Offeror by notice in writing within the said period of （…）days as hereinbefore provided，then the Offeree shall be deemed to have accepted the offer of the Offeror.

如果受要约人在上文所规定的（……）天内没有书面通知要约人，则受要约人被认为已经接受了要约人的要约。

### 4.1.5 本协议的 hereto

相当于 to this，可译成"本协议的"。

The parties hereto are fully aware that the best interests of their own and Joint Venture will be served by taking all reasonable measures to ensure increase in production and in order to achieve this goal, the Parties agree to retain sufficient earnings in Joint Venture for the expansion of production and other requirements, such as bonus and welfare funds.The annual proportion of the earnings to be retained shall be decided by the Board of Directors.

协议双方充分认识到，为了他们自己和合营企业的最大利益，必须尽一切可能增加生产。因此，双方同意合营企业保留足够的收益，用于扩大生产及其他需要，如奖金和福利基金。合营企业的年留用奖金比率由董事会决定。

Joint Venture shall employ competent treasurers and auditors to keep all books of accounts, which are accessible at any time to each Party hereto.

合营企业雇用合格的财务人员和审计人员，设立会计账目，合营各方可随时查看有关账目。

All disputes, controversies or differences which may arise between the Parties hereto, out of or in relation to this Agreement and which the Board of Directors fails to settle through consultation, shall finally be submitted for arbitration which shall be conducted by the Foreign Trade Arbitration Commission of the China Council for the Promotion of International Trade in accordance with the Provisional Rules of Procedure of Arbitration of the said commission, the decision of which shall be final and binding upon both parties.

本合同双方有关本协议的一切分歧与争议，若董事会不能通过协商解决，则提交中国国际贸易促进委员会对外贸易仲裁委员会，根据该会仲裁程序暂行规则进行仲裁。该委员会的裁决是终局的，对双方均具有约束力。

## 4.1.6 在本合同中的 hereof

相当于 of this contract，译成"在本合同中的……"。

Any failure or delay in the performance by either Party hereto of its obligations under this Agreement shall not constitute a breach hereof or give rise to any claims for damages if it is caused by the following occurrences beyond the control of the Party: earthquake, fire, floods, explosions, storms, accidents, war.

本协议任何一方因地震、火灾、洪水、爆炸、风暴、事故和战争等不可抗力事件，未能履行协议，不构成违约或索赔之缘由。

Whether the custom of the Port is contrary to this Clause or not, the owner of the goods shall, without interruption, by day and night, including Sundays and holidays (if required by the carrier), supply and take delivery of the goods.Provided that the owner of the goods shall be liable for all losses or damages including demurrage incurred in default on the provisions hereof.

不论港口习惯是否与本款规定相反，货主都应昼夜地，包括星期日和假日（如承运人需要），无间断地供货和提货。货主对违反本款规定所引起的所有损失或损坏，包括滞期应负担赔偿责任。

This Agreement shall begin on the date hereof, and shall continue for （…） years thereafter.

协议由本日开始，此后继续（……）年有效。

### 4.1.7　在此中 hereunder

相当于 under this，译成"在此中"。

The Principal shall not assign or transfer any of its rights, obligations or liabilities hereunder without the express prior written consent of the General Agent.

非经总代理人预先书面同意，委托人不得将本协议规定的任何权利、义务或责任予以转让或转移给他人。

The obligations of the Joint Venture hereunder shall be as follows：

合资企业各种义务如下：

### 4.1.8　此后，今后 thereafter

相当于 afterwards，after that，译成"此后""今后"。

This Agreement shall thereafter be automatically extended for further periods of（…）year（s）.

本协议此后应自动延长（……）年。

The parties shall organize and appoint the management committee, and thereafter, such management committee shall control the operation of the Joint Venture Company.

当事人双方应组织并委任管理委员会，而且今后该管理委员会应负责管理合资公司的经营。

### 4.1.9　因此，从而 thereby

相当于 by that means，in that connection，译成"因此""从而"。

Notice of termination shall be served by post or in person and the Agreement is thereby terminated.

停止协议的通知应通过邮寄或派人送去，至此该协议方可终止。

In the event of the death of any partner, this partnership shall not be thereby dissolved.

如果任何合伙人死亡，本合伙公司不因此而解散。

### 4.1.10　为此，therefor

相当于 for that，译成"为此"。

Before commencing the construction, the Contractor shall submit the plans and specifications therefor to the Owner for approval.

在开工之前，承包商应为此将各种计划、技术说明书一并提请业主批准。

The Engineer shall be paid therefor at standard prices fixed by the Parties hereto.

工程师应该为此按与约各方规定的标准价格得到报酬。

### 4.1.11　因此 therefore

译成"因此"。

It is, therefore, to the mutual benefit of AAA and ZZZ to establish high standard of quality in the merchandise.

因此，为了甲方和乙方的共同利益，应该为商品确立高的质量标准。

### 4.1.12　由此 therefrom

相当于 from that，译成"由此"。

"Products" means any and all agricultural products or any products derived therefrom.

"产品"一词，系指一切农产品或由此衍生的任何产品。

Additions thereto or deductions therefrom shall be made under this Article.

由此增加的条款或由此减少的条款可按照本条规定执行。

### 4.1.13　其，关于…… thereof

相当于 of that，from that source，表示"of the said Agreement"，译成"本协议的内容"。

Party A is the owner of the right to the Letter Patent together with any extensions thereof.

甲方是专利证书所有权及其任何引申权利的所有者。

The titles to the Articles in this Agreement and in the said Exhibits are for convenience of reference only, not part of this Agreement, and shall not in any way affect the interpretation thereof.

本协议的各条款和协议的附录中使用的标题，仅为了查阅方便，并非本协议的构成部分，绝不影响本协议内容的解释。

### 4.1.14　其中，在那里 therein

相当于 in that，译成"其中""在那里"。

The said Letter of Credit has just been received, but we find that some of the Clauses therein are not in agreement with the terms and conditions of the Contract.

我们刚收到该信用证，发现其中有些条款与合同条款不符合。

Royalty shall be paid if any patented invention of AAA is embodied therein.

一旦 A 方的任何专利发明在那里得以实现，那就应付给特许权使用费。

### 4.1.15　在其上 thereon

相当于 on that，译成"在其上"。

When the Licensed Products are sold，the royalty thereon shall be paid within a calendar month from the date of delivery.

特许产品售出后，该产品的专利权使用费从交货日算起，一个日历月度内付讫。

### 4.1.16　向那里，另外 thereto

相当于 to that，译成"向那里""另外"。

Written notice shall be sent to all directors，including copies of reports relating thereto.

应将书面通知送达所有的董事，其中包括有关各种报告副本。

The structure as well as equipments pertaining thereto shall be erected by the Contractor，on the Site set forth hereunder.

关于那里的建筑结构和设备应由承包商在下面所述场地建立起来。

### 4.1.17　凭此协议，凭此条款 whereby

相当于 by which，译成"凭此协议""凭此条款"。

In the event of accident whereby loss or damage may result in a claim under this Policy，immediate notice applying for survey must be given to our Agent.

所保货物，如发生此保险单项下负责赔偿的事故，应立即通知公司代理人查验。

译文中的 whereby 是关系副词引出定语从句。

This Agreement is made and concluded by and between A Corporation （hereinafter called Party A） and B Company （hereinafter called Party B） whereby the Parties hereto agree to enter into the compensation trade under the terms and conditions set forth below.

本协议由 A 公司（以下称甲方）与 B 公司（以下称乙方）签订，双方同意按下列条款进行补偿贸易。

## 4.2　　　法律词汇 "Shall" Legal Term "Shall"

shall 是国际商务合同中使用频率最高的词汇之一，它是构成独特英文合同文体的一个最主要的词汇。shall 主要用来表示合同中各项具体的规定和表示法律上应当履行的义务、债务和应承担的法律责任，这种情况下不使用 should，must 或 have to。shall 一词不受主语的人称影响，可根据合同的具体内容灵活翻译，可译成"须"、"应"、"应该"或"必须"，也可以翻译为"将""可以"或不译出来。

The employer shall make a prepayment of 20% of the Contract value to the Contractor within 10 days after signing the Contract.

雇主应于签约后 10 天内向承包人支付相当于承包合同价值 20% 的预付款。

The board meeting shall be called and presided over by the Chairman. Should the Chairman be absent, the vice-Chairman shall, in principle, call and preside over the board meeting.

董事会会议应由董事长召集并主持，如董事长缺席时，原则上应由副董事长召集并主持。

The Term of the Company shall be 5 years commencing from the date of issuance of the Company's business license.

公司条款于颁发营业执照之日起5年有效。

Any amendment to this Contract or to its appendices shall come into force after the written agreement is concluded and signed by the Parties hereto and approved by the original examination and approval authorities.

本合同及其附件的任何修改，必须经双方签署书面合同文件，并报原审批机构批准后才能生效。

If the Buyer fails to notify and/or forward full details within the period specified above, the Buyer shall be deemed to have waived their right to assert any claim.

如果买方未能在上述规定的期间内通知和（或）寄出完整的细节，那么买方将被认为放弃提出任何索赔的权利。

All residents shall be equal before the law.

法律面前人人平等。

Tenant shall pay for all utilities and/or services supplied to the premises.

租客须支付所有公用事业和/或服务设施的收费。

注意：一般的禁令用 shall not do…或 Nor…shall do…。

Tenant shall not change or install locks, paint, or wallpaper said premises without Landlord's prior written consent, Tenant shall not place placards, signs, or other exhibits in a window or any other place where they can be viewed by other residents or by the general public.

如未事先获得业主书面同意，租客不得更换或安装住所的门锁、油漆住所或贴换墙纸；也不得将招牌、告示牌或其他展示牌置放在窗户上或其他住客或公众看得见的任何地方。

在英文合同中，除了掌握"shall"的特殊法律内涵以外，还要了解其余的几个情态动词may，must，may not的准确应用。may，must，may not在合同中分别明确表示当事人的义务（应当干什么）、强制性义务（必须做什么）和禁止性义务（不得做什么）。

在合同中，以下几个句式有不同的含义：may do/have the right to do/be entitled to 表示"可以做什么或有权做什么"，shall do/be required to do/be obliged to/be obligated to/be under the obligation/responsibility to do 表示"应当做什么"，must do 表示"必须做什么"，而 may not do/shall not do 则被理解成"不得做什么"。

在合同翻译时，要注意，有时候是不可以调换 shall 和 may 在句中的位置的。如句子：The Parties hereto shall, first of all, settle any disputes arising in the execution of or in connection with the contract through amicable negotiations.If no settlement can be reached, such dispute may then be submitted for arbitration.

双方首先应友好协商解决在执行合同中或与合同有关的争议。如不能达成协议，争议可提交仲裁。

句中的 shall 和 may 很难互换。shall 表示当事人有权选择解决争议的方法。而句中的 may 如果用 shall 来替换，就被理解成当事人应当（明确当事人有这样的权利）诉讼解决，当事人方放弃诉讼，寻求其他解决途径的权利就给剥夺了，这显然不符合法律逻辑。

## 4.3　　　　　"系指"定义词 Defining Words

我们把表示定义的词称为"系指"定义词（defining words）。重要的合同，往往一开始就用系指定义词对合同中的关键名词的含义加以限定，给出一个统一的解释，以避免日后发生分歧。

在合同中经常使用的定义词有 mean, shall be, is, are, shall mean 等，表示"指"、"系指"和"含义为"等，但这些词使用起来是有区别的。如"定义词"是合同双方特别根据本合同约定的，那么就要用 mean, is, are；如果是"通常的定义"，即所有合同都用该定义词，shall 加上 mean, be 就是正确的表达。

"Licensed Products" are any and all the products as listed in Schedule A attached hereto and all improvements in such products which may be developed by the Licensor during the Effective Period.

"特许产品"的含义是指合同附件 A 中所列的所有产品和许可方在合同有效期内可能对这些产品做的全部改进。

In this Contract Force Majeure shall mean any ocurrence beyond the reasonable control of the parties preventing or delaying, the performance of this Contract including but not limited to：

本合同规定的不可抗力系指任何超出双方合理的控制力所发生的阻碍或延误本合同履行的事件，包括但不限于：

## 4.4　　　　　专用词汇 Terminology

在翻译国际商务合同时，我们不难发现一些我们平时不常用的却频频出现在合同中的一些词汇。这些词汇虽然数量不多，但却是法律合同和文件中专用的正式词汇，也是法律文体的特殊需要。

## 4.4.1　鉴于，就……而论 whereas

Whereas the first Party is willing to employ the second Party and the second Party agrees to act as the first Party's Engineer in…it is hereby mutually agreed as follows：

鉴于甲方愿意聘请乙方，乙方同意应聘为甲方在……（工程）的工程师。合同双方特此达成协议如下：

Whereas the Bank has agreed to extend a short-term credit loan for the purpose of providing general working capital to the Company，the Parties thereto do hereby agree as follows：

鉴于该银行同意向该公司提供短期信贷作为其周转资金之用，双方同意以下各点：

Whereas AAA represents and warrants that he is the owner of the sole and exclusive rights to use the secret process of ZZZ in（country）；

有鉴于甲方表示并保证他有独家的权利，可以采用乙方在（某国）的机密生产；

## 4.4.2　特此，因此 Now Therefore

Now therefore，the Conditions of this obligation are such that，if the Contractor will promptly and faithfully perform the said Contract（including any amendments thereto）then this obligation shall be null and void，otherwise it shall remain in full force and effect.

为此，本担保的义务条件是，如果承包人迅速地、忠实地履行上述合同（包括修改书），本保证书规定的义务无效，否则将生效实施。

Now therefore，in consideration of the sum of money paid，and of the terms and conditions set forth below，the parties mutually agree，as follows.

因此，考虑到所付款项的金额以及下列规定的条款和条件，双方相互同意如下。

"Now Therefore" 的句式紧接着鉴于条款之后，是序文与正文之间的桥梁，因此也被称为过渡条款（Transitional Clause）。

过渡条款大致包含三个内容：承接鉴于条款，对鉴于条款中的事实予以确认；确认合同对价；引出合同的正文部分。

Now therefore，in consideration of the premises and the covenants herein contained，the parties hereto agree as follows：

兹以上各点和契约条款为约因，订约双方协议如下：

Now therefore，in consideration of the payment to be made by Party A to Party B，Party B hereby covenants with Party A to complete the building in conformity with the provisions of the Contract.

乙方特此立约向甲方保证按合同规定完成工程建设，以取得甲方所付的报酬。

### 4.4.3　特此立（证）据，以此立（证）据 In Witness Whereof

In Witness Whereof/Thereof 特此立证，以此立证

In Witness Whereof the Parties hereto have caused this Agreement to be executed on the day and year first before written in accordance with their respective laws.

本协议书于上面所签订的日期，由双方根据各自的法律签订，开始执行，特立此据。

In Witness Whereof, stockholders of the Company have hereunto set his hands of the day and year first above written.

特此证明，公司股东已在此文本上签名，年月日已注明如上。

In Witness Whereof we have hereto signed this Documents on ＿＿（date）accepted on ＿＿（date）.

我方于＿＿年＿＿月＿＿日签署本文件，并于＿＿年＿＿月＿＿日已接受此文件，特此为证。

### 4.4.4　根据本文件，特此宣布 Know All Men by These Presents

Know All Men by these presents that we（bank's name）having our registered office at ＿＿（hereinafter called "the Bank"）will be bound unto（the Owner's name）（hereinafter called "the Owner"）in the sum of ＿＿for payment well and truly to be made to the said Owner, the Bank will bind itself, its successors and better assignee by these presents.

根据本文件，兹宣布，我行（银行名称）其注册地点在（注册地名）（以下简称银行），向（业主名称）（以下简称业主）立约担保支付（金额数）的保证金。本保证书对银行及其继承人和受让人均具有约束力。

## 4.5　其他特定用语 Other Specific Phrases

除了上述特定用语外，在英文的商务合同中还能常见到下面的一些用语，在翻译中仍要注意合乎合同的语言规范。

### 4.5.1　在……之前 prior to

The Contractor shall bear all costs and damages which may result from the ordering of any materials prior to the approval of the shop drawings.

承包商应承担未经施工图认可的物资订货所带来的一切花费与全部损失。

Not to make any structural alterations or additions to the said premises without first having obtained the written consent of the Landlord. In the event of any permitted alterations being made by the Tenant to the said premises during the said term the Tenant shall reinstate the said premises at his own costs and expenses prior to delivering up possession thereof to the Landlord at the expiration of the said term.

没有首先获得业主的书面同意，不得对该楼宇作任何结构上的改变或附加建筑。万一租户在所述期间对该楼宇进行任何获准的改变，租户须在所述期间届满而把楼宇所有权移交业主前，自费将楼宇复原。

## 4.5.2 作为……代替 in lieu of

A foreign or who is accustomed to sign his name may notify the company of his signature in lieu of the seal impression referred to in the preceding paragraph.

凡习惯于亲手签名的外商，可通知他签字的公司，以代替前段所述的印章。

## 4.5.3 根据…… in accordance with/according to…

The work shall be performed in accordance with the provisions of the Contract.
此工程应按合同条款完成。

The commission shall vary in percentage according to the kind of sale made by the salesman.

推销员的佣金要根据推销员所从事的销售种类的不同，其佣金的百分率也有所不同。

## 4.5.4 由于，因为 due to

The Landlord shall not be liable for any failure to supply such heat, water, or electricity, not due to gross negligence on its part.

如果不是因为房主方面的重大疏忽，房主对不能供应暖气、水、电不负责任。

## 4.5.5 以……为受益人，赞同 in favor of

This instrument shall inure to the benefit and run in favor of such Transferee, with the same force and effect as though such Transferee had originally been the Optionee herein.

本票据可供该受让人有效利用，其有效性一如该受让人原来就是取得优先选择权者。

## 4.5.6 按照……的要求 at the request of

The question of law shall be submitted to arbitration by the parties, or either of them, at the request of the expert.

在专家的要求下，有关法律问题应由各方或其中一方提交仲裁。

### 4.5.7　有关 pertaining to

Buyer shall be fully acquainted with all other matters and things pertaining to the operation of the business of Seller.

买方对卖方经营的有关情况应了如指掌。

### 4.5.8　依从，按照 in compliance with

In compliance with your invitation for bids of the above date，the undersigned hereby proposes to furnish all labor and materials.

遵照你方的上述日期投标，签字人特此建议提供全部劳动力和材料。

in conformity with 也表示 "依从" "按照"。

The financial statements shall present fairly the financial position of said companies in conformity with the generally accepted accounting principles.

财务报表必须遵照公认会计准则公正地展示该公司的财务状况。

### 4.5.9　但是，但规定 provided that

Instructions given by the Engineer shall be in writing，provided that if for any reason the Engineer considers it necessary to give any such instructions orally，the Contractor shall comply with such instructions.

由工程师发出的指令应为书面形式，但规定，如果由于任何原因，工程师认为有必要以口头形式发出指令，承包人应遵照执行。

The Owner may，at its discretion，approve or reject any change proposed by the Contractor，provided that the Owner shall approve any change proposed by the Contractor to ensure the safety of the Works.

业主可自行决定赞成或拒绝由承包人提出的变更，但应接受承包人提出的保证工程安全方面的变更建议。

### 4.5.10　该，这 in question

It is common for Tenders to be identified by such a tender reference or contract number as shall be added to link the Tender to the Project in question.

通常为了把投标书和有关工程项目联系在一起，投标书应标明投标参考编号或合同号。

### 4.5.11　上述的，前述的，是合同英语中的惯用词，用于指代上文中提及的事物 the above-mentioned，said，aforesaid

Party A shall make delivery of the goods in accordance with the above-mentioned arrangement.

甲方将按照上述安排交货。

Party A grants Party B an exclusive license to manufacture products by using the invention of the said Letter of Patent.

甲方授予乙方独占许可证，利用上述专利证书中的发明专利制造产品。

The Licensee shall keep full and adequate books of account containing all particulars that may be necessary for the purpose of showing the amount of royalty payable to the Licensor.The aforesaid books of account shall be kept at the licensee's place of business.

被许可方应完整地、详尽地记录会计账目，账目应包括所有旨在向许可方说明应付的使用费的细节，以上会计账目应在被许可方营业地保存。

### 4.5.12　以下签字方，署名的 undersigned

The undersigned promoters for the Company will prepare the Articles of Incorporation /Association.

署名的公司发起人将草拟公司组织条款。

The undersigned agrees to remain and continue to be liable for any unpaid balance remaining.

以下签字方同意继续负责支付未付清的欠款。

### 4.5.13　考虑到，鉴于，由于 in consideration of

In consideration of the Licenses and technical assistance provided herein，the Joint Venture Company shall pay Party A technical assistance fees in EURO.

考虑到许可证以及在此提供的技术援助，合资企业将以欧元的方式支付甲方技术援助费。

In consideration of such right to publish cheap edition，the Publisher shall pay to the Author 25 percent of the retail price of one copy sold of the edition.

考虑到有权出版这一平价版本，出版商每售出一本该书将付给作者零售价25%的版税。

### 4.5.14　基于……作为条件 subject to

subject to 的基本含义是 depending on…as a condition，在合同英语中应用较多。在翻译时，应根据其后宾语的具体内容，参照其基本含义，采用符合合同语言规范的翻译方法。

Subject to the terms of this Agreement，the Producer agrees to be bound by the terms to the following marketing agreement.

在本协议的条件下，制造商同意接受下列营销协议各项条款的约束。

Subject to Clause 5，no variation in or modification of the terms to the Contract shall be made except by written amendment signed by the parties.

根据第5条规定，合同的任何变更或修改，必须以双方签订的修改本为准。

Subject to the above stipulations, the profits, losses and risks of the Joint Venture Company shall be borne by the Parties in proportion to their respective contributions to the registered capital of the Joint Venture Company.

在上述规定的范围内，各方按各自对合资企业的注册资本出资比例分享合资企业的利润，并分摊合资企业遭受的损失和风险。

If any change is required regarding the terms and conditions of this Agreement, then both parties shall negotiate in order to find a suitable solution, provided that any change of this Agreement shall be subject to the approval by the Canadian Government.

如需对本协议条款进行修改，双方应协商解决，但对协议的任何修改内容必须经加拿大政府批准方为有效。

We make you the following offer, subject to change without notice.

我方报盘如下，如有变动不另行通知。

### 4.5.15　有权，有资格 to be entitled to

to be entitled to 在合同英语中表示 to give sb.the right to sth，翻译时可译成"有权""有资格"等，在表示权利的时候，体现出该权利在法律上的强制性，但还是要根据上下文的情况，来做具体的翻译。

Chairman and Directors are entitled to also have such positions in other companies, which will not be the competitors of the company.

公司的董事长及董事有资格在其他公司担任同样的职务，但其任职的公司不得是本公司的竞争对手。

If one or more of the following events of default shall occur and be continuing, the Agent and the Banks shall be entitled to the remedies set forth in Article 2 Item 3.

如果发生下列一种或几种以上违约事件，且违约事件正在继续，代理行以及各银行应行使第2条第3款规定的补救方法。

The Seller shall be entitled to terminate this license in the event of failure by the Buyer to comply with any of the conditions stated in this Article.

如果买方违反本条款所规定的条件，卖方有权终止这种特许权。

The Tenant shall not be entitled to any such reimbursement in accordance with the Clause 5.3 to this Agreement.

按照本协定第5条第3款的规定，承租人无权获得任何此类补偿。

### 4.5.16　尽管，即使 notwithstanding

介词 notwithstanding 在合同英语中的使用频率很高。该介词不能引导让步状语从句，但它的译法跟 although，though 和 even if 引导的状语从句没有太大的区别，基本上都可以译成"尽管""即使"，表示一种让步。

Notwithstanding the above provision，this Agreement shall terminate if the Joint Venture Company enters into liquidation.

虽有前述条款，但如合资企业停业清算，则本协议应终止生效。

Anything to the contrary notwithstanding，it is expressly agreed that on any default as provided in this paragraph，the Seller shall have the right to rescind this Agreement，and the Seller，at his option，may retake such Goods.

尽管有与之相反的情形，双方明确同意，如果违反本段条文规定，卖方有权废除本协议，且可自行决定收回这些货品。

### 4.5.17 除……外 save

save 在合同英语中，save 是一个与 except（for）相同的介词，译成"除……外"，不管是 save 还是 except（for）之后都可跟一个名词性短语，也可以跟一个从句或另一个介词短语。

The Contractor shall not cut or alter the work of any other Contractor save with the consent of the Engineer.

除非得到工程师的同意，否则该承包商不应削减或改变其他任何承包商的工程。

Save as is provided in this Ordinance，no claim within the jurisdiction of the Board shall be actionable in any court.

除非本条例另有规定，否则凡属仲裁处司法管辖权范围内的申诉，不得在任何法庭进行诉讼。

### 4.5.18 对于，关于，有关……的 in respect of

in respect of 在合同英语中使用较频繁，可译成"对于""关于""有关……的"。

The Voting Trustees shall，in respect of any stock possess all stockholders' right of every kind.

股权受托人拥有各类股票的全部股东权利。

Contractor shall not be relieved from any obligation，responsibility and/or liability under the Contract in respect of any part of the Work performed by a Subcontractor.

按照合同规定，由分包商执行的任何工程部分，承包商不能推卸其义务、责任和/或债务。

AAA will make，declare or pay any distribution or payments of any kind in respect of its capital stock.

甲方将实行、宣布或支付有关其股本的任何分配或各项支付。

### 4.5.19 按……，依……履行，执行 in pursuance of

All such advances or payments shall be deemed to have been made in pursuance of this Agreement.

应该把一切这一类预付款项看作是为了执行本协议而支付的。

### 4.5.20　相关的……the same

"the same"在英文合同中除了用作"the same…as"的固定短语外，主要用来代替前面已经表述过的事情或状态，从而避免重复。

The Contractor shall comply with the Owner's design and the management method and manuals, and any revision of the same.

承包商应遵守业主的设计、管理方法、手册以及对上述的修订。

Any repairs or replacements carried out as described above shall be deemed to be effected and made by the Manufacturer, and the guarantee concerned shall remain in effect provided that the same does not result in any detriment to the Equipment.

根据上述规定实施的维修或替换工作应视为是由生产商实施的，如果该维修替换并没有对设备造成损害，相关的担保仍然有效。

### 4.5.21　包括但不限于……including but not limited to/include without limitation

All intellectual property rights associated with the Products—including but not limited to trade marks, patents, designs, drawings, sketches, test results, and copyrights—remain the property of the Party B, provided that any such rights associated with particular specifications supplied by the Party A are not the Party B's property.

与产品相关的所有知识产权，包括但不限于商标、专利、设计、图纸、草图、实验结果和著作权，均属于乙方财产，但是甲方提出的任何与特别规定相关的权利不属于乙方财产。

All taxes and impost or customs duties and other taxes and duties, including without limitation VAT, in connection with the Contract levied on Importer by the relevant authority in China in accordance with the Chinese tax laws then in effect shall be paid by Importer.

中国有关部门按照当时适用的中国税法向进口商征收的所有与本合同有关的税款、进口税或关税，以及其他税费，包括但不限于增值税，应由进口商缴纳。

### 4.5.22　在不影响……的原则下，不妨碍……without prejudice to

Without prejudice to Article 21, the following authorization shall be treated as properly executed.

在不影响第21条的原则下，以下授权视为正式签署。

The Party A shall nevertheless have the right to cancel in part of in whole of the contract without prejudice to the Party A's right to claim compensation.

甲方取消部分或全部合同的权利并不妨碍其享有的索赔权。

## 4.5.23　自某日起 as of/as from

This Contract shall come into full force and effect as of the 31th day of December 2018.

本合同从 2018 年 12 月 31 日起生效。

This Agreement shall be in force for a term of three years as from the date of its execution and shall continue in effect thereafter for an indefinite term, even if either of the parties shall have otherwise communicated to the other party by written notice delivered to such other party at least three months in advance.

本协议自签字执行之日起生效，期限三年。此后除非一方至少提前三个月向另一方发出书面通知，否则协议效力不定期持续。

## 4.5.24　如果没有…… absent…

Absent a contractual provision to the contrary, consequential damages are generally not recoverable against the Indemnitor.

如果不存在相反的合同规定，通常不得向赔偿方要求赔偿间接损失。

## 4.5.25　反之亦然 vice versa

vice versa 是拉丁语，在英文合同中经常出现。

The Distributor shall inform the Manufacturer of any change in its management, and vice versa.

批发商应将本人经营中的任何变动告知制造商，反之亦然。

## 4.5.26　在……程度上，仅仅 to the extent

to the extent 常出现在英文合同中，表示达到一种程度和范围；有时候这个短语在英文合同中可以理解成"仅仅"。

The financial statement made and delivered by Operator shall not be in error to an extent to …% or more.

经纪人编制并提交的财务报表，其差错率不得超过……%。

Party A shall be subrogated to the rights to the extent of…

甲方应仅以……为限行使代位权。

If and to the extent that such work is attributable to any other cause, the Contractor shall be notified promptly by（or on behalf of）the Employer, and Sub-Clause 13.3（Variation Procedure）shall apply.

如果此类工作在归因于任何其他原因的范围，雇主（或其代表）应迅速通知承包商，并应适用第 13.3 款（变更程序）的规定。

### 4.5.27　在不限于上述一般性规定的情况下 without limiting the generality of the foregoing

Without limiting the generality of the foregoing，any of the following acts by the Distributor shall be deemed a violation of this Agreement.

对前述事项的普遍性不加限制的话，则经销商所采取的任何下列行动将被认为违反本协议。

### 4.5.28　被认为 be deemed

英文合同的正式用语。

Only the Defects Liability Certificate referred to in Clause 56，shall be deemed to constitute approval of the Works.

只有第56条规定的缺陷责任证书才能视为构成对工程的批准。

The headings and marginal notes in these Conditions shall not be deemed part thereof or be taken into consideration in the interpretation or construction thereof or of the Contract.

本合同条件中的标题和旁注不应视为合同条款的一部分，对合同条件或合同本身的解释或理解也不应考虑这些标题和旁注。

## 4.6　　　　　　　拉丁文的应用 Latin Words

在普通的英文写作中，很难见到如 "ad idem" 这样的生疏词汇。其实，这正是英文合同的语言特色。在法律文件中，像拉丁语这样的晦涩用词比比皆是。

下面是最常见的一些拉丁语词汇：

ab initio=from the beginning 自始

ad hoc=especially 特别地

ad idem=同前，同上

arguendo=为了辩论；在辩论的过程中

bona fide 善意的

de facto 事实上的

e.g.（example gratia）= for example 例如

ex contractu=因合同，由合同引起的

ex delicto=由于侵权；源自侵权

et al=等人，一起其他人

i.e.=that is to say

interalia=among other things 除了别的东西；除了其他事项；特别（是）；其中

per se=itself 本身，本质上

pro forma 形式上

pro tanto 至此为止，或至某个限制为止

subjudice=at bar 审判中；正在审理而尚未裁决；未决审理

viz=namely 即

void ab initio 自始无效

## Notes

1.provide v.供应，供给，准备，预防，规定

The Principal shall not have the right to share commissions with the Agent except as provided hereunder.

除下列规定者外，委托人无权同代理人分享佣金。

The Buyer is to be provided with complete and detailed operating statements and balance sheets.

应向买方提供完整和详细的营业损益表和资产负债表。

He shall have the right/be entitled to renew this sublease for further period, provided he shall notify the First Party in writing.

他应有权使转租契约展延一段时间，但他必须以书面通知甲方。

provided, providing conj.倘若，在……的条件下，如果

The Merger Agreement shall be filed with the government as soon as practicable thereafter; provided, however, that at the written request of either Buyer or Seller, the closing may be adjourned.

并购协议一旦执行之后，就应立即向政府备案，但是，如果买方或卖方提出书面要求，停业就可以推迟。

Final payment shall be due after completion of the work, provided the Contract be then fully performed.

如果合同到时已全部履行，则最后付款需在竣工之后。

provision 条款，规定

ZZZ shall make his best efforts not to fail to comply with the provisions of this paragraph.

乙方应努力遵守本节的各个条款。

Subject to the provision of（…）below, Seller shall have the right to have guarantee tests for products.

根据下列……条款，卖方应有权对产品进行保证性测试。

2.account n.账目，账款，账户；v.（与for连用）说明（原因等），是……的原因，（指数量等）占……

We keep an account with the Bank of China in Beijing.

我们在北京中国银行开有账户。

（1）for account of 为……，代……，受……委托

We hereby issue an irrevocable L/C in your favour for account of China Trading Co., Shanghai.

兹受上海中国贸易行的委托，开给你方不可撤销的信用证一份。

（2）（to be）for sb's account，for the account of sb. 由某人负担

The arbitration fees shall be for the account of the losing party.

仲裁费用须由败诉一方负担。

（3）on account of 由于，因为

On account of lack of direct steamer，please allow transhipment in your L/C.

因为没有直达船，在你方的信用证中请注明准许转船。

On account of difference in taste，your designs do not suit this market.

由于趣味不同，你的设计款式不适用于此市场。

（4）to take…into account 考虑，重视

You should take into account not only the price but also the quality.

你应予以考虑的不仅是价格，而且还有质量。

（5）on one's own account 为自己的利益，自行负责

We buy this commodity for a friend of ours，not on our own account.

此商品是我们代朋友买的而非为自己。

（6）not on any account 无论如何不

Not on any account shall the safe be opened without my express orders.

没有我明确的指示，无论如何不能打开保险箱。

| | |
|---|---|
| auditing of account | 查账 |
| capital account | 资本账户 |
| common account | 共同账户 |
| keeping current account | 流水账的登记 |
| running account | 流水账 |
| sales for account | 赊账 |
| accountancy | 会计职业 |
| accountancy firm | 会计机构 |
| accountancy law | 会计法 |
| accountancy section | 会计科，核算科 |
| accountancy service | 会计业务 |
| accountant | 会计师，会计员 |
| certified public accountant | 注册会计师 |
| chartered accountant | （英）注册会计师 |
| general accountant | 总会计师 |
| accounting | 会计学，会计，核算 |

| accounting period | 会计年度，会计结算期 |
| --- | --- |
| economic accounting | 经济核算 |
| managerial accounting | 管理会计学 |
| management accounting | 管理会计 |

（7）account for 说明，占……

Bank shall account for and deliver to such substitutes escrow agent all shares of stock and cash held by it.

银行应负责说明并向代管契据代理人交付它所握有的全部股票与现金。

Oil exports account for 30% of the total export bill.

石油出口额占出口总额的30%。

3.contrary n.相反，反面，对立面

on the contrary 正好相反，另一方面恰（好）

Cash zinc closed $29 up on the week； cash lead，on the contrary，closed $5 down.

现货锌（收盘价）周末上涨了29美元；而现货铅（收盘价）则下跌了5美元。

to the contrary （意思）相反的；（意思）相反地

Anything in this Agreement to the contrary notwithstanding，any commodities may be sold without reference to this Agreement in any of the following cases.

尽管有与本协议相反的情形，在下列情况下，任何商品可不必参照本协议予以销售。

Reference to Seller's bid shall not affect the items and conditions hereof，unless specifically provided to the contrary herein.

对卖主的报价进行查询（了解）并不影响本文规定的条款和条件，除非具体提供相反情况。

4.follow v.跟随，遵循

as follows=as what follows 表示"如下"。这是一习惯用语，不论前面的主语是单数或复数都用 as follows

| It is as follows： | 如下： |
| --- | --- |
| The telegrams read as follows： | 电文如下： |
| The items are as follows： | 项目列举如下： |
| We state as follows： | 兹陈述如下： |

ZZZ agrees to pay to AAA royalties as follows：

乙方同意对甲方支付提成如下：

The license herein granted is conditioned on ZZZ selling Licensed Device at prices no more favorable than those followed by AAA.

这里所给予的许可证是以乙方出售许可装置时，在价格上不比对甲方所采用的更优惠为条件的。

following pron.下面； adj.下列的，下述的； prep.随后

The following is（are）the points suggested.

下面是建议的要点。

We have sold you the following：

我们已卖给你的货物如下：

Please advise the position（status）of the following orders.

请告知下列订单执行情况。

Following the talks，a contract was signed.

谈判后签署了合同。

5.royalty n.特许权使用费，专利权使用费，矿区开采权使用费；版税

oil royalties 石油开采权使用费

copyright royalty 版税

patent royalty 专利权使用费

The Licensor shall have the right to reimburse itself from future royalties.

许可证发放者应有权从将来的专利权使用费中得到补偿。

The Second Party shall pay to the First Party a royalty of（…）% on the retail prices of all goods manufactured and sold by him.

乙方应按本方制造和销售的一切货物的零售价，向甲方支付百分之……的专利权使用费。

6. premises n. 上述各点，（企业的）房屋建筑及附属场地

The issue shall be submitted to the Patent Office in London on the basis of stipulated acts in accordance with the rules of practice as may be appropriate in the premises.

应该在各项规定的法令基础上，遵照可能使用的上述各点的实施规章，将这一问题及时提交伦敦的专利局处理。

All the food is made on the premises.

所有食品都是在场内生产的。

7. commence v. 开始（进行）

The parties to this Agreement shall commence collective bargaining negotiation on July 20th.

本协议缔约各方将于7月20日开始进行集体签约谈判。

The interest shall be paid monthly on the first day of each and every month commencing in 2019.

利息将自2019年开始于每月的第一天按月支出。

commencement n. 开始，开端，毕业典礼（美语）

The exact date of commencement of the term of this Agreement shall be reflected in the space provided at the top page of this Agreement.

本协议开始生效的确切日期必须在本协议第一页上空白处有所反映。

8.在合同的语言中，使用"and"或"or"会有不同的含义。有些合同中会出

现当事人必须提出"A，B and C"，则表示该事人必须提出 ABC 三者，缺一不可；相反，如果是"A，B or C"则只需要提出 A，B，C 其中之一（或按照合同约定，其中二者）。

注意合同文字的此类表达。比如"A and/or B"就代表 A 和 B 同时或单独出现都是符合合同规定的。

Supplier shall supply Goods and/or perform the Services in a professional manner and promptly correct，at no additional charge，no errors or deficiencies in the Goods and/or Services. Before each payment by Purchaser to Supplier in accordance with payment conditions，Purchaser or designated third parties shall evaluate the Goods and/or Services provided. The provision of Goods and/or Services shall be deemed to have been completed and accepted upon issuance by Purchaser or designated third parties of a notice confirming that the Goods and/or Services have been received and inspected and initially accepted.

供应商应当以专业标准及时准确地提供货物和/或履行服务。在货物和/或服务提供中无任何额外费用，无错误或缺陷。在买方向供应商根据付款条件之规定支付费用前，买方或其授权的第三人，应当检验供应商提供的货物和/或服务。买方或其授权的第三人应签发确认通知书表示货物和/或服务已收到，被检查且并被初步接受。

The Shipper shall be liable for all damage caused by such goods to the ship and/or cargo on board.

如果上述货物对船舶和（或）船上的其他货物造成任何损害，托运人应负全责。

9.compliance n. 依从，顺从，同意

Buyer may satisfy itself as to Seller's compliance with all of its obligations hereunder.

买方可以确认卖方履行了下述的全部义务。

The subcontractor shall furnish satisfactory evidence to verify compliance with the above requirements.

分包商应提供令人满意的证据，以证实符合上述要求。

in compliance with 遵照，按照

In compliance with your invitation for bids of the above date，the under signed hereby proposes to furnish all labour and materials.

遵照你方的上述投标日期，签字人特此申请提供全部劳动力和材料。

comply vi. 同意，依从，遵照

The Second Party shall strictly comply with all prescriptions and processes furnished by the First Party.

乙方应严格遵守甲方提出的所有规定和工艺程序。

It will comply with all of the requirements contained in any of such bulletins.

它将遵守任何该项公告中的一切要求。

10.except prep.除……之外，v.把……除外

except（for），but for，except the case 也表示除……以外

exception n.除外，例外；抗告，异议

No salary shall be paid to any officer or director of either party，except as the result of a mutual agreement.

除非相互同意，否则不向双方的任何负责人或董事支付薪水。

Except as/Unless otherwise provided herein，no charge for any extra work or material will be allowed.

除非本合同中有其他规定，否则任何额外工作或物资不允许另外收费。

The Contractor shall furnish all the materials，except as hereinafter specified.

除了下文载明者外，承包商应提供所有物资。

Subject to the exceptions herein provided，Seller will not engage in（country）in the manufacture of the products.

根据本文所规定的例外，卖方不应在该国从事制造这些产品。

## ● Exercises

I.Translate the following sentences into English：

1.董事会表决中如遇投票数均等平分，主席（董事长）可投一决定票。

2.如果任何一方有任何违反本协议之处，另一方有权索取因违反协议而造成的损失赔偿费。

3.合同价格意指第……款中所提及的总计价格，可根据下文所列条款酌情予以增减。

4.对于最低产量或有关专利费的支付的要求必须按比例分配。

5.此种买卖应服从下列条款。

6.考虑到包含于此的相互协议，缔约双方特此同意如下。

7.该项不动产包括土地连同地面上的一切建筑物和辅助设施。

8.工程师应该为此按公司规定的标准价格得到报酬。

9.高级职员或董事不得在卖方业务中使用的或从属于该业务的商标或商号中占有任何利益。

10.由于没有满足该项要求，这笔债务应视为到期应付款。

II.Translate the following sentences into Chinese：

1.By adding hereto one or more of the commodities，and fixing the current prices thereof，the Manufacturer may amend or change the price schedule.

2.When decisions are made by the Engineer，the Contractor shall comply therewith.

3.The Joint Venture Company shall have the Agreement executed and become bound thereby on the date.

4.The restriction provided for in this paragraph shall only apply to the Customers named in the aforesaid list.

5.If you are prepared to accept it，please indicate on the copy of this letter enclosed herewith in the space provided.

6.In the event of failure to the Operator to comply with the obligations to correct， the Company shall have the right to forthwith make such correction at the costs and expenses of the Operator.

7.The cost of such remedial actions will be for Contractor's account if and to the extent the aforesaid reasons are attributable to Contractor.

8.In the event of litigation against ZZZ on account of any claim of infringement arising out of the use of licensed products， AAA agrees to do so.

9.Testimony must be heard in the presence of all the parties relating to this License Agreement， unless a hearing is waived in the submission or by the written consent of the parties.

10.All and every other interest of or belonging to or due to each of the constituent corporations shall be deemed to be transferred to Buyer without further act or deed.

# Unit Five /合同句子的翻译

## Sentence Translation in Contracts

---

## 5.1 合同翻译的准则 The Principles of Contract Translation

在进行国际商务合同翻译时，要坚持两个基本要义：一是准确严谨；二是规范通顺。

### 5.1.1　准确严谨 Faithfulness and Accuracy

由于国际商务合同具有专业性和兼容性两个特点，因此，就要求合同的内容更加准确和完整，尽可能正确地使用法律名词、术语和用词，做到译文准确、严谨、无漏洞。

译文要忠实再现原文的含义，不能有任何的违反或错漏，尤其对一些重要的条款、术语或数据，更不能有丝毫的马虎，否则轻者容易造成误解和执行合同中的不必要的误会，重者会因小错而酿成巨大的经济损失。

如：Licensee shall furnish to Party A copies of insurance policies and / or the endorsements.

原译文：领有许可证者应给甲方提供几份保险政策和背书。

懂专业的人一看译文就知道 insurance policies 和 endorsement 在翻译时出错了，但不懂专业的人就会看得一头雾水。

事实上，insurance polices 是指 "保险单"，而不是保险政策，而 endorsement 并不是支付中的背书，而是保险单的另一种形式，称为 "保险批单"，即保险单的变更条款。

该句可以译为：受让人（受证人）应给甲方提供保险单和/或保险批单的复印件。

再如，

We regret to inform you that there is short weight of 6.9 metric tons only. Therefore, we raise a claim against you for the short weight of 6.9 metric tons as follows:

原译文：

我们遗憾地通知你们，（到货）仅仅短缺6.9公吨，因此，我们就此短缺6.9公吨一事提出索赔如下：

上述译文存在的问题是没有理解该句中的 only 一词。当 only 跟在数字后面时，表达的意思是汉语的"整"，而放到数字的前面则表示"仅仅"。所以，准确严谨的翻译才能专业地表达语义。

参考翻译：

我们遗憾地通知你们，（到货）短缺6.9公吨整。因此，我们就此短缺6.9公吨一事提出索赔如下：

## 5.1.2  规范通顺 Expressiveness and Smoothness

所谓规范通顺，就是要把理解了的东西，用规范通顺的、合乎合同语言要求的文字（英文或中文）表达出来。国际商务合同是具有法律约束力的正式文本，它的格式、条款和使用的语句、词汇、缩略语以及符号都要按照法律文书的行文习惯来翻译。

如：在"购货合同"中首先规定一条"兹经买卖双方同意按下列规定的条款出售和购买此货"，翻译时就要尊重合同的行文习惯，把合同中所说的"条款"用 terms and conditions 这两个词的连用来表达：

The undersigned Seller and Buyer have agreed to sell and buy the commodity according to the terms and conditions stipulated below.

再如：

Both Party A and Party B agree that Technology Transfer Agreement shall be signed between the Joint Venture Company and the Party B（or a third party）so as to obtain the advanced production technology needed for realizing the production scale stipulated in Chapter 6 to the Contract，including product design，manufacturing technology，means of testing，material prescription，standard of quality，and the training of personnel.

原译文：

甲、乙双方同意由合资公司与乙方（或第三方）签订技术转让协议，以取得为达到合同第六章规定的生产经营目的、规模所需要的先进生产技术，这些技术包括：产品设计、制造工艺、测试方法、材料的配方、质量标准以及人员培训。

原句中的"training of personnel"（人员培训）和"the advanced production technology"（先进生产技术）是并列的关系，搭配到一起就属于归类的错误。所以，在翻译的时候要秉承规范通顺的原则，理顺出逻辑关系。

参考翻译：

甲、乙双方同意由合资公司与乙方（或第三方）签订技术转让协议，以取得为达到合同第六章规定的生产经营目的、规模所需要的先进生产技术及人员培训，这些技术包括：产品设计、制造工艺、测试方法、材料的配方和质量标准。

# 5.2句子的翻译技巧 The Techniques of Sentence Translation

词是构成语言的基本单位。词性是词的一大特性，它直接决定词在句中的功能。由于英语与汉语之间的差异——词汇用法不同、句子结构不同、语言逻辑不同、表达方式不同等，在翻译国际商务合同时不可避免地遇到这样的问题，就是很难找到一个词性与英语原词相通，同时词义也与原词完全相同的汉语词汇进行翻译。这就需要进行词性的转化，让译者跳出原文的束缚对原文的句子成分和结构进行必要的调整和句子成分的转换，以达到严谨、准确和规范的翻译要求。

翻译合同常见的一个方法就是转化法，即将英语的某一成分转换为汉语的另一成分或将汉语的某一成分转换为英语的另一成分。

（1）Adjusting the Subject 主语的转换

a.主语转化为谓语：主语转换为谓语，往往是原文中的主语为动作性的名词，且采用被动语态。译成汉语时，进行转换翻译，将英语的被动语态调整为汉语的主动语态。

Delivery must be effected within the time stated on the purchase order，otherwise the Buyer must at its opinion cancel the order without cost to him，and charge the Seller for any loss incurred as the result of the latter's failure to make such a delivery.

卖方必须在购货订单规定的时间内<u>交货</u>，否则，买方可取消订货，而不承担任何损失，并要求卖方赔偿由于不交货所造成的一切损失。

原文的名词delivery作主语，转换为译文的动词"交货"作谓语，同时在主语的位置加译了"卖方"二字。

<u>Payment</u> shall be made by net cash against sight draft with Bill of Lading attached showing the shipment of the goods.Such payment shall be made through the Bank of China，Dalian Branch.The Bill of Lading shall not be delivered to the Buyer until such draft is paid.

凭即期汇票和所附表明货物发运的提单通过中国银行大连分行以现金<u>支付</u>。汇票未付之前，提单不交给买方。

原句中的payment作主语，可译为汉语的一个动词。

<u>Partial</u> shipments shall be allowed upon presentation of the clean set of shipping document.

可以允许<u>分批发货</u>，但须提示一套清洁的装运单据。

原文中的主语shipment转换为汉语的动词，原文中修饰主语的partial转化为状语。

b.主语转化为宾语：主语转化为宾语，原文的主语往往为普通名词，且常为被动语态。译成汉语时，将英语的被动语态改译为汉语的主动语态，主语转换为宾语。

Should <u>all or part of the Contract</u> and <u>its appendices</u> be unable to be fulfilled owing to the fault of one party, the breaching party shall bear the responsibilities thus caused.

由于一方过失，致使不能履行或不能完全履行<u>本合同及其附件</u>时，由过失方承担违约责任。

If <u>any terms and conditions of this Contract</u> are breached and the breach is not corrected by the breaching party within 30 days after a written notice thereof is given by the other party, then the nonbreaching party shall have the option to terminate this Contract by giving a written notice thereof to the breaching party.

如果一方违反<u>本合同</u>的<u>任何条款</u>，并且在接到另一方的书面通知后30天内不予以补救，未违约方有权选择向违约方书面通知终止本合同。

c.主语转化为定语：如果主语和宾语之间的关系密切，或宾语本身就是主语的一部分，译成汉语时，为使译文符合汉语的表达习惯，往往把原文的主语转换为定语。

<u>Each party is liable for the Joint Venture Company</u> only up to the limit of the capital subscribed by it.

各方对合营公司的责任以各自认缴的出资额为限。

<u>The Guarantee Period</u> shall start from the exact date on which the Purchaser received notification in writing from the Vendor that Plant is ready for dispatch from the Works.

<u>担保期限的具体日期</u>自买方收到卖方发出的告知可随时从工厂发运的书面通知起开始计算。

（2）Adjusting the Object宾语的转换

a.宾语转化为主语：英文合同中的某些动词宾语，是在逻辑上应说明的主体，为使其突出和醒目，翻译时一般将其转换为汉语的主语。

The Seller shall deliver <u>the Equipment and Materials</u> in accordance with the Contract from the 19（nineteenth）month to the 27（twenty‐seventh）month from the date of signing the Contract in 4（four）lots.

根据合同，卖方的<u>设备和材料</u>应当自合同签订之日起第19个至第27个月内分四批交货。

Party A shall send twice <u>its technical personnel</u> to Party B's factory for training, and the total number of the participants shall not exceed 200（excluding the interpreter）.

甲方的技术人员将分两批赴乙方工厂接受培训，参加培训人员的总数不超过200人（翻译人员除外）。

b.宾语转化为谓语：如果原文的谓语动词不宜处理成汉语的谓语，而原文中的宾语又是含有动作意义的名词，那么在汉译时可以将原文中的宾语转换成汉语的谓语，或与原文动词一起合译为汉语的谓语。

The Licensor will, at its own cost, <u>take such actions</u> to eliminate infringement of the Licensed Patents as may be reasonably necessary and proper in its own opinion.

许可方应在其认为有必要的时候，以适当的方式，自费采取行动，消除对特许产品的侵犯。

The Seller shall make delivery of the goods strictly within the period stipulated herein. In the event of delay in delivery, the Buyer may cancel the Contract and claim damages for breach of the Contract.

卖方应当严格按规定的期限交货，若迟交，买方有权撤销本合同，并向卖方提出由此所造成的损失赔偿。

（3）Adjusting the Predicative 表语的转换

a.表语转化为主语：在英语中，当用名词作表语时，主语和表语所表达的内容往往是一致的。在译成汉语时，为使上下文连贯，或突出表语所述的内容，可将原句中的表语转换为汉语的主语。

Agent oriented toward a single geographic market searching for products to import and market in the home Country is an import agent.

进口代理商是面向某一个地区市场，寻找能进口到本国销售的产品的代理人。

The date of registration of the Joint Venture Company shall be the date of the establishment of the board of directors of the Joint Venture Company.

合资公司董事会成立日期，以合资公司注册登记之日为准。

b.表语转化为谓语：当用介词短语作表语时，一般都应选择一个适当的汉语动词作谓语，这样有利于处理译文。

In the course of arbitration, the Contract shall be continuously executed by both parties except the part of the Contract which is under arbitration.

在仲裁过程中，除了正在仲裁的部分条款外，合同的其他条款应继续进行。

Whereas Party B is in the real estate business, and the two Parties are in consideration of the mutual convenances and agree to enter into this Contract under the terms and conditions set forth as follows：

鉴于乙方经营房地产业务，双方考虑相互的惯例，同意按下列条款签订本合同：

（4）Adjusting the Attributive 定语的转换

a.定语转化为谓语：在汉语里，形容词是能够作谓语的。因此，当英语的形容词作前置定语时，很难将其译成通顺的汉语。此时，如果把定语转换为汉语的谓语，使之和所修饰的名词一起构成汉语的主谓词组，则可以使译文流畅规范。

The sample of the machine submitted by the Seller is featured by novel shape, easy operation, high calorific efficiency and low fuel consumption.

卖方提交的样机的特点是造型新颖、操作简便、热效率高、油耗低。

We look forward to an ever increasing volume of business with your glass factories.

我方盼望与你方玻璃厂的交易额日渐增高。

We claim from shortage in weight and low quality on the consignment of wheat shipped per s.s. "Princess Victoria".

"维多利亚公主"号轮装运的小麦短重和质量低劣，我方对此提出索赔。

b.定语转化为状语：在英语中，如果将某一含有动作意义的名词转换为汉语的动词，那么，原来名词前的形容词或分词作定语，即可转为汉语的状语。

Any disputes arising from the execution of, or in connection with the Contract shall be settled through underlined friendly consultations between both Parties. In case no settlement can be reached through consultations, the disputes shall be submitted for arbitration.

凡由执行本合同所发生的或与本合同有关的一切争议，双方应友好协商解决，如果协商不能解决，应提交仲裁。

The Joint Venture's products to be sold in China may be handled by the Chinese Materials and Commercial Departments by means of agency or exclusive sales, or direct sale by the Joint Venture Company.

合资公司内销产品可由中国物资部门和商业部门代销或包销，或由合资公司直接销售。

（5）Adjusting the Adverbial 状语的转换

a.状语转化为主语：合同英语中有些介词短语在句中作状语时，往往在意义上和主语有密切的联系。为了强调其在句中的地位，翻译时常将这类状语转换为汉语的主语。

The conditions for establishment of the Joint Venture Company and the total amount of investment and registered capital are stipulated in this Contract.

本合同规定了设立合资公司的条件以及投资总额与注册资本。

For the purpose of this Contract, the Party B desires to introduce the Patent and engage in production cooperation in accordance with the technical know-how specified in the Patent.

本合同的目的在于乙方希望引进专利，按专利提供的技术诀窍进行合作生产。

The products fair will be held at the Standard Electrical Co., Madrid, Spain with the Buyer's representatives.

买方代表将参加在西班牙马德里标准电器公司举行的产品博览会。

b.状语转化为汉语的定语：英语中某些介词短语在形式上是状语，但实际上与句中的某个名词有密切的联系，这类状语在译成汉语时，处理成定语似乎更确切些。

In this Contract, the Packing Clause stipulates for one gross to the polythene bag, covered with paper box, 50 paper boxes to an inner carton, 2 inner cartons to a wooden case.

合同中的包装条款规定为：每一聚乙烯袋装一罗，然后装入纸盒，50盒装一纸箱，两纸箱装一木箱。

## 5.3　　被动语态的翻译 Translation of Passive Voice

由于主动语态比较自然、明确、直接和有力，所以合同英文中主动语态用得较多，以便表达法律责任。但英语合同中被动语态的使用也是在语言结构上必需的。在英文合同中被动语态所表达的概念，译成汉语时大多采用主动语态表示。在实际翻译工作中，要灵活运用翻译技巧，既做到在内容上忠实于原文，又在语言形式上规范通顺。被动语态的翻译方法有以下几种。

（1）被动语态的转换翻译 Transforming the Passive Voice

运用转化法翻译被动语态要注意以下几点：

a.把动作的发出者转换为汉语的主语：在合同英语中的一些被动句子中，往往会出现 by 或 between 引起的短语，在句中作状语，其中名词是本句涉及的行为当事人，为突出句中动作的发出者，可将它转换为主语。

This Contract is made <u>by and between the Buyer and the Seller</u>, whereby the Buyer agrees to buy and the Seller agrees to sell the under-mentioned commodity according to the terms and conditions stipulated below：

<u>买卖双方</u>同意按下列条款购买、出售下述商品，并签订本合同。

If any terms and conditions to this Contract are breached and the breach is not corrected by any party within 15 days after a written notice thereof is given <u>by the other party</u>, then the non-breaching party shall have the option to terminate this Contract by giving a written notice thereof to the breaching party.

如果<u>一方</u>违反本合同的任何条款，并且在<u>另一方</u>发出书面通知后15日内不予补救，未违约方有权选择向违约方书面通知终止本合同。

All the payments shall be made in the U.S.Currency <u>by the Buyer</u> to the Seller by telegraphic transfer to the Seller's designated account with the Bank of China, Beijing, China.

<u>买方</u>应以美元支付卖方货款，并以电汇的方式汇至卖方指定的在中国银行北京分行的账户。

b.把英语句中的某一状语转换为主语：在被动语态的状语与主语之间有包容关系时，为了使译文通顺，可将状语部分译成汉语的主语。

The cost of the nonreturnable containers of the goods sold under this hereunder Contract/hereunder is included <u>in the prices herein specified.</u>

<u>所定价格</u>包括依照本合同所售装货用的一次性容器费。

The production design, technology of manufacturing, means of testing, materials prescription, standard of quality and training of personnel shall be stipulated <u>in Chapter 4 in this contract.</u>

<u>本合同第4章</u>规定了产品设计、制造工艺、测试方法、材料配方、质量标准以

及人员培训。

The establishment，remuneration and the expenses of the staff of the preparation and construction office，when agreed by both parties，shall be covered <u>in the project budget.</u>

经甲乙双方同意后，<u>工程预算</u>应包括筹建处工作人员的编制、报酬及费用。

c.把英语句中的主语转换为宾语：如果原句中没有涉及合同的当事人，可将这样的英语被动句处理成汉语的无主语句，原句的主语被转换为宾语。

In case <u>the quality，quantity or weight of the goods</u> is found not in conformity to those stipulated in this Contract after reinspection by the China Import and Export Commodity Inspection Bureau within 15 days after the arrival of the goods at the port of destination，the Buyer shall return the goods to，or lodge claim against the Seller for compensation of losses upon the strength of Inspection Certificate issued by the said Bureau，with the exception of those claims for which the insurers or the carriers are liable.

货到目的港后15天由中国进出口商品检验局复检，如发现<u>货物的质量、数量或重量</u>与本合同规定不符时，除保险公司和船运公司负责赔偿的部分外，买方应凭中国进出口商品检验局出具的检验证明书，向卖方提出退货或索赔。

Upon the expiration of the duration or termination before the date of expiration of the Joint Venture，<u>liquidation</u> shall be carried out according to relevant law. The <u>liquidated assets</u> shall be distributed in accordance with the proportion of investment contributed by Party A and Party B.

合同期满或提前终止合营时，<u>应依照有关法律进行结算</u>，并根据甲、乙各方投资的比例分配<u>结算后的财产</u>。

（2）被动语态的顺序翻译 Translation of Passive Voice

在翻译国际商务合同时，为了使译文符合合同文体的汉语表达方式，可将原文中的某些被动语态，按原句的语序顺译。

a.译成汉语的主动语态：合同英文的某些被动语态，可在不改变原文主语的情况下，翻译时将被动语态改成主动语态，无须添加任何词。

<u>The Seller shall not be held responsible for</u> late delivery or non-delivery of the goods owing to generally recognized Force Majeure causes.

由于一般公认的人力不可抗拒的原因所造成迟延交货或不交货，<u>卖方不负责任</u>。

<u>The Seller shall be entitled</u> to terminate this Contract in the event of failure by the Buyer to comply with any terms or conditions stated in this Article.

如果买方违反本条所规定的任何条件，<u>卖方有权终止此合同</u>。

b.译成汉语的被动句：英语的被动句是由"be +v.+ed"构成的。因汉语的动词无词形变化，所以译成汉语被动语态时，只能通过添加一定的词汇手段来表示。

The term for the technology transfer agreement is signed <u>by</u> Joint Company and Party B and it shall be approved <u>by</u> the approval authority.

技术转让协议的期限由合资公司与乙方签订<u>并经</u>审批机关批准。

All the equipment and materials supplied <u>by</u> the Seller shall be inspected <u>by</u> the Buyer and the quality certificates and inspection and test records shall be issued <u>by</u> the manufacturer.

卖方所提供的全部设备和材料将<u>由</u>买方负责检验；质量合格证、检验和试验记录<u>应由</u>制造商出具。

c.It is +p.p.结构的翻译：合同英语中有时还常用一些特殊的被动句型，其结构为"It is+p.p.+ that clause"。这种句型已基本形成了固定的译法。

<u>It is mutually agreed that</u> the certificate of quality and quantity or weight issued by the manufacturer shall be part of the document for payment with the adopted Letter of Credit.

<u>双方同意</u>将制造商出具的质量、数量或重量检验证明书作为有关信用证项下付款的单据之一。

<u>It is essentially stressed that</u> the Buyers are requested to sign and return the duplicate of this Contract within 3 days from the date of receipt.In the event of failure to do this，the Sellers reserve the right to cancel the Contract.

<u>必须强调</u>：买方应于收到本合同之日起3日内签字并退还合同的副本，如买方不这样做，卖方保留撤消合同的权利。

<u>It is strictly understood that</u> the number of employees to be trained by the Contractor at any one time shall be no more than（…）.

<u>严格明确</u>承包商任何时候所训练的雇工人数不得超过（……）人。

## 5.4 从句的翻译 Translation of Clauses

合同英语中的从句翻译，除具有与其他文体从句翻译的共同点外，也有其不同点。通常来讲，英语的从句可分为名词性从句、副词性从句、形容词性从句三大类，而在合同英语中出现的主要是状语从句，其次是定语从句。

### 5.4.1 状语从句的翻译 Translation of Adverbial Clause

在合同英语中常用的状语从句有条件状语从句、时间状语从句和让步状语从句。

（1）条件状语从句的翻译

国际商务合同是合同各方就相互权利义务关系达成一致意见而订立的书面文件。这种书面文件主要约定双方应享有的权利和应履行的义务，但这种权利的行使和义务的履行，均附有各种条件，因此，在合同英语中大量地出现和使用条件状语从句。

引导条件状语从句的连词很多，我们重点来介绍以下几个。

a.if 若，如果

If the Force Majeure event lasts over 40 days, the Buyer shall have the right to cancel the Contract or the undelivered part of the Contract.

若不可抗力事件持续40天以上，买方有权撤销本合同或本合同中未完成的部分。

If any change is required regarding the terms and conditions to this Agreement, both parties shall negotiate in order to find a suitable solution, provided however, that any change to this Agreement shall be subject to the approval by the Chinese Government.

如需对本协议条款进行修改，双方应协商解决，但对协议的任何修改必须经中国政府批准方为有效。

Claims, if any, shall be submitted by fax within fourteen days after the arrival of the goods at destination.

若有索赔，买方应于货物到达目的地后14天内以传真方式提出。

注意：在合同英语中，常常会遇到if引起的省略句。这类if的省略句还有if required，if possible，if necessary，if agreeable等，但在翻译时要突出主语。

Contingent shares, if any, to be issued hereunder shall be determined on the basis of the after-tax consolidated earnings of Seller.

下述或有股票，如果有的话，是否发行，必须在卖方缴纳税金后的综合收入基础上来决定。

Said amount shall be reduced by the sum of the difference, if any, between the inventory value of small equipment and the closing inventory value thereof.

必须从上述金额中扣除小型设备的存货价值与期末存货价值间的差额，如果有这种差额的话。

b.in case 如，若，如果

in case 在表示条件状语从句的时候，通常是强调其条件成熟的可能性要比用if从句小。

In case the Buyer fails to carry out any of the terms or conditions to this Contract with the Seller, the Seller shall have the right to terminate all or any part of this Contract with the Buyer or postpone shipment or stop any goods in transit and the Buyer shall in every such case be liable to the Seller for all losses, damages and expenses thereby incurred.

倘若买方未能履行与卖方所订合同的任何条款，卖方有权终止与买方的全部或部分合同，或延期交货，或截留运输中的货物。在任何一种情况下，买方须负责赔偿卖方由此发生的损失、损坏和相应的费用。

注意：in case of 在合同英语中可用作状语，译成"若""如果"等。

In case of any divergence of interpretation, the Chinese text shall prevail.

若对解释产生异议，以中文文本为准。

In case of quality discrepancy, claims shall be filed by the Buyer within 30 days after the arrival of the goods at the port of destination.

若发生质量索赔，买方的索赔必须在货物到达目的港的30天内提出。

c.in the event that 若，如果，假如

In the event that deficiencies in the Equipment become evident, such deficiencies shall be corrected by ABC during the two days per week during which the Purchaser will not be testing.

若发现设备有明显缺陷，应由ABC用每周买方不进行实验的这两天时间对设备予以校正。

In the event that the Documents supplied by Party B are not in conformity with the stipulations in Sections 8.2, Party B shall, within the shorted possible time but not later than 30 days after the receipt of the Party A's written notice, dispatch free of charge to Party A the missing or the correct and legible Documents.

若乙方提供的技术资料不符合本合同第8条第2款的规定，乙方必须在收到甲方书面通知后30天内，尽快免费将所缺的或正确的、清晰易读的资料寄给甲方。

注意：in the event of 在合同英语中做状语，也表示"若""如果"。

In the event of graft（渎职）or serious dereliction（失职）of duty on the part of the general manager and/or deputy general managers, the Board of Directors shall have the power to dismiss them at will.

若总经理和/或副总经理有营私舞弊或严重失职时，董事会有权随时将其撤换。

d.should+主语+动词结构

这个结构属于非真实条件句。合同英语中使用这种条件句时，其主句一般为陈述语气。该结构表明，发生条件句中所述情况的可能性很小，如果该条件句所述的情况发生了，那么主句所设的事宜必须完成。

Should any of the stipulations to the Contract be altered, amended, supplemented or deleted, the same shall be negotiated between and agreed upon by both parties and written documents shall be signed by the representatives of both parties.

本合同条款的任何变更、修改或增删，须经双方协商同意，并由双方代表签署书面文件为有效。

Should the effect of Force Majeure continue more than one hundred and twenty（120）consecutive days, both parties shall settle the further execution of the Contract through friendly negotiations as soon as possible.

如不可抗力事件延续到120天以上时，双方应通过友好协商方式尽快解决继续履行合同的问题。

e.unless 相当于 if not, except if or except when，它引出的从句用现在时表示将来，一般不用虚拟条件句。Unless 从句中的主语和动词be常省去

Unless expressly agreed to, the port of shipment is at the Seller's option.

运货港由卖方选择，除非双方有明确规定。

在合同英语中，unless 与 otherwise 经常连用，表示"除另有……者外"，其后往往用过去分词。

Unless otherwise stated thereafter, the accounting principles employed shall be the same as those applied in the preceding years.

除非后文另有说明者外，所运用的会计原则应与以往各年所应用的会计原则相同。

Neither Party shall have the right to represent the other party unless otherwise arranged.

除另有安排者外，任何一方无权代表另一方。

f.provided that…引出从句表示条件时，常表示当事人所希望的条件

No salary shall be paid and charged against the operating expenses, provided that the commission or brokerage of the Second Party shall be paid and charged as a part of the operating expenses.

若想把支付乙方的佣金或回扣作为营业费用的一个部分，则不应在营业费用中支付和计算薪金。

Provided that Party B desires to continue leasing the flat, Party B shall notify Party A in writing two months in advance of expiry of the lease and a new contract shall be signed.

乙方若续租该套公寓，须于合同期满前2个月书面通知甲方并另订租赁合同。

注意：连词 where 和 when 在合同英语中还可以引出条件状语从句，表示"如果""若"等。

All disputes in connection with or in the execution of this Contract shall be settled through friendly negotiation. Where no settlement can be reached, the disputes shall be submitted for arbitration.

所有与合同有关的或在履行合同中发生的争议，均应通过友好协商的方式解决。如果得不到解决，应将争议提交仲裁。

When one party to the Joint Venture Company assigns all or part of his investment, the other party has preemptive right.

如果合资公司一方拟转让其全部或部分出资额，另一方有优先购买权。

（2）时间状语从句的翻译

在合同英语中，有两个表示时间的连词 after 和 before 是非常重要的。值得注意的是，这两个词的翻译方法，要合乎法律文书的行文习惯。

a.after

由 after 引出的时间状语从句，在合同英语中一般被翻译成"……之日起"，这合乎法律文书的语言严谨性。

After the Buyer receives the relative documents issued by the Shipping Company, the Buyer shall pay to the Seller within 20（twenty）days.

买方应在收到船舶公司出具的有关单据之日起，20天内向卖方支付款项。

b.before

由 before 引出的时间状语从句，一般被译成"……后，才能……"，这样的翻译方法，在合同中强调一方应尽的义务。

Both Parties shall apply to their respective government authorities for approval before the Contract is officially signed.

合同双方应分别向本国的政府当局申请，经批准后，才能签订正式合同。

### 5.4.2　定语从句的翻译 Translation of Attributive Clauses

定语从句可分为限定性定语从句和非限定性定语从句两大类。由于合同语言要求准确和规范，因此为了达到合同条款的语义完整，定语从句在合同英语中是不可缺少的。

（1）限定性定语从句的翻译

限定性定语从句和与先行词的关系十分紧密，在翻译时，要采用合译的方法，把这类句子译成汉语的"……的"，并置于被修饰词的前面。

Party B guarantees that the technical documents to be supplied by Party B are the latest technical information which has been put into practical use by Party B.

乙方保证所提供的技术资料是乙方经过实际使用的最新技术资料。

Shipment shall be commenced within 10 months counting from the date when the contract has come into force and completed within 16 months.

自合同生效之日算起，10个月内装运，16个月内交付完毕。

"Net Selling Price" means the price at which the product is sold by Party B from time to time after deduction of packing, installation and freight charges, trade and quantity discount, commission, insurance and commodity tax, if any, directly applicable of Product.

"净销售价"，是指在扣除合同产品的包装费、安装费、运输费、商业和数量折扣、佣金、保险费和商品税之后，乙方通常销售合同产品的价格。

注意：限定性定语从句的翻译方法，除最基本的合译法外，有时还可以根据情况采用分译的方法。分译时，可重复先行词，重复的方式可采用重复关系词所代表的意义，也可采用"该""其"等字以及采用省译关系词所代表的意义，也能达到层次分明的效果。

The Seller ensures that all the equipments listed in Appendix One to the Contract are brand-new products whose performance shall be in conformity with the Contract and which are manufactured according to current Chinese National Standards or Manufacturer's Standard.

卖方保证本合同附件一所列全部设备都是新产品，是根据现行的中国国家标准或制造商的标准制造的，其性能符合合同规定。

All drawings, designs, specifications and all other technical information made available under this Contract by Party B shall be kept strictly confidential by Party A who shall not sell, transfer or divulge it in any manner to anyone except those of its own employees who will be using it in a manufacture of the Product, without prior written consent of the Party B.

乙方根据本协议所提供的一切图纸、设计、说明书及其他技术资料，甲方均须严格保密，未得乙方的书面同意，甲方不得以任何方式出售、转让或泄漏给任何人，但不包括甲方生产合同产品使用技术资料的雇员。

（2）非限定性定语从句的翻译

非限定性定语从句与它所说明的先行词关系并不很密切，只是起一种补充说明的作用，因此，非限定性定语从句的翻译基本上是采用分译的方法处理。分译时可重复先行词或省译先行词。

If, through the Seller's default, the shipment is delayed beyond 30 days, the Buyer shall then be entitled to make other purchase of the same sort of goods at any lower market price; or he may cancel its order through a fax to the Seller, which is required to get to the latter prior to the beginning of any shipment.

如果由于卖方违约，装船延期超过30天，在此期间，买方有权以任何市场低价另行购买同类货物，买方也可以用传真通知卖方取消订货，但此电报须在装运之前到达卖方。

If within thirty days of the giving of such notice no successor Agent shall have been so appointed and accepted such appointment, the retiring Agent may appoint a successor Agent, which shall be a bank having a combined capital and surplus of at least USD 50,000,000, or the equivalent thereof in another currency, or an affiliate of such a bank.

如果在作出上述通知的30天内，接替的代理行没有被指定或没有接受这种指定，则已卸任的代理行可指定一个接替的代理行，或者是这家银行的附属机构这个接替代理行的联合资本和盈余至少有5,000万美元或与其值相当的其他外币。

## 5.4.3　句子及从句中的状语的翻译 Adverbial Translation in the Sentences and in Subordinate Clauses

（1）句子中状语的翻译

国际商务合同英语的句子有要求结构严谨、句子较长的特点，为了做到准确、严密、清楚、易解，句子中的状语有其自己一定的规则，其位置与基础英语中的频度副词的位置相同，一般应放在 shall 之后，行为动词之前。翻译时，按照汉语的合同语言习惯来做。

All disputes shall, first of all, be settled amicably by negotiation.

一切争端应首先通过友好协商进行解决。

The board meeting shall, under the Contract, be held on the location of the

Company.

按合同规定，董事会会议应在公司所在地举行。

The Contractor shall, throughout the execution and completion of the Works and the remedying of any defects therein, take all reasonable steps to protect the environment on and off the site.

在工程施工、竣工及修补工程缺陷的整个过程中，承包人应采取一切合理的措施，以保护现场内外的环境。

The Joint Venture Company shall, in the first three months of each fiscal year, work out the statement of assets and liabilities and losses and gains accounts of the past fisical year, and shall, after examined and signed by the auditor, submit the same to the Board meeting for approval.

合资公司应在每个会计年度头3个月编制上一个会计年度的资产负债表和损益表，经审计师审核签字后，提交董事会会议批准通过。

（2）从句中状语的翻译

如果合同中句子是复合句，那么从句中状语的位置与主句中状语的位置是不一样的。从句中状语通常应放在连词if或when等词的后面，但放在从句句子的前面。翻译时按照汉语的合同语言习惯来做。

If, during air transportation, the Documentation（technical information）is found lost or damaged, Party B shall, within 30 days after receiving Party A's written notice, supply Party A free of charge with the Documentation again.

如果技术资料在空运中丢失或损坏，乙方应在收到甲方书面通知后30天内，再次免费补寄或重寄给甲方。

If, for any reason beyond the reasonable control of the Consultant, it becomes necessary to replace any of the Personnel, the Consultant shall forthwith provide as a replacement a person of equivalent or better qualifications.

如果由于顾问不能正常控制的原因而有必要替换人员，顾问应替换同等或更有资质的人员。

If, in accordance with the delivery schedule as stipulated in Chapter 4 to the Contract, the goods fail to be delivered at dates due to the responsibility of the Seller, the Seller shall be obliged to pay to the Buyer penalty for such delay in delivery at the following rates.

如果由于卖方责任未能按本合同第4章规定的交货期交货时，卖方应按下列比例向买方缴纳因上述延误导致的罚款。

### 5.4.4　从句简略形式在句中的翻译 Translation of Ecliptic Clauses

若主从句中的从句是简略形式，从句应插入主句之中，应放在shall之后，行为动词之前。翻译时，按照汉语的合同语言习惯来做。

The Contractor shall, if called upon so to do, enter into and execute the Contract Agreement, to be prepared and completed at the cost of the Employer, in the form annexed to these conditions with such modification as may be necessary.

在被邀请签约时，承包人应同意签订并履行合同协议书，该协议书是由业主按照本合同条件所附格式拟订的，如有必要，可对其进行修改。该协议书的拟订和签订费用由业主承担。

The Contractor shall notify the insurers of changes in the nature, extent or programme for the execution of the Works and ensure the adequacy of the insurance at all times in accordance with the terms of the Contract and shall, when required, produce to the Employer the insurance policies in force and receipts for payment of the current premiums.

承包人应把工程施工的性质、范围或进度计划方面的变化情况通知承保人，并保证按合同条款在整个期间内有完备的保险，并在需要时，向业主出示生效保险单及本期保险费的支付收据。

## Notes

1.endorsement n.背书，签注（文件），签字；认可，批准，支持；保险批单

The athlete was highly paid to do endorsements of products.

运动员被付以高薪在产品上签名。

endorsement in blank 无记名背书

endorsement in full 记名式背书

Our products have met with wide endorsement.

我们的产品已得到广泛的赞许。

We are sending you herewith the requested endorsement to the policy.

兹寄去你方所需的保险批单。

endorse v.背书；批准，赞同

Bills of lading are to be written "to order and blank endorsed".

提单应注明"凭指示空白背书"。

Please cable us as soon as your application for import licence has been endorsed.

一旦你方进口许可申请得到批准请即电告。

The quality of this product has been widely endorsed.

这种产品的质量已得到广泛的赞许。

The Attorney shall endorse any bills of exchange on behalf of AAA.

代理人可代表甲方在任何汇票上背书。

endorsing party 批准方

2.fulfill vt.履行，执行，完成

The Contractor shall fulfill all of its duties and obligations in carrying out its work and services hereunder.

承包商在执行下述工作与劳务时，应履行一切职责与义务。

The person to whom any such shares of stock are to be transferred shall agree with the other parties to this Agreement to assume，fulfill and become subject to，and to carry out all of the agreements herein.

任何此类股票转让人应与其他方共同承担、履行、服从和执行本协议所有约定。

fulfillment n.完成，保证

On payment of（amount）to you upon fulfillment of the conditions will be in complete discharge of any and all obligations to you.

在你履行条件后支付给你的（……）数额，就是完全清偿了对你的一切债务。

All obligations of Buyer are subject to the fulfillment of each of the following conditions：

买方的全部责任是完成下列的每个条件：

在合同英语中，表示完成和履行的词还有execute，complete，perform，carry out。

Claims by the Contractor for extra cost must be made in writing before executing the work.

在实施该项工作以前，承包商所提出的额外费用的要求必须采用书面形式。

Upon execution of this agreement，ZZZ agrees to pay to AAA（amount）as advance royalties.

在执行本协议时，乙方同意对甲方支付一定数额的款项，作为预付的专利权使用费。

AAA shall have the right to complete any or all Contracts.
甲方有权完成任何或全部合同。

The Architect shall conduct inspections to determine the dates of substantial completion and final completion.

建筑师须进行检验以确定（施工）基本完工及最终完工的日期。

The following rules shall be faithfully kept，observed and performed by the tenant.
承租人必须忠实信守和履行下列各项规则。

The Licensee shall guarantee in writing the performance of the Contract.
许可证持有者必须书面保证履行本合同。

If either party shall be unable to carry out its obligations under this Contract，the party so failing shall give notice and full particulars of such cause in writing to the other party.

如任何一方未能履行本合同所规定的应尽义务，则应用书面详细说明其原因通知对方。

3.personnel

辨析：personnel，person，labour，worker，staff

personnel 是集合名词，以单数的形式表示复数，是任何团体的工作人员的总称，尤指各军种的军事人员。

person 可指自然人（男人或女人），也可指法人（legal person）。

labour 指工人，特别强调指从事体力劳动的工人。

worker 既可指劳工和技工，也可指脑力劳动工作者。

staff 指全体工作人员（其中不免也有工人，但主要是指"全体职员"）。

During the contracted period，the contractor shall have the right to appoint personnel for departments of the Company and the Refinery.

在承包期间，承包方有权委派本公司和炼油厂各个部门的人员。

Those persons and firms are licensed to produce licensed devices under patent.

兹许可这些人员和公司在专利证（的规定范围）下生产各种特许设备。

All shareholders are to be present in person or by proxy.

全体股东均须到会，由本人或全权代表出席。

| labour cost | 人工成本，人工费 |
| labour dispute | 劳资纠纷，劳资争议 |
| labour market | 劳动力市场 |
| labour and capital | 劳方与资方 |
| industrial workers | 产业工人 |
| skilled workers | 熟练工人 |
| foreign trade workers | 外贸工作人员 |
| office workers | 科室人员 |

Contactor shall provide such further supervisory staff at the site as are specified in the contract.

承包商必须按照合同的规定在工地现场提供这一类监工人员。

Trainee's travel expenses，living allowances and all remuneration to Owner's staff will be the responsibility of Owner.

受训人员的旅费、生活津贴和对雇主职工的一切报酬应由雇主负责。

4.eliminate vt.除去，排除，消除，剔除

All orders which have not been accepted by the customer and transmitted on to the Principal，are automatically eliminated from the payment of commission thereon.

凡尚未被顾客接受的，还没有传递给业主的一切订单，其佣金支付将自动取消。

This Agreement shall be executed with the valid protion thereof eliminated.

随着无效部分的删除，本协议应予执行。

5.infringement n.侵犯，违犯，损害

Know-how shall mean technical information，propriety to the Licensor.

"专有技术"应指为许可证持有方所专有的技术信息。

Whereas，AAA has certain rights and information，including patents，a trademark and information necessary for registration with（place）government of a product； and…

有鉴于此，甲方有某种权利与信息，包括专利权、商标以及在（某地）注册时所必要的产品信息，以及……

infringe vt.侵犯，违犯，损害

If the use or sale of Licensed Products infringes the patent，the royalty payable to the Licensor by the Licensee shall be reduced by the extent later agreed upon.

如果使用或销售特许产品时侵犯了专利权，则须按事后商定的数额扣除许可证持有者向许可证发放者应付的专利权税。

The Licensor represents that none of all patents and patent applications is being infringed or contested to the knowledge of the Licensor.

许可证发放人表示，据他所知，一切专利权和专利申请权均未发生侵权或争议。

6.gross adj.总的，毛重的；n.总额，罗（计数单位），等于144个即12打

The assets，liabilities and income，both gross and net，shall be ascertained.

资产、债务及收入，无论是毛额还是净额，均须加以查实。

No Voting Trustees shall be liable save only his own gross negligence.

投票受托人除了他自己的重大过失以外是没有责任的。

7.approval n.批准，赞成，同意，认可

We believe that quality will meet with your approval.

我们相信这种质量将会得到你的赞许。

The Second Party shall buy and sell，with the approval of the First Party，all goods and merchandise.

经甲方批准，乙方可购买或出售各类货物和商品。

All sales of Manufacturer's products shall be subject to prior approval by Manufacturer.

所有制造商产品的销售须经制造商事先批准。

approve v.批准，许可，赞成，满意

The Company shall approve standards of quality for all goods on the above-described premises.

公司应批准上述建筑物的一切物件的质量标准。

Replacement shall be properly manufactured in accordance with the specifications approved by AAA.

代用品应按甲方许可的规格准确地制造出来。

8.liable adj.常作表语用，表示（依法律）应负责的，有义务的；须交……的，应付……的，须受……的；有……倾向的，易于……的，有……可能的

The shipping company is the party liable for the damage of the goods.

轮船公司是应对货物残损负责的当事人。

Such commodities are liable to customs duties.

这类商品须缴纳关税。

Neither party shall be liable to the other with respect to orders so cancelled.

如果订单因此被撤销，则双方中的任何一方都不必对另一方负责。

We are liable to encounter difficulties in arranging the quantity required.

安排所需的数量，我们不免要遇到困难。

Mr.Johns is liable to visit Dalian after attending the Guangzhou Fair.

琼斯先生参加广交会后有可能前来大连。

辨析：liable, susceptible, subject, prone

这组词均含有人或事物在性质上、情势上处于某极易发生的状态之意。

liable 指人们遇到或可能遇到的事情是由于服从权势或因其生活状况，屈服于某种无法控制的力量而引起的后果。

susceptible 更强调人或事物的本质、特性、素质或性格。所有这些可以使事物失去抵抗力或容易遭受某种痛苦。

subject 由于某种原因（如生活状况、社会、经济或政治地位、性情特点）趋向于必须遭受、忍受或经历某事情。

prone 通常指人，很少指物，表示在不同程度上受到某事物的倾向性的制约，这种倾向性当情况顺利时必定会产生。

Prospective buyers are liable to judge the quality of goods by appearance.

有可能成为买主的人易于从外观判断货物质量。

The goods you packed in wooden cases are susceptible to damage by moisture.

装在木箱中的这批货很容易受潮损坏。

Perishable goods are subject to damage in transit.

易腐烂的货物在运输途中容易损坏。

One is more prone to make mistakes when one is tired.

当人们疲劳的时候做事就比较容易出错。

9.examine v.检验，检查；审查，审核

The goods were carefully examined before shipment.

货物在装运前经过仔细检查。

The Second Party shall not have the right to examine the books or records of the First Party.

乙方无权检查甲方的账册或记录。

辨析：examine, inspect, scrutinize, audit, check

examine表示严密调查，以确定某一事实、某事的真正性质、特征、状况或测定某事物的质量、效力、真实性或功能等。

inspect用于法律、军事、政府和工业方面时，指认真搜查可能出现的错误、缺陷或缺点。

scrutinize密切观察和关注微小细节。

audit认真检查账目，看其是否正确。

check认真仔细检查以便看到一切都正确。

The Contractor shall be responsible for checking and verifying all Drawings and Information supplied in writing by the Employer.

承包商应负责检查并核实由雇主所提供的一切书面信息及图纸。

The jeweler scrutinized the diamond of flaws.

珠宝商仔细察看钻石有无瑕疵。

The Franchisee agrees that all books and records shall be audited by Franchisor.

被特许人同意所有账册和记录均由特许人来查证。

Owner shall have the right at any time to inspect the Work as it is performed and more specifically any item of Materials whether or not during fabrication thereof.

业主有权在任何时候到工厂视察，以便检查工厂是否履行并生产明确规定由该厂生产的各种材料。

## ● Exercises

I.Translate the following into English：

1.每家银行每年都由政府部门的会计检查账目。

2.你最好派你公司会计去查对一下报表。

3.我方不得不为这批发货受损向你提出索赔。

4.法院判令甲方对乙方所受损失支付1万英镑赔偿费。

5.本合同规定的货物付款不意味着买方已完全接受货物的质量，所有货物要经过买方仔细检验后方可接受。

6.如果需要聘请其他国家的审计师对年度的财务进行审查，甲方应予以同意。其所需费用由乙方负担。

7.第一次技术服务应始于本合同生效之日起第6天。乙方应派遣一名技术人员赴甲方工厂，提供12个工作日的技术指导。

8.凡因为履行本合同而在甲方国家以外发生的一切税费，均由乙方负担。

9.倘若合同中的交货时间只是估计的时间，任何一方可在距估计日期尚有1/3的时间时，用书面要求另一方同意一个确定的时间。

10.制造商应对货物的质量、规格、性能及数量、重量进行一丝不苟和全面的检验，出具检验证明书，证实检验的技术数据和结论后，才能发货。

## II.Translate the following into Chinese：

1.Clean shipped on board Ocean Bill of Lading in full set made out to order of shipper and endorsed.

2. If the anticipated progress has not been maintained in accordance with the schedule， the Contractor shall advise the reasons therefore and suggest means to eliminate the causes of delay.

3.The issuing bank shall， have a reasonable time to examine the documents.

4.On close inspection， it was found out to be a forgery.

5. Progress review meeting will be held at the Seller's Plant with the Buyer's representatives as necessary during the manufacturing of the Equipment.At such meeting， the Seller shall report progress and indicate completion status against schedule.

6. Licensee shall keep true and accurate records， files and book of account containing all of the data reasonably required for the full computation and verification of the amount to be paid hereunder and the information to be given in the statements herein provided for.

7. The Contractor shall perform the inspection and examination of all equipment， machinery and materials including spare parts required for the construction of the plant.

8.This is the final arbitration award and binding on both Contracting Parties.

9.The Buyer is of the opinion that if the result of packing in cartons turns out to the satisfaction of the Buyer's clients， the Seller may continue using this packing in the future.

10. When either party contributes his capital goods or industrial property as investment， Party A and Party B shall conclude a separate contract to be a part of this main contract.

# Part Two

# 实践篇

# Practical Skills

# Unit Six /进出口货物买卖合同

## Import and Export Goods Contract

---

### 6.1    售货合同（1）Sales Contract（1）

CHINA NATIONAL CHEMICALS
IMPORT & EXPORT CORPORATION
GUANGDONG BRANCH

SALES CONTRACT （ORIGINAL）

Contract No.    Date：

Signed at：Guangzhou

Sellers：China National Chemicals Import & Export Corporation，Guangdong Branch

Address：61，Yanjiang Road（1），Guangzhou，China

Sellers：

……

Fax：

Tel：

Website：

E-mail：

Buyers：

Address：

Fax：

Tel：

Website：This Sales Contract is made by and between the Sellers and the Buyers whereby the Sellers agree to sell and the Buyers agree to buy the under-mentioned goods according to the terms and conditions stipulated as below：

| Name of Commodity Specifications & Packing | Quantity | Unit Price | Total Value |
|---|---|---|---|
| Lithopone ZnS content 28% min. Paper-lined glass-fibre bags | 50 m/tons | RMB ¥ 892 per M/T CIFC3% Singapore | RMB ¥ 44 600 |

（The Sellers are allowed to load 5% more or less and the price shall be calculated according to the unit price above）

Shipping Mark： To be designated by the Sellers.

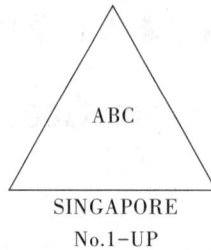

```
        /\
       /  \
      /    \
     /  ABC \
    /        \
   /          \
  /_____\
   SINGAPORE
   No.1-UP
```

Insurance： To be covered by the Sellers for 110% of invoice value against All Risks and War Risk as per the relevant Ocean Marine Cargo Clauses of the People's Insurance Company of China. If other coverage or an additional insurance amount is required， the Buyers must have the consent of the Sellers before shipment， and the additional premium is to be borne by the Buyers.

Port of Shipment： Guangzhou

Port of Destination： Singapore， with transhipment allowed.

Time of Shipment： During December， 20_____， allowing partial shipments.

Terms of Payment： The Buyers shall open with a bank acceptable to the Sellers an Irrevocable Sight Letter of Credit to reach the Sellers 30 days before the month of shipment， valid for negotiation in China until the 15th day after the month of shipment.

Commodity Inspection： It is mutually agreed that the Certificate of Quality and Weight issued by the China Import and Export Commodity Inspection Bureau at the port of shipment shall be taken as the basis of delivery.

Discrepancy and Claim： Any claim by the Buyers on the goods shipped shall be filed within 30 days after arrival of the goods at the port of destination and supported by a survey report issued by a surveyor approved by the Sellers. Claims in respect of matters within the responsibility of the insurance company or of the shipping company shall not be considered or entertained by the Sellers.

Force Majeure： If shipment of the contracted goods is prevented or delayed in whole or in part due to Force Majeure， the Sellers shall not be liable for non-shipment or late shipment of the goods under this Contract. However， the Sellers shall notify the Buyers by fax and furnish the latter within 15 days by registered airmail with a certificate issued by the China Council for the Promotion of International Trade attesting such event or events.

Arbitration： All disputes arising out of the performance of， or relating to this Contract， shall be settled amicably through negotiation. In case no settlement can be reached through negotiation， the case shall then be submitted to the China International

Economic and Trade Arbitration Commission, Beijing, China, for arbitration in accordance with its Rules of Procedure of Arbitration. The arbitral award is final and binding upon both parties.

Other Terms:

**参考译文：**

中国化工进出口公司广东省分公司

售货合同（正本）

合同号码：　　　　　　　　　日期：　　　　　签约地点：广州

卖方：中国化工进出口公司广东省分公司　　　　买方：

地址：中国广州沿江一路61号　　　　　　　　　地址：

传真：　　　　　　　　　　　　　　　　　　　传真：

电话：　　　　　　　　　　　　　　　　　　　电话：

网址：　　　　　　　　　网址：

电子信箱：　　　　　　　　　　　　　　　　　电子信箱：

兹经买卖双方同意由卖方售出买方购进下列货物，并按下列条款签订本合同：

1.商品基本条款。

| 商品名称、规格及包装 | 数量 | 单价 | 总值 |
|---|---|---|---|
| 锌贝白氧化锌含量至少在28%，用衬纸的玻璃纤维包装 | 50公吨 | 892元人民币/公吨，到岸价含佣金3%，新加坡港 | 44 600元人民币 |

（卖方可溢短装5%，价格仍按上述单价计算）

2.唛头：由卖方指定。

3.保险：由卖方按中国人民保险公司海洋货物运输保险条款按发票总值110%投保一切险及战争险。如买方欲增加其他险别或超过上述保额时须于装船前征得卖方同意，所增加的保险费由买方负担。

4.装船口岸：广州。

5.目的口岸：新加坡，允许转船。

6.装船期限：20_____年12月份装船，允许分批。

7.付款条件：买方应由卖方可接受的银行于装运月份前30天开立并送达卖方不可撤销即期信用证，至装运月份后第15天在中国议付有效。

8.商品检验：买卖双方同意以装运口岸中国进出口商品检验局签发的品质和重量检验证书作为品质和数量的交货依据。

9.异议和索赔：买方对于装运货物的任何索赔，必须于货到目的港30天内提出，并须提供经卖方同意的公证机构出具的检验报告。属于保险公司或轮船公司责任范围内的索赔，卖方不予接受。

10.不可抗力：如由于不可抗力的原因，致使卖方不能全部或部分装运或延迟装运合同货物，卖方对于这种不能装运或延迟装运不负有责任，但卖方须通知买方，并须在15天内用航空挂号信件向买方提交中国国际贸易促进委员会出具的证明此类事故的证明书。

11.仲裁：凡因执行本合同所发生的或与本合同有关的一切异议，双方应通过友好协商解决。如果协商不能解决，应提交北京中国国际经济贸易仲裁委员会根据该会的仲裁程序和规则进行仲裁。仲裁是终局性的，对双方都有约束力。

12.其他条款：

## 6.2　售货确认书 Sales Confirmation

CHINA NATIONAL LIGHT

INDUSTRIAL PRODUCTS IMPORT

AND EXPORT CORPORATION SHANGHAI BRANCH

128 Huqiu Road

Shanghai, China

Fax：

Tel：

http：//www.sinolight.com

E-mail：

SALES CONFIRMATION

（ORIGINAL）

No.CRE1890 Date：May 12，2018

Your Letter：30/4/2018

To Messrs

J.B.Lawson & Company

854 California Street

San Francisco，California 94104

Tel：

Address：

The undersigned Sellers and Buyers have agreed to close the following transaction according to the terms and conditions stipulated as below：

1.Commodity and Description： Canvas Folding Chairs with Wooden Frame

Quantity： 500 pcs

Unit Price： USD12.00 Per piece CFR San Francisco

Total Amount： USD 6 000

2.Loading Port and Destination： From China Ports to San Francisco.

3.Time of Shipment： During July，2018.

4.Packing： In cartons.

5.Shipping Marks：At the Sellers'option.

6.Insurance：To be effected by the Buyers.

7.Terms of Payment：By confirmed，transferable，divisible L/C with transhipment and partial shipment allowed，and with 5% more or less in quantity and value permissible，payable at sight and valid in China till the 15th day after shipment.

REMARKS：

（1）The Buyers shall establish the covering letter of Credit before June 1，2018，failing which the Sellers reserve the right to rescind this Confirmation without further notice，or to accept whole or any part thereof unfulfilled by the Buyers，or to lodge a claim for direct losses sustained，if any.

（2）Quality/Quantity discrepancy：In case of quality discrepancy，claim should be raised by the Buyers within 30 days after arrival of the goods at port of destination；while for quantity discrepancy，claim should be raised by the Buyers within 15 days after arrival of the goods at port of destination.It is understood that the Sellers shall not be liable for any discrepancy of the goods shipped due to causes for which the insurance company，shipping company，other transportation organization or post office is liable.

（3）The Sellers shall not be held liable for failure or delay in delivery of the entire lot or a portion of the goods under this Confirmation in consequence of any Force Majeure incidents.

（4）The Buyers are requested to countersign and return one copy of this Sales Confirmation immediately after receipt of the same.Objection，if any，should be raised by the Buyers within 5 days after receipt of this Confirmation，in the absence of which it is understood that the Buyers have accepted the terms and conditions of the Sales Confirmation.

Accepted by：

The Buyers                                              The Sellers

**参考译文：**

**售货确认书**

中国轻工业品进出口公司

上海市分公司

中国上海虎丘路 128 号

网址：http：//www.sinolight.com 　　电子信箱：××@sinolight.com

传真：

电话：

网址：

电子信箱：

编号：CRE1890 日期：2018 年 5 月 12 日

你方来信：2018年4月30日

我方去电：2018年5月12日

致： 加利福尼亚州旧金山市94104

加利福尼亚大街854号

劳森公司

电话：

地址：

签署本约的售买双方同意按下列条款成交：

1.商品名称规格　　数量　　　　　单价　　　　　　　总值

帆布木架折椅　　500把　　成本加运费到旧金山每把12美元　6 000美元

2.装货港和目的港：由中国港口至美国旧金山。

3.装船日期：2018年7月。

4.包装：纸箱装。

5.装运唛头：由卖方选定。

6.保险：由买方投保。

7.付款条件：保兑的、可转让的、可分割的信用证，准许转船和分批装运，允许价值和数量有5%的上下浮动，见票即付，且于装船后15天内在中国议付有效。

备注：

（1）买方须于2018年6月1日前开出本批交易的信用证，否则，卖方有权不经通知，取消本确认书，或接受买方对本契约未执行的全部或一部分，或对因此遭受的直接损失提出索赔。

（2）品质/数量异议：如买方提出索赔，凡属品质异议，须于货到目的地口岸之日起30天内提出；凡属数量异议，须于货到目的地口岸之日起15日内提出。对所装货物所提任何异议属于保险公司、航运公司、其他有关运输机构或邮递机构应负责者，卖方不负任何责任。

（3）本确认书内所述全部或部分商品，如因人力不可抗拒的原因，以至于不能履约或延迟交货，卖方概不负责。

（4）买方于收到售货确认书后请立即签字退回一份。如买方对本确认书有异议，应于收到后5天内提出，否则认为买方已同意接受确认书所规定的各项条款。

买方签字　　　　　　　　卖方签字

## 6.3　　售货合同（2）Sales Contract（2）

Contract No.： ××××××

Date： Aug.××，2018

The Buyer： ×××××××× （hereinafter referred to as ×××）

Legal Address： ×××××××××××

Representative：××××××××××××

Tel/Fax：×××××××××××

Website：

E-mail：

The Seller：×××××× （hereinafter referred to as ××××××）

Legal Address：×××××××××××

Representative：×××××××××

Tel/Fax：×××××××××××

Website：

E-mail：

WHEREAS：

This Contract is made by and between the Buyer and the Seller whereby the Buyer agrees to buy and the Seller agrees to sell the commodity in attached Annex according to the terms and conditions stipulated below：

1.SCOPE OF SUPPLY

Product： Inter-City Bus

Description：

Model：A

Length：12 000mm

Seats： 50

2.QUANTITY：10 000 Units

3. UNIT PRICE： FOB Xingang， Tianjin USD22 150.00 per unit （US Dollars twenty two thousand， one hundred and fifty only ）

GRAND TOTAL： USD221 500 000.00 （US Dollars two hundred and twenty one million and five hundred thousand ）

4.INCOTERMS

Unless otherwise stipulated in this Contract， the terms and conditions hereof shall be interpreted in accordance with "International Rules for the Interpretation of Trade Terms" （INCOTERMS 2010） provided by International Chamber of Commerce.

Risk of damage to or loss of the Product shall pass to Buyer upon delivery.Title to the Product shall be transferred to Buyer upon full payment to Seller.

5.TERMS OF PAYMENT

1） 20% （Twenty percent） of the contract value shall be paid by T/T （Telegraphic Transfer） as the advance payment within 10 days after contract signing date and the balance 80% （Eighty percent） of the contract value shall be paid against L/C at 360 days sight to be accepted by both parties.

L/C shall be passed via the Seller's bank as follows：

-Bank Name： ×××××××××

-Bank Address： ×××××××××

-Account Name： ×××××××××

-SWIFT Code： ×××××××××

2）Banking Charges.

The Seller shall bear the banking charges incurred in China， and all banking charges incurred outside China shall be borne by the Buyer， unless otherwise agreed by both parties.

6.TAXES

1）All taxes levied on the Seller or the Buyer shall be borne by the respective party in accordance with the applicable tax law/regulation in the territory.

2）All payments to be made by the Buyer to the Seller hereunder shall be paid without set-off， counterclaim or required withholding or deduction unless prohibited by any applicable law.In the event that a withholding tax or deduction is required， the Buyer shall pay the price net of the required withholding or deduction to the Seller.

7.TERMS OF DELIVERY

1）Time of shipment： Within 15 days after receipt of the advance payment and the L/C of balance value to be accepted by the ××× Bank.

2）Port of shipment： Chinese Port.

3）Port of destination： Singapore.

4）Partial shipment and transhipment shall be allowed.

5）All goods should be delivered by containers suitable package for sea freight.

8.DOCUMENTS REQUIRED FOR PAYMENT

1）Full set of three （3/3）Original OCEAN BILL OF LADING

2）3 Original COMMERCIAL INVOICE

3）3 Original detailed PACKING LIST

4）One （1）Original signed "CERTIFICATE OF QUALITY"

The certificate will indicate that the products being shipped have been inspected and meet the specifications and standards in all respects.

9.PACKING

Shipping/Packing Mark： The following information in sequence， should be clearly marked in English on a curable/waterproof tag and attached to each package：

1）The wording： HANDLE WITH CARE

2）Product Origin： Made in China

10.SHIPPING MARK

At the Seller's Option

11.WARRANTY

The Seller guarantees that the product conforms to the quality and specifications specified herein.The detailed Specifications shall be stipulated in Annex A hereto.

In no event shall the Seller and the Buyer be liable for any indirect and consequential damages, including loss of profits as per quality and specifications of the cargo agreed upon.

## 12.DISCREPANCY AND CLAIMS

The Seller shall accompany with the inspectors of （SGS） to examine and certify the quantity and quality of the cargo as per the specific order at the port of loading.

The Buyer shall notify the Seller in writing of such defects within 5 days after the detection supported by an Inspection Report issued by Societe Generale de Surveillance S. A. （SGS） and the Seller shall take all the measures necessary to remedy the defects.

## 13.DELAY

If Seller fails to deliver the Product according to the agreed schedule solely due to its own fault, Seller shall pay to Buyer liquidated damages/indemnities at a rate of 0.01% of delayed Product value for each day delayed, up to a maximum of ten percent （10%） of delayed Product value.Liquidated damages/Indemnities shall be the sole remedy of Seller in respect of late delivery by the Seller.

If any payment other than the advance payment is not paid on due date, the Buyer shall pay to the Seller interest at a rate of 8% per annum of the overdue amount accruing from the due date until the date of payment.

## 14.FORCE MAJEURE

Neither party shall be held responsible for failure or delay to perform all or any part of this Contract due to flood, fire, earthquake, snowstorm, rainstorm, drought, hailstorm, hurricane, war, government prohibition, or any other events that are unforeseeable at the time of the execution hereof and could not be controlled, avoided or overcome by such party.However, the affected Party shall give a notice to the other party of its occurrence as soon as possible and a certificate or a document of the occurrence of the Force Majeure event issued by the relevant authority shall be sent to the other party by airmail as evidence not later than 14 days after its occurrence.

If the non-performance due to the Force Majeure lasts for more than sixty （60） days, the parties shall immediately consult together in an effort to agree upon a revised Contract basis. If the parties are unable to arrive at a mutually satisfactory solution within one hundred and twenty （120） days from the beginning of such Force Majeure, then either of the Parties may terminate the Contract in respect of the unexecuted portion hereof.

## 15.TERMINATION

Except as provided elsewhere, this Contract may be terminated in either of the following cases:

1） Through mutual written agreement by both parties;

2）If the other party seriously fails to perform its obligations within the time limit stipulated herein，and fails to remedy such breach within 60 days following the receipt of the notice from the non-breaching party.In such case the non-breaching party shall give the other party a written notice to terminate this Contract.

In case the Contract is delayed or terminated due to the Buyer's cause，all the losses sustained should be taken by the Buyer.

16.GOVERNING LAW

The applicable law to this Contract is the United Nations Convention on Contracts for the International Sale of Goods，1980（the "CISG"）.

17.ARBITRATION

1）Any disputes arising from or in connection with this Contract shall be settled through friendly negotiation.

2）Should no settlement can be reached through negotiation，the case shall then be submitted to the Foreign Trade Arbitration Commission of the China Council for the Promotion of International Trade for Arbitration in accordance with its Provisional Rules in effect at the time of applying for arbitration.The arbitration tribunal shall be composed of three arbitrators.

3）The arbitrage/arbitral award is final and binding upon both parties.Neither party may bring a suit before a law court or make a request to any other organization for revising the arbitrage/arbitral award.

4）The arbitration fee shall be borne by the losing party.

5）The applicable law to this Contract is the United Nations Convention on Contracts for the International Sale of Goods，1980.

18.CONFIDENTIALITY

The parties commit not to divulgate any information resulting from this Contract during the execution of this Contract and for a period of 5 years after the termination hereof.

19.INTELLECTUAL PROPERTY RIGHTS

Intellectual Property Rights（"IPR"）in the Product and in all information relating to the Product made available to Buyer shall remain vested in the Seller.

Neither party assigns any of its IPR to the other party.The Buyer is granted a non-exclusive，non-transferable and non-sublicensing license to use the Product supplied hereunder within the territory of Singapore.

20.EFFECTIVENESS OF THE CONTRACT

This Contract shall come into force on the date of signing by both parties and the receipt of the advance payment by the Seller.

21.MISCELLANEOUS

1）The language shall be in English.

2）All attachments，Annexes and Appendices hereto are integral parts of this Contract.

All definitions，specifications and details not mentioned in this Contract will be attached in annex and will constitute an integral part of this contract. In case of contradiction，wording of this Contract shall prevail.

3）Any amendments，supplements and alterations to the terms and conditions of this Contract shall be made in written form and signed by the authorized representatives of both parties upon the agreement which has been reached between the Seller and the Buyer，and they shall form integral parts of this Contract and have the same force as the Contract itself.

IN WITNESS THEREOF，this Contract is made in TWO originals，one for each party.

××××××××××××

××××××××××××

（Buyer）（Seller）

Date Date

**参考译文：**

合同号：×××

日期：2018年8月××日

买方：××××××××（以下称为×××）

注册地址：××××

代表人：×××××

电话号码/传真号码：××××××××××

网址：

电子信箱：卖方：××××××××（以下称为×××）

注册地址：××××××××××

代表人：×××××

电话号码/传真号码：××××××××××

网址：

电子信箱：

鉴于：

买卖双方同意按照如下条款签订本买卖合同：

1.货描

产品：城际公共汽车

描述：

型号：A

长：12 000毫米

座位：50个

2. 数量：10 000 辆

3. 单价：FOB 天津新港每辆 22 150 美元

总价： 221 500 000.00 美元

4. 贸易术语

除非在合同中有其他约定，本合同采用的贸易术语遵循国际商会颁布的《国际贸易术语 2010 通则》的规定。

货物的风险在交货后转移给买方。所有权在买方全额付款后转移。

5. 付款方式

1）合同金额的 20% 作为预付款在合同签署后的 10 日内以电汇的方式支付。合同金额的 80% 以远期信用证的方式在交单后的 360 天支付。

卖方的银行信息为：

银行名称：

银行地址：

账户名称：

SWIFT 编码：

2）银行费用。

除非双方有其他约定，在中国境内产生的银行费用由卖方负责，在中国境外产生的银行费用由买方负责。

6. 税费

1）所有的税费由买卖双方按照所在国当地法律的要求进行缴纳。

2）除非法律要求，否则买方不能够对向卖方支付的货款进行任何的抵扣、反诉、预提或者抵减。如果法律规定了预提税款或者抵减，买方支付的货款为预提完毕或者抵扣之后的金额。

7. 交货

1）装运日期：在收到预付款且信用证被当地银行接受的 15 天内装运。

2）装运港：中国港口。

3）目的港：新加坡港口。

4）允许分批发货和转船。

5）所有的产品都要采用适合海运的包装，以集装箱来运输。

8. 付款文件

1）三份正本提单。

2）三份正本商业发票。

3）三份详细的装箱单。

4）一份签字的"质量合格证明"。

此证明表明货物在装运时已经经过检验且符合合同约定的技术规范。

9. 包装

包装标识：以下信息应该按照顺序用英文，以防水标签的形式标示在每个包装盒上。

1）轻拿轻放。

2）原产地：中国制造。

10.唛头

由卖方选择。

11.质保期

卖方承诺所交付的产品符合本合同约定的质量和技术标准。详细的技术标准在附件A中进行了约定。

买卖双方在任何情况下都不会对由于质量或者技术标准引起的任何间接损失如利润损失等承担责任。

12.异议和索赔

卖方在装运港要配合检验方瑞士通用公证行进行产品质量和数量的检验。

买方在发现产品缺陷的5天内，将由瑞士通用公证行出具的问题报告书面告知卖方。卖方应该采取一切方法解决问题。

13.延期

如果由于卖方的原因，导致货物不能按期交货，则卖方需要每日支付延期货物价值的0.01%作为滞期罚金，最多支付至延期货物价值的10%。滞期罚金为卖方对买方延迟交货的唯一补救措施。

如果买方没有按期支付货款，买方需要按照年利息的8%支付延期罚金，计算周期为应付款日至付款日期。

14.不可抗力

买卖双方因洪水、火灾、地震、暴雪、暴雨、干旱、冰雹、飓风、战争、政府禁令或者其他无法预见的事件导致合同无法履行或者延迟履行，双方都不承担任何责任。尽管如此，受影响的一方应该将官方发布的不可抗力的证明在事件发生后的14日之内通过邮件通知另一方。

如果由于不可抗力的原因导致合同在60日之内无法继续执行，则双方应该尽快协商是否需要修改合同。如果双方在120天之内无法达成一致，双方中的任意一方都有权终止合同未完成的部分。

15.合同终止

除了其他的约定，本合同可以在以下情况发生时终止：

1）双方书面终止合同；或者。

2）如果合同一方在合同允许的缺陷弥补期限内无法履行相关责任，或者在收到非违约方通知60日之后没有做出弥补。在这种情况下，非违约方可以书面通知违约方终止合同。

如果完全由于买方的原因导致合同延误或者终止，则由此造成的所有损失由买方负责。

16.适用法律

本合同适用法律为1980年版《联合国国际货物销售合同公约》。

17.仲裁

1）本合同的所有争议都遵从友好协商的方式解决。

2）如果友好协商无法解决，则此案件需提交中国国际贸易仲裁委员会，依据仲裁规则进行仲裁。仲裁成员由三人组成。

3）仲裁为终局性的，对双方都有约束力。任何一方不得将此案件诉诸法院或者申请复议仲裁结果。

4）仲裁费由败诉方承担。

5）合同的适用法律为1980年版《联合国国际货物销售合同公约》。

18.保密

合同双方承诺在合同执行期和合同终止后的5年内不向外界披露此合同的任何信息。

19.知识产权

产品中的知识产权和相关信息授权给买方使用，但是所有权仍然归卖方所有。

任何一方不得转让其知识产权给另外一方。卖方授予买方在此合同项下、在新加坡国境内，非排他的、不可转让的、不可授权的使用权。

20.合同生效

此合同在双方签字和卖方收到预付款的情况下生效。

21.其他

1）此合同语言为英语。

2）所有的附属文件都作为此合同的一部分。所有在附属文件中的定义、技术规范和其他约定都构成此合同的一部分。如果发生了冲突，此合同优先。

3）所有针对此合同的修订、补充和变更应该以书面的形式，经过双方授权签字人签字后生效，构成有效合同的一部分。

特立此证，此合同一式两份，双方各执一份。

买方　　卖方

日期　　日期

## 6.4　　　　购货合同 Purchase Agreement

Contract No.： 123456

Signing Date： August 26th，2018

Signing Place： Indonesia

The Buyer： PT ABCD

Address： ××××××.Indonesia

Tel：×××××××

Fax：×××××××

Website：

E-mail：

The Seller： China ABCD

Address： Beijing，P.R.China

Tel： ××××××××

Fax.： ×××××××

Website：

E-mail：

As the equipment of the contract is discussed and fixed by and between PT ABCD and the manufacturer. Both the seller and the buyer agree that China ABCD buy the commodity from the manufacturer and sell it to PT ABCD.

China ABCD shall not be held responsible for all the issues concerning the commodity name, model, country of origin, manufacturer, quantity, packing, time of shipment, port of destination, technical specification, technical documents and / or technical standard, erection, commissioning, performance test-run and acceptance etc.

This Contract is made by and between the Buyer and the Seller; whereby the Buyer agrees to buy and the Seller agrees to sell the under-mentioned commodity according to the terms and conditions as stipulated below：

Article 1.DESCRIPTION OF THE COMMODITY

| Item No. | Commodity，Specifications | Unit | Quan. | Unit Price （USD） | Amount （USD） |
|---|---|---|---|---|---|
| 1 | FX | Set | 4 | 1,000,000 | 4,000,000 |
| Total | | | | | |

Total Value： USD 4,000,000.CIF Jakarta port，Indonesia （Say in U.S.Dollars four million only）

The above contract price is calculated on the basis of the exchange rate of CNY （Chinese Renminbi） against U.S.dollars at 6.55：1.If the exchange rate of CNY against the U.S.dollars fluctuates by the time of the date of the bill of lading, the buyer should make compensation to the seller, and the compensation plan is as follows：

1.1　If the appreciation of the CNY against U.S.dollars is less than 2%, the buyer needn't make compensation to the seller；

1.2　If the appreciation of the CNY against U.S.dollars is between 2% and 5%, the buyer shall make compensation to the seller.The amount of compensation is calculated as follows：

The amount of compensation = Contract amount × 85%× （Appreciation percentage−2%）

1.3　If the appreciation of the CNY against U.S.dollars is more than 5%, the buyer shall make partial compensation to the seller.The amount of compensation is calculated as follows:

The amount of compensation = Contract amount × 85%×3%+Contract amount × 85%× (Appreciation percentage−5%) ×50%

The compensation should be paid by the buyer when the final repayment is affected.

Article 2.COUNTRY OF ORIGIN

P.R.China

Article 3.TERMS OF PAYMENT

3.1　Down Payment:

15% of the total contract price shall be paid by telegraphic transfer by the Buyer to the Seller not later than 30 days after the Buyer has received the following documents from the Seller.

1.Commercial invoice;

2.Proforma invoice covering the total Contract price.

3.2　Payment after Shipment:

1.15% of the total contract price shall be paid by telegraphic transfer by the Buyer to the Seller within 180 days after the first shipment date;

2.20% of the total contract price shall be paid by telegraphic transfer by the Buyer to the Seller within 360 days after the first shipment date;

3.25% of the total contract price shall be paid by telegraphic transfer by the Buyer to the Seller within 540 days after the first shipment date;

4.25% of the total contract price plus the compensation amount shall be paid by telegraphic transfer by the Buyer to the Seller within 720 days after the first shipment date.

3.3　Shipping Documents:

1.Original Bill of Lading: Full set;

2.Commercial Invoice: 3 Copies;

3.Packing List: 3 Copies;

4.Insurance Policy: Full Set.

3.4　All banking charges incurred in China shall be borne by the Seller and those incurred outside of China shall be borne by the Buyer.

Article 4.SHIPMENT

4.1　Port of Shipment:

Any Chinese seaport at Seller's option.

4.2　Port of Destination:

Jakarta Port, Indonesia.

4.3　Time of Shipment:

Within 360 days after effectiveness of the contract.

4.4　The Seller shall, immediately upon the completion of the loading of the goods, advise by fax the Buyer of the Contract No., commodity, quantity, invoice value, gross weight, name of vessel or flight No., date of sailing, etc.

Article 5.PACKING

The Seller shall have the goods packed in wooden case (s) or in carton (s), suitable for long distance ocean or air transportation.

Article 6.INSURANCE

The insurance should be covered by the Seller for the full invoice value plus 10% against All Risks/Institute Cargo Clauses （A）.Should the Buyer desire to cover for any other extra risks besides the above-mentioned, the Seller' s approval must be obtained beforehand and all the additional premiums thus incurred shall be for the Buyer' s account.

Article 7.INSPECTION

It is mutually agreed that the equipments supplied by the Seller shall be inspected by the buyer before each shipment, and the letter of acceptance should be signed after inspection.

If the buyer does not inspect the equipments before each shipment, it means the quality of the equipments have been accepted by the buyer.After shipment, the buyer should make payment as per stipulated in Article 3.

Article 8.ERECTION, COMMISSIONING, PERFORMANCE TEST-RUN

The seller shall not be held responsible for the issues concerning the Erection, Test Run, Commissioning, and Performance Test-Run.

Article 9.FORCE MAJEURE

Should any cases happen and prevent either party from executing the Contract, such as war, serious fire, typhoon, earthquake, floods and other cases which could not be foreseen, controlled, avoided and overcame, the party concerned shall notify the other party by fax and send by registered airmail a certificate issued by competent authority concerning confirmation of the Force Majeure within fourteen （14） days following the occurrence of the case of force majeure.

The party concerned shall not be held responsible for any delay or failure in performing any or all of the obligations due to the event of force majeure.However, the party concerned shall inform the other party by fax the termination or elimination of the case of force majeure as soon as possible.

The parties shall proceed with their obligations immediately after the date when the case of force majeure has ceased or the effects have been removed.The performance of those obligations shall be extended by a period equal to the effect of such cases.Should the effect of the force majeure mentioned above last for more than 90 days, either party shall be entitled to terminate the Contract.

Article 10.TAXES AND DUTIES

1. All taxes in connection with the execution thereof levied by the Chinese Government on the Seller in accordance with the tax laws in effect shall be borne by the Seller.

2.All taxes arising outside of China in connection with the execution thereof shall be borne by the Buyer.

Article 11.ARBITRATION

All disputes in connection with this Contract or the execution thereof shall be settled through friendly negotiations.In case no settlement can be reached, the case may then be submitted for arbitration to China International Economic and Trade Arbitration Commission in accordance with its Rules of Arbitration promulgated by the said Arbitration Commission.The Arbitration shall take place in Beijing and the decision of the Arbitration Commission shall be final and binding upon both parties; neither party shall seek recourse to a law court nor other authorities appeal for revision of the decision. Arbitration fee shall be borne by the losing party.In the course of arbitration, both parties shall continue to execute the present Contract except those under arbitration.

Article 12.EFFECTIVENESS OF CONTRACT

This Contract will come into effectiveness upon the following items are completely occurred:

1.The signature by all parties ;

2.The Seller receives 15% of the contract value as the down-payment ;

This contract shall remain valid until all parties finish a the obligations defined in the contract.

Article 13.OTHER TERMS

Unless otherwise stipulated herein the terms and conditions of the Contract shall be interpreted in accordance with International Rules for the Interpretation of Trade Terms (2010 edition), ICC Uniform Customs and Practice for Documentary Credits 600 and Uniform Rules For Collections （Publication No.522）.

IN WITNESS THEREOF, this Contract is made in English and signed by both parties in two originals; each party holds one original.

For the Seller： For the Buyer：

**参考译文：**

合同号：123456

签约日：2018 年 8 月 26 日

签署地：印度尼西亚

买方名称：PT ABCD

地址：印度尼西亚××××××

电话：××××××××

传真：××××××××

网址：

电子信箱：

卖方名称：中国 ABCD

地址：中国北京市××××××××

电话：××××××××

传真：××××××××

网址：

电子信箱：

兹经 PT ABCD 和生产商已经确定合同的标的设备。买卖双方同意中国 ABCD 从生产商购买设备销售给 PT ABCD。

中国 ABCD 对于设备名称、型号、原产地、生产商、数量、包装、运输时间、目的港、技术规范、技术文件和/或技术标准、安装、试运行、性能测试和验收等不负任何责任。

本合同经买卖双方同意，按下列条款签订本合同：

条款1                    **产品描述**

| 条目号 | 产品型号 | 单位 | 数量 | 单价/美元 | 总价/美元 |
|---|---|---|---|---|---|
| 1 | FX | 台 | 4 | 1,000,000 | 4,000,000 |
| 合计 | | | | | |

总价值：4,000,000美元. CIF 雅加达港，印度尼西亚（400万美元整）

以上约定的合同价格基于人民币兑美元6.55：1的汇率测算，如果在提单日之前汇率发生了波动，买方应该按照如下约定补偿卖方汇率损失：

1.1　如果人民币兑美元升值不超过2%，买方无须补偿；

1.2　如果人民币兑美元升值在2%到5%之间，买方需要补偿汇率损失，补偿金额的计算方式如下：

补偿金额=合同金额×85%×（汇率升值比例-2%）

1.3　如果人民币兑美元升值幅度超过5%，买方需要部分补偿汇率损失，计算方法如下：

补偿金额 = 合同金额×85%×3%+合同金额×85%×（汇率升值比例-5%）×50%

补偿金额由买方在最终付款支付时偿付。

条款2.原产国

中华人民共和国

条款3.付款条款

3.1  预付款：

合同金额的15%在买方收到卖方提供的如下材料后30天内以电汇的方式支付。

1.商业发票；

2.包含合同金额的形式发票。

3.2  出运后付款：

1.合同金额的15%在出运日之后的180天内由买方以电汇的方式支付给卖方；

2.合同金额的20%在出运日之后的360天内由买方以电汇的方式支付给卖方；

3.合同金额的25%在出运日之后的540天内由买方以电汇的方式支付给卖方；

4.合同金额加上补偿金额的25%在出运日之后的720天内由买方以电汇的方式支付给卖方。

3.3  装运单据：

1.提单原件：全套；

2.商业发票：3份；

3.装箱单：3份；

4.保险单：全套。

3.4  所有在中国产生的银行费用都由卖方承担，中国之外产生的费用由买方承担。

条款4.装运

4.1  装运港：

卖方指定的任意中国港口。

4.2  目的港：

雅加达港，印度尼西亚。

4.3  装运日：

合同生效日后的360天以内。

4.4  卖方应在装船完成后立刻以传真的方式通知买方合同编号、产品名称、数量、发票金额、毛重、船名或者航班号、开船日等信息。

条款5.包装

卖方应将货物以适宜长途海运或者空运的木箱以及硬纸板箱包装。

条款6.保险

卖方应购买覆盖发票金额110%的海洋运输一切险/协会货物保险条款A。如果买方欲增加的风险范围覆盖并超过上述保险范畴，需预先征得卖方同意，且所增加的费用由买方承担。

条款7.检验

双方同意买方在出运前进行检验，验收证书在检验合格后出具。

如果买方没有在出运前进行检验，则意味着买方接受了货物。出运后，买方应该按照条款3的约定进行付款。

条款8.安装，试运行，性能测试

卖方不负责设备的安装、性能测试和试运行。

条款9.不可抗力

在合同执行过程中，如因发生无法预见、无法控制和无法避免的事件，如战争、严重火灾、台风、地震、洪水等，导致合同一方无法履行合同，合同方应在不可抗力发生时尽快电告另一方，并在事故发生后14日内将主管机构出具的事故证明书挂号航空邮寄给另一方。

合同双方对于由不可抗力导致的延迟或者违约不承担任何责任。尽管如此，受阻方应在不可抗力结束或影响减弱时，尽快以传真方式通知另一方。

在不可抗力影响减弱或者消除时，双方应尽快履行各自的义务。合同履约期相应顺延。如果不可抗力持续时间超过90天，合同任何一方都有权终止合同。

条款10.税费和关税

1.在合同执行过程中，所有由中国政府按现行税法征收的税费由卖方承担。

2.在合同执行过程中，所有在中国境外涉及的税费由买方承担。

条款11.仲裁

所有关于本合同和本合同执行过程中的纠纷都应本着友好协商的方式解决。如果协商无法解决纠纷，双方应将案件提交中国国际贸易仲裁委员会，按照委员会的仲裁规则仲裁。仲裁地在北京，仲裁效力为终局的，对双方都具有约束力；仲裁后，双方都不可再将案件诉诸法院或者找寻其他权威机构。仲裁费用由败诉方承担。在仲裁期间，除仲裁事项外，双方应正常履约。

条款12.合同生效

本合同的生效条件如下：

1.合同双方签字；

2.卖方收到合同金额15%的预付款；

本合同的有效期至双方履约完毕后结束。

条款13.其他条款

除非合同中另有约定，本合同的条款受以下惯例约束：《2010年国际贸易术语解释通则》、《跟单信用证统一管理600》和《托收统一惯例522》。

合同以英文书写，由双方签署两份原件；一方保留一份，特此为证。

卖方：　　　　　　　　　　买方：

# Notes

1.This Sales Contract is made by and between the Seller and the Buyer…

双方制定合同除了……is made by and between ，还有其他写法，如 enter into the contract。

2.as per 按照

3.stipulate v.规定，作为合约的条件规定，按合同要求；在约定中指出或安排

The retail list price shall be those stipulated in written schedules.

零售定价表应当以书面明细表的形式规定下来。

Final payment shall be paid by the Owner to the Contractor, unless otherwise stipulated in the Certificate.

除非在交工证书中另有规定，否则，业主应将最终付款交给承包商。

在合同中，表示"规定"的词还有 provide 和 prescribe 等。

The formal agreement will provide for an escrow fund of … % of the securities to be delivered by the Buyer.

正式协议应规定卖方提供保险金……%的代管基金。

This Association shall admit applicants to membership in the Association upon such uniform conditions as may be prescribed by the Board of Directors.

本协议按照董事会所规定的同一条件，接纳申请人取得该协会的会员资格。

The Committee shall have the right to prescribe an organization fee to be paid by each person.

该委员会应有权规定每个成员缴纳的组织费。

其他的一些表示"规定"的同义词还有：

show, state, specify 以及 set forth 和 set out

4.coverage n.保险范围，承保险别，保险总额，投保条款

We want broader coverage to include some extraneous risks.

我们需要较广泛的保险，包括一些附加险。

coverable adj.可投保的，可承保的

Please let us know the premium at which breakage is coverable by the insurer on your side.

请告知你处保险商承保破碎险的保费。

The Company shall furnish to the Operator a statement as to the coverage limits as well as the then present premium upon said Company.

公司须给业务经营人提供一份报表，以说明保险总额的限度（额）以及该公司当时应付的保险费（标准）。

This coverage shall provide for both bodily injury and property damage.

此项保险总额既适用于肉体损伤又适用于财产损毁。

cover n.（保险业）保险；v.保险，投保

insurance cover 保险

We have arranged the necessary insurance cover.

我们已安排了必要的保险。

Does your policy provide adequate cover against breakage?

你们的保险单是否提供适当的破碎险？

Cover 作及物动词时，宾语除可为所保的货物和投保的险别外，还可以是保险和被保险人。

We shall cover the goods against all risks.

我们将对此货投保一切险。

We shall cover all risks and war risk for you.

我们将为你方投保一切险和战争险。

Insurance is to be covered by the buyers.

保险应由买方办理。

This insurance policy covers us against breakage.

这份保单给我们保了破碎险。

5.bear vt.负担，承担；带有，具有，标明；承受，经得起，耐（得住）

Corporation will conduct such national publicity as it may deem fit and bear all expenses.

公司将进行适当的全国性的宣传推广（工作），并承担一切费用。

The Contractor shall bear all costs or damages which may result from the ordering of any materials.

承包商须负担由于订购材料而造成的一切费用或损坏赔偿费。

Extra expenses are to be borne by you.

额外费用将由你方负担。

Each package is to bear the shipping mark.

每件货须带有此唛头。

Our product bears tests.

我公司产品经得起检验。

bearer n.持票人，不记名

The payment shall be made in checks payable to the bearer.

付款将以付给持票人支票的方式支付。

6.partial shipment 分批装运

If partial shipment is allowed，we will space out consignments over two months.

如允许分批装运，我方将在2个月内分期装运货物。

7.transhipment n.转船

We，therefore，deem it necessary to request you to amend your L/C to allow transhipment.

因此，我方认为有必要请你方把信用证修改为允许转船。

tranship v.转船

Therefore，with the exceptions of unusual condition of China which may happen accidentally，the goods will be transhipped from Hong Kong without delay.

因此，除非有特殊情况发生，否则，货物将在中国香港转船，不得有误。

8.valid adj.有效的，生效的

The payment shall be effected by cash or by valid check

订货必须用现金或即期支票付款才能生效。

No assignment shall be valid or binding, if the same shall be in contravention of any terms or provisions of this Agreement.

如果转让书违反了本协议中的任何条款或规定，那么该转让书是无效的，或者说是没有约束力的。

This offer will be valid for your acceptance until （date）, after which date the offer shall be deemed withdrawn.

在（某日）之前，该报价对你是有效的，（某日）以后该报价便被认为业已撤销。

validate v.证实，使生效

No agreement shall be valid or shall in any manner alter or modify any provisions by the government authority thereof unless validated.

除非协议在法律上生效，否则，协议是无效的，协议也不能变更或修改政府当局所定的条款。

For validating warranty, the Purchaser shall fill up in the enclosed form and send it to the Seller.

为使保证书生效，买方应填写附表一份，随函送达卖方。

validity n.合法性，有效性

Licenses shall not contest the validity of the registrations of these trademarks at the Patent of Office of （country）.

许可证持有方不应对（某国）专利局注册的这些商标的有效性提出异议。

This Agreement shall be governed by the laws of （country）, including all matters of construction, validity and performance.

本协议应受（某国）法令所制约，其中包括对协议的解释、合法性及其履行等问题。

Because of the recent fire in the factory, all the stocks were destroyed.In this case, we cannot make shipment as arranged before.Please extend the date of shipment and the expiry date of L/C No.44779 to 30 April and 15 May respectively.

由于最近工厂发生火灾烧毁了全部库存，已不能按照原安排发货。请将44779号信用证的交货期和有效期分别延展至4月30日和5月15日。

9.negotiable adj.（票据等）可转让的，可流通的，可议付的；可谈判的，可商议的

Whereas the Corporation is empowered to enter into, make and perform contracts of every kind with any person, execute and issue negotiable instruments, so far as may be permitted by the laws of （country）…

有鉴于此，只要（某国）法律许可，该公司有权与任何人缔约、制定和履行各种合同，有权签署与发行流通票据……

All negotiable set of B/L made out to order must be endorsed by the shipper.

所有可转让的、空白抬头的提单都要由托运人背书。

Part time barman required，hours and salary negotiable.

招聘兼职酒保，工作时间和薪水面议。

This Bill of Lading is issued in a negotiable form，so it shall constitute title to the goods and the holder，by endorsement of this B/L.

所签发的提单可为转让的，故只要在提单上背书，便确定了货物和持票人的所有权。

non-negotiable adj 不可商议的，不可转让的

non-negotiable copy of B/L 提单副本

negotiation n.谈判，商议，议付

in negotiation with，under negotiation 在谈判中

negotiate vt.

negotiate with sb/over/for sth 与某人商议，谈判某事，议付

We will send a representative to negotiate the business with you in person.

我们将派代表与你方商洽此事。

We are willing to negotiate with you on your proposal to act as our agent.

我们愿就你方充当我方代理的建议同你方商议。

10.inspection n.检验

The Inspection Certificate covering this shipment states clearly that the goods were in sound condition when shipped.

此货的检验证书清楚地说明货物在装出时情况良好。

inspection certificate 检验证书

CCIB=China Commodity Inspection Bureau 中国商品检验局（现国家质检总局）

Such dispute in respect of the result of the tests shall be immediately referred to a reliable and agreeable third party inspection institute operating in （country）.

关于这些试验结果的争论，应该马上提交给一个可信赖的、被认可的在（某国）开展业务的第三方检查机构。

11.survey report 鉴定报告

survey n.检查，调查，鉴定；现场调查

surveyor n.鉴定人，鉴定行

customs surveyor　　海关检验人员

engineer surveyor　　工程检验员

insurance surveyor　保险检验员

marine surveyor　　海事鉴定人

survey report　　　鉴定报告

surveyor's report　鉴定行报告

surveying agent　　检验代理

A survey report is requested.

需要一份检查报告。

Please survey the business possibilities and advise your findings.

请调查交易可能性并告知结果。

Please survey the situation closely and keep us informed of developments.

请密切关注形势并将发展情况随时告知。

12.delivery n.交付，交货，移交

在远洋贸易中表示交货期时 delivery 和 shipment 可以互相换用，如 June delivery =June shipment，但是 take delivery "提货" 和 make delivery "交货" 则不能用 shipment 代替。

We will take delivery of the goods as soon as they are released from the Customs.

一旦海关放行我们即将货提出。

When we made delivery to the buyers, they refused it on seeing the damaged condition.

当我们向买方交货时，他们见到残损情况拒绝收货。

The first of such monthly installments shall be paid simultaneously with the execution and delivery of the Agreement.

按月分摊的第一批分期付款将于协议的执行及交付时支付。

The aggregate of such price shall be payable in cash, upon delivery of possession of the property.

产权一经移交，总价格即可用现金支付。

actual（physical）delivery　实际交货

forward delivery　　远期（交货）

near delivery　近期（交）货

partial delivery　分批交货

short delivery　短交

deliver vt.递送，投递，交付，交（货），交（船）

The quantity to be delivered next month must not be less than 2 000 tons.

下月应交付的数量不得少于 2 000 吨。

The documents have already been delivered to the bank.

单据已交付银行。

ZZZ may terminate this Agreement by giving written notice of termination delivered to AAA.

乙方将终止协议的书面通知递交给甲方后即可终止本协议。

Optionor agrees, upon the request of Optionee, to deliver to the Optionee all of its rights in and to the following property.

经优先财产人请求，产权出让人同意将其对下列财产的全部权利移交给优先财

产人。

deliverable adj.可交付的，可发货的

Stock certificate shall be deliverable before （date）.

在某年某月某日前交付股权证书。

The Seller is not entitled to realize any taxable income until he places the good in a deliverable state or passes title to the Buyer.

在他将货物置于可发货状态或将所有权移交给买方之前，卖方无权获得应税收益。

13.attest v.证明

attesting witness 文件（书）见证人

辨析：attest，certify，witness，vouch，corroborate

attest：（1）暗指知情者口头或书写的证词，但通常并不一定必须用起誓或自己的名誉担保的方式做出证言。（2）在法律上主要指验证官方证明（如遗嘱、契约或案卷）或由有资格的代理人（如公证人或契约管理人员）保证签字、证书、誓言的真实性。

certify通常指书写的证明，特别是带有签名、印章或二者兼备而在法律上生效的证明。

witness暗指对某个签名（如声明的、遗嘱的或契约的）的确认或证实，但不一定是正式的或经过公证的。可以是由实际目睹签名的人来证实，亦可由在文件上署上本人名字的人来证明其真实性。

vouch（常和 for 连用）与其他词不同，很少指官方或法律证明，但意指证明人是个有法定资格的或可靠的人，能坚持其证言并在必要时进一步证实其的证言。

corroborate用其他证据来增强或支持某种理论或信仰。

The accounts were certified （as） correct.

账目被证明正确无误。

This is to certify that… 兹证明……

While reimbursing, the negotiating bank is required to certify that all the credit terms have been duly complied with.

议付行在索偿时须证明，信用证所有条款业已完全照办。

When the Contractor shall have completed the work, he shall certify, in writing, completion of the work to the Owner.

当承包商的施工（工程）完成时，他须向业主提出书面完工证明。

I can attest to the absolute truth of his statement.

我可以证实他的话是千真万确的。

The expert attested to the genuineness of the document.

专家证明该文件系真品。

The corporator parties hereto have caused this Agreement to be attested by their respective secretaries.

缔约各方共同促使本协议得由各自的秘书来鉴定。

Heavy enquires are a witness to the popularity of our product.

大量的询盘证明我公司产品深受欢迎。

This gift witnesses to his generosity.

这件礼物证明了他的慷慨。

I am ready to vouch for his ability to pay.

我愿保证他的付款能力。

Upon checking your statement, it has been impossible to corroborate the facts.

经审查，你所用申诉的事实不能得到证实。

14.amicably adv.友好地，亲切地

In the event of any disputes, controversies or differences between the parties for the breach thereof, both parties shall use their best efforts to settle such disputes, controversies or differences amicably by negotiation.

因违约在各当事人之间引起的争端、争辩或分歧，双方应尽最大的努力，通过友好协商来解决此种争端、争辩或分歧。

amicable adj.友好的，亲切的

All disputes arising out of this Contract shall be settled in any amicable manner.

由合同引起的一切争端应以友好的方式来解决。

15.submit v.提交，提供

All advertising matter shall be submitted to and approved by the Company.

公司应提供并批准一切有关广告宣传事宜。

Any decision of the Engineer which is subject to arbitration shall be submitted for arbitration.

工程师的决定是凡属由仲裁解决的问题应提交仲裁。

在英文合同中，表示"提供"的动词还有 render, provide, offer, furnish, supply。

The Buyer shall render all assistance to enable the Seller to correct any defects.

买方应提供一切援助，以使卖方纠正缺点。

The Buyer is to be provided with complete and detailed operating statements and balance sheets.

要向买方提供完整和详尽的营业报表和资产负债表。

These commodities may be offered for sale.

这些日用品可供销售。

The Contractor shall furnish samples to the Contracting Officer when he directs to do so.

承包商在进行指导时应为合同职员提供样板。

AAA agrees to supply ZZZ with a complete copy of all the necessary documents relating to the ongoing license negotiation between the parties.

甲方同意供给乙方一切必要的文件的完整文本。该文件与正在进行的当事人各方的许可证谈判有关。

16.packing n.包装；打包；包装法

| | |
|---|---|
| export packing | 出口包装 |
| improper/faulty/poor/insufficient packing | 包装不良 |
| inner packing　内包装 | |
| outer packing　外包装 | |
| packing charges/expenses　包装费 | |
| packing list　装箱单、花色码单 | |
| seaworthy packing　适合海运的包装 | |

pack n.小包、小箱、小盒，包装；v.包装，把……打包或装箱等

a six-pack of beer 半打装啤酒

a pack of canned goods 一小箱罐头食品

We will make you an offer when the new pack is available.

有新货时定给你方报盘。

The goods are to be packed in iron drums.

货物须以铁桶包装。

The shirts will be packed each in a polyethylene bag, five dozen to a cardboard case.

每件衬衫装一塑料袋，5打装一硬纸板箱。

package n.（中、小型的）包裹，包，捆；包装（用料）；打包

When the shipment arrived, the packages were all intact, but many of them were found short of weight.

到货时，包装完整无损，但其中有很多包被发现短重。

These two functions are not separable in view of the fact that the franchise is granted as a complete service package deal.

鉴于该项特许权是作为一揽子全面服务贸易而授予的，所以这两种作用是不可分的。

packaging n.（包装方面的）装潢，（效率高的、美观的）包装法，打包

packaging designing　装潢设计

packaging industry　包装装潢业

You are outdistanced in the packing and packaging of the material.

在货物的包装和包装材料方面你方大大落后。

17.L/C 是信用证的缩写形式

Letter of Credit 信用证是可数的普通名词，大写缩写成 L/C；复数形式的信用证 Letters of Credit 大写缩写成 Ls/C。

有关信用证的部分常见词组：

confirmed L/C　　　　　　　　保兑信用证

transferable and divisible L/C 可转让与可分割信用证

documentary L/C　跟单信用证

revolving L/C　循环信用证

back to back L/C　背对背信用证

reciprocal L/C 对开信用证

30 days L/C　　见票后30天议付的信用证

即期信用证是 letter of credit available by draft at sight，letter of credit payable against draft

at sight 书信中常简称 sight L/C。

远期（或迟期）信用证是 usance L/C 或 time L/C 或 term L/C。

见票后多少天议付的说法很多，以见票后30天议付的信用证为例。下面是较常见的几种说法：

L/C available by draft at 30 days after sight

（usance/time/term）L/C at 30 days after sight

（usance/time/term）L/C at 30 days

30 days（usance/time/term）L/C

18.rescind v.废除，取消，解除

rescind an agreement　　取消协议

rescind a rule　废除一项规则

Either party may rescind this contract by notice in writing.

任何一方都可用书面通知解除本合同。

The Agreement shall stand cancelled and rescinded，in default on the either party to …

双方中任何一方对……违约时，本协议应告作废和取消。

rescission n.废约，解约

Such rescission of the Contract shall not impair any right.

本合同的如此解约不应损害任何权利。

辨析：rescind，annul，cancel，withdraw，revoke

rescind 表示运用正当的权利进行废除或废止活动。在法律上，指合同的废止，并且表示该合同似乎从未生效。

annul 宣布在法律上不再有效（最常见的词），可用于某种权力、婚姻、契据、凭证、法规或条例等。

cancel 表示彻底否定某事物的行为，通过法律宣布无效或者撤销，解除或通过某事物的对立面抵消其自身的影响。

withdraw 发出去的东西又追回

revoke 表示召回、废除或取消

If you fail to effect shipment at latest by the end of this month, the contract is to be considered annulled.

若你方最迟至本月末仍不发运，该项合同应被视做无效。

As the time of shipment you proposed is too late for our customer to accept, we wish to cancel our order No.123.

由于你方所提装运期太晚，我方客户不接受，因此撤销我方第123号订单。

We should withdraw dirty banknotes from circulation.

收回破旧钞票使之不再流通。

revoke a cheque 撤销支票

revoke a driving licence 吊销驾驶执照

The king revoked his decree.

国王取消了他的法令。

19.discrepancy n.不同，差异，不符合，不一致

There are several discrepancies between your statement of account and our records.

你方对账单与我方记录之间有几笔不符之处。

There are some discrepancies between our two sides.

我们双方的意见有些分歧。

In the event of any discrepancy between the two said versions, the language of (host country) shall prevail.

如该两种文本之间发生差异，则以（东道国）的语言（文本）为准。

20.claim vt.索赔，索汇，索款，要求（应得）权利；声称，宣称，自称，主张。vi.索赔，提出要求。n.（对权利等的）要求，索赔，索款，索汇

to lodge/file/enter/register/make/raise/put in a claim against/with sb on a certain shipment for a certain reason for amount of money…

对某批发货由于某种理由向某人提出索赔金额为……

Only the holder of the B/L may claim to be the owner of the shipment.

只有提单持有人才能要求取得货物的所有权。

Our customer claims 8 pence reduction per 1b on the 85 bales of Goathair shipped by M/V "Star".

对由"星"号轮运来的85包山羊毛，我方客户要求每磅减价8便士。

We have to claim from you £400 on this shipment for inferior quality.

对这批发货由于质次我方不得不向你方索赔400英镑。

The firm claims to be well placed for promoting the sales of your product.

对于推销你公司产品，该公司声称处于有利地位。

Buyers have claimed on us for short shipment.

买主已因短装向我方（提出）索赔。

Our users have claimed upon us for inferior quality.

我方用户已因质量差向我方索赔。

Buyers have lodged a claim on this shipment for RMB ￥1 500 for （on account of） short weight.

由于分量短少，买主对此批货索赔人民币 1 500 元。

We have already raised a claim against the insurance company for $310 for damage in transit.

因运输中受损，我们已向保险公司提出要求赔偿 310 美元。

Our claim on your L/C No.84 has not been paid.

我们对你的第 84 号信用证索汇没有得到支付。

21.《2010 年国际贸易术语解释通则》（International Rules for the Interpretation of Trade Terms 2010），缩写 Incoterms 2010，是国际商会根据国际货物贸易的发展，对《2000 年国际贸易术语解释通则》的修订，2010 年 9 月 27 日公布，于 2011 年 1 月 1 日起实施。

相对于 Incoterms 2000，Incoterms 2010 的主要变化有以下几点：

（1）术语分类的调整。EFCD 四组分别改为两组，分别适用于所有运输方式的用语包括 EXW、FCA、CPT、DAT、DAP 和 DDP，以及适用于水路运输的用语，包括 FAS、FOB、CFR、CIF。

（2）贸易术语的数量由原来的 13 种变为 11 种。

（3）《2010 年国际贸易术语解释通则》删去了《2000 年国际贸易术语解释通则》中的 4 个术语：DAF（Delivered at Frontier）——边境交货、DES（Delivered Ex Ship）——目的港船上交货、DEQ（Delivered Ex Quay）——目的港码头交货、DDU（Delivered Duty Unpaid）——未完税交货。

（4）新增了两个术语。

DAT（Delivered at Terminal）在指定目的地或目的港的集散站交货、DAP（Delivered at Place）在指定目的地交货。

DAT 类似于 DEQ 术语，取代了 DAF、DES 和 DDU 三个术语，且扩展至适用于一切运输方式。DAT 指卖方在指定的目的地卸货后将货物交给买方处置即完成交货，术语所指目的地包括港口。卖方应承担将货物运至指定的目的地的一切风险和费用（除进口费用外）。本术语适用于任何运输方式或多式联运。目的地包括码头、仓库、堆场、车站、空港。

DAP 类似于 DAF、DES 和 DDU 术语，指卖方在指定的目的地交货，只需做好卸货准备无需卸货即完成交货。术语所指的到达车辆包括船舶，目的地包括港口。卖方应承担将货物运至指定的目的地的一切风险和费用（除进口费用外）。本术语适用于任何运输方式。

（5）修订后的《2010 年国际贸易术语解释通则》取消了"船舷"的概念，卖方承担货物装上船为止的一切风险，买方承担货物自装运港装上船后的一切风险。

在 FAS、FOB、CFR 和 CIF 等术语中加入了货物在运输期间被多次买卖（连环贸易）的责任和义务的划分。考虑到对于一些大的区域贸易集团内部贸易的特点，Incoterms 2010 不仅适用于国际销售合同，也适用于国内销售合同。

根据运输方式，Incoterms 2010 可以分成两大组：

第一组：适用于任何运输方式的术语有七种：EXW、FCA、CPT、CIP、DAT、DAP、DDP。

EXW（Ex Works）工厂交货

FCA（Free Carrier）货交承运人

CPT（Carriage Paid to）运费付至目的地

CIP（Carriage and Insurance Paid to）运费/保险费付至目的地

DAT（Delivered at Terminal）目的地或目的港的集散站交货

DAP（Delivered at Place）目的地交货

DDP（Delivered Duty Paid）完税后交货

DAT 卖方要负责卸货，但不负责进口通关事宜与费用。

DDP 卖方要负责进口通关事宜与费用，但不负责卸货。

DAP 由买方负责卸货和进口通关事宜与费用。

第二组：适用于水上运输方式的术语四种：FAS、FOB、CFR、CIF。

FAS（Free Alongside Ship）装运港船边交货

FOB（Free on Board）装运港船上交货

CFR（Cost and Freight）成本加运费

CIF（Cost Insurance and Freight）成本、保险费加运费

使用 Incoterms 2010 贸易术语需要注意的问题：

（1）使用贸易术语的格式要求

在使用任何贸易术语时都需要将"Incoterms 2010"或"国际贸易术语解释通则 2010"作为后缀或者贸易术语选择的必要构成要件在合同中说明。例如，尽可能对地点和港口作出详细说明。例如，"FCA Dalian International Port Zone Incoterms 2010"。

说明："FCA"（货交承运人）是贸易术语，"Dalian International Port Zone"是地点或地址，"Incoterms 2010"是对所选的贸易术语最新版本的说明。

（2）贸易术语中地点的重要性

在使用贸易术语 Ex Works（EXW，工厂交货）、Free Carrier（FCA，货交承运人）、Delivered at Terminal（DAT，运输终端交货）、Delivered at Place（DAP，目的地交货）、Delivered Duty Paid（DDP，完税后交货）、Free Alongside Ship（FAS，船边交货）和 Free on Board（FOB，船上交货）时，指定地点是指风险从卖方转移到买方的交货地点。

在使用贸易术语 Carriage Paid To（CPT，运费付至）、Carriage and Insurance Paid To（CIP，运费、保险费付至）、Cost and Freight（CFR，成本加运费）和

Cost，Insurance and Freight （CIF，成本、保险费加运费）时，指定地点并非交货地点。在使用此四种贸易术语时，指定地点是指运费已付至的目的地。

（3）术语指明地点的法律意义

在 EXW、FCA、DAT、DAP、DDP、FAS 和 FOB 术语中，指定地点是交货（delivery）地点，即风险转移地点，建立了风险承担的认定基础。

在 CPT、CIP、CFR 和 CIF 术语中，指定地点是指运费已付至的地点，风险如何承担尚不清楚，即还需要明确交货地点。

"交货（delivery，也可译为交付）"的特定法律意义：法律意义上控制权的转移，可成为风险转移的基础，可成为所有权转移的基础。

使用 CPT、CIP、CFR、CIF、DAT、DAP 和 DDP 术语时，卖方需安排货物运输至指定目的地。运费虽由卖方支付，但买方为实际支付方，因为实际上运费已包含在货物总价之中。运输费用有时会包括在港口或集装箱码头设施内处理和移动货物的费用，而承运人或港口运营人很可能向接收货物的买方索要这些费用。除非另有约定，卖方承担"交货"前费用。

22.curable tag 粘贴

description tag 描述标签； 叙述标签； 描写标签； 说明标签

luggage tag 行李牌； 行李签 ； 行李标签； 行李吊牌

tag paper 标签纸； 封口条

price tag 价格标签；标价

23.liquidate v.清算，清理

liquidated damages=indemnities 违约赔偿金

liquidated damages clause 违约金条款

liquidated damages and penalties 约定损害赔偿金

liquidated damages delay 误期损害赔偿

the punitiveness liquidated damages 补偿性违约金

partial liquidated damages 部分赔偿金

liquidated damages by agreement 约定违约金

overall liquidated damages 整体违约赔偿金 ； 整体算定损害赔偿

labor contract liquidated damages 劳动合同违约金

The Contractor agrees to make no demand for liquidated damages or penalties for delay to the Contractor.

承包商同意，如转包商发生延误，其不要求收取违约赔偿金。

The Seller shall pay to the Buyer the sum of …as liquidated damages for each and every breach of this covenant.

卖方每违反本契约一次，就须向买方支付……金额的违约赔偿金。

liquidator n.清盘人，清算人

The board has appointed liquidators to wind up the company.

董事会已委托清算人将公司清盘。

liquidation n. 清算，清理

This firm has gone into liquidation.

这家公司已清盘。

Shareholders are worried that the group will be put into liquidation.

股东担心这个集团将会停业清理。

24.accrue vi. 自然增加；积累；生成； vt.积累，应计

accrue payable 应付款

Interest on interest-bearing claims shall cease to accrue thereon at the time of acceptance of the bankruptcy petition.

附利息的债权自破产申请受理时起停止计息。

"Liabilities" shall mean any and all debts, liabilities and obligations, whether accrued or fixed.

"责任"是指各种债务、责任及义务，无论其属于衍生责任还是固有责任。

In the event of termination of this Agreement by Sponsor before expiration of the project period, Sponsor shall pay all costs that the Institute has accrued as of the date of termination.

如果在项目期间届满前发生由资助人终止本合同的任何事件，资助人应向机构支付自终止日起产生的所有费用。

25.arbitrage award= arbitral award 仲裁结果

arbitration n.仲裁，公断

arbitration tribunal 仲裁院

arbitration clause 仲裁条款

voluntary arbitration 自愿仲裁

arbitration committee 仲裁委员会

submit a matter to arbitration 把某事提交仲裁

compulsory arbitration 强制仲裁

settle by arbitration 由仲裁解决

We wish to submit the case for arbitration and to abide by its decision.

我们愿将此案提交仲裁并遵守其裁决。

Any differences between the parties may be submitted for arbitration by the committee.

各方之间的任何分歧可提交委员会仲裁。

All disputes which may arise between the parties shall be finally settled by arbitration, either in （Place A） or in （Place B）.

各方之间可能引起的争端，无论在甲地或乙地，都应通过仲裁最后解决。

arbitrate vt.公断，仲裁

This Agreement so to arbitrate shall be enforceable under the law.

经过这样仲裁的本协议在法律上有效。

The two parties agreed to arbitrate their dispute.

双方同意把争议提交仲裁。

arbitrator n.仲裁人

The award rendered by the arbitrators shall be final.

仲裁人的裁决应是最后的裁决。

If negotiations are deadlocked, an arbitrator must be called in.

如果谈判陷入僵局，就必须请一位仲裁人。

26.合同中的代词用法

注意英文合同中一些代词，如 each，every，either，neither，both 的翻译。either，neither 和 both 在合同中还可以当作连词和介词使用。

The Guarantor hereby waives presentment, demand for payment, protect, and notice of protest, of each and every one of the note.

票据担保人特此声明自动放弃对每一张票据的提示、付款要求，予以保护及发拒付通知书等权利。

Each assistant, to whom duties have been assigned or authority has been delegated, shall only be authorized to issue instructions to the Contractor to the extent defined by the delegation.

已被指派任务或付托权力的每个助手，应只被授权在付托的范围内向承包商发出指令。

neither（不带 of）用于没有冠词、物主词或指示词的单数名词之前，动词是单数。neither of 放在带有冠词、物主代词或指示代词的复数名词之前，动词可以是单数或复数。

During the term of operation of the company, neither party has the right to announce unilaterally the cancellation or termination of this Contract.

在合营期限内，双方均无权单方面宣布撤销或终止本合同。

Neither party shall be liable to the other party for any failure to perform or delay in performance of the terms of this Agreement, other than an obligation to make payment, caused by any circumstances beyond its reasonable control.

除付款义务外，任何一方当事人均不能对因超出其合理控制的因素造成的未能履行或延迟履行负责。

Neither Party shall assign the whole or any part of the Contract or any benefit or interest in or under the Contract.However, either Party: may assign the whole or any part with the prior agreement/consent of the other Party, at the sole discretion of such other Party。

任一方都不应将合同的全部或任何部分，或合同中或根据合同所具有的任何利益或权益转让他人。但任一方在另一方完全自主决定的情况下，事先征得其同意后，可以将全部或任何部分转让。

　　either 用作代词，可单独用，也可以和 of 同用，后接复数名词短语。当 either of 后接名词词组时，一定要再加一个限定词（人称代词、指示代词或冠词），你可以说 either of the rooms 或 either of my rooms，但是不能说 either of rooms。在人称代词前总是用 either of。在带有 either of 的句子中，动词一般是单数的。

　　Either of the parties is responsible for the loss of the damage.

　　（合约）两方都对损失负责。

　　In either case, the Contractor must proceed with the Works unless and until he receives a response or is instructed otherwise.

　　无论哪一种情况，承包商必须继续施工，除非并直到他收到回复或得到其他指示。

　　Both Parties shall treat the details of the Contract as private and confidential, except to the extent necessary to carry out obligations under it or to comply with the applicable Laws.

　　除了根据合同履行义务和遵守适用法律的需要以外，双方应将合同的详情视为私人的和秘密的。

　　27. vest vt. 授予；赋予；vi. （财产、权力等）属；归属（in）

　　vest something in somebody 授予，赋予

　　vest somebody with authority，rights in an estate，etc 授予某人权力、产权等

　　The Agent is vested with only the powers specially granted to him.

　　代理商被授予专属于他的各种权力。

　　All rights vested in AAA shall forthwith become null and void.

　　赋予甲方的一切权利应立即宣告无效。

　　28.contradiction n.矛盾，抵触

　　If there is any apparent contradiction or ambiguity between the drawings and specifications, the Contractor shall bring the fact to the attention of the Engineer.

　　如在图纸及技术规格之间有什么明显的矛盾或含糊不清之处，承包商应将此情况提请工程师注意。

　　29.commissioning n.委托，代理；试运行，试车，试运转

　　AECOM has begun pre-construction activities and shall provide project，procurement，construction and commissioning management services for the project.

　　艾奕康科技已经开始施工前的准备工作，并将负责该项目的规划、采购、施工和委托管理服务等。

　　The Contractor shall be responsible for and shall carry out all maintenance work during commissioning period.

　　在代理期间承包商应负责一切维修工作。

China ABCD shall not be held responsible for all the issues concerning the commodity name, model, country of origin, manufacturer, quantity, packing, time of shipment, port of destination, technical specification, technical documents and / or technical standard, erection, commissioning, performance test-run and acceptance etc.

中国ABCD对于设备名称、型号、原产地、生产商、数量、包装、运输时间、目的港、技术规范、技术文件和/或技术标准、安装、试运行、性能测试和验收等不负任何责任。

30.incur v.招致，遭受

It is mutually agreed that all the cost and expenses incurred by trainees such as salaries, costs of travelling and accommodation, etc. shall be borne by Foreign (Local).

双方同意，实习生所需诸如工资、差旅费和生活费等一切成本及费用，均由外国（当地）负担。

Broker shall not be liable to the salesman for any expenses incurred by him, or for any of his acts.

经纪人对推销员所花的任何费用或推销员的任何行动概不负责。

In case his age exceeds 16 years old, the extra average insurance premium thus incurred shall be borne by the Party B.

如果他的年龄超过16岁，则由乙方承担因此产生的平均保险费以外的费用。

31.set off 抵消

Each of the Guarantors hereby agrees that the Company may set off any sum at any time owing or payable by the Company to the Guarantors or any of them (whether or not then due) against any sum then due from them or him / her to the Company under this Guarantee and unpaid.

保证人均特此同意，公司可在任何时间，抵消公司依照本保证合同规定向保证人到期应付的款项全部或其中一部分，无论届时是否到期。

32. consitute v. 组成

同义词还有compose 和 make up.

另外还有一组词comprise，consist of，contain，include 和 involve 也表示"组成"或"构成"。

所不同的是，constitute，compose 和 make up 是由小单位组成了大单位。而comprise，consist of，contain，include 和 involve则表示大的和整体的是由哪些部分构成。

Technical specifications which are attached hereto constitute an integral part of this proposal.

所附的技术规格构成本计划的整体组成部分。

The Internet composes more than 4 billion IP addresses.

互联网有40多亿个IP地址组成。

Old workers make up 18% of our staff.

年纪较大的占员工的18%。

The reorganization shall comprise the acquisition by Buyer of substantially all of the property, assets, good will, and business as a going concern of Seller.

此次改组将包括由买方获得卖方的全部财产、资产、商业信誉以及继续经营的业务活动。

The components of the said device shall consist of the items listed on Exhibit A.

该装置的部件应由附件A中所列的品目构成。

Their clients included Unilever and Coco-Cola.

他们的客户包括联合利华公司和可口可乐公司。

The atlas contains forty maps.

这个地图集有40幅地图。

## ● Exercises

I.Translate the following into English：

1.如果双方不能达成协议，该争议案件就得提交仲裁。

2.由于这一条与合同不符，请尽早从信用证中删除。

3.我方不得不指出你方在信用证中加列了一项不符合合同条件的条款。

4.大多数分析家认为，大规模交易的时机尚未成熟。

5.交货条件：需附品质、数量、重量、产地证书，买方有权在货到后由中华人民共和国广州出入境检验检疫局进行复检，有关复检证书，可作为买方向卖方提出索赔的依据。

6.今附上我方第3674号购货合同，我方已签字，请审查和会签，并尽快寄回一份存档。

7.这笔交易的达成当然不是结束。它仅仅是个开端，并且是我们之间长期友好业务关系的开端。

8.经过长时间断断续续的谈判，我们现在终于达成了协议。

9.在谈判过程中，我们都给予双方很好的谅解，这对我们今后的业务很有意义。

10.我们的迟延付款是由于在清理账务上的暂时困难所致。金额……元将在下周全部支付给你公司。

II.Translate the following into Chinese：

1.Contractor shall execute with owner a secrecy agreement the terms and conditions of which will be agreed upon by both parties.

2.AAA will give performance bond with sufficient surety.

3. Assignment shall not be effective until the transferees assume all AAA's

obligations.

4.In the event of any discrepancy between the two versions，the English version shall prevail.

5.This contract shall be void，if Seller fails to provide good title as provided herein.

6. Withdrawal of any party from this agreement shall not affect the rights and obligations of the remaining parties.

7.The documents shall be made in duplicate and sealed.

8.The right of the Joint Company to use the trademarks is an exclusive right.

9.The Seller agrees to deposit in the Seller's special account with a bank.

10. The Association shall be organized with suitable Articles of Incorporation and bylaws as determined by an organization committee.

# Unit Seven /包销协议

## Offtake Agreement

## ABCD金属公司与EFGH公司的包销协议
## Offtake Agreement of ABCD Metals Limited and EFGH Co., Ltd.

This Agreement is made between ABCD Metals Ltd. (hereinafter referred to as the Seller) and EFGH Co., Ltd. (hereinafter referred to as Buyer)

Whereas: The Seller agrees to sell and deliver Iron Ore to the Buyer and the Buyer agrees to purchase, accept delivery and pay for Iron Ore from the Seller, in accordance with the terms and conditions set forth in this Agreement.

Governing Law: Australia, see clause 24

Date of Agreement: See Signing page

## General terms

### 1.Definitions

In this Agreement the following definitions apply unless the context requires otherwise:

Agreement means this agreement including its schedules as may be amended from time to time;

Business Day means a day not being Saturday, Sunday or a public holiday in Australia, or the PRC;

Certificate of Analysis means the certificate issued by the Seller pursuant to clause 12.1;

Certificate of Weight means the certificate issued by the Seller pursuant to clause 11.1;

CIQ means the Entry-Exit Inspection and Quarantine of PRC;

Commencement Date means the later of:

(a) the date on which all of the Conditions are satisfied or waived; and

(b) the date on which the first transhipment of Product from the Loading Port to a Panamax vessel in Port of Darwin, Northern Territory is completed;

Conditions means the conditions listed in clause 2.1;

Contract Year means the period of 12 months commencing on 1 January in any year during the Term and ending on 31 December in the same year thereafter except the first Contract Year will commence on the Commencement Date and end on the immediately following 31 December and the last Contract Year will commence on the last date, 1 January falling within the Term and end on the last day of the Term;

Discharge Port means the port where the Buyer or its agent will unload the Product;

DMT means a tonne on a dry basis (Dry Metric Tonne);

Dry basis when applied to Product means Product dried at 105° Celsius;

End Date means the date six years after the date of this Agreement;

Final Certificate of Analysis means the certificate issued by the Umpire pursuant to Clause 12.3;

Final Invoice means the invoice for the sale of a shipment of Product based on a weight determination made pursuant to clause 11.3 and a physical and chemical analysis made pursuant to clause 12.3;

CFR has the meaning ascribed to it in the Incoterms;

Force Majeure Event has the meaning given to that term in clause 17;

Government Agency means a government or a governmental, semi-governmental or judicial entity or an authority. It also includes a self-regulatory organisation established under statute or a stock exchange;

Incoterms means Incoterms 2010 published by International Chamber of Commerce;

IMSBC Code means the International Maritime Solid Bulk Cargoes Code 2009;

Insolvency Event means, in relation to a party, that any of the following events or circumstances have occurred:

(a) the affected party becomes insolvent or is declared insolvent or notifies the other party or creditors generally that it is insolvent;

(b) proceedings are commenced to appoint a liquidator or provisional liquidator to the affected party (not being for the purposes of amalgamation or reconstruction of the affected party);

(c) the affected party enters into a deed of company arrangement with its creditors;

(d) any receiver (as that term is defined in the Corporations Act 2001 (Cth) ) is appointed over, or any mortgagee takes possession of any material part of, the affected party's assets;

ISM Code means the International Management Code for the Safe Operation of Ships and for Pollution Prevention, adopted by the International Maritime Organisation in 1993;

ISO means International Organisation for Standardisation standard for the analysis of iron ore;

ISPS Code means the International Ship and Port Facility Security Code, an addendum to the Safety of Life at Sea（SOLAS）Convention；

Loading Port means the Port of Darwin，Northern Territory；

Natural basis when applied to Product means Product in its natural or wet state；

Notice of Readiness means a notice of readiness to load a vessel；

Party means a party to this Agreement；

Place of Loading means the relevant place of loading onto the Panamax vessel within the Loading Port；

Price means the price to be paid for the product as determined in accordance with clause 6.3（c）；

Price Agreement Date means in respect of each shipment of Product the day falling 10 days prior to the last day by which the Buyer must open the irrevocable Letter of Credit in accordance with clause 13.1；

Price Index has the meaning given to that term in clause 6.2；

Pricing Period has the meaning given to that term in clause 6.1；

Product means magnetite concentrates produced by the Seller from its Project known as "PERFECT Magnetite Concentrates"；

PRC means the People's Republic of China；

Provisional Invoice means the invoice for the sale of a shipment of Product based on a weight determination made pursuant to clause 11.1 and a physical and chemical analysis made pursuant to clause 12.1；

Specifications has the meaning given to it in Clause 5；

Umpire means a third party who performs sampling and analysis to the level generally accepted in the mining industry；

Weather Working Day means any day or part of a day where weather conditions do not prevent transhipment operations and includes any day or part of a day：

（a）where temperature is between−45° Celsius and+45° Celsius；

（b）when the wind speed is less than or is reasonably forecast to be less than 20 nautical miles per hour；

（c）where wave conditions are less than 1.5 metres in height；and

（d）where visibility is at least 0.5 nautical miles.

Wet Basis when applied to Product means Product in its natural or wet state；and

WMT means a Wet Metric Tonne on a Natural Basis.

## 2. Conditions Precedent

2.1　Conditions

This Agreement and the obligations of the Parties hereunder are subject to the satisfaction of the following conditions：

（a）the Seller needs proceeding to financial close of its proposed project finance facility with financier； and

（b） the Seller needs obtaining all necessary approvals and consents for the transportation， storage and loading of Product derived from the Project at the Loading Port.

2.2 Failure to Satisfy the Conditions

If the Conditions are not satisfied or compliance with the Conditions waived by the Seller by the End Date， then either Party may terminate this Agreement by written notice to the other Party， in which case this Agreement shall terminate and be of no further force or effect （save in respect of any antecedent breach of this Agreement） .

**3.Term**

Subject to satisfaction or waiver of the Conditions， the obligations of the Seller to sell Product and of the Buyer to buy Product under this Agreement shall commence on the Commencement Date and shall continue for six years.

**4.Quantity**

In each Contract Year， the Seller shall sell to the Buyer and the Buyer shall purchase from the Seller the quantities and type of Product set out in Schedule 1 in Appendix 1 （each quantity being， except as specified， an annual quantity and on Wet Basis） .

**5. Specifications**

5.1 Specifications Applicable in the Initial Contract Year

The specifications （on Dry Basis） for Product to be delivered under this Agreement in the initial Contract Year on the basis of samples drawn at the Loading Port in accordance with clause 12.1 hereof shall be as follows：

| Chemical Composition (On dry Basis) | Typical (Percentage by Weight) | Maximums and Minimums (Percentage by Weight) |
|---|---|---|
| Fe | 64.0% | 60.0% min |
| $SiO_2$ | 8.00% | 10.0% max |
| $AL_2O_3$ | 0.59% | 1.0% max |
| P | 0.01% | 0.05% max |
| S | 0.32% | 0.35%max |
| Moisture | 8.0% | 8.0% max |

5.2 Physical Specifications

Physical specifications （on wet basis） of Product as set out in the table below：

| | | Typical | |
|---|---|---|---|
| Oversize | >100um | 15.0% | 20% max (Oversize Maximum) |
| Undersize at Discharge Port | < 10um | 20.0% | 25% max (Undersize Maximum) |

## a) Oversized Ore

In relation to each shipment, if the Product delivered under this Agreement exceeds the Oversize Maximum, a penalty at the rate of US$0.50 per DMT shall be applied to such quantity of the oversized ore in each shipment that exceeds the Oversize Maximum.

## b) Undersized Ore

In relation to each shipment, if the Product delivered under this Agreement exceeds the Undersize Maximum, a penalty at the rate of US$0.50 per DMT shall be applied to such quantity of the undersized ore in each shipment that exceeds the Undersize Maximum.

5.3 Specifications Applicable in Subsequent Contract Year

The specifications for Product delivered in subsequent Contract Years may vary from the Typical Specifications given in clause 5.1 and 5.2 hereof in accordance with the then applicable typical specifications as from time to time published by Seller in its Product Data Sheets. The Seller shall provide the Buyer with prior written notice of any such variation. The Specifications as varied under this Clause shall be the "Specifications" for the purposes of this Agreement.

### 6.Prices

6.1　Pricing Period

In respect of each shipment of Product the Pricing Period will be the 30 days period up to the Price Agreement Date.

6.2　Price Index

The Parties agree the Platts Index to be used for the purposes of establishing the Price pursuant to this clause 6 will be the Platts INDEX 62% Fe CFR North China (Price Index), published in Platts Steel Markets Daily.

If Platts ceases to be published or is substantially modified, another alternative market Index shall be adopted by mutual agreement.

6.3　Determination of Price

(a) By no later than the Price Agreement Date, the Seller and the Buyer shall, for the purposes of determining the amount of the Letter of Credit required for a shipment of Product, agree the Price for the applicable Product. Such agreement shall be based on the average of the daily prices for the Price Index published in Platts Steel Markets Daily over the Pricing Period

(b) If the Price has not been agreed by the date specified in 6.3 (a), then the Price for the previous Pricing Period shall be used on a provisional basis until the Price has been agreed or determined (Provisional Price). When the new Price is agreed or determined, the Parties shall make retroactive adjustments for all sums owed due to any difference between the Provisional Price and the Price as agreed or determined.

(c) Price = Platts CFR

Platts CFR means average of the applicable daily prices of Platts INDEX 62% Fe CFR North China published in Platts Steel Markets Daily over the Pricing Period plus or minus price adjustment.

### 7.Price Adjustments

7.1  Specifications and Price Adjustments

The Seller's liability for failure to deliver Product conforming to the then applicable Specifications shall be limited to the remedies described in clause 7.2.

7.2  Price Adjustments for Non-Conformance With Specifications

In the event that the analysis of a particular shipment of Products, determined in accordance with clause 12 (Sampling and Analysis) does not meet any one or more of the Specifications as evidenced by the Certificate of Analysis (or the Final Certificate of Analysis if applicable) issued in respect of such shipment, the Buyer shall accept such shipment, subject to the price adjustments set out in the table below, such adjustments to be the sole and exclusive remedy for such non-conformance in respect of that shipment.

| Element | | Adjustment (US$ per DMT) | Payable per Fractions pro rata |
|---|---|---|---|
| Iron | Fe content | Reduction of each Platts Index per 1% Fe Differential published by Platts Steel Markets Daily in Pricing Period per 1% Fe below 62% | For each 1.0% below the 62% Fe payable per Fractions pro rata |
| Silica plus Alumina | $SiO_2$+ $Al_2O_3$ | Reduction of $ 0.20 | For each 1% above 10.0% |
| Phosphorous | P | Reduction of $ 0.20 | For each 0.01 % in excess of 0.05% |
| Sulphur | S | Reduction of $ 0.20 | For each 0.01 % in excess of 0.10% |

7.3  Free Moisture Loss

If in respect of any particular shipment, free moisture loss at 105 Celsius as determined pursuant to clause 12 for the Product exceeds the relevant maximum Specification, the Buyer shall accept such shipment but the Price for that shipment shall be reduced by the an amount equal to the Buyer's actual increased cost resulting from the additional weight represented by the excess moisture.

7.4    Bonus Price Adjustment

If the analysis of iron for a particular shipment of Products, determined in accordance with clause 12 (Sampling and Analysis) is higher than the typical Specification, as evidenced by the Certificate of Analysis (or the Final Certificate of Analysis) issued in respect of such shipment, the Buyer shall make bonus price adjustment in respect of that shipment as follows:

| Element | | Adjustment (US$ per DMT) | Payable per DMT |
|---|---|---|---|
| Iron | Fe above 62.0% | Price to be increased by each Platts Index per 1%, Fe Differential published by Platts Steel Markets Daily in Pricing Period per 1% Fe over 62% over agreed price | For each 1.0% above 62.0% Fe payable per Fractions pro rata |

## 8. Delivery, Title and Risk

(a) Unless agreed otherwise in an Addendum to this Agreement, delivery of the Product hereunder shall be CFR (Spout Trimmed) at the Loading Point.

(b) All risk of loss, damage or destruction to the Product shall pass to the Buyer at the time the Product passes over the rail of the vessel, arranged by the Buyer under clause 9, at the Discharge Port.

(c) Title shall pass from the Seller to the Buyer when the total Price has been paid.

(d) In the event of inconsistency between the provisions of this Agreement and the provisions of Incoterms, the provisions of this Agreement shall prevail.

## 9. Shipping Schedule and Arrival Notifications of Vessels

9.1    Shipping Schedule

(a) The Seller will use reasonable efforts to ensure shipments of Product are evenly spread throughout the Contract Year, with the agreed shipping schedule attached hereto as Appendix 3 to apply for the first Contract Year.

(b) the Seller shall agree an annual shipping schedule which shall specify:

(i) a tentative 30 laydays spread for each vessel;

(ii) the quantity of Product to be loaded on board each vessel.

(c) At least 45 days prior to the commencement of each calendar quarter the Buyer shall submit to the Seller for approval by the Seller a quarterly shipping schedule by months. Both parties shall endeavour to agree upon the quarterly schedule no later than 30 days prior to the commencement of each quarterly period. The quarterly shipping schedule shall:

(i) specify a 15 laydays spread for each vessel; and

(ii) confirm the quantity of Product to be loaded on board each vessel.

9.2　Vessel Nomination，Notification of Arrivals and Ship's Agency

(a) Seller shall nominate the performing vessel no later than 20 days before the first day of the nominated laycan specifying to the Buyer：

(i) the name of the vessel，its age and flag；

(ii) the estimated date of arrival；　and

(iii) the full vessel description and General Agreement or hold layout plan.

(b) Vessel substitution may be made，at the latest 10 days prior to the estimated time of arrival for the vessel at the Discharge Port and subject to the conditions of clause 9.2 hereof.

(c) Unless the Seller's nominated vessel does not comply with the requirements of clause 9.2，the Buyer must accept the nominated vessel by notice to the Seller within 24 hours upon receipt of the nomination.

(d) The Seller shall ensure that with all vessels nominated by it pursuant to this Agreement，the Seller appoints the shipping agent (Seller's Agent) to attend to all regulatory and customary agency requirements at the Discharge Port.

(e) The Seller shall further notify the Buyer of the expected date of arrival of each vessel at the Discharge Port and of the declared tonnage of Product at least 10 days in advance of the arrival of the vessel.

**10.Discharging Terms**

10.1　Letter of Credit provided prior to loading

The Buyer must establish the Letter of Credit referred to in clause 13.1 hereof，not less than 14 business days prior to commencement of loading or laytime whichever occurs first.

10.2　Discharging Conditions

(a) The Seller shall deliver the Product to the Buyer in bulk，CFR，Spout Trimmed at one of the Buyer's nominated safe anchorages. The tides，draft，passages to and from and currents at these anchorages will be provided prior to Laycan. The Seller shall have the right to require any vessel which has presented Notice of Readiness or is discharging at Discharge Port to transfer or to cease discharging and transfer from such place of discharging to another place of discharging (where such vessel's draft will permit) . All additional expenses incurred by the Seller as a result of the Buyer complying with such requirement shall be for the Buyer's account. Shifting time shall count as laytime.

(b) If any expenses other than fuel，ship consumables，provisions and crew cost are incurred by the Seller in fulfilling this obligation to transfer from one Place of Discharging to another Place of Discharging and if any such expenses are incurred as a result of regulatory requirement by authorities in PRC，then such expenses shall be to the account of the Buyer.

(c) Any taxes, dues, port charges or other charges levied against the vessel and/or freight at Discharge Port shall be for Buyer's account.

(d) The Buyer shall also pay for the pre and post discharging draft survey and the hold cleanliness inspection.

10.3  Discharging Rates

The Buyer shall cause all Product delivered under this Agreement to be loaded aboard vessels at 40,000 WMT per Weather Working Day of 24 consecutive hours, including Saturdays, Sundays and holidays.

10.4  Demurrage or Despatch Money

If the Buyer fails to meet the discharging requirements specified in clause 10.3 hereof, the Buyer shall pay demurrage to the Seller for all time lost after the expiration of allowable laytime at the rates in United States dollars to be agreed each Contract Year at the time of Price negotiation in accordance with clause 6.3 hereof, such demurrage rate to be documented in an Addendum hereto.

**11. Weight Determination**

11.1  Weighing at Loading Port

At the Loading Port, the Seller at its own expenses shall appoint an independent surveyor to determine the weight of the shipment of Product by draft survey and the Seller shall issue a Certificate of Weight accordingly, such certificate to be the basis for the Seller's provisional invoice. The Buyer may at its own expense have its representative (s) present during the draft survey.

11.2  Weighing at Discharge Port

At the Discharge Port in China, the Buyer at its own expense shall arrange for CIQ, or an alternative third party to be mutually agreed upon by the Parties, to undertake weighing of the shipment by draft survey. The weight thus determined shall, subject to clause 11.3 hereof, be final as to the wet weight of the shipment. The dry weight shall be determined by deducting the free moisture referred to in clause 12.2 hereof from such wet weight.

11.3  Weight Difference

If the difference between the Loading Port and Discharge Port weights for a particular shipment as determined in accordance with clauses 11.1 and 11.2 hereof respectively exceeds 0.50 per cent on Wet Basis then the Buyer and the Seller shall consult to settle the difference. If after consultation the difference cannot be reconciled, then the relevant weight shall be determined by averaging the Loading Port and Discharge Port weights and the average weight so determined shall be deemed the final weight of the shipment, such final weight to be set out in a certificate which shall be the basis for the Seller's Final

Invoice.

### 12.Sampling and Analysis

12.1    Sampling and Analysis at Loading Port

At the Loading Port the Seller shall, at the Seller's expense, take a representative sample of each shipment of Product, divide the sample into 3 parts, one for the Seller, one for the Buyer and one for Umpire analysis. The sample for Umpire analysis shall be sealed and kept by the Seller or its representative. The Seller will analyse one part for chemical and physical composition and for free moisture content and provide a Certificate of Analysis accordingly which shall be the basis for the Seller's Provisional Invoice. All sampling and analysis shall be carried out in accordance with the standards of ISO effective on the date of delivery. The Buyer may, at the Buyer's expense, have its representative (s) present at the time of such sampling and analysis.

12.2    Sampling and Analysis at Discharge Port

At the Discharge Port in China, the Buyer at the Buyer's expense shall arrange for CIQ, or an alternative third party to be mutually agreed upon by Parties, to take a representative sample of each shipment of Product and analyse such sample for chemical and physical composition and for free moisture content. All sampling and analysis shall be carried out in accordance with the standards of ISO effective on the date of delivery.CIQ (or the third party) shall divide the sample into three parts, one for the Buyer, one for the Seller and one for a potential Umpire. The Seller may at the Seller's expense have its representative (s) present at the time of sampling and analysis. CIQ (or the third party) shall analyse the sample for the Buyer. The Buyer shall promptly forward to the Seller by email a certificate issued by CIQ (or the third party) showing the percentage of chemical contents, the percentage of free moisture loss at 105 degrees Celsius and the relevant screen analysis. The CIQ (or third party) certificate shall be final except as otherwise provided for in clause 13.3 hereof.

12.3    Analysis Differences

If the difference in Fe content between the CIQ (or third party) analysis determined at the Discharge Port in accordance with clause 12.2 hereof and the Seller's analysis determined at the Loading Port in accordance with clause 12.1 hereof is more than 0.50 % but less than or equal to 1%, or if there exists a significant difference between the two analyses in respect of any one or more chemical contents other than Fe which materially affects the Price, then the relevant chemical content shall be determined by averaging the analysis results at the Loading Port and at the Discharge Port.

If the difference in Fe content between the CIQ (or third party) analysis determined at the Discharge Port in accordance with clause 12.2 hereof and the Seller's analysis determined at the Loading Port in accordance with clause 12.1 hereof is more than 1 %, the Seller and the Buyer shall consult to reconcile the difference. If after consultation the difference cannot be reconciled, an Umpire Laboratory shall be appointed by the mutual agreement of Parties. An Umpire analysis shall then be undertaken using the third sample from both the Loading and Discharge Ports and the average of the results of said analysis shall control and be used as the final analysis. The final analysis of a shipment determined in accordance with clauses 12.1 to this clause 12.3 shall be set out in a certificate which shall be the basis for the Seller's Final Invoice （Final Certificate of Analysis）.

12.4　Cost of Umpire

The cost of the Umpire must be borne by the party whose sampling result has the greater variance from that of the Umpire, except where the Umpire's analysis is equal to the exact mean of the original sampling results in which case the cost of the Umpire must be borne equally by the parties.

**13. Payment**

13.1　Letter of Credit

（a）Payment of invoices issued by the Seller to the Buyer for each delivery of Product shall be made under an irrevocable Letter of Credit.

（b）Not less than 14 Business Days prior to the commencement of the planned laydays at the Loading Port notified by the Seller in accordance with clause 10.1 hereof, the Buyer shall open an irrevocable without recourse to drawer and workable Letter of Credit acceptable to the Seller and able to be confirmed by Seller's Bank, payable at sight, in favour of the Seller in an amount in United States dollars equal to one hundred and ten （110） per cent of the expected value of the shipment, and with provision for 10% plus both in quantity and amount.

（c）Should the Buyer fail to provide the Letter of Credit within the 14 Business Days prior to commencement of laycan then the Seller shall have the immediate right to cancel that shipment contract and reduce the Buyer's annual Product allocation by the nominated amount for that shipment.

（d）The Letter of Credit shall remain open for not less than 60 days after the ocean bill of lading date. If necessary, the validity of the Letter of Credit shall be extended by the Buyer in order to allow the performance of the respective shipment. All banking charges outside the PRC or charged by the issuing bank after establishment of the Letter of Credit shall be paid by the Seller. The Buyer shall arrange for its bank to provide the Seller with a copy of the Letter of Credit by facsimile on the day on which it is opened.

13.2　Provisional Payment

（a）The Letter of Credit shall be payable at sight against the presentation of the Seller 's copy for the amount of 95% of the value of the shipment.

（b）When drawing against the Letter of Credit for its provisional payment, the

Seller shall present the following documents to the Seller's Bank for negotiation:

（i）a full set of clean on board ocean bills of lading issued to order, blank endorsed;

（ii）The Seller's Provisional Invoice in one original and four copies, indicating contract number, Letter of Credit number and name of carrying vessel;

（iii）The Seller's Certificate of Analysis issued in accordance with clause 12.1 hereof in one original and three copies;

（iv）draft survey report in one original and two copies issued by the independent surveyor appointed in accordance with clause 11.1 hereof, certifying the weight of Product loaded;

（v）the Seller's Certificate of Weight based on the independent surveyors draft survey report in one original and two copies; and

（vi）a certificate of origin in one original and four copies issued by the Seller attesting that the Product is of Australian origin.

13.3　Final Payment

（a）The Seller shall prepare a final invoice for each shipment, based on the certificates provided in clauses 11.3 and 12.3 hereof. The Seller may draw against the Letter of Credit for any balance due to the Seller on presentation of the Seller's Final Invoice.

（b）The Certificate of Weight and the Certificate of Analysis at the Loading Port, in accordance with clauses 11.1 and 12.1 hereof, shall be conclusive as to the weight and/or analysis of the shipment or Product and the provisional invoice issued under clause 13.2 （b）（ii）shall be considered the Final Invoice if:

（i）a determination of weight in accordance with clause11.2 hereof or analysis in accordance with clause 12.2 hereof is not undertaken at the Discharge Port;

（ii）the relevant certificates issued in accordance with clause 11.1 and/or clause 12.2 hereof is not received by the Seller within 60 days after the vessel arrives at the Discharge Port;

（iii）all or part of the Product is lost after loading into the vessel; or

（iv）the Product is damaged or contaminated （including by seawater） whilst on the vessel or being discharged.

（c）Any amount found to be due from one Party to the other as a result of a difference between the Provisional Invoice and the Final Invoice on any deliveries already made during a Contract Year shall be immediately settled by the Parties and paid upon presentation of the original debit note or complementary invoice. If the Buyer fails to pay any amount due to the Seller as a result of a difference between the Provisional Invoice and Final Invoice on any deliveries already made during a Contract Year, the Seller shall have the right to delay the loading of the Buyer's vessel until such payment is made by the Buyer and received by the Seller even if the vessel is within the agreed laydays. In this case any time, risk and expense related to the vessel shall be for the Buyer's account and the vessel shall have this laytime counted as from the beginning of loading operations.

13.4   Despatch and Demurrage

The Buyer and the Seller shall agree despatch and demurrage calculations within 30 days of the departure of the shipment from the Discharge Port and the applicable adjustment payments will be made within 5 Business Days of receipt of the appropriate invoice.

13.5   Interest

Where a payment under any part of this clause 13 has not been received by a party by the due date, the other party may, at its own discretion, charge interest at the LIBOR Rate in effect on that due date plus 2% per annum for the period beginning on that due date and ending on the date funds are received by that party.

### 14. Taxes and Dues

（a）Any existing or future taxes, duties or levies on the Products （including on freight or shipping）or on this Contract in the country of origin shall be for the Seller's account.

（b）Any existing or future taxes, duties or levies on the Products （including on freight or shipping）or on this Contract out of the country of origin shall be for the Buyer's account.

### 15. Licences

The Buyer shall be responsible for obtaining and maintaining in force any necessary import licences and the Seller shall be responsible for obtaining and maintaining in force any necessary export licences. The failure to obtain or to maintain in force such licences shall not be grounds for a claim of Force Majeure if the regulations in force at the time when the Agreement was made called for such licences to be obtained.

### 16. Non Delivery

In the event that the Seller fails to effect delivery of the total quantity of Products in any relevant Contract Year during the Term, as stipulated in Clause 4, due to a cause or causes for which Seller is found responsible, the Buyer shall have an option either to cancel the undelivered quantity, or to discuss an alternative to effect such delivery in a manner to be mutually agreed between the Buyer and the Seller.

### 17. Force Majeure

The Seller shall not be liable to the Buyer nor shall the Buyer be liable to the Seller for any delay or failure in the performance of obligations hereunder if such delay or failure is due to or results from war （whether declared or undeclared）, act of terrorism, revolution, riot, insurrection, civil commotion, act of God, fire, flood, storm, tempest, requirements or injunctions of governments or governmental authorities, strike, lockout, failure of supply of materials including power, electricity and fuel, epidemic or quarantine, accidents to or closing at railroads, harbours, docks, canals, or any other cause or causes beyond the reasonable control of the Seller or the Buyer, covering and including mine to Place of Loading （"Force Majeure Event"）.

### 18. Dispute Resolution

18.1　Resolution by Mutual Accord

（a）The Parties shall seek to resolve any dispute or claim arising out of or in relation to this Agreement by mutual accord. If the dispute or matter cannot be settled by mutual accord between the Parties, such dispute or claim shall be referred to arbitration in accordance with the Rules of Conciliation and Arbitration of the International Chamber of Commerce.

（b）The board of arbitration shall be composed of three arbitrators, one of whom shall be chosen by the Buyer, one by the Seller, and a third by the two so chosen.

18.2　Location of Arbitration

The place of arbitration shall be Singapore pursuant to the relevant rules of the Singapore International Arbitration Centre and the arbitration shall be conducted in the English language. The arbitration award shall be final and binding upon the Parties . The costs of arbitration shall be borne by the unsuccessful Party unless decided otherwise by the board of arbitration in accordance with the said Rules.

### 19. Entire Agreement and Amendment

19.1　Entire Agreement

This instrument contains the entire agreement between the Parties in relation to the sale and purchase of Product hereby agreed and supersedes all prior negotiations, understandings and agreements, whether written or oral in relation to that Product.

19.2　Amendment

This Agreement shall not be modified, amended, or supplemented except by an instrument in writing duly executed by the Parties to this Agreement.

### 20. No Consequential Loss

Subject to anything to the contrary elsewhere in this Agreement, the Parties hereby agree that no Party is in any circumstances liable in respect of any breach of this Agreement to the other Party for any indirect or consequential loss.

### 21. Further Assurances

Each Party shall do anything necessary or desirable （including executing agreements and documents） to give full effect to this Agreement and the transactions contemplated by it.

### 22. Costs and Stamp Duty

Each Party shall bear its own costs arising out of the negotiation, preparation and execution of this Agreement. All stamp duty （including fines, penalties and interest） payable on or in connection with this Agreement and any instrument executed under or any transaction evidenced by this Agreement shall be borne equally by the Parties.

### 23. Severability

If the whole or any part of a provision of this Agreement is or becomes void, unenforceable or illegal in a jurisdiction the offending provision is severed for that jurisdiction. The remainder of this Agreement shall have full force and effect and the validity or enforceability of that provision in any other jurisdiction shall not be affected.

### 24. Governing Law and Jurisdiction

This Agreement shall be governed by the laws of South Australia, Australia. Each Party submits to the jurisdiction of courts exercising jurisdiction there.

### 25. Counterparts

This Agreement may be executed in any number of counterparts. All counterparts together will be taken to constitute one instrument.

### 26. Language

This Agreement is in English language and no translation into Chinese or any other language shall affect its meaning or interpretation. The parties hereby acknowledge and agree that they have understood and shall be legally bound only by the English language version of this Agreement.

### 27. Signatories Page

Executed this ················. day of ·················20××.

| BUYER: | SELLER: |
|---|---|
|  |  |
|  |  |
|  |  |
| ····························· . | ····························· . |
| SIGNED | SIGNED |
| Authorised Signatory of the Buyer | Authorised Signatory of the Seller |
| In the presence of: | In the presence of: |
|  |  |
|  |  |
| ····························· . | ····························· . |
| Signature of Witness | Signature of Witness |
|  |  |
| ····························· . | ····························· . |
| Name of Witness (block letters) | Name of Witness (block letters) |

## 28. Appendix

Schedule 1：Yearly Quantity

The quantity expressed in WMT of the Product to be sold and purchased during each Contract Year of the Term is set out in the table below.

| Contract Year | Quantity |
| --- | --- |
| 2015 | 500,000 tonnes |
| 2016 | 500,000 tonnes |
| 2017 | 500,000 tonnes |
| 2018 | 500,000 tonnes |
| 2019 | 500,000 tonnes |
| 2020 | 500,000 tonnes |
| 2021 | 185,650 tonnes |

The quantity of the Product to be delivered in each Contract Year may be varied by plus or minus ten percent （+/-10%） at the Seller's option.

The above product quantities are derived from the Seller's production plans as at the date of this Agreement. Should these production plans significantly change, the Seller shall consult with the Buyer to determine mutually acceptable quantities.

Schedule 2：Shipping Schedule and Quantity

| Scheduled Delivery Month（2015—2020） | Total Scheduled Monthly Quantity （WMT） |
| --- | --- |
| February | 71,500 tonnes |
| April | 71,500 tonnes |
| June | 71,500 tonnes |
| August | 71,500 tonnes |
| September | 71,500 tonnes |
| October | 71,500 tonnes |
| December | 71,000 tonnes |
| Scheduled Delivery Month（Year 2021） | Total Scheduled Monthly Quantity （WMT） |
| February | 71,500 tonnes |
| April | 71,500 tonnes |
| June | 42,650 tonnes |

**参考译文**

本协议是由 ABCD 金属有限公司（以下简称卖方）和 EFGH 公司（以下简称买方）订立的。

鉴于本协议达成的条件，卖方同意向买方出售并交付铁矿石，买方同意购买，接受且向卖方支付铁矿石贷款。

管辖法律：澳大利亚法律，请见第 24 条。

合同签署日期：请见签署页。

**通用条款**

1.定义

本协议中，除非文本中另有说明，否则以下定义为准：

协议包括本文件及后续修订的附件；

工作日为除去星期六、星期日和澳大利亚、中国公共假期的日期；

产品检验证书为卖方依据合同 12.1 条款签发的证书；

重量检验证书为卖方依据合同 11.1 条款签发的证书；

CIQ 为中华人民共和国出入境检验检疫局；

执行日以以下日期晚者为准：

（a）条款 2.1 中条件全部满足或者双方同意豁免；和

（b）第一批货物从装运港移交到达尔文港的巴拿马货船上的时间。

条件为条款 2.1 中列明的条件；

合同年为同一年从 1 月 1 日至 12 月 31 日 12 个月的时间。第一个合同年也可从合同执行日至当年 12 月 31 日止。最后一个合同年从最后一个 1 月 1 日起算，至合同终止日结束；

卸货港口为买方或者其代理卸货的港口；

DMT 为干态下一公吨；

干态指在 105 摄氏度下干燥过的矿石产品；

终止日为本合同签署日 6 年后的日期；

最终验收证书为由检验方依据条款 12.3 出具的证书；

最终发票为基于条款 11.3 中要求的重量标准和条款 12.3 经物理和化学分析结果开具的货物销售发票；

CFR 为国际贸易术语规则中描述的含义；

不可抗力为条款 17 中描述的含义；

政府机构为一国政府，或者政府的、半政府的机构或司法当局。它还包括依据法律设立的协会组织或者证券交易所；

Incoterms 为国际商会出版的国际贸易术语规则 2010 版；

IMSBC 规则为 2009 年国际海运固体散货规则；

破产事件为以下任意一种事件或者状况发生，对合同一方产生的影响：

（a）受影响的协议一方无偿债能力或公告破产，或者正式通知协议其他方或者债权人无力偿还债务；

（b）受影响的一方已经开始进入安排清算人或者临时清算人程序（不是为了公司合并或者改组）；

（c）受影响的协议一方与债权人达成公司重组安排；

（d）任何接管人（依据2001年公司法规定）已经指定完毕或者因受影响，协议一方的抵押资产被接管；

ISM规则为1993年国际海事组织制定、为了安全航行和防止污染的国际安全管理规则；

ISO为制定铁矿石分析标准的国际标准组织；

ISPS规则为国际船舶和港口设施保安规则，为海上人命安全公约修正案；

装运港为北部地区，达尔文港口；

当应用于产品时，自然状态为产品处于自然状态或者潮湿状态；

装卸准备就绪通知为货物装运就绪的通知书；

一方为本协议中的一方；

装运地为在装运港口中将货物装运到巴拿马船上的地方；

价格为按照条款6.3（c）中需要支付的合同价格；

价格协议日为按照条款13.1的要求，买方开出不可撤销信用证最终日期的前10日；

价格指数为按照条款6.2中约定的含义；

价格期限为按照条款6.1中约定的含义；

产品为卖方从其"PERFECT磁铁矿项目"中生产的磁铁矿精矿；

PRC为中华人民共和国；

暂付发票为按照条款11.1约定的重量要求和条款12.1约定的物理和化学分析结论开具的货物销售发票；

技术标准为按照条款5中约定的含义；

检验方为在矿产行业中，从事取样和产品分析并评定的第三方；

晴天工作日为天气条件适合转运工作且包含以下情况：

（a）温度处于摄氏零下45度至零上45度；

（b）风速低于或者合理预计低于每小时20海里；

（c）海浪高度低于1.5米；

（d）能见度不低于0.5海里。

湿态为产品处于自然状态或者潮湿状态；

湿吨为自然状态下矿石的重量。

2.前提条件

2.1　条件

本协议和协议中各方义务的履行需满足以下条件：

（a）卖方针对本项目的融资需要完成；和

（b）卖方需要获取所有在装运港涉及运输、存储和装运的许可。

2.2　无法满足以上前提条件

如果在协议终止日之前无法满足或者卖方主动放弃满足以上条件，协议任何一方可以通过书面通知的方式终止此协议，在此情况下本协议立即终止（除非之前有违约事件发生）。

3.协议期限

基于前提条件的满足或者双方对相关条件同意豁免，买卖双方的协议执行日自协议执行日起算，有效期6年。

4.数量

在每一个合同年，买卖双方需要根据附件1计划列表1（除非明确说明，否则都是按照年度数量和湿态标准进行约定的）中对于产品数量和类型的约定进行交易。

5.产品规格

5.1　第一个合同年的产品规格要求

第一个合同年要求交货的矿石产品的规格（干态）按照条款12.1规定，在装货港提取的样品需满足以下条件：

| 化学成分<br>（干态） | 标准<br>（重量百分比） | 最高和最低<br>（重量百分比） |
| --- | --- | --- |
| 铁 | 64.0% | 最低60.0% |
| 二氧化硅 | 8.00% | 最高10% |
| 三氧化二铝 | 0.59% | 最高1% |
| 磷 | 0.01% | 最高0.05% |
| 硫 | 0.32% | 最高0.35% |
| 水分 | 8.0% | 最高8.0% |

5.2　物理规格

矿石的物理规格（湿态）如下：

| | | 标准 | |
| --- | --- | --- | --- |
| 超大 | 大于100微米 | 15.0% | 最多不超过20% |
| 在卸货港低于标准大小 | 小于10微米 | 20.0% | 最多不超过25% |

a）超大矿石

在每船货物中，如果矿石大小超过了合同中要求的最高比例，则对于超量部分按照每一干公吨0.5美元进行罚款。

b）低于标准大小矿石

在每船货物中，如果矿石大小超过了合同中要求的最高比例，则对于超量部分按照每一干公吨0.5美元进行罚款。

5.3　其他合同年的产品规格要求

其他合同年交付的货物的产品质量如果与协议条款5.1和5.2中的规定不同，则需按照卖方在产品数据清单中的描述进行调整。卖方需提前书面通知买方相关变化情况。按照此条款调整的产品规格即视为满足本合同要求的产品规格要求。

6.价格

6.1　价格期限

对于每一批运输的货物，价格期限为协议价格日期前30天。

6.2　价格指数

协议双方同意依照条款6采用普氏指数确定价格，即采用普氏钢铁日报中发布的62%铁矿石品位，CFR中国北方（普氏指数）作为定价基础。

如果普氏指数停止发布或者其后进行了实质性的变更，双方将会协商其他替换的市场指数。

6.3　价格确定

（a）在价格协议日前，买卖双方需确定所运输矿石的价格以确定信用证金额。此价格为价格期限内普氏钢铁日报中发布的普氏指数的平均值。

（b）如果矿石价格不能在约定期限内按照6.3（a）达成一致，则前价格期间

仅作为临时价格参考，直至价格最终达成一致（临时价格）。当新价格达成一致后，双方

需要按照临时价格和最终价格进行调整。

（c）价格为CFR普氏价格

CFR普氏价格为在价格效期内普氏钢铁日报中发布的62%铁矿石，CFR中国北方（普氏指数）的平均价格加上或者减去调整后的价格。

7.价格调整

7.1　规格和价格调整

如果卖方没有按照协议约定的标准交货，则其仅需按照条款7.2中的约定进行调整。

7.2　因矿石规格不符导致的价格调整

按照条款12（样品和分析）中的约定，且依据出具的分析证书（或者最终分析证书），如果交付的矿石不符合协议中约定含量标准，则需通过以下方式进行价格调整，买方需要按照以下价格调整购买该船矿石，价格调整为卖方交货不一致的唯一补偿方式。

| 元素 | | 价格调整<br>（每干吨美元数） | 按比例计算 |
|---|---|---|---|
| 铁 | 铁元素含量 | 如果铁元素低于62%，则每降低1%含铁量，价格期内普氏价格平均指数降低1% | 低于62%，价格同比例下降 |
| 硅和铝 | 二氧化硅和三氧化二铝 | 降低0.2美元 | 超过10%部分每超过1% |
| 磷 | P | 降低0.2美元 | 超过0.05%部分每超过0.01% |
| 硫 | S | 降低0.2美元 | 超过0.1%部分每超过0.01% |

7.3　自然水分流失

按照条款12的约定，如果任意一船货物的自然水分在105摄氏度下流失比例超过产品规格中的最高值，则买方需要购买此船货物，但货物价格需要按照相关金额进行递减，递减的金额为买方由于水分流失过多而实际增加的购买成本。

7.4　价格奖励

按照条款12（样品和分析）中的约定，且依据出具的分析证书（或者最终分析证书），如果交付的矿石高于协议中约定含量标准，则需通过以下方式进行价格调整，买方需要按照以下价格调整购买价格，给予价格奖励。

| 元素 | | 价格调整（每干吨美元数） | 每干吨应付 |
|---|---|---|---|
| 铁 | 铁元素含量超过62% | 如果铁元素高于62%，则每提高1%含铁量，价格期内普氏价格平均指数提高1% | 对于高于62%部分的铁含量，每1%含量对应1%价格调整 |

8.交付、所有权和风险

（a）除非本协议附件中另有约定，产品的交付采用CFR（平仓）装运港。

（b）依据条款9的约定，所有关于产品的损失、损坏或者破坏的风险转移到买方的时点为当产品在卸货港越过买方安排的船的船舷时。

（c）产品所有权需要买方支付完货款进行转移。

（d）如果本协议的约定与Incoterms发生冲突，则以本协议为准。

9.运输计划和船舶到达通知

9.1　运输计划

（a）卖方应尽力确保在合同年中交付的货物按照预计的运输计划进行安排，如附件3中对第一个合同年的明确运输计划。

（b）至少在一个合同年起始日前90天，买卖双方需就年度运输计划进行明确，运输计划中应明示：

（i）对于每艘船暂定30天的受载期限；

（ii）每艘船的装载量。

（c）至少在每个季度起始日前45天，买方应向卖方提交按月安排的季度运输计划。

双方应于季度起始日前30天就季度计划达成一致。季度运输计划应：

（i）明确每艘船15天的受载期限；并

（ii）确认每艘船的装载量。

9.2　船舶信息，到达通知和船公司代理

（a）卖方应在不晚于受载期前20日明确指定具有承运能力的船舶信息给买方：

（i）船舶名字、船龄和国籍；

（ii）预计的到港日；且

（iii）船舶的详细描述和总布局图或者平面图。

（b）船舶更换也是允许的，按照条款9.2中的约定，需在船舶到达卸货港前10日前提出。

（c）除非卖方指定的船舶无法满足条款9.2中的需求，否则买方必须在收到指示的24小时内将接收通知发给卖方。

（d）卖方需确保其指定的船舶符合本协议的要求，且卖方需在卸货港指定运输代理（卖方代理）参与相关清关工作

（e）卖方应在每艘船到达卸货港10日前通知买方货物重量。

10.卸载条款

10.1　装货前须提供信用证

以装运日期或者受载期早者为基准日，买方需在基准日前14个工作日开出条款13.1中提到的信用证。

10.2　卸载条件

（a）卖方应在买方指定的安全锚地进行交货，货物为散货，需进行平整，且按照CFR贸易术语交付。在受载期前，需提供安全锚地的潮汐、吃水、进出通道和水流信息。卖方有权要求任何出具装卸准备就绪通知的船舶或者在卸货港正在卸货的船舶停止卸货，并转移至其他卸货地（船舶的吃水可满足）。因卖方满足相关条件而产生的费用均由买方负责。转移时间计算在受载期内。

（b）除去燃油费用、船舶消耗品、给养和船员成本，如果由转移卸载地所导致的其他费用，且如果相关费用应中国政府管理机构要求而支付，则相关费用由买方负责。

（c）买方应负责在卸载港所发生的所有税费，港口费用或其他针对船舶的费用。

（d）买方还需负责卸载前后的水尺检量费用和清洁度检验费用。

10.3　卸载费用

买方需要支付本协议项下的装运费用，费用基数为每连续24个小时的晴天工作日，包括周六、周日或者节假日，装运能力为平均4万湿吨。

10.4　滞港费或速遣费

如果买方不能按照条款10.3的约定满足卸载要求，买方需在每个合同年根据条款6.3确定的价格，在受载期到期后，以美元向卖方支付滞港费，相关滞港费需要列示在附件中。

11. 重量测定

11.1　装运港测重

在装运港，卖方应自费指定独立第三方就船运货物重量测重，测重方法为水尺检量，卖方应依据测重签发重量证书，此证书为卖方暂付发票的计算基础文件。在水尺测重阶段，买方也可自费让其代表出席测重过程。

11.2　卸载港测重

在中国的卸货港口，买方应自费安排CIQ或者其他双方同意的第三方通过水尺测量的方式进行测重。依据条款11.3的约定，此次测重为终局性的湿吨重量。干吨重量为依据条款12.2的约定，由湿吨重量减去自然水分流失后计算得出。

11.3　重量差异

依据条款11.1和11.2的约定，如果装运港和卸载港重量存在差异，且超过了湿吨重量的0.5%，则买卖双方将协商解决重量差异。如果双方无法对重量差异达成一致，则最终重量以二者的平均值为准，该最终重量将作为出具给卖方的最终发票计算依据。

12. 取样和分析

12.1　装运港的取样和分析

在装运港，卖方应自费对每一船货物进行取样，将样品分成三部分，一份给卖方，一份给买方，另一份给第三方检验方。送给第三方检验方的样品应该密封保存，由卖方或其代表持有。卖方需对样品的化学和物理成分、自然水分含量进行分析，并提供分析证书，该证书为开具暂付发票的依据。所有的取样和分析工作需在交货日按照ISO的标准进行。买方也可自费安排其代表出席取样和分析过程。

12.2　卸载港的取样和分析

在中国的卸货港，买方应自费安排CIQ或者其他双方同意的第三方针对每船货物取样，并对样品的化学和物理成分、自然水分含量进行分析。所有的取样和分析工作需在交货日按照ISO的标准进行。CIQ（或者第三方）需将样品分为三份，一份给卖方，一份给买方，另一份给潜在的第三方检验方。卖方也可自费安排其代表出席取样和分析过程。CIQ（或者第三方）为买方进行分析工作。买方应尽快通过邮件给卖方提供CIQ签发的证书，证书内容应包括在105摄氏度下产品的化学成分百分比、自然水分含量百分比和颗粒分析结果。除了条款13.3的要求外，CIQ（或者第三方）证书为最终证书。

12.3　分析差异

如果依据条款12.2在卸货港由CIQ（或者第三方）出具的铁含量检验结果和依

据条款12.1在装运港卖方出具的检验结果存在差异，且差异数额高于0.50%，低于或等于1%，或者对其他化学元素的含量差异影响了产品价格，则化学元素含量应为两个检测结果的平均值。

如果依据条款12.2在卸货港由CIQ（或者第三方）出具的铁含量检验结果和依据条款12.1在装运港卖方出具的检验结果存在差异，且差异数额高于1%，买卖双方需通过协商解决。如果双方无法达成一致，则需由双方同意的第三方实验室进行检测。第三方需对买卖双方留存的第三份样品进行检验，两份样品的平均值为最终检测结果。依据条款12.1和12.3，最终检测结果需出具检测证书，该证书为卖方开具最终发票的依据（最终分析证书）。

12.4　聘用检验方的成本

聘用检验方的成本由样品结果差异较大的一方承担，如果双方样品差异一致，则费用由双方分摊。

13. 付款

13.1　信用证

（a）对于每一笔卖方向买方的支付采用不可撤销的信用证的方式。

（b）依据条款10.1的约定，卖方应在装运港受载期执行日不少于14个工作日前通知买方，买方应开立以卖方为受益人的不可撤销、无追索的即期信用证，信用证需经卖方同意，且经过卖方银行的确认，信用证币种为美元，金额为预估货物价格的110%，数量和金额浮动10%。

（c）如果买方不能在装运港受载期执行日前14个工作日开出信用证，卖方可立即取消本次运输合同，且在买方的年度产品计划中减去相关金额。

（d）信用证有效期需在获取海运提单后至少60日内依然有效。如有必要，为了保证每船货物的运输，买方需就信用证有效期进行延展。开立信用证之后，所有在中国以外或者由开证行收取的费用应由卖方负责。买方需在信用证开立日通过传真向卖方提供信用证副本。

13.2　暂付款项

（a）在卖方提交相关单据后，货物95%的款项通过信用证即期支付。

（b）当卖方向卖方银行提交暂付款项议付时，需提供以下材料：

（i）套凭指示，空白背书的清洁海运提单；

（ii）卖方的暂付发票，一份正本，四份副本，发票上需明示合同号、信用证号和承运船舶的名字；

（iii）依据条款12.1的约定卖方出具的分析证书，一份正本，三份副本；

（iv）依据条款11.1的约定，由独立方出具的水尺检量报告证明装载货物的重量，报告正本一份，副本两份；

（v）基于独立方报告由卖方出具的重量证书，正本一份，副本两份；和

（vi）卖方出具的原产地证书，证明原产地为澳大利亚，正本一份，副本四份。

13.3 最终付款

（a）卖方需基于条款11.3和12.3约定的证书，对每船货物准备最终发票。在卖方按照信用证要求递交单据后议付。

（b）依据条款11.1和12.1的约定，装运港出具的重量证书和分析证书对于货物的重量或者含量分析为终局性的，依据条款13.2（b）（ii）出具的暂付发票如果满足以下条件，则应被认为是最终发票：

（i）条款11.2要求的卸货港的测重和条款12.2要求的取样或分析不需再进行；

（ii）当货船到达卸货港60天内，卖方未收到条款11.2和/或12.2要求的相关证书；

（iii）部分或者全部货物在货物装运完成后损失；或者

（iv）货物在船上或者卸载时被损坏或者污染（包括被海水污染）。

（c）如果在一个合同年中，暂付发票和最终发票价格存在差异，则双方应通过递交原始付款通知单或者补充发票的方式立刻解决。如果买方不能支付给卖方相关差额，即使货船已经在约定的受载期内，卖方依然有权推迟将货物装至买方船舶。在此情况下，货船相关的风险和费用将由买方承担，且货船的装货时间需从开始装货日起算。

13.4 滞港费和速遣费

买卖双方同意当货船离开卸载港后30天内计算速遣费和滞港费，适当的调整费用需在收到相关发票后5个工作日内支付。

13.5 利息

如果按照条款13的约定协议一方未如期收到相关款项，则另一方需按照Libor+2%的年化利率支付利息，利息起始日为应付款日，终止日为收到款项的日期。

14.税费

（a）本协议中所有在原产地产生的税费、关税或者其他货物税费（包括运输过程）由卖方负责。

（b）本协议中所有在原产地之外产生的税费、关税或者其他货物税费（包括运输过程）由买方负责。

15.许可

买方应负责获取和持有有效的进口许可，卖方应负责获取和持有有效的出口许可。如果在协议执行时，相关许可即需要办理，则未获取有效的许可不能被认可为不可抗力事件。

16.未交付货物

如果由于卖方原因，卖方不能按照条款4的约定，在相关合同年中无法交付承诺数量的货物，买方有权选择取消未交付部分的货物或者与卖方探讨双方可接受的针对未交付货物部分的其他交付方式。

17.不可抗力

买卖双方对以下事件引起的损失均不承担任何责任，相关事件包括战争（无论是宣布的还是未宣布的）、恐怖事件、革命、骚乱、起义、暴动、不可预知的自然事件、火灾、洪水、暴风雨、暴风雪、政府或政府机关的要求或禁令、罢工、停工，相关能源无法获取供应，包括能源、电力和燃料，传染病或者隔离，铁路、港口、码头、运河或其他超出买卖双方合理控制的任何其他事件，覆盖地点包括从矿山至装运港（"不可抗力事件"）。

18.争端解决

18.1　双方协商解决

（a）协议双方应通过协商的方式解决协议项下相关争议或者索赔。如果无法通过协商达成一致，则双方可以依据国际商会调解和仲裁规则通过仲裁解决。

（b）仲裁委员会由三名仲裁员组成，买卖双方各指定一名仲裁员，第三名仲裁员由前两名仲裁员指定。

18.2　仲裁地

仲裁地为新加坡，仲裁规则为新加坡国际仲裁中心规则，仲裁语言为英语。仲裁为终局性，且对双方有效。仲裁费用由败诉方承担，如果仲裁庭另有判决，依据仲裁庭判决为准。

19.完整协议和补充协议

19.1　完整协议

本协议代表了买卖双方对于本次买卖货物的完整协议，之前无论口头还是书面谈判、达成的一致都无法律效力。

19.2　补充协议

本协议在未获得双方同意的情况下不可被更改、修订或者增加，除非按照本协议以书面补充协议形式进行更改。

20.无间接损失

除非与本协议中的其他条款相违背，否则协议一方不得对另一方因合同违约主张任何间接损失。

21.其他保证

协议中各方应尽全力促使本协议生效，并执行相关交易。

22.成本和印花税

协议中各方应承担各自在合同谈判、准备和执行中产生的成本费用。本协议或本协议执行过程中产生的印花税（包括罚款、违约罚金和利息）由双方均等承担。

23.协议可分割性

如果本协议某个条款全部或者部分失效，无法执行或者在法律管辖权内不再合法，合同中的其他条款依然有效且有效部分的执行不应受到任何影响。

24.管辖法律和管辖权

本协议受南澳大利亚法律管辖。协议任何一方应提请有管辖权的法院行使管辖权。

25.副本

本协议可能会签署多份副本。所有副本视同与原本完全一致。

26.语言

本协议采用英文书写，中文或者其他语种的翻译不能影响本协议的含义和解释。协议双方同意英文版本为合法版本。

27.签署页

签署日：20××年　月　日

| 买方： | 卖方： |
| --- | --- |
| | |
| | |
| ……………………… | ……………………… |
| 签字 | 签字 |
| 买方授权签字人 | 卖方授权签字人 |
| | |
| 在场人： | 在场人 |
| | |
| | |
| ……………………… | ……………………… |
| 证明人签字 | 证明人签字 |
| | |
| | |
| ……………………… | ……………………… |
| 证明人名字（印刷体） | 证明人名字（印刷体） |

28.附录

附表1：年度数量

每一个合同年中预期交付的采用湿吨计算的货物数量如下表所示：

| 合同年 | 数量 |
| --- | --- |
| 2015 | 500,000 吨 |
| 2016 | 500,000 吨 |
| 2017 | 500,000 吨 |
| 2018 | 500,000 吨 |
| 2019 | 500,000 吨 |
| 2020 | 500,000 吨 |
| 2021 | 185,650 吨 |

卖方可以对每一个合同年交付的货物数量进行调整，调整数量范围为+/-10%。

以上货物交付数量来源于本协议签署时卖方的生产计划。如果生产计划发生重大变化，则卖方需及时与买方沟通交付货物数量，并获取买方同意。

附表2：运输数量

**运输计划和数量**

| 计划交货月份<br>（2015 至 2020 年） | 每个月计划交货数量 |
| --- | --- |
| 2 月 | 71,500 吨 |
| 4 月 | 71,500 吨 |
| 6 月 | 71,500 吨 |
| 8 月 | 71,500 吨 |
| 9 月 | 71,500 吨 |
| 10 月 | 71,500 吨 |
| 12 月 | 71,000 吨 |
| 计划交货月份<br>（2021 年） | 月度计划交货数量 |
| 2 月 | 71,500 吨 |
| 4 月 | 71,500 吨 |
| 6 月 | 42,650 吨 |

# Notes

1. umpire n.检验方

2. insolvent adj. 无力偿还债务的，周转不灵的

The company has been declared insolvent.

这家公司已被宣布破产。

This bank's liabilities exceed its assets，making it technically insolvent.

该银行的负债超过其资产，技术上它已破产。

If the Buyer becomes insolvent，the Seller may refuse to make further deliveries.

如果买方变成无偿还能力时，卖方可以拒绝交货。

insolvency n. 破产，无力偿还债务，周转不灵

insolvency n. 无偿还能力

有两种含义：一是企业的总负债超过总资产的破产式的无力偿还；二是总资产超过总负债，但因一时的周转不灵而对到期的债务无法偿付。

insolvency clause           破产条款

insolvency law              破产法

insolvency proceedings     破产程序

This agreement shall automatically terminate upon the bankruptcy or insolvency of Joint Venture Company.

合资公司破产或无力偿付时，本协议将自行宣告终止。

It is expressly understood and agreed that bankruptcy or insolvency causes the termination of this Agreement.

大家明确地认识到并同意，破产或无能力偿还造成本协议的终止。

关于"破产"还有一个词 bankruptcy。

Bankruptcy      n. 破产

bankruptcy law          破产法

bankruptcy proceedings    破产程序

There are ten bankruptcies in the city last year.

该市去年有10家企业破产。

As a result of the bankruptcy of this factory，hundreds of workers have become charges on the public.

由于这家工厂的破产，数百名工人成为社会赈济的人。

Bankruptcy or insolvency shall cause the termination of this Agreement.

破产或无支付能力促使本协议终止。

The lawyer shall take necessary proceedings under Bankruptcy Act.

律师根据破产法的规定提起必要的诉讼。

bankrupt n.破产，破产者；vt.使破产

In the event Licensee be adjudicated a bankrupt，AAA forthwith terminate this Agreement.

如果宣判许可证持有方为破产者，那么甲方可立即终止本协议。

If the Sales Agent becomes bankrupt，the Pincipal may terminate this Agreement.

如果推销代理人成为破产者，那么该委托人可终止本协议。

关于公司的"解散"、"重组"、"合并"以及"清算诉讼"，有下列的表达词汇：

dissolution n. 解散

解散指一个企业自愿或非自愿的结束。合并或政府吊销执照等属于非自愿的结束。

dissolution of a legal entity 法人解散

dissolution of juridical person 公司（法人）解散

dissolution of partnership 合伙企业解散，拆股

Upon the dissolution of the partnership a full account of the assets and liabilities of the partnership shall be taken.

合伙关系一经解除，合伙人的资产和负债须全部登账。

Upon dissolution，the equity interests of members and patrons shall be determined as provided in the bylaws.

在公司解散时，其成员及赞助人的股息将按公司章程来核定。

modification n. 变更，企业的变更或重组

It is expressly understood that any modification to the Agreement must be made by an instrument in writing.

双方明确理解，本协议如有任何修改，都须以书面文件为凭。

The Salesman agrees to accept it upon these terms and conditions and upon such modification that may be made by the Sales Company.

推销员同意按这些条款和条件以及按照销售公司可能作出的这种修改来接受（这笔交易）。

consolidation n. 合并

指两个或两个以上的公司合并成立一个新公司，接管原来各公司的全部资产和业务。它与 merger（兼并）的含义不同。merger 是指一个公司兼并或收买另一个或数个公司，被兼并的公司宣告解散，其资产和负债全部由进行兼并的公司接收，业务也由其继续经营。

consolidation by lease 租赁合并

consolidation by merger 吸收合并

consolidation by purchase 购买合并，受盘合并

consolidation policy 合并方针

amalgamation n. 联合，合并

In the event of the Employer becoming bankrupt or being a company going into liquidation other than for the purpose of a scheme of reconstruction or amalgamation, the Contractor shall be entitled to terminate his employment under this Contract.

如果雇主行将破产或由于其他原因而不是为了要完成重建计划或合并计划而将停业清理，承包商将有权终止他在合同规定下的就业权利。

receivership proceedings 清算诉讼

指由法院指派财产清理人，依法接管和处理破产企业的全部资产。

3.possession n. 所有权，财产，领地

Part B shall receive and accept possession of the goods upon the terms and conditions stipulated below.

根据下文规定的条款和条件，乙方应接收并接受该批货物的所有权。

possess v. 拥有

Party A shall possess of any right to take over the Patent.

甲方应拥有一切接取专利的权利。

possession n. 所有权，财产，领地

Part B shall receive and accept possession of the goods upon the terms and conditions stipulated below.

根据下文规定的条款和条件，乙方应接收并接受该批货物的所有权。

possess v. 拥有

Party A shall possess of any right to take over the Patent.

甲方应拥有一切接取专利的权利。

4. visibility n. 能见度，可见性

The advertisements were intended to increase the company's visibility in the marketplace.

这些广告旨在提高该公司在市场上的知名度。

5. Conditions Precedent

precedent n.先例；adj.在先的

precedent condition（合约生效前的）先决条件

This must not be taken as a precedent for future business.

此事不得作为今后交易的先例。

The decision of the arbitrators shall be a condition precedent to any right of legal action that either party may have against the other.

双方中的任何一方向对方行使采取法律行动的权利时，仲裁人的决定应该是一种先决条件。

Conditions Precedent 先决条件或所附生效条件，指只有该条件发生，合同才生效。

This Agreement and the obligations of the Parties hereunder are subject to the satisfaction of the following conditions：

（a）the Seller proceeding to financial close of its proposed project finance facility with financier;

本协议和协议中各方义务的履行需满足以下条件：

（a）卖方针对本项目的融资需要完成；

如上文所述，在由供应商向业主提供垫资形式的合同中，应首先落实资金安排，把融资问题作为合同的先决条件之一，并约定违反该条件的法律后果。

6. terminate

辨析：terminate, close, end, conclude, complete, finish

作及物动词时，这组词均含有使结束、使完成之意；作不及物动词时，这些词（complete除外）含有接近终了之意。

terminate 指时间上的期限或空间上的界线的终止。

close 通常指其行为尚有潜力，在某种意义上讲，该行为是针对悬而未决或尚未完成的事情而言。

end 侧重指最终结束，经常用以表达某一发展过程被认为已经结束。

conclude 是正式用语，特指用正式或特殊的方式来结束事情、活动或文章。

complete 指消除一切缺陷或完成所有要做的事。

finish 表示完成了要做的事，经常指做完一系列程序中的最后一项工作。

The Union shall forthwith terminate the existing strike against the corporation.

工会应立即终止目前对公司的罢工。

Upon payment of the agreed sum, all of the buyer's rights and obligations shall terminate.

在支付已经同意的款额以后，买方的一切权利和义务应告终止。

I want to close my account.

我想结账。

The board of directors of the corporation may provide that the stock transfer books shall be closed for a stated period but not to exceed, in any case, （…） days.

公司董事会可规定，股票转让簿得暂告中止一段规定的时间，但无论如何不得超过……天。

Income can be reduced by holding off deliveries in the closing on weeks of the years.

在临近年终的几个星期，用拖延交货的办法可以使收入减少。

The dividend which accrued in the previous year ended on June 30 will be paid early next month.

到6月30日为止的上一年度应付的股息下月初即予支付。

The buyer with whom you will conclude such a transaction shall be required to sign the Contract as attached hereto.

将与你方达成这笔交易的买主必须在此所附的合同上签字。

The woodwork is beautifully finished, smoothed and polished.

那件木器漆得很精美。

The workers finished the dyke with remarkable speed.

工人们以惊人的速度筑成了堤坝。

The work hasn't been completed yet.

这个工作尚未完成。

AAA shall have the right to complete all contracts.

甲方有权去达成（完成）全部合同。

7.waiver n. 弃权，弃权声明书

A waiver by either party of any breach under this Contract shall not prevent a subsequent enforcement of such term.

双方中的任何一方如对违反本协议的某一条款弃权，不应有碍于今后该条款继续执行。

8.modify v. 修改

辨析 alter，change，modify，vary

这组词均含有使事物变得与以往不同之意。

alter 与 change 有时可以互换。

alter 只强调某些特殊方面（如形式或细节）的变化，而不暗指失去原有特性。

change 通常暗指本质上的变化，或指一事物取代了另一事物。

modify 常指缓和严重程度或降低过分程度等的变化，有时还表示较小的改动或不作根本的改变。

vary 常指由于变化（如移动、改变或生长）而产生的一个或一系列差别，有时指偏离常规或惯例。

The design of this lathe must be altered to meet the new requirements.

这台车床的设计必须改动一下，以适应新的要求。

The ship altered its course.

这艘船改变了方向。

Can you change this five-pound note?

你能兑换这张5英镑的钞票吗？

The wind has changed from north to east.

风由北风转为东风。

He won't modify his demands.

他不减少他的要求。

We have modified a few terms of your draft agreement.

你方协议草案中有些条款已被我方作了修改。

This plan must be modified if it is to be carried out successfully.

这项计划要想得到顺利贯彻必须加以修改。

A driver can vary the speed of an automobile.

司机可以改变汽车的速度。

Customs vary with the times.

风俗随时代而变。

9. alternative adj. 两者挑一的，可供替代的

If Platts ceases to be published or is substantially modified，another alternative market Index shall be adopted by mutual agreement.

如果普氏指数停止发布或者其后进行了实质性的变更，双方将会协商其他备选的市场指数。

They are provided with the choice of two alternative flights.

有两个航班可供他们选择。

10. laydays n.受载期（船舶预计到达装货港口的时间）

laytime 装卸货时间（超过装卸货规定的时间就会产生滞期费 demurrage，提前完成装卸就有速遣费 despatch money）

laycan 是 layday and cancelling date 的缩写，表示以一段时间作为受载期，过此期限，承租人有权决定是否解除合同。

14 Business Days prior to the commencement of the planned laydays at the Loading Port notified by Seller in accordance with clause 10.1 hereof，the Buyer shall open the L/C.

依据条款10.1的约定，卖方应在装运港受载期执行日不少于14个工作日前通知买方，买方应开出信用证。

In this case any time，risk and expense related to the vessel shall be for the Buyer's account and the vessel shall have this laytime counted as from the beginning of loading operations.

在此情况下，货船相关的风险和费用将由买方承担，且货船的装货应从开始装货日起算。

Should the Buyer fail to provide the Letter of Credit within the 14 Business Days prior to commencement of laycan then the Seller shall have the immediate right to cancel that shipment contract and reduce the Buyer's annual Product allocation by the nominated amount for that shipment.

如果买方不能在装运港受载期执行日前14个工作日开出信用证，卖方可立即取消本次运输合同，且在买方的年度产品计划中减去相关金额。

11. layout plan 平面图

12. substitution n. 代替品，替换

This Agreement，its extensions and renewals or substitutions shall be binding upon the parties hereto.

本协议、本协议的增补和续订，或本协议的替代协议，都将对协议各方具有约束力。

substitute v. 代替

Preferred stocks shall be substituted for common stocks，where approporiate.

在适当的情况下，优先股得由普通股代替之。

13. anchorage n. 下锚；停泊，锚地；泊地

There is enough room for the anchorage of thirty ships here.

这里足可停泊30艘船。

This is a secure anchorage.

这是个安全的锚地。

14. reconcile v. 对账，核查

Reconciling bank statements and cash accounts took a long time.

核对银行对账单和现金账户花了很长时间。

15. dispute resolution 争端（纠纷）解决

"争端解决条款"是几乎所有商务合同中的约定条款。通常，解决合同争端有三种方法：协商（negotiation）、仲裁（arbitration）、诉讼（lawsuit）。在国际商务领域，仲裁使用的频率往往大于协商和诉讼。根据《纽约公约》，仲裁的效力是受各国司法强制力保障实施的，这就避免了"协商"不具有强制性以及"诉讼"结果不被他国承认并予以执行的难题。

If any controversies of disputes should arise out of the effectiveness，construction，interpretation or performance of this Agreement，the parties hereto agree to use their best efforts in good faith，for a period of sixty（60）days，or such other period as shall be mutually agreed upon by them，to resolve all such controversies or disputes in an amicable manner.

因本协议效力、解释或履行所发生的任何纠纷，双方同意以最大的善意与努力，在60天或双方同意的期限内，以友好的方式协商解决。

When any dispute occurs and when such dispute is under arbitration，except for the part under dispute that is subject to the arbitration，the Parties hereto shall，in accordance with the provisions hereof，continue to exercise their respective rights and perform their respective obligations.

在发生争端并将争端提交仲裁的过程中，除所提交的争端部分外，双方都应按照本协议的规定，继续执行各自的权利并履行各自的义务。

16. entire agreement and amendment 完整协议及补充协议

"完整协议条款"的目的是在于确立合同当事人之间的书面合同有至高无上的地位。"完整协议条款"通常会与"补充协议条款"连用，表示书面合同包含当事人的所有约定，优于之前订立的任何口头和书面约定；对合同的条款进行补充必须以书面文件的形式进行。

17. severability n. 可分割性

Severance/Severability Provision 可分割条款

"可分割性条款"是指合同的各个条款都是可分的，效力是互不影响的。某一条款被司法部门宣布无效，并不影响其他条款的有效性。换言之，该条款的功能就在于通过当事人的意思自治请求法院把不具有法律效力的条款与合同的其他有效部分分割开来。

If a court finds any provisions of this Agreement invalid or unenforceable, the remainder of this Agreement shall be interpreted so as best to effect the intent of the parties.

若法院发现本协议的任何条款无效，余下的部分应被视为与约各方的意图。

The invalidity, in whole or in part, of any term of this Agreement does not affect the validity of the remainder of the agreement.

本合同条款中一部或全部被法院判决无效，则不影响其他有效部分条款的执行效力。

A judicial determination that any provision of this Agreement is invalid, in whole or in part, shall not affect the enforceability of those provisions unaffected by the finding of inability.

本合同一部分或全部内容无效不影响合同剩余部分内容的有效性。

This Agreement constitutes the entire agreement between the parties pertaining to the subject matter hereof, and fully supersedes any and all prior proposal (oral or written), negotiations, conversations, and discussions between or among the parties relating to the subject matter of this Agreement.

本协议完全表达了与约各方对合同标的物的理解并替代了先前的书面意向书、陈述和理解。本协议除非有双方的书面签署，否则不得修改。

All the appendices to this Agreement shall be an integral part of this Agreement. This Agreement and all its appendices shall constitute the entire Agreement between the Parties with respect to the subject matter set forth herein and supersede any and all pervious oral and written discussions, negotiations, notices, memoranda, documents, agreements, contracts and communications between the Parties relating to such subject matter.

本合同的所有附件是合同不可分割的一部分。本合同及其附件构成双方就本合同规定的标的达成的完整协议，并取代双方先前与该标的的相关一切口头和书面的洽谈、谈判、通知、备忘录、文件、协议、合同和通信。

● Exercises

I. Translate the following into English：

1.本合同条款为当事人完整的合意内容，效力超越当事人缔约前所有关于本合同标的之建议（口头或书面）、协商、会谈与讨论。

2.如果买方不能按照条款11.3的约定满足卸载要求，买方需向卖方根据条款6.3确定的价格，在受载期到期后，以美元支付滞港费，相关滞港费需要列示在附件中。

3.买方需要支付本协议项下的装运费用，费用基数为每连续24个小时的晴天工作日，包括周六、周日或者节假日，装运能力为4万湿吨。

4.有两个航班可供他们选择。

5.这些广告旨在提高该公司在市场上的知名度。

6.该银行的负债超过其资产，技术上它已破产。

7.该产品的商标由甲方供给，如有法律纠纷，甲方应付全部责任。

8.卖方和中间人共同向买方提供一份协议副本，其中包括协议有效期。

9.请告知这一商品在贵地市场是否有销路（或适销）。

10.核对银行对账单和现金账户花了很长时间。

## II. Translate the following into Chinese：

1. The issuing bank shall be responsible for any consequences arising from its failure to follow this procedures.

2.We take pleasure in informing you that we have shipped today on m/v "Browick" 100 tons of the Product in pursuance of our S/C No.123.

3. ABC Company shall take the responsible alone of the company's operation as stipulated in Article 2.5 hereof.

4. Income can be reduced by holding off deliveries in the closing on weeks of the years.

5.A buyer with whom you will conclude such a transaction shall be required to sign the Contract as attached hereto.

6.The ship altered its course.

7.This bylaw shall apply to all presently existing and future shops， during the time his agreement is in effect.

8.The Purchaser shall not be entitled to any abatement in the purchasing price， if such assignment cannot be effected.

9.The reminder of the profit shall be divided between the Buyer and the Seller.

# Unit Eight/独家代理协议

## Sole Agency Agreement

This Agreement is entered into by and between the parties concerned on the basis of equality and mutual benefit to develop business on terms and conditions agreed upon as follows:

1.The Parties Concerned

Supplier: China National ××× Import and Export Corporation (hereinafter called Party A); Agent: ××× Company (hereinafter called Party B).

2.Commodity and Quantity

Party A hereby appoints Party B as its Sole Agent for the sales of···Party B shall undertake to achieve the sales of the aforesaid commodity not less than···in the duration of this Agreement.

3.Territory

In···only.

4.Confirmation of Orders

The quantities, prices and dates of shipment concerning the commodity stated in this Agreement shall be confirmed in each transaction, the particulars of which will be shown in Party A's S/C.

5.Payment

After confirmation of an order, Party B shall arrange to open a 100% L/C available by draft at sight in favour of Party A within the time stipulated in the relevant S/C. Party B shall also notify Party A immediately after the L/C is opened, so that Party A may make preparations for shipment.

6.Commission

A···percent (···%) commission on invoice value against each shipment will be remitted to Party B by party A after receipt of the payment.

7.Reports on Market Conditions

Party B shall have the obligation to forward once every three months to Party A detailed reports on current market conditions and on consumers, comments. For Party A's reference, Party B shall, from time to time, forward to Party A samples of similar commodity offered by other suppliers, together with their prices, sales position and advertising materials.

8.Advertising & Publicity Expenses

Party B shall bear all expenses for advertising and publicity within the aforementioned territory in the duration of this Agreement and submit to Party A all drafts and/or drawings intended for such purposes for prior approval.

9.Validity of Agreement

This Agreement, when duly signed by the parties concerned, shall remain in force for⋯ to be effective as from⋯ to⋯ If a renewal of this Agreement is desired, notice in writing should be given by either party one month prior to its expiry. Should one of the parties fail to comply with the terms and conditions of this Agreement, the other party is entitled to terminate this Agreement.

10.Arbitration

All disputes arising from the execution of this Agreement shall be settled through negotiation between both parties. In the event that no settlement can be reached, the case in dispute shall then be submitted for arbitration to the China International Economic and Trade Arbitration Commission, Beijing, China, in accordance with its Rules of Procedure of Arbitration. The decision made by this Commission shall be regarded as final and is binding on both parties.

11.Other Terms & Conditions

1）Party A shall not supply the contracted commodity to other buyers in the above mentioned territory. Direct enquiries, if any, will be referred to Party B. However, should any other buyers insist on dealing direct with Party A, Party A shall have the right to do so. In the latter case, Party A shall send to Party B a copy of relevant S/C and reserve ⋯per cent （⋯%） commission for Party B on the net invoice value of the transaction concluded.

2）Should Party B fail to send their orders to Party A for a minimum of⋯ for a period of⋯ months, Party A shall not be bound to this Agreement.

3）For any business transacted between governments of both Parties, Party A shall have full right to handle such direct dealings as authorized by Party A's government without binding themselves to this Agreement. Party B shall not interfere with such direct dealings, nor shall Party B bring forward any demand for compensation or commission thereof.

4）Other terms and conditions shall be subject to those specified in the S/C signed by both parties.

This Agreement is made out in quadruplicate, each party holding two copies.

Party A （Supplier）　　　　　　Party B （Agent）

## 参考译文：

### 独家代理协议

有关双方在平等互利发展贸易的基础上签订本协议并达成条款如下：

1.有关当事人

供货人：中国××进出口公司（以下简称甲方）

代理人：××公司（以下简称乙方）

2.商品及数量

甲方委任乙方为某商品的独家销售代理人。乙方保证在协议期间推销上述商品不少于……销售额。

3.地区

以……地区为限。

4.订单的确认

协议商品的有关数量、价格和装船期，应在逐笔交易中确认，其细节详见甲方销货确认书。

5.付款

在订单确认后，乙方应于有关销货确认书规定的时间内，安排开立以甲方为受益人的百分之百金额的即期信用证，并于开证后立即通知甲方，以便甲方准备装运。

6.佣金

甲方于收妥货款后，按每批货物发票价值的百分之……向乙方汇付佣金。

7.市场情况报告

乙方有义务每3个月向甲方寄送一次详细的报告，反映当地的市场情况和消费者意见。乙方还应随时将其他供货人所报同样商品的样品，连同价格、销售情况、广告资料等寄给甲方参考。

8.广告宣传费用

乙方应负担协议期间在上述地区的一切广告宣传费用。所有用作广告宣传的草稿和绘图必须送交甲方取得事前同意。

9.协议有效期

本协议经有关双方签字后保持有效……年，从某日期起到某日期止。如果一方需要延长协议，必须在满期前一个月书面通知另一方。如果一方未能履行协议条款，另一方有权终止本协议。

10.仲裁

凡执行此协议引起的一切争议，应通过双方协商解决。如解决不了，应提交北京中国国际经济贸易仲裁委员会，按其仲裁规则进行仲裁。该委员会的裁决是终局的，并约束双方。

11.其他条款

1）甲方不应向上述地区的其他客户供应协议商品。如有任何直接询盘，均要转介乙方。但是，如有任何客户坚持要与甲方直接交易，甲方有权直接成交。在后一情况下，甲方应送给乙方销货确认书副本一份，并按该笔交易发票净值的百分之……为乙方保留佣金。

2）如果乙方未能在……月内向甲方寄送至少……数量或金额的订单，则甲方不再受本协议的约束。

3）对于双方政府间的交易，甲方有权按其政府授权直接成交而不受本协议的约束。乙方不应干涉这种直接交易，也不应对此提出索赔或佣金的要求。

4）其他条款应以双方签订的销货确认书为准。

本协议共写成一式四份，每方各执两份。

甲方（供货人）　　　　　乙方（代理人）

## Notes

1. abide vi. abide by 遵守，服从；vt.与 can 连用，表示忍受

We assure you that we will abide by all the rules and regulations.

我们向你们保证我们将遵守所有的规章制度。

We cannot abide your breach of contract.

我们不能容忍你方违约。

2. aforesaid adj. 上述的

也可用 aforementioned，与 above-mentioned 和 above-said 同义。 aforesaid 或 aforementioned 是法律用语。

The restriction provided for in this paragraph shall apply only to the customers named in the aforesaid list.

本节所得的限制仅适用于列入上述名单中的那些客户。

AAA hereby grants to ZZZ a license under the Letters Patent aforesaid.

根据上述专利证书规定，甲方特向乙方颁布一许可证。

3. 在合同的翻译中要特别留意下面的一些句式：

（1）no more …than…的含义是"同……一样不……"

not more…than…的意思是"不比（或不如）……（更）"，专用于指前者不如后者的场合。

He is no more able to read Spanish than I am.

他和我一样，都不懂西班牙文。

He is not more able to read Spanish than I am.

他的西班牙文没有我懂得多。

（2）no more than 只不过，不到

We had walked no more than three li when the rain came pouring down.

我们走了不到三里路就下大雨了。

John is no more than a traffic cop.

约翰只不过是个交通警察而已。

（3）more than…can 这种句型形式上是肯定，实际上有否定含义

The beauty of the place is more than I can describe.

那地方美得无法形容。

This is more than I can tell.

这我简直不懂。

He has bitten off more than he can chew.

他承担了力所不及的事。

（4）as many …as…； as much …as 这两个词组中均可加名词，用来表示数量或其他

We need as many records as possible.

I find I haven't got as much money as I thought.

（5）no less…than… 在含义上相当于 as well as 。它所强调的对象是 no less 之后的事物，而不是 than 之后的人物

Anita is no less an actress than a singer.

Anita is an actress as well as a singer.

Anita is not only a singer but also an actress.

以上三个句子都译成"安妮塔不但是个歌唱家，而且也是个演员"。

（6）no less…than 和 as…as 都作为 "和……一样" 解

She is no less beautiful than her sister.= She is as beautiful as her sister.

她长得并不比她的妹妹差。

Mr.Lee is no less enthusiastic and active than he used to be.

李先生还是和以前一样热情和积极。

（7）如果把 no less than 连在一起使用，其意为："不少于"或"竟有……之多"，相当于 as many as

By 1880，there were no less than fifty-six coal mines in England.

到了1880年，英国的煤矿已有56个之多。

No less than 150 people were injured or killed in the crash.

在此次空难中，至少有150人伤亡。

（8）not less than… 不低于，至少

The Insuring Party shall insure the Contractor's Equipment for not less than the full replacement value，including delivery of Site.

应投保方对承包商设备投保，保险额不低于全部重置价值，包括运至现场的费用。

4. dispute n.争议，争执；vi.争论，争议；vt.争议，辩论

trade dispute 贸易纠纷，劳资纠纷，行业纠纷

in/under dispute 在争议中的

Either of the parties in dispute may authorize the Maritime Arbitration Commission to choose for him an arbitration.

争议当事人的任何一方都可以委托海事仲裁委员会选定仲裁员。

All disputes arising from the execution of, or in connection with this contract shall be settled amicably through friendly negotiation.

凡因执行本合同或与本合同有关的一切争议，应通过友好协商解决。

The disputing parties shall choose the arbitrators within the time fixed by the Maritime Arbitration Commission or agreed upon between the parties.

争议当事人应在海事仲裁委员会规定的期限内，或在双方议定的期限内选定仲裁员。

The committee disputed whether the firm is entitled to the credit.

委员会对该公司是否有资格获得信贷进行了辩论。

5. agreement

辨析 agreement 与 contract

agreement 协议，contract 合同

（1）协议往往着眼于宏观，重在把原则性问题作出规定，涉及的标的比较广泛，内容和条款则不很具体，书写格式也较为灵活多样；协议的重要性不等，可以指普通的非正式协议，也可指国与国之间的正式协定。

（2）合同多致力于微观，重在把具体问题作出明确详细的规定，往往是一个标的签订一个合同，书写格式也多基本相似，有的甚至可以格式化；协议多数是见诸文字并且受法律保障的正式契约。

（3）在实际经贸业务中，双方对某一项目往往是先达成的原则性问题订立一个协议，然后据以签订一个或多个合同，以全面确定具体执行的细节，并说明合同是根据协议签订，或者协议是合同的组成部分。

● Exercises

Ⅰ.Make sentences with the following words and expressions：

| | |
|---|---|
| appoint sb. | give assistance to sb. |
| above-mentioned | for sale |
| exclusive agent | on sale |
| push the sales of sth. | draw up |
| to the contrary | on the contrary |
| act as | specialize in |
| at the get-acquainted stage | take sth into consideration |
| try out | annual turnover |
| valid | null and void |

**II .Put in the missing words：**

1.We are offering a general agency_____our textiles in Canada.How about you?

2.For the area…we are looking for a young man to act_____our representative.

3. I am well acquainted_____ local conditions and have excellent business connections.

4.We are seeking a reliable representative who would undertake to buy_____us _____commission.

5.We should be glad to know_____what terms you would be willing to represent us，also the terms_____which business is generally conducted in your country.

6.We are very happy to appoint you_____our representative.

7. We would like to discuss the duration of the contract with you_____ the interview.

8. The salary as agreed_____ the contract will be transferred monthly to the representative's account.

9.We are already represented by our_____agent in your city for the_____of our Enamelware.

10.We believe that through_____efforts business can be_____to our mutual _____.

**III .Make corrections of the following inappropriate words and expressions：**

1.When opportunity matures，we will consider to entrust you as our exclusive agent for the U.K.

2.The trial period for agency seems fairly too long for us.

3.In consideration of your extensive experience in the fields，we are glad to point you as our agent.

4.I，who is the pioneer in introducing the new product of yours into this market， should be entitled to being appointed as your agent.

5.It was two years ago when we entrusted them as our sole agents.

6.We shall be glad to offer you a sloe agent for the sale of our products in New York.

7. The agreement automatically comes into force again at expiration for a similar period unless notice is given to the contrary.

8.Please advise us of if you are interested in representing us and whether you consider the volume of business you can obtain would warrant as us granting you a sole agency.

9.We shall pay you a commission of 5% for the net value for all sales against orders received through you，which would be added a delcredere commission of 2.5%.

10. After we have agreed to all terms and conditions can we start to prepare the contract.

Ⅳ.Translate the following into English：

1.我们愿意担任你们现行出口商品的代理，因为我们拥有一个广阔的国内市场。

2.我们深信，担任你们海外贸易的进口代理，能起重要作用。

3.代理问题尚在考虑中，希望在现阶段继续努力推销我们的产品。

4.我们认为讨论代理问题的时机还未成熟。

5.我们已委托ABC公司为你地区的代理。

6.得知你方推销瓷器很有经验，非常荣幸能和你们打交道。

7.对你们想担任独家代理的请求，我们正在仔细考虑。同时，我们很想了解你方推销我们产品的计划。

8.在产品的广告方面我们尽了很大努力，营业额仍不能令人满意。

9.我们所有做这类商品的代理都只拿5%的佣金。

10.如果情况令双方满意，协议有效期可以延长。

Ⅴ.Translate the following letter into English：

我们仔细研究了你方9月10日函，现愿与你方进一步商谈你方要求在苏格兰建立代理处的建议。你方为詹姆士·内尔公司工作的情况，我们不了解，但鉴于你方在苏格兰的贸易关系，我们认为你方在该地发展我们的业务是可以大有作为的。

我们的最后决定取决于条款是否合适。因你公司史密斯先生将于下月访问我地，我们愿与史密斯先生面谈而不愿进行旷日持久的通信往来。为此，请告知史密斯先生何时来面谈。

# Unit Nine /雇佣合同

## Employment Contract

## 9.1　雇佣合同（1）Employment Contract（1）

The Foreign Languages Department of the AA University, Canberra, Australia（the engaging party） has engaged Professor Li Ming（the engaged party） as a teacher of the Chinese classics. The two parties, in the spirit of friendship and cooperation, hereby sign this Contract subject to the following terms and conditions：

1.The term of service is one year beginning on September 1, 2018 and ending on August 31,2019.

2.The work of the engaged party is decided through mutual consultation as follows：

1） Training teachers of Chinese, research students and students having advanced studies；

2） Conducting Chinese classical literature for senior and advising students on extracurricular activities of Chinese；

3） Compiling Chinese textbooks and supplementary teaching material；

4） Having 8 to 10 teaching periods a week.

3.The engaged party works five days a week and seven hours a day. The engaged party will have legal holidays as prescribed by both Chinese and Australian Governments. The winter vacation is fixed by the school calender.

4.The engaging party pays the engaged party a monthly salary of 2 000 Australian dollars and provides him with various benefits as prescribed by Australian Government for foreign teachers working in Australia.

5. The engaged party shall abide by the laws and regulations of the Australian Government concerning residence, wages and benefits, and travel for foreigners when entering, leaving and passing through the territory of the country, and shall follow the working system of the engaging party.

6.Neither party shall cancel the Contract without reasonable causes.If the engaging party finds it imperative to terminate the Contract, then, in addition to bearing the above-mentioned wages and benefits，it shall pay the engaged party three months' extra salary as compensation allowance，and arrange at its own cost for him and his family to go back to their country within one month.

If the engaged party submits his resignation in the course of his service，the engaging party shall stop paying him salary from the date when his resignation is approved by the engaging party，and the engaged party will no longer enjoy the benefits. When leaving Australia，the engaged party and his family will have to pay for everything by themselves.

7.This Contract comes into effect on the first day of the engaged party's arrival at the AA University and ceases to be effective at its expiration.If either party wishes to renew the Contract，the other party shall be notified in writing one month before it expires. Upon agreement by both parties through consultation，a new contract may be signed between two parties.

8.This Contract is made in English and Chinese，both versions being equally valid.

The engaging party                    The engaged party

Signed at Guangzhou，China on August 10，2018

**参考译文：**

### 聘请合同（1）

澳大利亚堪培拉AA大学外语系（聘方）聘请李明教授（受聘方）为中国古典文学教师。双方本着友好合作的精神特签订本合同，其条款如下：

1.聘期为1年，自2018年9月1日起，至2019年8月31日止。

2.受聘方的工作任务，经双方协商确定为：

1）担任汉语教师、研究生和进修生的培训工作；

2）担任高年级中国古典文学教学，指导学生开展汉语课外活动；

3）编写汉语教材和补充读物；

4）每周授课8~10课时。

3.受聘方的工作时间每周5天，每天7小时。受聘方按照中国、澳大利亚两国政府规定的节假日放假，寒假按本校校历规定。

4.聘方每月支付给受聘方工资2,000澳元，并按照澳大利亚政府对在澳工作的外籍教师的规定提供各种福利待遇。

5.受聘方在入境、离境或过境时，必须遵守澳大利亚政府有关外国人居住、工资福利及旅行等的法律、规章，并遵守聘方的工作制度。

6.双方均不得无故撤销合同。如果聘方要求中途终止合同，除按上述条款承担工资福利待遇外，须给受聘方增发3个月的工资作为补偿金，并于1个月内安排受聘方及其家属回国并承担有关费用。

如果受聘方中途提出辞职，聘方自同意之日起即停发工资；受聘方不再享受各项福利待遇；受聘方及其家属回国的一切费用均由本人自理。

7.本合同自受聘方到校之日起生效，到聘期届满时失效。如一方要求延长聘期，必须在合同期满前1个月用书面向对方提出，经双方协商同意后另签延聘合同。

8.本合同用中英两种文字写成，两种文本具有同等效力。

聘方： 受聘方：

签字地：中国广州 日期：2018年8月10日

## 9.2　　雇佣合同（2）Employment Contract（2）

We hereby offer you a contract of employment with ABCD （the "Company"）subject to the terms and conditions set out in this Employment Contract.

EMPLOYMENT CONDITIONS

PREREQUISITE　This contract is only valid upon the outcome of a satisfactory result of medical checkup on you as directed by the Company.

JOB TITLE　The Company shall employ you and you shall be employed by us as Commercial Manager.

WORKING HOURS　Your normal working hours is between：

［Monday—Friday（9：00—17：00）］ except public holidays.

However, you might be required to work overtime if necessary for the proper discharge of your duties according to the reasonable requirement of the Company.

COMMENCEMENT DATE　20 Apr., 2018.

SALARY Your salary will be USD 3 000 per month payable in arrears normally on the 5th of every calendar month.

PROBATIONARY PERIOD　The first 6 months of your employment will be treated as probationary period. The employment may be terminated during such probationary period by you or the Company according to the Labour Laws of Singapore.

A. IT IS AGREED THAT THROUGHOUT YOUR EMPLOYMENT WITH THE COMPANY：

a.You shall abide by the Company's rules and regulations in force from time to time.

b. You shall not engage or be interested or concerned in any other business or commercial activity that will affect your work at the Company, damage the image of the Company, or create a conflict of interest with the Company, either on a paid or unpaid basis without the Company's prior consent in writing.

c. You shall not do any matter which may violate the Company's proprietary interests.

d. You shall not contravene the laws or act in opposition to safeguard the Company's reputation.

e. You shall not solicit or receive any gift or benefits at any time from clients or persons having business relationship with the Company.

f. As for absence from work without notification, the Company shall reserve the right to take disciplinary action or even dismiss without compensation.

B.CONFIDENTIALITY

a. You are aware that in the course of employment under this Agreement, you shall have access to and be entrusted with information in respect of the business, financing and other data of the Company and its dealings transactions and affairs (and likewise in relation to the Company's parent company, subsidiaries and associated companies, suppliers, agents, distributors or customers) all of which information is or may be confidential.

b.You shall not during or at any time after the period of your employment under this Agreement divulge to any person whatsoever or otherwise make use of (and shall use your best endeavors to prevent the publication or disclosure of) any information of the Company or any of the Company's parent company, subsidiaries and associated companies, suppliers, agents, distributors or customers unless the information can be available in public domain.

c. You shall not cause or permit anything which may damage or endanger the Company's intellectual property or the Company's title to it or assist or allow others to do so during or at any time after the period of your employment under this Agreement.

C. OTHER TERMS

TERMINATION Your employment shall be terminated:

a.After probation by you provided that you should serve on the Company a 3 months' notice in writing or payment in lieu thereof; or

b.After probation by the Company provided that the Company should serve on you a 3 month's notice in writing or payment in lieu thereof; or

c.By the Company without notice or payment in lieu thereof in the event of serious misconduct or neglect of duty or serious breach of any rules or regulations made by the Company.

MEDICAL BENEFITS You are entitled to have medical benefits according to the Company's policy after successful completion of your probationary period.

ANNUAL LEAVE You are entitled to have 15 working days leave with pay upon completion of one full calendar month's service with the Company, the timing of the leave thereof is to be mutually agreed between the Company and the employee. No annual leave can be accumulated, unless otherwise approved by the Company in writing in advance.

COMPENSATION & BENEFIT You are entitled to the mandatory retirement scheme according to the laws of Singapore.

END OF YEAR BONUS End of year payment including double pay, i. e. the thirteenth month salary, if any, will depend on both the Company's business result and your individual performance and is at total discretion of the Company.

If you agree to the above terms and conditions，please sign and return the duplicate copy of this Employment Contract to us on or before 31st May，2018.

For and on Behalf of                    Confirmed & Signed by：

ABCD
_____                        _____
Andrew                                 [ Name ]
Head of Human Resources                ID / Passport No.　[　]

**参考译文：**

我方特雇用您为我 ABCD 公司雇员，相关协议如下。

雇佣条件

先决条件　本合同生效的前提条件为您医疗检查的结果符合公司的要求。

工作岗位　公司雇用您的工作岗位为商务经理。

工作时间　您的日常工作时间为周一到周五，上午9点到下午5点，公众假期除外。根据公司的合理要求，为了完成您的工作，您也许会在额外时间加班工作。

聘用日期　2018年4月20日

月薪　　　您的月薪为3 000美元，将在第二个月的5日为您支付上个月的工资。

试用期　　前6个月为您的试用期。在试用期内，根据新加坡法律的规定，您和公司都可以随时解除雇佣协议。

1.在雇佣期内，您需要遵守以下规定

（1）您应该时刻遵守公司规章制度。

（2）在没有公司书面同意的情况下，不论是否取得报酬，您不得从事任何对公司有影响的商业活动，破坏公司形象，损害公司利益。

（3）您的任何活动不得侵害公司的所有权益。

（4）您的行为不得违反法律规定，不得作出有损于公司声誉的事情。

（5）您不得从与公司有业务往来的企业收取任何礼品或者好处。

（6）如果您未经请示擅自离岗，公司有权在不承担任何赔偿责任的前提下对您进行处分甚至解雇。

2.保密

（1）在工作过程中，您应该知晓您会接触到公司的保密信息，包括商业信息、财务信息和公司的相关交易信息（比如针对母公司、子公司和关联公司、供应商、代理商、分销商或者客户的交易）。

（2）在工作过程中，除非可以从公共领域获取的信息，您不得泄露或者使用任何本公司或者本公司的母公司、子公司和关联公司、供应商、代理商、分销商或者客户的任何信息，并应该尽力阻止信息的泄漏。

（3）在工作过程中，您不能作出任何对公司知识产权侵权的行为，亦不可协助他们或者允许他人在本合同失效后作出对公司不利的行为。

3.其他条款

合同终止　　您的雇佣协议在以下情况下会被终止：

（1）试用期后，如果您决定辞职，请提前3个月通知公司，否则需要支付3个月的工资作为补偿；或者

（2）试用期后，如果公司决定解雇您，公司会提前3个月通知您，否则需要支付3个月的工资作为补偿；或者

（3）如果由于您的玩忽职守、重大过失、没有履行员工义务或者严重违背公司管理规定，公司不需要提前通知，也不需要支付任何补偿金。

医疗福利年休假　　在试用期结束之后，您将享有公司的医疗福利政策。

在您签约的1个月后，您就开始享有15天的带薪休假，休假的时间由您和公司共同确定。请注意，除非经过公司的批准，否则您的年休假天数不能跨年累计。

补偿和权利年度奖金　　您有权利享受新加坡法律规定的强制退休计划。在年底，依据您的个人绩效和公司的运行情况，

公司将决定是否支付年度奖金，比如13个月的工资。

如果您同意以上条款，请您签署两份协议，并在2018年5月31日前送还我公司。

代表ABCD公司　　　　　　　签字

安德鲁　　　　　　　　　　　姓名

人力资源总监　　　　　　　　身份证/护照号码

## 9.3　　实习协议 Internship Agreement

Article 1 Purpose of the Agreement

This Agreement governs the host organization's relationship and the intern.

Article 2 Objective of Internship

The internship is a temporary period of work in a professional environment, where the student will acquire professional skills and put into practice the knowledge gained from his education in view of earning a diploma or certificate, and facilitating his professional integration. The intern will be given one or more tasks, in conformance with the educational plan established by the educational institution and approved by the host organization.

The educational institution and the host organization will establish the schedule based on the general training program being offered.

Article 3 Terms of Internship

The weekly duration of the intern's presence at the host organization will be…hours, on a full time / part time basis（*cross out the inappropriate item*）

If the intern's presence at the host organization is to be required at night， or on Sunday or during a public holiday， specify the specific cases：

Article 4 Intern Hosting and Supervision

The intern will be supervised by his academic advisor， as designated in this agreement， as well as by the institution's internship program office.

The intern shall be permitted to return to his educational institution during the internship period in order to take the courses specifically required by the program， or to attend meetings； the institution shall notify the host organization of the corresponding dates.

Article 5 Stipend – Benefits

The organization may decide to pay a stipend for interns.

In case of a suspension or termination of this agreement， the amount of the stipend due to the intern shall be prorated based on the duration of the internship conducted.

Internship durations qualifying for the payment of a stipend are determined in consideration of this agreement and any amendments thereto， as well as the number of days of the intern's physical presence within the organization.

THE AMOUNT OF THE STIPEND is set at RMB⋯ per hour / day / month.

Article 6 Social Welfare Coverage

For the duration of his internship， the intern shall remain covered under his previous former social welfare protection framework.

Article 7 Discipline

The intern shall be subject to the applicable internal disciplinary and regulatory terms， of which he shall be made aware prior to the start of the internship， particularly in regard to schedules and to the health and safety regulations in effect at the host organization.

In case of a particularly serious breach of discipline， the host organization reserves the right to terminate the internship， while respecting the provisions set forth in article 8 of this agreement.

Article 8 Leave – Internship Interruption

Time off or of absence are possible for internships lasting more than 2 months but less than 6 months.

The host organization shall notify the educational institution of any other temporary interruption of the internship（illness， unjustified absence， etc.）by mail.

Notice of any interruption of the internship shall be provided to the other parties to the agreement and the academic advisor.

A postponement of the internship end date is possible， if approved by the parties to the agreement, so as to permit the full duration of the internship as originally planned. This postponement will be the subject of an amendment to the internship agreement.

If any of the three parties (host organization, intern, educational institution) wish to put an end to the internship, such party must immediately inform the other two parties in writing. The reasons given will be examined in close consultation. The definitive decision to terminate the internship shall be made at the end of this consultation phase.

Article 9 End of Internship – Report – Evaluation

1) Internship certificate: at the end of the internship, the host organization shall issue a certificate, indicating as a minimum the effective duration of the internship, and, if applicable, the amount of the stipend paid.

2) Internship quality: Once the internship has ended, the parties to this agreement are invited to submit an assessment of the quality of the internship. The intern will send a document to the appropriate department of the educational institution in which he will evaluate the quality of the reception he was given by the host organization. This document will not be taken into consideration in his evaluation, or in awarding his diploma or certificate.

3) Evaluation of the intern's activity: Once the internship has ended, the host organization shall fill out an assessment form on the intern's activity, which it will return to the academic advisor.

Article 10 Applicable Law – Competent Courts

This agreement shall be governed exclusively by ××× law. Any disputes that cannot be amicably resolved shall be subject to the jurisdiction of the competent ××× courts.

**参考译文：**

条款1　本协议的目的

本协议用于管理实习生和实习机构。

条款2　实习的目标

实习为一项在专业领域临时性的工作，为了撰写学术论文或者获取相关证书，增强专业水平，学生将会获取专业的技能并将所学知识用于工作实践。基于教育机构和实习机构达成的实习计划，实习生将会授予一项或者多项工作任务。

教育机构和实习机构会针对培训要求设计实习计划。

条款3　实习期限

实习时间为每周××小时，全职或者兼职（划掉不适合的项）

如果实习时间需要在晚间，或者周日或者公共假期，则具体要求为：

条款4　实习生的托管和监管

实习生将由在本协议中指定的学术导师和实习机构的实习项目办公室共同监管。

在实习期内，如果为了实习项目需要返回教育机构进行学习或者参加会议，实习生可以离岗。教育机构需要通知实习机构相应的离岗时间。

条款5　实习报酬

实习机构将会对实习生支付实习报酬。

如果本协议暂停或者终止执行，基于实际的实习期限，实习报酬将进行同比例的调整。

实习生实习报酬的支付取决于本协议及补充协议中列明的要求，和实习生在实习机构的时间。

实习报酬为每月/每日/每小时×××人民币。

条款6　社会保险覆盖

在实习期内，实习生的社会保险仍旧由原有社会保险覆盖。

条款7　实习纪律

实习生应在实习期前学习实习机构内部的纪律和管理规定，尤其是实习计划和关于健康和安全的要求，并在实习期内严格遵守。

如果违反了相应的纪律要求，依据本协议条款8的约定，实习机构保留终止实习协议的权利。

条款8　离岗-实习终止

在实习期内，临时离岗时间可以在2个月以上，但是不能超过6个月。

实习机构将会通过邮件通知教育机构任何实习期的临时中止（因为疾病，缺席等）。

依据本协议的规定，任何实习期的中止通知需要由协议一方提供给其他方和学术导师。

实习终止日期的延期是可行的。如果协议相关方同意延期，整个实习期将进行相应的顺延。实习期的延期将通过实习协议补充协议的方式重新约定。

如果三方（实习机构、实习生、教育机构）中的任何一方想要终止此协议，一方应立即书面通知其他两方。终止原因将由其他两方进行密切磋商。在磋商期结束时，最终决议将提供给提出终止的一方。

条款9　实习结束-报告-评估

1）实习证明：在实习期结束时，实习机构将会签发实习证明，证明中将明确有效的实习期限和实习报酬（如果要求的话）。

2）实习质量：在实习期结束时，本协议的相关方将对实习质量提交评估报告。实习生将向相关教育机构的负责部门提交书面文件，文件中需对实际机构的接待质量进行评价。本文件对实习期内的评估、获取学位或实习证明不做任何影响。

3）实习行为的评价：在实习期结束时，实习机构将填写实习工作的评估表，并将该表格反馈给学术导师。

条款10　适用法律-法院

本协议受×××法律管辖。任何争议如果无法通过友好协商解决，可上诉×××法院。

## 9.4　不支付报酬的实习协议 Unpaid Internship Agreement

In exchange for the opportunity to study ××× activities from with the _____ ［Agency］ _____ organization：

I agree to comply with the office routines of the business and follow any reasonable instructions that I may be given.

I understand that my status at the agency is not that of an employee and I do not expect any compensation in connection with my activities at the agency.

I will hold ［Agency］ and its employees blameless for any personal injury that I might experience during the period I choose to be an unpaid intern at their office.

I agree that I will advise the agency of，and may decline to participate in，any undertaking for which I am not confident or qualified to perform the activity requested.

I acknowledge and accept responsibility for my own acts and will hold ［Agency］ blameless should my conduct lead to the physical injury or property damage of others.

I understand that I will be reimbursed for any personal funds I expend that benefit the agency during my internship.

I understand that I may be asked to perform useful activities in the office area，but that I will not be used as an unpaid laborer to perform the work routines ordinarily performed by paid staff.

I understand that my status as an unpaid intern may be maintained only for so long as 6 Months for my activities at the agency，and I will advise the agency if this status changes.

INTERN'S SIGNATURE _____ DATE

AGENCY'S REPRESENTIVE _____ DATE

**参考译文：**

为了获取在XX机构进行学习XX的机会，我同意遵守公司办公室管理规定和其他的公司要求。

我知晓自己作为非正式员工，不会获得其他任何报酬补偿。

如在实习期间受到人身伤害，我个人将承担全部责任，公司及公司其他员工将免责。

如果在实习期间，我自己不能胜任相关工作，我将及时告知公司，不再参与相关工作。

我确认且为自己的所有行为承担责任，如果我的过失造成其他人员伤害或者财产损失，则公司将对我的行为进行免责。

我知晓在实习期间个人为公司支付的相关费用将会获得报销。

我知晓我可能会在办公区域进行相关活动，但作为非正式员工，我不会从事正式职员的日常工作。

我知晓我的实习期最长为6个月，如果发生任何变化，我将及时通知贵公司。

实习生签字 日期

实习机构代表签字 日期

# Notes

1.engage vt. 雇用，聘请；保证，约定（接不定式或 that 从句）；吸引（注意力）。vi. 从事于（与 in 连用）

The Managing Director is worried about an employer - employee dispute and has decided to engage a lawyer to argue the case in court.

常务董事（总经理）正为劳资纠纷而忧虑，已决定聘请一位律师上法庭辩论。

We hereby engage with the drawers, endorsers and bona fide holders of draft （s） drawn under and in compliance with the terms of the Credit that such draft （s） shall be honoured on due presentation and delivery of documents as specified.

本行兹向根据本信用证及符合本信用证条款所开立的汇票的出票人、背书人及合法持有人保证，一旦提交规定的有关单据，本行即如期支付汇票。

The company has engaged itself to finish the building by May.

该公司曾经约定到5月份建好大楼。

Your proposal of making a personal visit here to smooth the way for our future cooperation has engaged our particular attention.

你提出亲自前来访问为将来合作铺平道路的建议引起我们特别的注意。

We engage in construction business in China.

我们在中国从事建筑业。

engagement n.聘请，聘任期；约会；契约；债务（复数）

An agreement for engagement of legal adviser was signed by and between our company and International Economic and Trade Law Office.

我们公司与国际经济贸易律师事务所签订了聘请法律顾问的协议。

The engagement of the managing director has been terminated.

这位总经理（常务董事）聘任期已满。

The two parties entered into a binding engagement for employment of 10 skilled workers.

双方订立了一份雇用10名技术工人的契约。

They found difficulty in meeting their engagements （obligations）.

他们在偿还债务上发现困难。

2.service n.服务，贡献；行政部门、服务机构及其全体人员的总称；（商品售后的）保养、维修，（饭店、旅馆等的）服务情况；劳务（复数）。vt.保养维修，提供服务。adj.服务的

His services to the country are immense.

他对国家的贡献是非常大的。

The job of the Fire Service is to put out fires.

消防局的任务是灭火。

Please send your car in for service every 3,000 kilometres.

每行驶3 000公里，请把你的汽车送厂检修。

The food is good at this hotel, but the service is poor.

这家饭店的菜饭很好，但服务情况很差。

The value of a country's goods and services is its GNP（gross national product）.

一国的全部产品和劳务的总价值就是该国的国民生产总值。

Three transportation lines will service the fair.

三条交通线将为交易会提供服务。

Here is an all-night service store.

这里是一家通宵服务商店。

| | |
|---|---|
| service charge（fee） | 服务费 |
| service center | 服务中心 |
| service cost | 劳务成本 |
| service desk | 服务台 |
| service firm | 服务性企业 |
| service man | 服务员 |

3. consultation n. 协商，商量，磋商，（专家等的）会议

to hold a consultation to make decision

举行会议以便作出决策

consult vi. 商量，商议，磋商，协商

vt. 请教，咨询

We have to consult with our manufacturers about/on this point.

这一点我方须与厂方商量。

You may consult your lawyer on the details.

你可请教你的律师有关细节。

consultancy n. 咨询业务，咨询服务

consultancy service 咨询部门，咨询服务

consultancy expert 咨询专家

4. extracurricular activities of Chinese 汉语课外活动

5. supplementary teaching material 补充读物

6. law

（1）用作可数名词，指某项或各项法律，与动词搭配

draft a law　　　　　　　　　　　　起草法律

| pass/adopt a law | 通过法律 |
|---|---|
| promulgate a law | 颁布法律 |
| enact/formulate/institute/make a law | 制定法律 |
| observe/obey/abide by a law | 守法 |
| break/violate/flout a law | 犯法 |
| execute/enforce/administer/apply a law | 执行法律 |
| annul/repeat/revoke a law | 取消（废止）法律 |

We must study the laws relating to foreign trade.

我们必须学习有关外贸的各项法律。

（2）用作不可数名词，表示法律通称或整体，其前常加定冠词；但表示法律学科或某类法律时，则不加定冠词。

| business law | 商业法 |
|---|---|
| constitutional law | 宪法 |
| corporate law | 合伙法 |
| trademark law | 商标法 |
| labour law | 劳动法 |
| maritime law | 海事法 |
| audit law | 审计法 |
| insolvent law | 破产法 |

He is an authority on the subject of international economic and trade law.

他是国际经济贸易法律的权威。

辨析：law，constitution，decree，rule，regulation

law（法律）是法律的通称和总体。

constitution（宪法）：是国家的根本大法，居于各种法律的最高地位，具有最高效力，是普通法的立法基础，普通法不得在精神上与条款上违反根本法，否则无效。宪法通常由制宪会议、宪法起草委员会制定并以特定多数通过为有效，有的还要通过全民讨论或表决。

decree（法令）泛指法律、命令、条例等；通常以条例、决定等形式出现，其效力仅次于law（法律）的规范性文件。

rule（条例）是法律形式的一种，是国家机关发布的单行法规。在我国，条例可由人大常务委员会、国务院及所属各部委以及地方国家机关制定。

regulation（规则）是国家机关、社会团体、企事业单位对某一事项制定的规章和准则。国家机关颁行的规则具有法律的性质。

Great Britain has an unwritten constitution; the United States has a written constitution.

英国的宪法是不成文法；美国的宪法是成文法。

We demand that carriers be sent to all the departments to notify them of the decrees that you proclaim here.

我们要求派人到一切部门去传达你们在这里公布的各项指令。

International Rules for the Interpretation of Trade Terms

国际贸易术语解释通则

rules relating to bills of exchange

有关汇票的法则

The present Rules shall come into force from the date of its adoption by the China Council for the Promotion of International Trade.

本规则自中国国际贸易促进委员会通过之日起施行。

AAA agrees to abide by all regulations and bylaws governing the association.

甲方同意遵守一切管理该协会的规章和条例。

The Contractor agrees to comply with the regulations, rulings and interpretations of the Labor Department of the Government.

承包商同意遵守政府劳动部的各种规章、规定和解释。

7. in arrears 拖欠

He was two weeks in arrears with the rent.

他已拖欠了两个星期的房租。

I'm in arrears with the homework.

我的作业还拖欠着呢。

In this aspect, we are very much in arrear (s) of Europe.

在这方面，我们远远落后于欧洲。

They were in arrears with their mortgage, so their home was repossessed.

他们未按时还按揭贷款，所以房子被收回了。

8.violate v.侵犯；违反

breach n. v.违反

The company was accused of breach of contract.

这家公司被控违约。

TEP may terminate this Agreement at any time if you violate its terms.

如果您违反了协议的条款，TEP 公司可随时终止本协议。

9.contravene v.违反；相抵触；否定

The content of the settlement agreement shall not contravene the law.

调解协议的内容不得违反法律规定。

All those that may contravene WTO rules or our commitments will be abrogated.

不合世界贸易组织规则和中国的承诺的要加以废除。

10.Your employment shall be terminated by the Company without notice or payment in lieu thereof in the event of serious misconduct or neglect of duty or serious breach of any rules or regulations made by the Company.

如果由于您的玩忽职守、重大过失、没有履行员工义务或者严重违背公司管理规定，公司不需要提前通知，也不需要支付任何补偿金。

11.presence n. 到场，出席

This Agreement has been signed by both parties in the presence of AAA.

本协议已在甲方出席的情况下由双方签署。

Should Buyer be unable to send its representatives in time for such scheduled tests, Seller may, at its option, carry out the tests without the presence of Buyer's representatives.

如果买方未能及时派出自己的代表参加这种规定的测试，则卖方可以在买方代表不到场的情况下自行进行调试。

12. stipend n.薪水；定期津贴

We offer a monthly stipend plus a travel allowance.

我们提供每月的薪水，外加旅游津贴。

13.undertaking n. 保证，许诺

He was required to give a written undertaking not to disclose the details of their contract.

他被要求出具书面保证不披露他们的合同的细节。

undertake vt.承担，答应，担保

ZZZ undertakes that it will not sublicense the rights to any other party.

乙方答应不得将许可证权转给任何他方。

The object of the company shall be to undertake manufacture, sale, export and import of the products.

公司的目标应该是承担产品的生产、销售和进出口业务。

14.property n.财产

| | |
|---|---|
| property insurance | 财产保险 |
| property dividend | 财产股利 |
| real property | 不动产 |
| community property | 夫妻共有财产 |

The Seller does sell and convey to the Buyer all the property and assets, both tangible and intangible.

卖方向买方出售和转交全部财产和资产，包括有形财产和无形财产。

The merchandise so delivered by the consignor shall be held and cared by the consignee as the property of the consignor.

收货人应把发货人发送的商品作为发货人的财产加以保管和保护。

15.routine n. 例行公事，常规，无聊；adj. 常规的，例行的，乏味的

We must introduce some system into our office routine.

我们须在日常公务中建立一些制度。

Routine office jobs have no relish at all for me.

我对坐办公室那种刻板的工作毫无兴趣。

## ●Exercises

I.Translate the following into English：

1.中国提出"平等互利、讲求实效、形式多样、共同发展"的四项原则，作为中国与第三世界进行经济和技术合作的指导方针。

2.关于劳务合作，我们愿意提供任何行业的工程师、技术工人，为任何工厂或矿物生产线进行工程建设、设备安装和技术指导。

3.劳务合作的方式包括草拟可行性研究、勘探、设计、建筑、设备安装和技术指导。

4.当前承包工程的世界市场很大，中国的劳务合作公司有着广阔的前景。

5.如果雇员死亡，雇主应负担其尸体保存和运送的费用。

6.如果工程师因公在国内出差，雇主应提供最好、最快的交通设施，并负担一切费用。

7.关于售后服务，在你方地区有我方代理……商行将为你服务，请放心。该行有熟练技术人员，能协助你方维修我方所供应的任何机器。

8.雇主应出钱为工程师安排医疗服务，必要时安排住院治疗。

9.如果本协议暂停或者终止执行，基于实际的实习期限，实习报酬将进行同比例的调整。

10.雇主应向雇员提供免费食宿。

II.Translate the following into Chinese：

1. In the event of termination for cause，Employer shall pay Employee's wages through the effective date of the termination and shall purchase a one-way ticket for the return of Employee to his/her point of hire.

2. In case of an emergency involving serious illness，accident or death of Employee，Employer shall notify Empolyee's next-of-kin immediately.

3. Chinese construction firms have qualified technical and managerial personnel. They are capable of undertaking a whole range of work，including design，research，consultancy and construction.

4.Our instrument is warranted against defective materials or workmanship for a period of one year from the date of its arrival at your warehouse.Their warranty does not hold good for any damage to the instrument caused by accident or improper use.

5. In the interest of our clients，we would train their technical staff at request.The training may be carried out in this city or at your end，depending upon specific conditions. The training courses include operation and maintenance of individual machines and also industrial administration of a shop up to a complete plant.

6. If any of the three parties（host organization， intern， educational institution）wish to put an end to the internship， such party must immediately inform the other two parties in writing. The reasons given will be examined in close consultation. The definitive decision to terminate the internship shall be made at the end of this consultation phase.

7. Party A shall pay the premium and effect Accident Insurance with …Insurance Co. for each engineer， assigning the engineer or his family member as the beneficiary， for the minimum amounts given below.

8. Party B's personnel shall abide by the laws and decrees prevailing in …（country），respect the local habits and customs and not partake in local political activities. The Employer shall respect the personnel's habits and personalities and not interfere in their activities in off-duty time.

9. Party B's personnel shall be on probation for 90 days. In case any of them is found incompetent， he will be repatriated to China.Party B shall replace him with a suitable person and pay tvavelling expenses for the replacement.

10. Party B's personnel shall be entitled to 20 days leave with pay after completing one year's service in …（country）.No such leave can be given to those who have served less than one year.

# Unit Ten /技术转让和设备材料进口合同

# Contract for Technology Transfer and Importation of Equipment and Materials

China Broadcasting Products Import & Export Corporation and Better Broadcasting Products Factory of Guangdong Province, People's Republic of China (hereinafter referred to as "SINO") as the first part, and Foreign Advance Broadcasting Ltd., Holland (hereinafter referred to as "INVESTOR") as the second part, and Good-Trade Trading Ltd, Italy (hereinafter referred to as "GTT") have entered into contract with the terms and conditions as follows:

### Article 1.Technology Transfer

1.SINO shall introduce the technology necessary to produce INVESTOR's A type and B type products in Guangzhou. These products are referred to as "PRODUCTS" hereinafter.

2.INVESTOR shall offer, at SINO's request in accordance with this Contract, the technology and information possessed by INVESTOR which are necessary to produce PRODUCTS.

3.Actual names and specifications of PRODUCTS are shown in Appendix 1.

4. INVESTOR shall offer SINO the information concerning trade secret, manufacturing technique and know-how which are necessary to produce PRODUCTS. Details of the information offered by INVESTOR to SINO are shown in Appendix 2.

### Article 2.Facilities Planning

1.SINO shall prepare the facilities for production of PRODUCTS in accordance with INVESTOR's suggestions.

2.In order to assist preparation for production facilities in Guangzhou, INVESTOR shall provide assistance including supply of the following data and information:

a.Plan for production line

b.Plan for production manpower arrangement

c.Plan for equipment layout

d.Plan for infrastructure, e.g.water supply, electricity, air-conditioning, transportation, communication

e.Plan for installation and operation of equipment

f.Plan for production management

g.Plan for market promotion.

Above data and information shall be offered to SINO by INVESTOR within 60 days after the effective date of this Contract.

3. Production line is subject to the production schedule attached to this Contract which is named as Appendix 3.

4.SINO shall prepare production planning by itself, but shall be able to request for INVESTOR's cooperation if deems to be necessary.

### Article 3.Payment of Royalty

1.The royalty concerning technology transfer from INVESTOR to SINO shall be as follows:

a. SINO shall pay INVESTOR US $ ···as initial payment for buying the production rights from INVESTOR.

b.SINO shall pay INVESTOR 3% of the sales price on each product sold.

2.All payments shall be made in accordance with this Contract and the Agreements relating to this clause.

3.All payments shall be made through Bank of China.

4.Method of payment shall be by Irrevocable Letter of Credit payable at sight, in U.S.currency.

5. SINO shall open an Irrevocable Letter of Credit for the above initial payment payable to INVESTOR, within one month after the effective date of this Contract.

6.Within 30 days after the arrival of the above Letter of Credit, INVESTOR shall supply all the technical data specified in this Contract.

7.When SINO places purchase orders with INVESTOR for the materials stipulated in this Contract, SINO shall add the royalty equivalent to 3% onto the amount of Letter of Credit, each time, or shall open a separate Letter of Credit equivalent to the royalty, at the same time of payment for purchase order.

8.SINO shall be responsible for the induced fees arising in China, and INVESTOR shall be responsible for such fees arising outside China.

### Article 4.Marketing

1.INVESTOR shall assist SINO concerning marketing of PRODUCTS produced by SINO, by means of trade show, seminar, advertisement, etc..However, expenses incurred shall be borne by SINO.

2. INVESTOR's logo shall be allowed for use in advertisement, etc., if SINO necessitates.However, INVESTOR shall not participate in SINO's profit or loss relating to

it，nor shall be responsible.

### Article 5.Quality Control

1.Quality of PRODUCTS finished in Guangzhou shall be judged in accordance with INVESTOR's quality control standards.

2.Quality check on the PRODUCTS produced in Guangzhou at the initial stage shall be carried out jointly by SINO's and INVESTOR's engineers. Details are shown in Appendix 4.

3. Quality check on the PRODUCTS shall be done twice，if needed. In case PRODUCT's quality does not meet the targeted specifications at the second inspection，and if causes are judged to be at INVESTOR's side，INVESTOR shall solve the problem at its own cost.

4. In case quality inspection of PRODUCTS is satisfactory，both SINO's and INVESTOR's engineers shall sign an inspection certificate in duplicate and each party shall keep one copy.

### Article 6.Delivery of Equipment

1. SINO shall purchase from INVESTOR the equipment necessary to produce the PRODUCTS.

2.Details of items and specifications of the equipment are shown in Appendix 5.

3.Details of prices of equipment which SINO shall purchase from INVESTOR，shall be determined between SINO and INVESTOR and contract（s）for equipment shall be signed separately.

4.Equipment delivered by INVESTOR shall be of latest type and brand new.

5.Settlement for the cost of the equipment delivered by INVESTOR to SINO shall be by Irrevocable Letter of Credit at sight，CIF a China port in US currency.

6.INVESTOR shall deliver equipment as per delivery schedules，in accordance with this Contract.

7.INVESTOR shall offer SINO the technical information concerning the equipment，as per stipulated by this Contract.

8.Official delivery dates of equipment shall be the dates on bills of lading.INVESTOR shall inform SINO of the bill of lading numbers，execution dates，packing list，arrival dates，etc. without delay. At the same time INVESTOR shall send duplicate of the documents on which above information is described.

9.In case equipment and technical information，which are requested in the Contract，are found missing，SINO shall be able to request INVESTOR for replacement.

10. INVESTOR shall deliver equipment by rigid packing to endure a long distance transportation.

11.INVESTOR's packing list for the deliveries shall bear the following:

a.Contract no.

b.Consignee's name

c.Destination

d.Shipping mark

e.Weight

f.Case numbers

g.Consignee mark

12.INVESTOR shall include duplicate of details of the content in the packing.

## Article 7.Acceptance of Equipment

1.SINO shall prepare facilities and place to receive the equipment delivered from INVESTOR and store it.

2.INVESTOR shall despatch engineers to SINO within three weeks after SINO's request for installation and testing of the equipment arrived.In this instance, SINO shall provide necessary assistance like interpreter, etc. for INVESTOR.

3.INVESTOR's engineers' stay at SINO, in this instance, shall be two (2) weeks.

4.Acceptance test of the delivered equipment shall be carried out by engineers from SINO and IINVESTOR as well as surveyor from China.Details are shown in Appendix 6.

5.In case initial test is unsatisfactory, a second test shall be carried out.If the second test is again unsatisfactory, INVESTOR shall replace the equipment involved at its own cost, within two months after the second test.

6.In case test results are satisfactory, SINO and INVESTOR shall sign a test certificate in duplicate and each party shall keep one copy.

7.Stay expenses of INVESTOR's engineers despatched to SINO for installation and test shall be all borne by INVESTOR.

## Article 8.Training for Operation and Maintenance of Equipment

1.INVESTOR shall implement training programs concerning the operation and maintenance of the equipment, when engineers are despatched to SINO for installation and test.In this instance, SINO shall provide necessary assistance like interpreter, etc. for INVESTOR.

2.Duration of training shall not exceed two weeks including the time for installation and test referred to in the previous item.

3.Training programs shall be conducted mainly in English language, with Chinese as a supportive language.SINO shall prepare interpreter (Chinese-English) at SINO's cost, if such arrangement is needed.

4.Stay expenses of INVESTOR's engineers at SINO for training for operation and maintenance of the equipment shall be all borne by INVESTOR.

## Article 9.Guaranty for Equipment Delivered

1.In accordance with the international customary standards, the warranty period for the equipment delivered shall be eight (8) months after the completion date of the acceptance inspection at SINO.

2.In case defect of the delivered equipment is found within the warranty period, INVESTOR shall take appropriate action for settlement without delay, upon SINO's request.

3.In the above instance, INVESTOR shall request SINO for payment of the actual costs of transportation, when such defect is judged to be due to inexperienced operation by SINO, or due to inappropriate handling, or due to an article of consumption.

4.INVESTOR shall offer its maximum services to SINO concerning the equipment delivered.

5.Maintenance of the equipment after the warranty period shall be at SINO's cost, however, INVESTOR shall endeavor to offer its maximum cooperation and lowest cost.

## Article 10.Procurement of Materials

1. SINO shall purchase, from INVESTOR, materials necessary to produce PRODUCTS in accordance with this Contract.

2.INVESTOR shall deliver the necessary materials at SINO's request in accordance with this Contract.

3.INVESTOR shall endeavor to supply these materials at a cost as low as possible.

4.Actual and detailed items of materials to be purchased by SINO shall be determined by separate purchase contract (s).

5.INVESTOR shall supply newest materials and guarantee their quality.

6.SINO shall supply INVESTOR with its monthly production plan and monthly need of materials eight months in advance, so that materials' delivery may be guaranteed.

7. INVESTOR shall endeavor to deliver the materials ordered by SINO as per specified delivery schedules.

8.Payment for the materials supplied by INVESTOR to SINO shall be effected by Irrevocable Letter of Credit in US currency.

## Article 11.Exportation Methods of Materials (Omitted)

## Article 12.Acceptance of Materials (Omitted)

## Article 13.Training of SINO's Engineers

1.INVESTOR shall accept 10 SINO's engineers, and provide three-month technical training at INVESTOR's cost.

2.In above regard, INVESTOR shall bear costs of lodging and food for SINO's engineers during their stay in Italy, excepting round-trip expenses between China and Italy.

3. SINO's engineers to be despatched to INVESTOR shall be able to comprehend practical English, with fundamental knowledge of electronic engineering.

4. Educational programs shall be carried out mainly in English language, with Chinese as a supportive language. INVESTOR shall prepare an interpreter (Chinese - English) at SINO's request and at SINO's cost.

5. INVESTOR shall compile educational programs promptly and shall notify SINO in advance. Items relating to technical education programs are shown in Appendix 7.

6. GTT shall despatch, at the same time, one engineer to attend the above educational programs together.

### Article 14. Despatch of INVESTOR's Engineers

1. INVESTOR shall despatch a number of engineers to SINO twice. At the first time, two engineers shall be despatched to SINO for two months in order to effect this project. At the second time, four engineers shall be despatched to SINO for three months in order to achieve production target.

2. Tasks of INVESTOR's engineers at SINO shall be carried out mainly in English language, with Chinese as a supportive language. SINO shall prepare an interpreter (Chinese-English) at SINO's cost, if necessary.

3. In above regard, SINO shall bear expenses for stay and trip within China of INVESTOR's engineers, excepting round trip expenses between China and Italy.

4. SINO shall be able to request for continued technical support from INVESTOR, if necessary, even after completion of the above despatch of INVESTOR's engineers. However, in this instance, INVESTOR shall be able to request SINO for the cost of such additional technological cooperation. Terms and conditions shall be subject to mutual discussion and agreement between SINO and INVESTOR, in future.

5. Details of the technical services requested by SINO from INVESTOR are shown in Appendix 8.

### Article 15. Technological Cooperation in Future

1. INVESTOR shall cooperate with SINO in future technological developments including high resolution display, etc..

2. Terms and conditions of the above technological cooperation, including its cost, shall be determined by a separate contract which shall be discussed in future among SINO, INVESTOR and GTT.

### Article 16. Role of GTT

1. GTT shall be responsible for transmission of information, being an intermediary, in communication, etc. between SINO and INVESTOR, and shall offer necessary assistance to SINO.

2. GTT shall be rewarded reasonably for such activities by SINO.

### Article 17.Duties of GTT

1.GTT shall act as a bridge between SINO and INVESTOR.

2. GTT shall assist SINO in marketing in China of products finished by SINO by means of trade show, seminar, technical training program, etc..

3. GTT shall consider marketing finished products to Europe and Africa when the quality turns out to be satisfactory.

4. GTT shall provide free facilities for engineers when SINO dispatches them to Europe for product development. However, SINO shall be responsible for all cost for engineers in Europe.

### Article 18.Arbitration（Omitted）

### Article 19.Taxes

During the effectiveness of this Contract, SINO shall be responsible for any taxation arising in China, whilst INVESTOR and GTT shall be responsible for any taxation arising in Europe respectively.

### Article 20.Effectiveness of this Contract

1.Unforeseen matters shall not affect the execution of this Contract.

2. SINO, INVESTOR and GTT shall apply for permissions to import/export the related products to their own governments. The effective date of this Contract shall be the date of the last party being approved. Three parties shall try their best to obtain approval within eighty（80）days.

### Article 21.Cancellation of Contract

1.Three parties shall reserve the right to cancel this Contract in case there is no effect for six months after the effective date of this Contract.

2. This Contract shall be valid for two years after its effective date, and shall be renewable for further two years thereafter.

### Article 22.Languages Used in Contract

This Contract is written in both Chinese and English, and both versions shall have the equal validity.

### Article 23.Documents Attached to this Contract

1.In case any amendment occurs to this Contract, the three parties concerned shall agree and sign official documents and shall consider same as a part of this Contract.

2.Appendices shall be valid and form a part of this Contract.

Dated this 3rd day of March, 2018

Signatures（Omitted）

**参考译文：**

### 技术转让和设备材料进口合同

中国广播产品进出口公司和广东省优良广播产品厂（以下简称"中方"）与荷

兰对外先进广播有限公司（以下简称"投资人"）和意大利兴隆贸易有限公司（以下简称"GTT"）签订本合同，其条款如下：

第1条 技术转让

1.中方为在广州生产投资人的甲型和乙型产品而引进必要的技术，这些产品以下简称为"产品"。

2.投资人应中方要求按合同提供其拥有的制造产品所需的技术和资料。

3.产品的名称规格详见附件一。

4.投资人应向中方提供制造产品所需的商业秘密、制造技术和专有技术方面的资料。投资人向中方提供的资料详见附件二。

第2条 设备规划

1.中方必须按照投资人的建议准备产品生产设施。

2.为了帮助在广州准备生产设施，投资人应提供援助，包括提供下列资料和信息：

a.生产线计划；

b.生产劳动力安排计划；

c.设备布局计划；

d.基础设施计划（如水电供应、空调、运输、通信等）；

e.设备安装操作计划；

f.生产管理计划；

g.市场推广计划。

上述资料和信息应于本合同生效后60天内由投资人提供给中方。

3.生产线必须符合附于本合同的生产进度表，即附件三（略）。

4.中方应自行准备生产计划，但必要时可要求投资人给予合作。

第3条 许可费的支付

1.投资人向中方转让技术的许可费如下：

a.中方各投资人购买产品生产权应交入门费……美元。

b.每件出售的产品应向投资人交付售价3%的提成费。

2.一切付款应按照本合同及本条款的有关约定事项办理。

3.一切付款应通过中国银行办理。

4.支付方式采用不可撤销的即期信用证，用美元支付。

5.中方应在本合同生效后1个月内开立不可撤销的信用证，向投资人支付入门费。

6.投资人应在收到上述信用证后30天内提供合同规定的一切技术资料。

7.中方每次向投资人订购合同规定的材料时，应在信用证的金额中加上3%的提成费；也可在支付货款时为该提成费另开一份信用证。

8.中方负责在中国发生的一切费用；投资人负责在国外发生的一切费用。

第4条 销售

1.投资人应帮助中方举办展销会、研讨会、广告宣传等，以推销中方生产的产品，但费用应由中方负担。

2.在开展广告宣传等活动中，中方如有需要可以使用投资人的广告标识，但投资人既不分担中方的盈亏，也不对此承担责任。

第5条　质量控制

1.在广州制造产品的质量必须按照投资人的质量控制标准进行鉴定。

2.在广州制造的产品的质量检验，在开始阶段应由双方工程师联合进行，其细节详见附件四。

3.在广州制造的产品的质量检验必要时应进行两次。如果第二次检验未能达到规格指标而且原因又是在投资人方面，则投资人应自费解决存在的问题。

4.如果产品质量检验合格，双方工程师应签署产品质量检验证明书一式两份，双方各执一份。

第6条　设备交货

1.中方应向投资人购买生产产品所需的设备。

2.生产产品所需设备的品名、规格详见附件五。

3.中方向投资人购买设备的价格细节由双方商定，并另签设备购买合同。

4.投资人运交的设备应该是最新型的、未用过的。

5.投资人向中方运交设备的价款应以不可撤销的即期信用证按CIF中国口岸条件用美元支付。

6.投资人应按本合同的交货计划表运交设备。

7.投资人应按本合同的规定，向中方提供与设备有关的技术资料。

8.设备正式交货日期为提单的日期。投资人应将提单号码、装船日期、装箱单、抵达日期等及时通知中方。同时，投资人还应将上述资料单据副本寄给中方。

9.合同规定的设备和技术资料如有遗失，中方得要求投资人补交。

10.投资人运交设备应使用坚固的包装，足以经受长途运输。

11.投资人的装箱单应写明：

a.合同号码；b.收货人姓名；c.目的港；d.装船唛头；e.重量；f.箱号；g.收货人标记。

12.投资人应将装货内容清单的副本放入包装内。

第7条　接受设备

1.中方应准备设施和场地以接收和保管投资人运来的设备。

2.投资人应在中方提出对运到的设备进行安装和调试的要求后3周内派出工程师。中方应就此事向投资人提供翻译之类的必要帮助。

3.投资人的工程师应为安装调试任务停留两周。

4.运交设备的验收工作，应由双方工程师和中国检验官员一起进行，详细规定见附件六。

5.如果初次检验不合格应进行第二次检验。如果第二次检验仍不合格，则投资人应在2个月内自费调换有关设备。

6.如果检验合格，双方应签署检验证明书一式两份，双方各执一份。

7.投资人派往中方安装调试的工程师的居留费用均由投资人负担。

第8条 设备操作和保养的培训

1.投资人在派遣工程师到中方安装调试设备时，应举办关于设备操作和保养的培训。中方应为此事对投资提供诸如翻译之类的帮助。

2.培训的时间，包括前款所讲的安装调试在内不得超过2周。

3.培训主要用英语进行，但也用汉语作为辅助语言。中方如有需要应自费准备汉英翻译员。

4.在中方进行设备操作保养培训的工程师的居留费用均由投资人负担。

第9条 对运交设备的保证

1.按照国际惯例标准，运交设备的保证期为8个月，从中方完成验收工作之日起算。

2.如果在保证期内发现运交的设备有缺陷，投资人必须按中方的要求，及时适当解决。

3.在上述情况下，该缺点经鉴定是由于中方操作经验不足、搬运不当或某一物品的消耗所致，则投资人应要求中方支付实际运输费用。

4.投资人应向中方提供与运交设备有关的最大限度的服务。

5.保证期以后的设备保养需要向中方收取费用，但投资人应努力提供最大的合作和收取最低的费用。

第10条 物资的采购

1.中方应按本合同的规定向投资人采购生产产品所需的材料。

2.投资人应按本合同的规定向中方运交所需的材料。

3.投资人应力求以尽可能低的价格供应这些材料。

4.中方采购材料的实际详细品名，另以购买合同规定。

5.投资人应该供应最新的材料，并保证质量。

6.中方应提前8个月向投资人送交月度生产计划和月度材料采购数量，以便材料的交货得到保证。

7.投资人应尽力按照交货计划运交中方采购的材料。

8.中方对投资人运交材料的付款，必须采用信用证，以美元支付。

第11条 材料的出口方法（略）

第12条 接受材料（略）

第13条 培训中方的工程师

1.投资人应接待10名中方工程师，并提供3个月的技术培训。

2.投资人对中方工程师为此在意大利居留期间承担给食宿费用，但中意之间的来回旅费除外。

3.派出受训的中方工程师应懂得实用的英语，具有电子工程学的基础知识。

4.教学主要用英语进行，但以汉语为辅助语言。投资人应按中方要求准备一名汉英译员，费用由中方负担。

5.投资人应立即编写教育计划并提前通知中方。有关技术教育计划项目详见附件七。

6.GTT应同时派遣一名工程师去照料上述培训事宜。

第14条　派遣投资人的工程师

1.投资人应派遣多名工程师去中方两次，第一次派2名去2个月，以实施这项转让计划。第二次派4名去3个月，以达到生产目标。

2.投资人派往中方的工程师主要用英语进行工作，但也以汉语为辅助语言。中方必要时应自费准备一名汉英翻译员。

3.中方应负担投资人的工程师为此而在中国国内居留和差旅的各种费用，但中意之间的旅费除外。

4.在投资人派遣工程师的任务完成以后，中方如有必要仍可要求投资人继续给予技术支持，但投资人应要求中方为这种增加的合作支付费用。合作的条款由双方将来讨论约定。

5.中方要求投资人技术服务的细节，见附件八。

第15条　将来的技术合作

1.投资人应为将来的发展与中方进行合作，包括高分辨率显示器等在内。

2.上述技术合作的条款，包括它的费用，应由中方、投资人、GTT三方面在将来商定并另签合同。

第16条　GTT的作用

1.GTT负责中方和投资人之间的信息传递、交往媒介等，并对中方提供必要的援助。

2.GTT应为此适当向中方收取报酬。

第17条　GTT的责任

1.GTT是中方和投资人之间的桥梁。

2.GTT应协助中方用展销会、研讨会、技术培训等办法在中国推广销售产品。

3.GTT应在产品质量合格时考虑把这些产品销往欧洲和非洲。

4.GTT应在中方派遣工程师到欧洲进行产品开发时，向他们提供免费使用的设施和工具，但中方应负担他们在欧洲的一切费用。

第18条　仲裁（略）

第19条　税款

在合同有效期内，在中国发生的税款由中方负责，而在欧洲发生的税款由投资人和GTT负责。

第20条　合同的生效

1.不可预见的问题不应影响本合同的执行。

2.中方、投资人、GTT三方应向各自的政府申请允许有关商品的进口和出口。最后一方获得批准之日即为本合同生效之日。三方应尽最大努力争取在80天内取得批准。

第21条 合同的撤销

1.如果在合同生效后6个月没有见到效果，三方保留撤销本合同的权利。

2.本合同从生效之日起有效2年，期满后可延长2年。

第22条 使用的文字

本合同用中文和英文写成，两种文本具有同等效力。

第23条 合同附件

1.如要修改合同，有关三方应同意签订正式修改文件，并作为本合同的一部分。

2.所有附件均有效，并应成为本合同的一部分。

签订于2018年3月3日

签字（略）

## Notes

1.know-how技术诀窍，是拥有人自己秘密使用的实际技术知识，未向政府申请专利和公开内容，不受法律保护但可自由买卖，因此它被称为非专利技术，俗称技术诀窍。know-how一经向政府申请专利和公开内容就成了专利技术（patented technology），在规定年限内受法律的保护，并且可以自己买卖或转让。

The Franchiser is to make available to the Franchisee advice, guidance and know-how, with respect to management of this franchise.

特许权拥有人应就有关本项特许的经营管理问题向特许经销代理人提供意见、指导和技术诀窍。

2.logo n.（企业、公司等的）专用标识，标记，商标（如用于广告中的）

If it does meet those standards, it can then use the name and advertising symbol, the logo, as it is called, for the group.

验收合格，方可使用此名称和广告标志，即所谓的标识。

3.warranty n.根据；理由；保单，保证（书），担保书

warranty clause 保证条款

express warranty 明示保证

What warranty do you have for saying so?

您这样说有什么根据吗？

Can you give me a warranty of quality for these goods?

您能为我担保这些货物的品质吗？

Company's obligation under this warranty is limited to repair and replacement.

公司对本保单所承担的责任，只限于修理和更换。

Distributor shall make no express warranty, unless authorized by the Manufacturer.

除非制造商授权让经销商提出保证，否则，经销商不提供明确的保证。

This warranty is expressly made in lieu of all other warranties.

该保证书的签订明确替代一切其他保证。

辨析:warranty，guarantee

在实行合同中，如违反了warranty，很大程度上会导致受损方向违约方提出索赔，而违反了guarantee，其后果极有可能是受损方提出终止合同。

4.defect n.缺点、欠缺

Licensed Devices which are found to have defects shall not be sold in the market.

凡经发现有缺陷（毛病）的特许装置不得在市场上出售。

The Buyer may be required to notify the Seller of defects within a specified period of time for making goods thereof.

买方有必要将缺点通知卖方，以便在规定期限内弥补缺点。

5.intermediary n.中介人

Certain precautions shall be required to protect the interest of buyer，prospective sellers and their designated intermediaries.

必须采取某些预防措施，用以保护买主、未来卖主以及他们指定的各种中介人的利益。

6.whilst=while conj.用以表示对比或相反的情况。

## ● Exercises

I.Translate the following into English:

1.技术，人类劳动的成果，由于可以交换而成为一种商品；技术作为一种商品，由于可提高生产率而具有很高的价值。

2.技术应当商品化，即买和卖，以便技术成果能够广泛应用于生产。

3.技术合同涉及专利的，应当注明发明创造的名称、专利申请人和专利权人、申请日期、申请号、专利号以及专利权的有效期限。

4.技术合同的价款、报酬或使用费的支付方式有:

1）一次总算一次总付；

2）一次总算分期支付；

3）提成支付；

4）提成支付附加预付入门费。

5.非法垄断技术、妨碍技术进步或者侵害他人技术成果的技术合同无效。

6.技术转让合同包括专利权转让、专利申请权转让、技术秘密转让、技术实施许可合同。

7.技术转让合同的让与人应当保证自己是所提供的技术的合法拥有者，并保证所提供的技术完整、无误、有效，能够达到约定的目标。

8.让与人未按约定转让技术的，应当返还部分或者全部转让费，并应承担违约责任。

9.技术咨询合同包括为特定技术项目提供可行性论证、技术与专题技术调查、分析评价报告等合同。

10.供方不得强迫买方接受不合理的限制性要求，如要求买方购买不需要的技术、技术服务、原材料、设备、产品等。

## II.Translate the following into Chinese:

1.Since the successful recovery of the 17th satellite on October 26，1985，we have been ready to place our satellite-launching service on the international technology market. Our Long March-2 Rocket，32-meter-long，two-stage，can carry a two-ton satellite into orbits near Earth.Our most advanced rocket，the three-stage Long March-3，43-meter-long，has a payload capability of 1.4 tons for loads to be put into long-distance geostationary orbits.Furthermore，the Chinese People's Insurance Company is ready to provide insurance cover at internationally competitive rates for foreign clients making use of our launching service.

2.In addition，we have a lot of traditional technologies，such as those involved in making pottery and porcelain，arts and crafts and traditional medicines. As these technologies are rare in the international market，they may turn out to be good sellers in your country.

3.We are glad to learn that you are willing to export your advanced technology and equipment to our country.There is no doubt that China's rich experience in developing her national economy and technology will be very useful to our country.We share your country's view to supply each other's needs on the basis of equality and mutual benefit that is an important way to promote South-South cooperation.

4. We used to purchase technology and equipment from developed countries at exorbitant prices. Seeing that as China belongs to the Third World，she naturally understands our problems and difficulties and her technology and equipment are likely to be more suitable to our needs.Our company is prepared to switch our purchases to you if your terms and conditions are favorable and prices are reasonable.

5.The invention and creation shall mean invention，utility model and design.

6.No patent right shall be granted for any invention-creation that violates the laws of the state，goes against social morals or is detrimental to the public interests.

7.Any entity or individual exploiting the patent of another must conclude a written licensing contract with the patentee and pay the patentee a fee for the exploitation of the patent.

8.If any Chinese entity or individual intends to file a patent application in a foreign country for the invention-creation made in China，it or he shall file first a patent application with the patent administration department under the state Council and appoint a patent agency designated by the said department to act as its or his agent.

9. The dispute on the infringement of the patent right shall be settled through

consultation by the parties concerned.If the consultation fails, the patentee may institute legal proceedings in the people's court.

10.Where any person passes the patent of another person off as his own, he shall bear his civil liability according to the laws and his illegal earnings shall be confiscated.

# Unit Eleven /国际商标许可合同

## Agreement for Trademark Licence

This Agreement becomes effective on the 16th day of June, 2018 between _____ a corporation organized under the laws of the People's Republic of China, hereinafter called "Party A", and_____, a company organized under the laws of the Republic of Peru, hereinafter called "Party B".

Whereas, Party A possesses proprietary technical information including designs, techniques, processes, formulas, skills and other data useful in the manufacturing and marketing of certain products; and

Whereas, Party B desires to acquire the right and license to use the aforesaid technical assistance, and the right to receive continuing technical assistance for the purpose of manufacturing, using and selling such products; and

Whereas, Party B desires to use the following trademarks owned by ONRINCO, Party A (Symbol).

Now, therefore, the parties hereto do hereby agree as follows:

**A.TRADEMARK LICENSE**

1.In the present contract, the term PRODUCTS shall be interpreted as the Party A Series Family of vehicles released for left hand drive application and the term "Licensed Products" is meant to include all components as improved, added to or modified, which now form or may hereafter form an integral part of the Licensed Product (s).

Party B shall identify Licensed Products as being made under licence from Party A. The form and location of such identification shall be approved by Party A.

2. Party B has requested permission to use the above mentioned trademarks upon goods made by itself, and Party A is willing to grant such permission on the terms and conditions hereinafter set forth.

3.Party A hereby grants to Party B the exclusive right to use the Trademarks in the Republic of Peru, only on PRODUCTS made by Party B Provided, however, that such exclusive right applies only to the use of the trademarks in connection with the PRODUCTS, the parties understand that the trademarks may be used by others, but not on the PRODUCTS. This license is personal to Party B and shall not be assignable to anyone else.

4. Party B agrees and undertakes to use the above mentioned trademarks strictly in accordance with the instructions and directions of Party A and in conformity with the process and methods of manufacture given directly by Party A to Party B as technical assistance, so that the PRODUCTS on which the trademarks will be used by Party B shall conform to the standards and specifications established by Party A and be in uniform in quality with PRODUCTS on which Party A uses the said trademarks.

5. Party B recognizes Party A's ownership of and title to the said trademarks and will not at any time do or suffer to be done any act or thing which will anyway impair the rights of Party A in and to the said trademarks. Party A through any of its officers or agents shall have the right at any time during business hours to inspect Party B's factory and any PRODUCTS manufactured by Party B under the licensed trademarks and to the extent necessary to protect the said trademarks, the right to reject for sale any such PRODUCTS, after complying with the provisions of Section C of this Agreement, which in the judgment of Party A are not of quality to that of similar PRODUCTS manufactured and sold by Party A under the said trademarks.

6. Party B agrees and undertakes to use the aforementioned trademarks strictly in accordance with the legal requirements in Peru and to use such markings in connection therewith as may be required by the applicable_____Law and any other pertinent legal provisions. The manner in using with said Party A trademarks on the PRODUCTS will be submitted to Party A for its approval prior to being used as a product graphic on the PRODUCTS.

## B.SUPPLY OF DOCUMENTATION AND TECHNICAL ASSISTANCE

1. Party A shall furnish two sets of documents in 90 days after received written request, one of which will be reproducible:

a. All drawings for assembly in possession of Party A to support the specific models to be produced in Peru.

b.i. With respect to components contained in Licensed Products which are obtained by Party A from outside suppliers, Party A shall furnish such drawings and/or specifications as are made available by Party A's suppliers and as are required but subject, however, to any Limitation placed upon the use of such drawings by suppliers.

ii. For supplier components, Party A shall supply physical dimensions, performance characteristics, design parameters and such other information Party A may have developed regarding such supplier components in order to permit Party B to source components of equivalent specifications in Peru.

iii. Party A shall not be liable for the unwillingness of any outside supplier to provide technical documentation for use by Party B.

c. Material and manufacturing specifications for all parts produced to the design and specifications of Party A.

d. Tolling and equipment drawings which may be available in the files of Party A.

2. The technical documentation and know-how will be supplied in accordance with the standard manufacturing techniques used by Party A. All drawings will be in the language and dimensions of the country of origin. Any conversion to metric dimensions will be the responsibility and cost of Party B.

3. For the term of this Agreement and commencing with a date mutually agreed upon for each Licensed Product, Party A undertakes to release to Party B details of major improvement engineering changes made by Party A to the licensed Product.

4. Party A will provide and arrange training for Party B personnel at appropriate factories of Party A or its subsidiaries, affiliates or licensees. Periods of time may be mutually agreed upon by Party A and Party B.

## C.ENGINEERING

1. Party B agrees to manufacture and/or assemble Licensed Products in accordance with the documentation, know-how and technical assistance supplied to Party B by ONRINOC. Party B will adhere to Party A's design except for compelling and necessary reasons caused by manufacturing capability, performance failures, or material availability.

Alterations or changes will be processed in the following manner:

a. Version drawings, that is, conversion to metric, material substitutions, and language, will be handled by Party B.

b. Compelling alterations or changes required by Party B may be processed by Party B provided, however, that advance written notice is given to Party A about such alteration or change and advance approval is given by Party A. Party B will furnish Party A with drawings, sketches, test results, or any necessary data, in English to enable an immediate response. The function, performance quality and interchangeability of changed parts will be Party B's responsibility.

c. Substitution of locally purchased, such as seals, bearings, hardware, etc. will be responsibility of Party B.

2. Party A has the right at any time to inspect the Licensed Products or components manufactured by Party B or Party B's suppliers to determine that the materials and workmanship conform to the standard of drawings and specifications supplied by Party A. Party B agrees to cooperate and make available the necessary facilities for such inspections.

3. It is understood and agreed by Party B that Licensed Products manufactured by Party B shall be manufactured strictly in accordance with the design, drawings, and

specifications furnished by Party A unless modified pursuant to C. 1.and in any event the Licensed Products will possess the same characteristics in quality and performance as products produced by Party A. Party A, however, does not assume any warranty obligations with respect to Party B's Licensed Products if they have not been manufactured strictly in accordance with the design, drawings, and specifications furnished by Party A.

4. Party B agrees to maintain and protect drawings, specifications, and other technical data identified with proprietary markings of Party A in strict confidence and agrees not to disclose any of this information to any person except whomsoever may be necessary to secure materials or components for the production of Licensed Products made by Party B.Party B also agrees to impose similar restrictions on its suppliers to whom such drawings, specifications, and production information are made available for the production of parts or components required by Party B for such purpose.

It is agreed that for manufacturing and purchasing convenience Party B may, at its option, redraw or convert Party A's drawing to metric measures and Party B's part number and description.Party B further agrees to cause the following legend to appear on all Party A's drawings redrawn by Party B.

"This print is provided on a restricted basis and is not to be used in any way detrimental to the interests of Party A."

5.Party B further agrees to maintain drawings, specifications, and other technical data, which are marked or otherwise designated as proprietary to the outside suppliers of Party A and made available by these outside suppliers and forwarded to Party B, in complete confidence. Party B also agrees not to disclose any of this information to any person whomsoever without the permission of Party A.Party B further agrees not to use any of the information furnished to it pursuant to this Agreement in a manner inconsistent with the intent of this Agreement.

### D.IMPROVEMENTS AND LIMITS

1.Each party hereto agrees to immediately and fully communicate to the other party any subject matter comprising an improvement, modification, further invention or design with respect to manufacture and assembly of the Licensed Products or components thereof.

The party which discovers, makes or develops such subject matter may, at its own expense and its own name file application for Letters Patent or take other necessary legal steps to protect the same one, and any patent issuing thereon will belong to the party so filing. Said the other party, during the life of the Agreement may make use, and sell products utilizing such improvement, modification, further improvement or design (whether patented or unpatented) without charge and royalty fee in any manner nor inconsistent with this agreement.

2.Party A shall not be obligated to defend or save harmless Party B against any suit, damage claim, or demand based on actual or alleged infringement of any patent or any unfair trade practice resulting from the exercise of use of any right or license granted hereunder.

3.Nothing in this Agreement shall be construed:

a. As conferring right or imposing an obligation on either party to bring or prosecute actions against third parties for infringement.

b.So as to require or impose on either party any duty or obligation, which will violate any proprietary or patent rights of any third party.

## E.TERMS OF THE AGREEMENT

The term of this Agreement shall be five years from the date first above written.This Agreement may be renegotiated for renewal after four years.Either party may terminate this Agreement by ninety (90) days prior written notice.

1. It is deemed a material condition of this Agreement that Party B shall actively pursue the manufacture and sale of Licensed Products in accordance with the terms of this Agreement.Annual manufacturing objectives shall be mutually agreed upon by Party A and Party B as of the date first above written. Either party reserves the right to review this Agreement in the event that Party B fails to meet the annual manufacturing objective mutually agreed upon by Party B and Party A.

2.Either party may terminate this Agreement forthwith in the event of the bankruptcy or insolvency of the other party.

3.This Agreement may be terminated forthwith by the mutual consent of both parties.

4. Upon termination of the present contract, Party B will, within twelve (12) months thereafter, discontinue the use of the trademarks or any similar marks.In the event that Party B fails to discontinue the use of one or more of Party A's marks within twelve (12) months from the termination of this Agreement, Party B shall pay Party A the sum of_____ in U.S.currency for each month during such unauthorized use of Party A's trademarks.

## F.PRICE (omitted)

## G.GENERAL PROVISIONS

1.Until otherwise notified in writing, the mailing addresses of the parties hereto for notices and communications, are as follows (unless otherwise specified in this Agreement):

Party A:_____ Party B:_____

2.Party B hereby acknowledges the ownership of the Trademarks in Party A, and admits the validity of the Trademarks and all registrations in Peru and foreign countries thereto now or hereafter issued with respect to the Trademarks owned by Party A or a related company.Party B agrees that it will not attack directly or indirectly such validity or ownership and will not permit the same to be done，both during the term of the Agreement or thereafter. Party B further agrees that in the event it acquires， during the term of this Agreement or thereafter， any right in the Trademarks in Peru or elsewhere in the world， except these granted by this Agreement， it will， at Party A's request， assign such rights and goodwill associated with such rights to Party A along with.

3. Party B agrees that it will not use or acquiesce in the use of any trademarks which are likely to be confusingly similar to the Trademarks.

4. Party B shall promptly notify Party A of any conflicting use of， or act of infringement upon the Trademarks of which it may become aware and agrees to cooperate with Party A in every reasonable way in prosecuting all acts that Party A may deem advisable to protect the validity of Party A's rights in the Trademarks. It is expressly understood that Party B shall take no action independently of Party A without first obtaining the written approval of Party A.

H. DISPUTES

This Agreement is submitted to the Law of_____.

Except as is otherwise expressly provided herein， all disputes， controversies or differences arising between the parties out of or in relation to or in connection with this Agreement， or any breach or default hereunder （including but not limited to， a dispute concerning the existence or continued existence of this Agreement， and the validity of the arbitral provision） which cannot be settled amicably shall be subjected to arbitration.

Arbitration shall be conducted in accordance with the procedures and rules set forth in the Civil Code of_____ and Civil Procedure Code of_____. The arbitral tribunal shall have its seat， and arbitration proceedings shall take place in_____.

The arbitral tribunal shall consist of three arbitrators. Party B and Party A shall each appoint one arbitrator and will be subject to the rules and regulations of UNCTRAL.

In witness whereof， the parties hereto have respectively caused this instrument to be executed in duplicate， as of the date first above written.

Party A_____    Party B_____
By_____     By_____

**参考译文：**

### 国际商标许可合同

本协议于 2018 年 6 月 16 日生效，由_____公司（依中华人民共和国法律设立，以下简称"甲方"）与_____（依秘鲁共和国法律设立，以下简称"乙方"）双方共同签署。

鉴于甲方拥有合同产品的生产及销售所涉及的技术信息，包括设计、技术、工艺、配方、技能和其他资料的专有权；

鉴于乙方希望获得使用上述技术协助的许可权利，以及以生产、使用和销售合同产品为目的的持续的技术协助的权利；

鉴于乙方希望使用甲方所有的下述商标:甲方（标志）。

双方就下列内容达成一致：

A.商标许可

1.在本合同项下，产品意指甲方系列左驾驶车辆，"许可证产品"意指包括所有改进、增补、改良之后的部件，其现有形式和将来可能采用的形式均为合同产品不可分割的一部分。

乙方应表明许可证产品是依照甲方许可形式制造，而且这一标志的形式和位置应经甲方确认。

2.乙方要求就其所生产的货物许可使用上述商标，且甲方同意依后述条件和条款做出许可。

3.据此甲方授予乙方在秘鲁共和国境内使用甲方商标和独占权利，这一权利仅限于由乙方所生产的许可证产品的范围。由于此独占权利仅适用于与产品有关的范围之内使用商标，双方确认，该商标可以由他方使用，但不得使用于许可证产品的范围之内。该许可仅向乙方授予而不得向任何第三方再行转让。

4.乙方同意并允诺严格依甲方的指令、指导和甲方在向乙方技术协助中规定的生产工艺和生产方法使用上述商标，以使由乙方标识商标的产品符合由甲方设立的标准和规格，并且与甲方商标系列的产品具有统一的质量。

5.乙方知晓甲方对上述商标拥有所有权，并且允诺在任何情况下不做出或不默许他人做出对于上述甲方商标权利有害的行为。在工作期间的任何时间内，甲方有权派员或通过代理商基于商标许可检查乙方的工厂和由乙方生产的任何许可产品，并确定上述商标的必要保护范围。在依本协议第三款规定由甲方判定产品未能与甲方在同类商标项下生产和销售的产品质量一致的情况下，甲方还享有停止许可证产品销售的权利。

6.乙方同意并允诺严格依照秘鲁的法律使用上述商标并且在相关产品上使用此类标志应符合_____适用法律及任何其他法律条文。在产品上使用甲方商标的方式应在正式使用之前交由甲方进行批准。

B.提供资料及技术协助

1.在收到书面请求之后90天内，甲方向乙方提供如下两套资料，其中一套应是可复制的：

a.由甲方所拥有的为支持秘鲁生产指定型号产品的全部组装用图纸。

b.i.对于包含甲方自外部供应商所获得的部分许可证产品部件、甲方提供依从供应商所制作的图纸和/或规格，但应依从于供应商对于图纸使用的限制条件。

ii.对于供应部件，甲方应提供外观尺寸、性能特性、设计参数以及其他甲方可能开发的为使乙方在秘鲁得到相同规格的供应部件的相关信息。

iii.甲方对于任何外部供应商不愿向乙方提供技术资料的后果不承担责任。

c.材料和依甲方的设计和规格生产全部零件所需的规格。

d.工具及设备图纸，其应依甲方现有可能存档图纸为限。

2.技术资料和专有技术将依甲方所使用的标准生产技术为准；所有图纸均以原有国家语言和度量制为准；全部资料度量制式转换为公式的责任和费用由乙方承担。

3.在本协议期间以及每一个许可证产品由双方达成一致的起始日之后，甲方承诺向乙方披露由甲方就许可证产品所做出的主要改进细节。

4.甲方将提供并负责安排在适当的工厂或其子公司、分支机构或特许权受让人所在地对乙方的职工进行培训。此类的培训期将由双方商定。

C.操作

1.乙方同意依甲方向其提供的资料、专有技术和技术协助生产及装配许可证产品。除非因生产能力、履行能力或材料适应性方面的原因之外，乙方均应依从于甲方的设计。

变更均依以下方式进行：

a.翻译图纸，即公制转换、材料替代、语言翻译等工作由乙方承担。

b.依乙方要求所作的强制性变更应由乙方进行，但应事先向甲方发出书面通知并就此变更得到甲方的认可。乙方将向甲方提交图纸、草图、实验结果或其他必要的数据，并以英文做成以尽快得到回复。更换零件的性能、工作质量及可替换性均由乙方负责保证。

c.由当地购买的零件，如密封件、轴承、五金件等，均由乙方负责保证。

2.甲方有权在任何时间检查由乙方或其供应商生产的许可证产品或部件，以决定其材料和工艺是否符合甲方提供的图纸和规格。乙方同意为此检查提供合作和便利。

3.乙方确认由其所生产的许可证产品必须严格按照甲方所提供的设计、图纸及规格生产，除依第c条第1款规定的修改内容以外，在任何情况下许可证产品均应具备与甲方所生产的产品相同的质量与运行性能。如果乙方未严格依照甲方的设计、图纸及规格生产，则甲方对于乙方生产的许可证产品不承担任何担保责任。

4.乙方同意保持并严格保护带有甲方专有标记的图纸、规格和其他技术资料的秘密，并同意不向任何人披露任何上述信息，除非其是属于保证乙方许可证产品生产的材料和部件所必需者。乙方亦同意将同样的限制加于依同样目的乙方要求生产零部件而使用此类图纸、规格及生产信息的供应商。

双方同意为生产及采购的便利，乙方可依需要重新描绘或转换甲方的图纸为公制度量并依要求加注乙方的零件序号和乙方的说明。乙方进而同意在由其重新描绘的甲方图纸上均标明如下文字说明：

"本文仅属限制使用并不得用于任何有害甲方的用途。"

5.乙方同意对于由甲方的外部供应商向乙方提供并标明的图纸、规格和其他技术资料进行完全的保密，乙方也同意未经甲方的许可不向任何人披露上述信息。乙方还同意不以与协议目的相矛盾的方式使用协议所提供的信息。

D.改进和限制

1.各方同意对于有关生产及装配许可证产品或部件所进行的改进、修正、更新发明或设计均应立即全部通知另一方。

开发改进的一方可以自负费用并以自身名义申请专利或其他类似的法律保护程序，由此产生的专利将属于该方所有。在本协议的有效期内，另一方可以与本协议不相矛盾的方式无偿使用和销售利用改进、修正、更新发明或设计（无论其是否取得专利权）生产的产品。

2.甲方无义务保证乙方在由于行使或使用下述许可权利而事实上或被指控侵犯任何专利权或不正当贸易惯例所引起的诉讼、索赔及其他要求的情况下不受到损害。

3.本协议不包含如下内容：

a.授予任何一方权利或强加于任何一方义务从事某种对第三方侵权的行为。

b.要求或强迫任何一方承担义务侵犯第三方的专有权利或专利权。

E.协议的期限

本协议期限为自签字之日起5年。本协议可在4年之后由双方商议延长。任何一方可在90日前以书面通知终止本协议。

1.作为本协议的重要条件，乙方须依照本协议条款积极从事许可证产品的生产和销售。年度生产目标将由甲方与乙方在协议生效后商定。任何一方保留在乙方未能完成依乙方与甲方双方达成的年度生产目标时对协议重新审查的权利。

2.在一方破产或资不抵债的情况下，另一方可以终止本协议。

3.双方合意可终止本协议。

4.与终止协议相对应，乙方将在终止协议后12个月内停止使用商标或任何类似标记。如果乙方未于协议终止后12个月内停止使用一个或数个甲方的标记，则乙方要为未经授权使用甲方商标而向甲方支付总额为　　　　　美元的赔偿。

F.价格（略）

G.一般条款

1.除非另有书面通知，则双方的邮政通信地址依下述为准（除本协议另有约定之外）：

甲方：_____　　乙方：_____

2.乙方确认甲方对于其商标的所有权，并承认由甲方或某个相关公司所属的商标在秘鲁或其他国家的商标登记及商标的有效性。乙方同意在本协议期间或其后的时间内，不直接或间接地否认甲方商标的有效性及所有权，并不允许此类行为发生。乙方进而同意在本协议期间或其后的时间内，其在秘鲁或世界上任何地方所获得的与本协议所指商标有关的任何权利，除依本协议授权之外均应依甲方的要求而将此类权利及与此类权利相关的商誉让与甲方。

3.乙方同意不使用或不默许使用可能与本协议商标相类似易混淆的商标。

4.乙方应在发生任何对于商标侵权行为及冲突性使用的情况时，立即通知甲方并与甲方合作以采取合理手段对此类行为进行举报，而使甲方及时地保护其商标权的合法性。双方明确在未得到甲方的书面许可之前，乙方不得单独采取任何行动。

H.争议

本协议依_____法律解释。

除非另有明确表示，则与本协议有关或无关的协议双方的所有争议、纠纷或歧义，以及任何违约或过失（包括但不限于有关本协议存续的争议和仲裁条款有效性的争议），如不能以友好协商的方式解决，则提交仲裁。

仲裁应依_____民法的程序及_____民事诉讼法规进行。仲裁有固定的仲裁庭，在_____进行。

仲裁庭由三名仲裁员组成，乙方与甲方各依联合国国际贸易法委员会规则及规定指定一名仲裁员。

本文件一式两份，由双方分别于文首日期订立，特此为证。

甲方公司_____　　　　　　　乙方公司_____

代表：_____　　　　　　　代表：_____

# Notes

1.identify v.确定，认定；验明

It is agreed that the seller sells and delivers and the buyer purchases from the seller all products identified as follows.

经同意，由卖方出售及运送，买方向卖方购买下文明确的一切产品。

identification n.鉴定

The First Party gives the Second Party the exclusive right to lease a certain land for identification by the respective parties to this Agreement.

第一方承诺第二方享有独家租借某块土地的权利，供本协议有关各方鉴定之用。

2.grant v.准予，让与

AAA grants the Joint company the rights to use trademarks and trade names.

甲方给予联合公司使用各种商标以及商标名称的权利。

AAA hereby grants to ZZZ a license under the aforesaid letters patent.

根据上述的专利证书，甲方特此给予乙方一份许可证。

在商务英语乃至英文合同中，表示"准予""让与"的其他词汇还有 give 和 allow。

The company agrees allow the Distributor a commission of … % of the retail selling price.

公司同意给予经销商一笔零售价格的……%的佣金。

You are to allow us the actually amounts of cash discounts given to you by the parties with whom you do business on our account.

你方应将由我方负担损益而与之进行交易的当事人各方所允许给予你方的一笔实际的现金折扣总额，给予我方。

3. ownership n. 所有权，所有制

The seller may retain ownership of the container, if they are reusable and expensive.

如果这些容器可以再利用并且价格昂贵的话，卖方可以保留它们的所有权。

The stockholders shall have no ownership rights in any of the domestic or foreign patents.

股票持有人在国内外专利方面都不具有所有权。

4. judgement n. 判断，审判，判决

ZZZ will not be bound to do the marketing of any licensed device which in its judgement have become obsolete.

任何根据乙方的判断认为过时的特殊设计，乙方可以不必销售。

The distributor shall discontinue any advertising, in the sole judgement of the distributor, that may be objectionable.

经销商根据他的独立判断，应该放弃任何不能令人满意的广告宣传。

judge n. 法官，审判员，鉴定人；vt. 审理，鉴定，判断，判决，断定，认为；vi. 下判断，作评价

The members of the jury are the sole judges of what the truth is in this case.

陪审团的成员们是判断这个案件真相的唯一审判员。

5. trademark n. 商标，商标专用权

The licensee shall take all necessary measures to protect the licensor's trademark.

许可证受让人应采取一切必要的措施以保护许可证发证人的商标专用权。

The Manufacturer is the owner of the trademark, which has been duly registered in the Patent Office.

制造商是商标的拥有人，该商标业已在专利局登记注册。

6. pertinent adj. 有关系的，中肯的

The data so furnished shall be supplemented as additional pertinent data become available.

当更多的有关数据用上之后，那里所提供的数据就可得到补充。

7. equivalent adj. 相等的，相当的，相同的

Such commission shall be payable in installments equivalent to … % of the down payment.

这笔佣金应分期摊付，每次付款相当于第一次分期付款额的……%。

These charges, appearing on Seller's invoice, must be supported by a paid freight bill, or equivalent.

卖方发票上所示的这些费用必须用已付讫的运货单据，或相等物（单据）来证实。

undertake

8.affiliate vt.接纳……为会员，合并，联号，附属于

The offeror party shall have the right to purchase all of the shares of the joint company owned by the offeree party and its affiliated corporations.

发盘人一方有权收购（买下）合营公司中受盘人一方及其附属公司（分号）所拥有的全部股票。

affiliated company 附属子公司

9.know-how 专有技术，技术秘密，技术诀窍

Improvement refers to new findings and/or modifications made in the validity period of the Contract by either party in know‐how in the form of new designs, formulas, recipes, ingredients, indices, parameters, calculations, or any other indicators.

改进是指在合同有效期内由合同的任何一方以新设计、程式、处方、成分、数值、参数、计算或任何其他指标的形式对本专有技术进行的新发明和/或修改。

Know‐how refers to any valuable technical knowledge, data, indices, drawings, designs and other technical information, concerning the design, manufacture, assembly, inspection of contract products, developed and owned or legally acquired and possessed by Licensor and disclosed to Licensee by Licensor, which is unknown to either public or Licensee before the Date of Effectiveness of the Contract, and for which due protection measures have been taken by Licensor for keeping know‐how in secrecy. The specific description of know-how is set forth in Appendix 2.

专有技术是指本合同生效前尚不为公众或被许可方所知晓，由许可方开发、所有或合法取得、占有并由许可方披露给被许可方的关于设计、制造、安装、合同产品的检验等方面的任何有价值的技术知识、资料、数值、图纸、设计和其他技术信息，许可方已采取了适当措施使专有技术处于保密状态，专有技术的具体描述规定在附件二中。

10.patent n.专利权，执照，专利品；adj.特许的，专利的；vt.取得……的专利权，给予专利权

Licensed Patents shall mean all patents and patent applications owned and controlled by the Licensor.

经许可的专利意指许可方所有和所控制的专利权和专利申请。

AAA shall have the right to grant releases for past infringement of ZZZ under the patent of AAA.

甲方有权豁免乙方过去侵犯甲方专利权的过失。

Seller shall not be liable to Buyer because of the infringement of any patent application, patent or certificate of invention.

卖方不应由于任何专利申请、专利权或发明证明受到侵犯，而对买方负责任。

a patent right 专利权

patent law 专利法

proprietary adj.所有的，私人拥有的；n.所有者，所有权

Whereas，the company is desirous of securing assignments of the inventions and proprietary rights of Inventor in and to the identified applications…

有鉴于公司急欲获得发明转让的保证以及验证申请书中发明人专利权的保证……

The Architect represents and guarantees that the work is free from defects and contains no matter that infringes any of proprietary right at（country）laws.

建筑师表示并保证，工程没有缺陷，并且没有侵犯（某国）法律的所有权问题。

11.detrimental adj.有害的，不利的

Whereas，the Manufacturer desires to increase the public consumption of the product and to prevent detrimental，injurious and uneconomic practices in its distribution…

鉴于制造商希望增加产品的公共消费量以及在经销中防止出现不利的、有害的和浪费的经营方式……

detriment n.有损于，损害

All information received by Buyer from Seller shall not be disclosed by Buyer to others to the detriment of Seller.

买方从卖方（那里）收集到的一切信息不得由买方泄露给别人，以致有损于卖方。

12.royalty n.特许开采权，特许开采权利金；版税，专利权税，租费

AAA grants ZZZ a royalty-free nonexclusive license.

甲方授予乙方一张豁免特许权使用费的非独家许可证。

The lessee agrees with the lessor to pay to the lessor，as royalty upon all products that may be mined，shipped or sold from the property…% of the net mill value.

承租人同意从对此资源的开采、装运或出售的全部产品中，将净产值的……%作为租费支付给出租人。

13.construe vt.分析，翻译，解释，结合；把……看作

This guarantee shall be governed and construed in accordance with the laws of（country）.

本保证书按照（某国）法律予以执行与解释。

Nothing contained herein shall be construed to entitle ZZZ to any deduction of the price.

本文内容不能解释为授权乙方进行任何折价。

The provisions herein shall not be construed as the grant of a license on such trade mark.

本条款不得解释为该项商标已取得许可证。

14.confer vt.授予，商议

The failure of the Owner to exercise any option herein conferred shall not be construed as a waiver of any option.

不能把业主在行使其所得之优先买卖权上的失利，看成是放弃优先买卖权。

Class B preferred stock shall have no voting power, except in such cases where the name specifically is conferred by statute.

除非有条文明确规定，否则，B级优先股不应有选举权。

The company's supervisonary personnel shall have the right to enter the same conferring with the operator's employees.

公司监督人员应有权过问与经营者的雇员协商的上述事件。

15.renewal n.更新，复兴，恢复，续借，重申，补充

AAA becomes liable for the damages upon any renewal of the Agreement.

甲方对因协议的任何改变所造成的损失负有责任。

This Agreement shall enter into force on the signing of both parties.At least three（3）months before the expiration of the term, both Seller and Agent shall consult each other for renewal of this Agreement.If the renewal of this Agreement is agreed upon by both parties, this Agreement shall be renewed for another_____year（s）period under the terms and conditions herein set forth, with amendments, if agreed upon by both parties, unless this Agreement shall expire on_____.

本协议经双方签字生效。在本协议终止前至少3个月，卖方或代理商应共同协商协议的续延。如果双方一致同意续延，在上述规定的条款、条件下，附上补充文件，本协议将继续有效_____年。若不续延，本协议将于_____年月_____日终止。

renew vt.使更新，使恢复，重申，补充，续借，复兴；vi.更新，重新开始

The mortgage on the land shall be renewed as long as the payment is fully completed.

只要全部款项付清，土地抵押契约应当重订。

AAA shall have the right, privilege and option of renewing this Agreement.

甲方应享有重订协议的权利、特许权和选择权。

This Agreement shall automatically renew from year to year.

本协议应逐年自动更新。

renewable adj.可更新的，可恢复的，再开始

renewable resource　可再生资源

renewable energy　可再生能源

a one-year renewable contract 为期一年可续订的合同

16.acknowledge vt.承认，答谢

The Second Party borrows and acknowledges having received the sum of amount from the First Party.

乙方借到并承认收到甲方这笔款项。

The parties acknowledge and agree that Joint Venture Company shall be formed forthwith upon satisfaction of the following conditions.

各方确认并同意，在下述条件具备时应立即组成合资公司。

acknowledgment n.承认收悉，收到通知书

Claims for loss or damage will not be considered unless supported by railroad agent's acknowledgment on freight bill.

对损失或损坏的赔偿将不予考虑，除非铁路货运代理人确认货运单据。

The acknowledgment shall be in the form prescribed by the law of jurisdiction where executed.

承认将采取执行地区管辖范围内的法律所规定的形式。

17.prosecute vt.执行，控告

AAA and ZZZ shall jointly prosecute applications for patent.

甲方和乙方应联合执行专利权申请。

The First Party was injured on（date），while repairing a machine in the plant of the Second Party and desires to employ an attorney to prosecute his claim and cause of action against any person answerable for such injury.

甲方在乙方工厂修理机器（某日）受到损害，想聘请一名律师针对负有损害责任的人，依法提出索赔要求与诉讼原因。

prosecution n.执行，实行，起诉

Prosecution beyond such conditions of insurance shall be subject to further discussion.

超过保险条件的执行尚待进一步讨论。

The distributor shall save harmless the manufacturer from any claim that it may be liable for by reason of the institution and prosecution of such suit.

经销商要免除制造商因起诉而遭受的债务损失。

18.controversy n.争论，辩论，论战

The arbitrator shall promptly proceed to hear and determine the controversy.

仲裁人应迅速从事审理并裁决这一争论。

The controversy arising out of the contract shall be settled by arbitration.

因合同而产生的任何争议应由仲裁解决。

● Exercises

I.Translate the following sentences into English:

1.第一方承诺第二方享有独家租借某块土地的权利，供本协议有关各方鉴定之用。

2.甲方给予联合公司使用各种商标以及商标名称的权利。

3.任何根据乙方的判断认为过时的特殊设计，乙方可以不必销售。

4.许可证受让人应采取一切必要的措施以保护许可证发证人的商标专用权。

5.许可方应有权从将来的特许权使用费中得到补偿。

6.甲方应享有重订协议的权利、特许权和选择权。

7.在一方破产或资不抵债的情况下，另一方可以终止本协议。

8.许可方依照协议双方另行约定的费用和其他条款，就许可软件的使用，向被许可方提供培训。

9.许可方应于双方签订每个单立合同之日起60天内，向被许可方交付许可软件。

10.被许可方承认，许可方对许可软件的版权和作者的道德权享有所有权或控制权。

II.Translate the following sentences into Chinese:

1.The Manufacturer is the Owner of the trademark, which has been duly registered in the Patent Office.

2.Improvement refers to new findings and/or modifications made in the validity period of the Contract by either party in Know-how in the form of new designs, formulas, recipes, ingredients, indices, parameters, calculations, or any other indicators.

3.The Architect represents and guarantees that the work is free from defects and contains no matter that infringes any of proprietary right at （country） laws.

4.Whereas, the Manufacturer desires to increase the public consumption of the Product and to prevent detrimental, injurious and uneconomic practices in its distribution…

5.Each party hereto agrees to immediately and fully communicate to the other party any subject matter comprising an improvement, modification, further invention or design it may discover, make or develop with respect to manufacture and assembly of the Licensed Products or components thereof.

6.For the term of this agreement and commencing with a date mutually agreed upon for each Licensed Product, Party A undertakes to release to Party B details of major improvement engineering changes made by Party A to the Licensed Product.

7.Party B has requested permission to use the above-mentioned trademarks upon Goods made by itself, and Party A is willing to grant such permission on the terms and conditions hereinafter set forth.

8.Licensor shall provide a replacement copy of the Licensed Software if the medium on which the Licensed Software is delivered is defective and prevents the Licensed Software from being used.

9.With regard to rendering the actual services related to information technologies,

Licensor reserves the right to use any external resources for the fulfillment.

10.Licensee agrees not to copy，modify，enhance or merge the Licensed Software or any portion thereof，except as expressly permitted by this Agreement，and not to decompile or reverse engineer the Licensed Software.

# Unit Twelve /股权转让协议

# Agreement for the Transfer of Shares

A Company's Equity Assignment Agreement dated as of_____ , 2018, by and between B Company, the Assignor and C Company, the Assignee.

A Company, a foreign-funded company, was established with investment from B Company. A Company was registered in the Administrative Bureau for Industry and Commerce of Dalian with a registered capital of USD ×××, the total investment capital is USD ×××.

Whereas, the Assignor desires to sell and assign the equity interests of A Company, and the Assignee desires to acquire and accept assignment from the Assignor, the legal ownership of A Company's shares. Now, therefore, after amicable negotiation, the parties hereby agree as follows:

### Article 1.Parties Hereinafter Include

The Assignor:

B Company's official address:_____ ;

Legal representative:_____

Position:_____ ;

Nationality:_____

The Assignee:

C Company's official address:_____ ;

Legal representative:_____

Position:_____ ;

Nationality:_____

### Artice 2.The Price and Percentage of the Equity Interests Assigned

B Company assigns all its shares of 'A' Company to C Company at a cost of _____ , to be paid in the currency of_____.

### Article 3.Closing Date and Mode of the Equity Assignment

This Agreement shall become effective after the approval by the relevant endorsing authority, and the Assignee has paid the assignment fee specified in Article 2 to the Assignor within one month after the successful change of registration of the business license.

## Article 4.Representations，Guarantees and Covenants

4.1 The Assignor hereby represents，guarantees and covenants that it has all requisite power，authority and legal capacity to execute and deliver this Agreement，and the equity interests is free from any lien or hypothec，and without any third party recourse. Otherwise，the Assignor shall bear all legal liabilities herein arise.

4.2 The Assignor acknowledges that the date of the determineation of the Assignment Price shall be_____ （date），and that the contents of its audited financial statements as at the Relevant Date are true，accurate，complete，without omission or falsehood；and

4.3 After the assignment of the equity interests，the Assignee shall recognize and accept the contracts，memorandum，articles and appendixes of the original 'A' Company，and shall assume and execute all the rights，obligations and liabilities of the Assignor in 'A' Company.

## Article 5.Creditor and Debtor Responsibilities

5.1 After the parties have affixed their signatures to the Agreement，the Assignor shall be free from any liabilities of 'A' Company and benefit no more from the earnings of 'A' Company；the Assignee shall receive the unappropriated profits，inclusive of contributed surplus，retained earnings，reserve funds before the assignment and the profits after the assignment.

5.2 After the parties have affixed their signatures to the Agreement，the Assignee shall receive the profits and assume the risks and loss in proportion to the equity share of 'A' Company （including the debts and credits before the assignment）.

## Article 6.Expenses

All the expenses incurred in relation to the execution of this Agreement shall be absorbed by the Assignee.

## Article 7.The Appointment of Directors

The original directors appointed by the Assignor shall resign automatically and be replaced by directors appointed by the Assignee.

## Article 8.Breach of Agreement

In the event of the Assignee does not effect payment within the stipulated time specified in Clause 3，the Assignee shall pay the Assignor a penalty sum of 1% of the assignment amount for every overdue month，if the breach exceeds three months，the Assignor reserves the right to terminate this Agreement and demands indemnification，other than the penalty sum from the Assignee.

## Article 9.Governing Law and Dispute Resolution

9.1 This Agreement and its effectiveness，validity，interpretation，execution and settlement of disputes shall be governed by and construed in accordance with the laws of the People's Republic of China.

9.2 In the event of any dispute, claim, question or difference arises with respect to this Agreement or its performance or enforcement, the parties will use their reasonable efforts to attempt to settle such dispute amicably; if the parties cannot resolve the dispute, then it shall be resolved by the China International Trade Arbitration Commission based on the prevailing arbitration rules. The award of the arbitrators will be final and binding as to all parties; the losing party shall bear all the arbitration costs.

### Article 10.Rights of the Unassigned Party

The unassigned party voluntarily waives the priority rights on the assigned shares of the Assignor and agrees to the assignment in accordance with the terms and conditions of this Agreement.

### Article 11.Binding Effect and Other Matters

This Agreement shall become effective after the Assignor and the Assignee have affixed their signatures to it and approved by the relevant endorsing authority. This Agreement is in quintuplicate, the Assignor, the Assignee, 'A' Company, the endorsing authority and the registration department shall hold one copy each.

In witness whereof, the parties hereto have caused this Agreement to be executed by their respective duly authorized officers, as of the date first written above.

The Assignor:

_____ ( signature and seal of the company )

Legal Representative:_____

The Assignee:

_____ ( signature and seal of the company )

Legal Representative:_____

**参考译文:**

### 股权转让协议

A公司的股权转让协议签于2018年_____，B公司为出让方，C公司为受让方。

出让方:B公司

受让方:C公司

A公司是由B公司投资设立的一家外资企业。A公司在大连市工商行政管理局登记，注册资本为××万美元，投资总额为××万美元。

鉴于出让方有意出售并转让A公司的合法股权，受让方有意购买并接受转让方的出让。因此，经过友好协商，双方达成协议如下:

第1条 出让方和受让方的基本情况

出让方:

B公司，法定地址:_____；法定代表人:_____；职务:_____；国籍:

_____。

受让方：

C公司，法定地址：_____；法定代表人：_____；职务：_____；国籍：_____。

第2条 股权转让的价格和百分比

B公司将其所持A公司的全部股份，转让给C公司，转让价格为_____，支付币种为_____。

第3条 股权转让交割期限及方式

本协议由审批机构批准后生效，受让方将第二条约定的转让款项自营业执照变更后一个月内缴付给出让方。

第4条 声明、保证及承诺

4.1 出让方在此声明、保证并承诺所转让的股权为其合法拥有，具有完全、有效的处分权，且没有设置任何抵押权或其他担保权，并免遭任何第三人的追索，否则，出让方应承担由此而引起的所有法律责任。

4.2 转让方确认，转让价确定日期为_____（日期），于相关日期编制的经审计的财务报表真实、准确、全面、无遗漏或虚假。

4.3 上述股权转让后，受让方承认原A公司的合同、章程、条款及附件，愿意承担并履行原转让方在A公司中的一切权利、义务及责任。

第5条 债权债务的承担

5.1 自本协议各方签字之日起，出让方不再负担A公司的任何责任，也不再享有A公司的任何收益，公司转让前的未分配利润，包括资本公积、盈余公积、储备基金及转让后的收益，归受让方所有。

5.2 自本协议各方签字之日起，受让方按其在A公司中股份比例分享利润和分担风险及亏损（包括转让前该股份应享有和分担之公司的债权债务）。

第6条 费用

本协议实施所发生的有关费用，由受让方承担。

第7条 董事的委派

原出让方委派的董事会成员自动退出A公司，改由受让方委派。

第8条 违约责任

受让方若未按本协议第三条规定的期限如数缴付出资时，每逾期1个月，受让方需缴付应出资额的1%的违约金给出让方，如逾期3个月仍未缴付的，除向甲方缴付违约金之外，出让方有权终止本协议，并要求受让方赔偿损失。

第9条 适用的法律及争议的解决

9.1 本协议以及效力、合法性、解释、签署、争议的解决应适用中华人民共和国法律。

9.2 凡因履行本协议所发生的或与本协议有关的一切争议、索赔、质疑或歧义，各方应通过友好协商解决；如果协商不能解决，应提交中国国际贸易仲裁委员会，根据该机构的仲裁规则进行仲裁。仲裁裁决是终局的，对各方都有约束力。仲裁费用由败诉方负担。

第10条　未受让方的权益

上述出让方转让的股份，未受让方自愿放弃所享有的优先权，同意根据本协议的条款而进行的转让。

第11条　协议的生效与其他事宜

此协议经出让、受让各方正式签署后报原审批机关批准后生效。本协议一式五份，协议各方各执一份，A公司一份，报审批、登记机关各一份。

协议双方于前文所述日期签署本协议，特此证明。

出让方：　　　　　　　　　受让方：

_____公司（盖章签字）：　　_____公司（盖章签字）：

法定代表人：　　　　　　　法定代表人：

## Notes

1.memorandum 公司章程

公司章程的其他表示法有：

the articles of association

the memorandum of association

the articles of incorporation

Memorandum and Articles of Association　（M&A）

2.affix n.附录，附件；v.附加，加（附言），附上（签名等），（尤指在末尾）添上；盖（印章）

The notary's seal or stamp must be affixed.

须经公证人盖章。

He affixed his signature to the document.

他在那份文件上签了名。

affix a seal

盖上图章

3.assign v.转让，主要用于对某财产或权利的转让；分配；指定

assignor 出让人

assignee 受让人

assignment n.转让，转让书，分配的任务

Neither the Owner nor the Architect shall assign or sublet his interest in this Agreement.

无论业主或建筑师都不得将其在本协议中的股权（利益）转让或转租（给他人）。

Assignor shall continue to be liable and assignee shall assume liability for the due performance of the Contract.

为了正当履行合同，转让人将继续负责，受让人也得承担义务。

The Purchaser shall not be entitled to any abatement in the purchase price，if such assignment cannot or may not be effected.

如转让未能或不可能生效，则买主无权降低购买价格。

4.absorb v.承担

The cost shall be absorbed by the seller.

费用由卖方承担。

5.resign vt.& vi.辞职，放弃

The trustees shall not resign before the termination of the trust.

在托管期满以前，托管人不应辞职。

He resigned his directorship and left the firm.

他放弃了董事职务，离开了公司。

resignation n.辞职

Upon resignation of Individual A，the First Party and the Second Party jointly shall have full power to appoint any other persons to act as trustee，in the place of Individual A.

甲某辞职以后，第一方和第二方应共同享有全权去委任其他人员出任托管人，以取代甲某的位置。

6.英语合同中常见的"优先权"表示法，可以翻译成"优先购买权"。

right of preemption

right of preference

right of priority

right of first refusal

The third party agrees to purchase…shares of common stock together with all dividends，incomes and issues therefrom，and all right of preemption.

第三方同意购买……股普通股以及一切股息、收益和有权权益以及一切优先购买权。

Orders placed by the Buyer shall receive first priority in the Manufacturer's production schedule.

买方所下的订单在制造商的生产日常表中应享有第一优先权的待遇。

● Exercises

I.Translate the following into English:

1.本股权转让（简称"转让"）总对价（简称"转让价"）详见协议双方约定的本协议附件三第二条。

2.转让价不含下述第二条第3款规定的应付的转让（可能的）税款。

3.受让人应于下列第三条第1款第1项所述交割日期，向转让方支付转让价格。

4.受让人应提交与转让相关的所有必要文件供盖印，应代表转让方依照相关法律，向有关税务部门纳税。

5.在风险投资中，公司章程是一个重要文本。

6.公司章程设定了包含但不限于不同种类、不同序列的公司股票所对应的权利、优先权、特权及限制。

7."衍生证券"指任何可转换、执行或兑换为普通股的有价证券或权利，包括期权和认股权证。

8."股东"指持有可登记证券的、为本协议当事方的股东。

9."发起股东"指根据本协议适当地发起登记申请的股东之统称。

10."首次公开招股"指公司根据《证券法》首次将它的普通股公开销售。

II.Translate the following into Chinese:

1. "Key Employment" means any executive-level employee （including division director and vice president-level positions） as well as any employee who, either alone or in concert with others, develops, invents, programs, or designs any Company Intellectual Propery （as defined in the Purchase Agreemnt）.

2. "Major Investor" means any Investor that, individually or together with such Investor's Affiliates, holds at least … shares of Resigtrable Securities （as adjusted for any stock split, stock dividend, combinations, or other recapitalization or reclassification effected after the date hereof）.

3.In the event there is more than one closing, the term "Closing" shall apply to each such closing unless otherwise specified.

4. "Company Intellectual Property" means all patents, patent applications, trademarks, trademark applications, service marks, tradenames, copyrights, trade secrets, licenses, domain names, mask works, information and proprietary rights and processes as are necessary to th conduct of the Company's business as now conducted and as presently proposed to be conducted.

5. "Shares" means the shares of Series A Preferred Stock issued at the Initial Closing and any （Milestone Shares or ） Additional Shares issued at a subsequent Closing under Section 1.3.

6. For the purposes of these representations and warranties （other than those in Sections 2.2, 2.3, 2.4, 2.5, and 2.6）, the term "the Company" shall include any subsidiaries of the Company, unless otherwise noted herein.

7. With respect to the property and assets it leases, the Company is in compliance with such leases and, to its knowledge, holds a valid leasehold interest free of any liens, claims or encumbrances other than those of the lessors of such property or assets.

8. The Financial Statements have been prepared in accordance with generally accepted accounting principles applied on a consistent basis throughout the periods

indicated.

9. The share of capital stock of the Corporation shall not be sold， pledged， hypothecated， or transferred.

10.By the contract B shall be entitled to have a general lien on all of the merchandise.

# Unit Thirteen /关于马来西亚A项目的三方合作协议

## Tripartite Cooperation Agreement

## in relation to Project A，Malaysia

dated: 10th April，2018

于2018年4月10日签署

### Parties

（A）ABCD a company incorporated under the laws of Malaysia with Commercial Registration Number [567] and whose registered address is at PO Box 123，Malaysia （ABCD）；

（B）CDEF a company incorporated under the laws of Malaysia with Commercial Registration Number [789] and whose registered address is PO Box 234，Malaysia （CDEF）；and

（C）EFGH a company incorporated under the laws of Malaysia with Commercial Registration Number [678] and whose registered office is PO Box 345，Malaysia （EFGH）

each a Party and together the Parties.

### Introduction

（A）ABCD is the owner of the real estate development known as City of Square （more particularly defined below as the Development）.

（B）ABCD and CDEF have entered into a sale and purchase agreement with certain addendum under which CDEF shall purchase the above mentioned building within the Development（the "Building"）.

（C）ABCD employed EFGH to carry out certain construction works at the Development in accordance with the terms of a building contract dated [Feb 1st，2018] （the "Construction Contract"）.The construction works under the Construction Contract are inclusive of the Building.

（D）ABCD，CDEF and EFGH have had several discussions with the objective of finding a solution to expedite the remaining works for completion of the Development （the

"Works") by addressing the financial requirement of the Works and have agreed to act reasonably and in good faith to achieve the completion of such Works in accordance with the terms of this Agreement.

## Agreed Terms

### 1.Interpretation

1.1    The singular includes the plural and vice versa, and words of one gender include any other gender.

1.2    The headings above the clauses and the contents pages of this Agreement are for reference only and do not affect its construction.

1.3    Any reference to a clause or schedule without further designation is a reference to a clause or schedule of this Agreement.

### 2.Cooperation

2.1    As soon as practicable after the date of this Agreement, ABCD and EFGH shall execute either a new construction contract or an agreement amending the terms and conditions of the Construction Contract (the "New Construction Agreement") under which EFGH shall agree to carry out the Works.

2.2    In consideration of EFGH agreeing to execute the New Construction Agreement and carry out the Works, ABCD and CDEF severally covenant with EFGH that from the date of this Agreement they shall comply with their respective undertakings, responsibilities, obligations and covenants in this Agreement and agree to act reasonably and in good faith to provide such comfort to EFGH and its financiers that the monies due under the New Construction Agreement.

2.3    In the event of a breach of clause 2.2 by either or both ABCD and CDEF, EFGH shall be able to exercise and enforce their rights under this Agreement for non-performance by ABCD or CDEF (as appropriate).

2.4    The Parties agree (so far as each is able) to take all such steps and do all such acts and things as may be necessary or desirable and execute any ancillary agreements as are necessary or desirable (in EFGH's sole discretion) to give effect to the Parties' intentions as detailed in this Agreement.

### 3.Undertakings

3.1    From the date of this Agreement until the date that all monies that shall or may be claimed by EFGH under or in connection with the New Construction Agreement are paid or settled in full, CDEF agrees and irrevocably undertakes that:

3.1.1    notwithstanding any direction or instruction from ABCD or any third party, to transfer all remaining monies payable to ABCD according to Schedule 4 (as amended) of the respective purchase agreement to such bank account as is notified by EFGH to CDEF in writing.For the avoidance of doubt, the total of all remaining monies payable under the purchase agreements by CDEF to ABCD is USD 50, 000, 000;

3.1.2 to pay all such monies in full and not to make any deduction or set-off from such monies in any circumstance. Any dispute of whatsoever kind under or in connection with the purchase agreements (including any right of deduction or set-off that CDEF may have) shall not affect or prejudice EFGH's right and entitlement to the monies referred to in Clause 3.1.1. Such dispute shall be separately dealt with and settled between CDEF and ABCD under the respective purchase agreement subject to the terms of this Agreement; and

3.1.3 without the written consent of EFGH, amend the purchase agreements or enter into any agreement with ABCD or any third party relating to the Buildings.

3.2 From the date of this Agreement until the date that all monies that will or may be claimed by EFGH under or in connection with the New Construction Agreement are paid in full, ABCD acknowledges and agrees that:

3.2.1 all remaining monies payable to ABCD in accordance with the purchase agreements will be assigned to EFGH and paid to such account as is determined by EFGH in accordance with clause 3.1 and ABCD shall not direct CDEF to pay the monies due under the purchase agreements to any other bank account; and

3.2.2 provided that such monies are paid in full (without set-off or deduction) and on their due date for payment, payment by CDEF of all monies due to be paid to ABCD under the purchase agreements to EFGH in accordance with clause 3.1 will form satisfaction of CDEF's obligations under clause 4 and Schedule 4 (as amended) of the purchase agreements and ABCD shall not bring any claim or action against CDEF for non-performance of clause 4 of the purchase agreements; and

3.2.3 without the written consent of EFGH, amend the purchase agreements or enter into any agreement with CDEF or any third party relating to the Buildings.

3.3 Notwithstanding the terms and conditions of this Agreement, CDEF undertakes, acknowledges and agrees that:

3.3.1 The Parties do not intend that this Agreement shall create any direct contractual relationship between CDEF and EFGH in respect of the execution, delivery or handover of the Works; and

3.3.2 CDEF shall not bring any claim or proceedings directly against EFGH in respect of late delivery of the Buildings or any other matters dealt with under the terms and conditions of the New Construction Agreement.

3.4 If prior to the date of this Agreement, CDEF has assigned its rights and obligations under the purchase agreements to a lender or financier in accordance with clause 6 of the purchase agreements or otherwise secured any monies against the Buildings or the provisions of the purchase agreements, within fourteen days of the date of this

Agreement, CDEF shall procure an acknowledgment and acceptance by such lender or financier of the terms of this Agreement (in a form acceptable to EFGH acting reasonably).

3.5 Following the date of this Agreement, CDEF shall not assign its rights and obligations under the purchase agreements to a lender or financier in accordance with clause 6 of the purchase agreements or otherwise secured any monies against the Buildings or the provisions of the purchase agreements, without procuring the prior written acknowledgment and acceptance by such lender or financier of the terms of this Agreement (in a form acceptable to EFGH acting reasonably).

### 4.Other Agreements

In the event of any ambiguity or discrepancy between the provisions of this Agreement and either the purchase agreements or the New Construction Agreement, then it is the intention of the Parties that the provisions of this Agreement shall prevail. Accordingly, each Party (so far as each is able) shall take all such steps and do all such acts and things as may be necessary or desirable, so as to give effect to the provisions of this Agreement.

### 5.Representations and Warranties

5.1 Each Party warrants and represents to the other Parties that:

5.1.1 it has duly executed and delivered this Agreement;

5.1.2 it has the full power and authority to execute, perform and observe this Agreement;

5.1.3 it has obtained all necessary governing body and shareholder approvals and all other necessary governmental and other consents, approvals and registrations to authorise the execution, performance and observance of this Agreement;

5.1.4 the execution of, performance of and observance by this Agreement will not result in any breach of its constitutional documentation, or any provision contained in any agreement or instrument to which it is a party or by which such company is bound or any law applicable to it;

5.1.5 this Agreement will, when executed, constitute legally valid and binding obligations on such Party, be enforceable in accordance with its terms;

5.1.6 there is no pending or, action, suit, investigation, arbitration or other proceeding that would impair the ability of that Party to perform its obligations under this Agreement; and

5.1.7 that all information furnished to the other Party at any time prior to the execution of this Agreement relative to the subject matter of this Agreement was at the time it was provided (and remains at the date hereof) true and accurate in all material aspects.

5.2 Each Party acknowledges that the other Parties are entering into this Agreement in reliance upon each of the warranties in clause 5.1.

## 6.Confidentiality

6.1    This clause applies to:

6.1.1    all information of a confidential nature disclosed （whether in writing, verbally or by any other means and whether directly or indirectly） by one Party to the other Parties whether before or after the date of this Agreement；

6.1.2    any information concerning the business affairs of one Party or other information confidential to that Party which the other Parties learn as a result of the relationship between the Parties pursuant to this Agreement；

6.1.3    including any information relating to any Party's products， operations， processes， plans or intentions， product information， know-how， design rights， trade secrets， market opportunities and business affairs （together Confidential Information） .

6.2    In this clause， in relation to a particular item of Confidential Information:

6.2.1    the Disclosing Party means the Party by whom （or on whose behalf） that Confidential Information is disclosed or （where there is no such disclosure） the Party to whom the Confidential Information relates， or to whom the Confidential Information is proprietary or who otherwise desires that the confidentiality of the Confidential Information is respected； and

6.2.2    the Receiving Parties means the other Parties.

6.3    During the term of this Agreement and after termination of this Agreement for any reason whatsoever， the Receiving Parties shall:

6.3.1    keep the Confidential Information confidential；

6.3.2    not disclose the Confidential Information to any other person other than with the prior written consent of the Disclosing Party or in accordance with this clause 6； and

6.3.3    not use the Confidential Information for any purpose other than the performance of its obligations and the exercise of its rights under this Agreement.

6.4    Notwithstanding clause 6.3， the Receiving Parties may disclose Confidential Information as follows:

6.4.1    to its professional advisers （each， a Recipient） providing the Receiving Parties ensure that each Recipient is made aware of and complies with all the Receiving Parties' obligations of confidentiality under this Agreement as if the Recipient was a party to this Agreement； and

6.4.2    to other parties to this Agreement and to their Affiliates， and where disclosure is required by Law， by any court of competent jurisdiction or by any appropriate regulatory body.

6.5    This clause 6 does not apply to any Confidential Information which:

6.5.1    is at the date of this Agreement or at a later date comes into the public domain other than through breach of this Agreement by the Receiving Parties or any Recipient;

6.5.2    was known by the Receiving Parties before receipt from （or on behalf of） the Disclosing Party.

### 7.General

7.1    Any notice given under this Agreement must be in writing and must be served by delivering it personally or sending it by registered post to the address detailed at the beginning of this Agreement.

7.2    The Parties do not intend that a third party should have the right to enforce any provision of this Agreement.

7.3    No failure or delay by a Party in exercising any right under this Agreement will operate as a waiver thereof nor will any single or partial exercise of any right preclude its further exercise or the exercise of any other right.

7.4    No Party shall assign， transfer， charge， underlet or otherwise deal with its interest under this Agreement in whole or in part without the other Parties' prior written consent.

7.5    Each of the provisions of this Agreement is severable and distinct from the others and if at any time one or more of such provisions is or becomes invalid， illegal or unenforceable， the validity， legality and enforceability of the remaining provisions of this Agreement will not in any way be affected or impaired thereby.

7.6    This Agreement may only be amended with the prior written agreement of all of the Parties.

### 8.Governing Law and Jurisdiction

8.1    This Agreement will be governed by and construed in accordance with the laws of the Malaysia.

8.2    All disputes which may arise will， if they cannot be amicably settled， be finally settled by arbitration and either Party may refer such disputes to the China International Economic and Trade Arbitration Commission. Any arbitration shall be conducted pursuant to the rules of the China International Economic and Trade Arbitration Commission incorporating any amendments or modifications published on or before the date of this Agreement.Any arbitration shall be conducted in the English language.

This Agreement has been executed on the date stated at the beginning of this Agreement.

**参考译文**:

**签约方**

（1）ABCD公司在马来西亚法律下成立，营业执照注册号码为:567，注册地址为马来西亚邮箱123（以下简称ABCD）；

（2）CDEF公司在马来西亚法律下成立，营业执照注册号码为789，注册地址

为马来西亚邮箱234（以下简称 CDEF）；和

（3）EFGH公司在马来西亚法律下成立，营业执照注册号码为678，注册地址为马来西亚邮箱345（以下简称 EFGH）

以上每一方为合同一方，几方共同构成多方。

## 背景介绍

（A）ABCD 公司为城市广场（以下简称"开发物业"）地产开发项目的所有者。

（B）ABCD 和 CDEF 已经达成了销售协议，销售协议约定 CDEF 将会购买上述开发物业的部分楼宇（购买的楼宇）。

（C）ABCD 与 EFGH 于2018年2月1日签署针对开发物业的工程建设合同，工程建设范围包括上述购买的楼宇。

（D）ABCD，CDEF 和 EFGH 已经对目前在建物业通过融资解决剩余工程的解决方案探讨过多次，并且三方同意将在不违反其他合同约定的情况下，积极采取行动按照本协议的约定来将物业开发完毕。

## 合同条款

### 1.说明

1.1　本协议使用单词单数与复数形式互指，指代某一性别的词语包含其他性别。

1.2　上述条款和协议内容中的标题仅作参考，不影响其项下的内容。

1.3　如果没有进一步的说明，任何对条款或者附件的参考都是对本协议中相关条款和附件的参考。

### 2.合作

2.1　在本合同签署后，ABCD 和 EFGH 会签署一个新的建设合同（以下简称"新建设合同"）或者针对之前的建设合同进行修订，在此合同项下，EFGH 将会继续执行此项目。

2.2　鉴于 EFGH 将继续执行此项目，ABCD 和 CDEF 共同承诺将遵守各自的约定、责任，履行各自的义务，并在此协议项下积极配合 EFGH 和融资人的工作。

2.3　如果 ABCD 和 CDEF 中的任何一方违反了条款2.2的约定，EFGH 有权向双方中的任何一方进行索偿。

2.4　以上各方将会尽一切努力，行一切必要之事或者在 EFGH 的要求下签署必要的补充协议来促使本协议的执行。

### 3.承诺

3.1　从本协议签署之日起至全额支付给 EFGH 所有的新建设合同的款项过程中，CDEF 承诺：

3.1.1　一旦收到 ABCD 或者任何第三方的指示或者要求，CDEF 将按照之前销售协议附件4中的约定支付给 ABCD 相应的款项，款项将支付到 EFGH 书面指示的账户中。为了避免任何可能出现的歧义，在销售协议项下由 CDEF 支付给 ABCD 的金额预计为5 000万美元。

3.1.2 将全额支付所有的应付工程款，且在任何情况下不会做出抵扣或者冲减。销售协议中的任何纠纷（包括 CDEF 可能拥有的抵扣或者冲减权）都不能影响 EFGH 在本协议条款 3.1.1 项下的权利。这些纠纷由 CDEF 和 ABCD 基于本协议的约定和签署的销售协议单独处理解决。

3.1.3 没有 EFGH 的书面同意，不会更改销售协议或者与 ABCD 或其他第三方签署与购买的楼宇相关的任何协议。

3.2 从本合同签署之日起至全额支付给 EFGH 所有的新建设合同的款项过程中，ABCD 承诺：

3.2.1 所有在销售协议项下 ABCD 的应收账款将按照条款 3.1 的约定转让给 EFGH，并且支付到 EFGH 指定的账户，同时 ABCD 承诺不会指示 CDEF 支付到其他任何账户。

3.2.2 只要 CDEF 在销售协议下的合同款项按照本协议条款 3.1 的约定付给 ABCD 的全额且及时支付（没有抵扣或者冲减）给 EFGH，就认为 CDEF 履行了销售协议条款 4 和销售协议下附件 4 所要求的义务，并且 ABCD 也不能以未履行销售协议条款 4 的义务提出任何抗辩。

3.2.3 没有得到 EFGH 的书面同意，ABCD 不会修改销售协议且也不会与 CDEF 或者其他第三方签署任何关于购买楼宇的协议。

3.3 尽管本协议的条款已有所约定，CDEF 依旧承诺：

3.3.1 各方承诺本合同的签署不构成 CDEF 和 EFGH 之间的直接合同关系，不会限制 EFGH 的项目执行、交付和移交。

3.3.2 如果购买的楼宇延迟交付或者在新建设合同项下存在纠纷，CDEF 不会将这些纠纷或者权利主张直接面向 EFGH。

3.4 如果在本协议签署之前，CDEF 按照销售协议条款 6 的约定或者由于需要确保购买楼宇的款项，或者确保销售协议条款的正常履行，已经转让了其销售协议下的权利和义务给借款方或者融资人，那么在本协议签署后的 14 日之内，CDEF 将寻求借款方或者融资方的确认和接受（按照 EFGH 可接受的方式）。

3.5 在本协议签署之后，CDEF 在未获得本协议项下借款方或者融资方的同意的前提下（按照 EFGH 可接受的方式），不能转让任何权利和义务，即使其按照销售协议条款 6 的约定或者由于需要确保购买楼宇的款项，或者确保销售协议条款的正常履行。

### 4.其他约定

如果本协议条款与销售协议或者新建设合同有任何冲突或者模糊的地方，本协议的条款具有优先效力。因此，协议的每一方都应该尽最大努力来履行本协议的约定。

### 5.陈述和保证

5.1 协议每一方都对其他方作如下保证：

5.1.1 协议方都正式认同并履行本协议。

5.1.2　协议方有权力或者已得到授权来执行、履约和遵守本协议。

5.1.3　协议方已经取得了所有必要的管理机构的许可和股东的授权，或者得到了相关政府机构的同意、审批并进行了登记要求，以执行、履约和遵守本协议的规定。

5.1.4　本协议的执行、履约和遵守不能违反国家宪法的规定，或者其他合同及法律对本协议方的约束。

5.1.5　本协议的执行具有法律效力，对各方形成约束，协议执行需要按照条款的约定进行。

5.1.6　各方不存在未决的纠纷、案件、诉讼、调查、仲裁或者其他事项对协议方的履约造成影响。

5.1.7　在执行本协议之前和签署本协议时所提供给其他方的信息务必是真实的、准确的。

5.2　协议方知晓其他方签署此协议都是基于5.1条款的承诺。

## 6.保密

6.1　本条款要求以下信息需要保密:

6.1.1　不论协议签署之前还是之后，所有由一方披露给其他各方的保密信息（不管是通过书面、口头或者其他方式，直接或者间接披露）。

6.1.2　所有关于协议一方商业运营的保密信息或其他由于本协议项下的关联关系得到了相关的披露的信息。

6.1.3　任何关于协议方的产品、运营、流程、商业计划或意向、产品信息、技术诀窍、设计权、贸易秘密、市场机会和商业活动的信息（总称为"保密信息"）。

6.2　本条款中，对于保密信息的特殊项进行说明:

6.2.1　信息提供方是指提供保密信息方或者指信息提供方，或者即使没有信息提供，与保密信息有关的相关方，或者保密信息的所有人，或者对保密信息有保密要求的相关方。

6.2.2　信息接受方指除了信息提供方的其他方。

6.3　在本协议的执行期和协议终止后，信息接受方应:

6.3.1　确保保密信息保持机密。

6.3.2　依据本协议条款6的约定，在没有信息提供方的书面同意前，不得将保密信息泄漏给任何人。

6.3.3　不得将保密信息用于非本协议履约项下的目的。

6.4　尽管有条款6.3的要求，信息接受方可以在以下情况下披露保密信息:

6.4.1　将信息披露给其专业顾问（每位顾问作为一个信息接受方），只要信息接受方确保每位顾问都知晓其应被视为协议的一方遵守本协议项下信息接受方的保密义务。

6.4.2　在法律要求、法院判决要求或者其他管制机构要求下将保密信息披露给其他第三方或者其关联方。

6.5　本条款6不适用于以下保密信息：

6.5.1　在协议签署日或者签署后，信息流入到公共领域，而非由信息接受方披露所致。

6.5.2　在信息提供方提供之前，信息接受方已经知晓。

### 7.综合要求

7.1　本协议项下的所有通知必须以书面的形式提供，且需要亲自递交或者通过挂号信的方式邮寄到本协议前面所述的地址。

7.2　协议方不得引入任意第三方来执行本协议。

7.3　任何一方未能或延迟行使本协议规定的任何权利不得视为该方放弃该权利，行使或部分行使任何权利亦不得排除其对该权利的进一步行使。

7.4　在未获得其他方书面同意的情况下，任何一方不得转让、转移或者廉价处置合同相关的权益。

7.5　本协议的每一个条款都是可分割的，如果协议中的某些条款失效，违反法律要求或者无法执行，则其他条款不受这些条款的影响，且其他条款依然有效。

7.6　本协议在得到其他协议方书面同意的情况下可以进行相应的更改。

### 8.适用法律和管辖

8.1　本协议适用于马来西亚法律且按照马来西亚法律解释。

8.2　凡本协议的任何争议如果无法通过友好协商解决，则需要通过仲裁解决，仲裁机构为中国国际贸易仲裁委员会，申请仲裁时按照现行有效的仲裁规则进行仲裁。仲裁语言为英语。

本协议的生效日在协议前面有所说明。

# Notes

1.other than conj.除了，除了……以外

The Joint Company shall have no obligation to pay for the costs of such training, other than to pay for their salaries.

除了支付他们的薪金以外，联营公司并无责任支付这类培训的费用。

Nothing contained in this Agreement shall prevent the Seller from selling goods of the kind specified in this Contract to persons other than the Buyer.

本协议所列条款，不应妨碍卖方将本合同中所提的那种货物出售给（本协议中）买方以外的人士。

2.intend v.意愿

Prior to filling application, B shall advise A of its decision to file application for such patents and the countries in which it intends to file.

在申请专利之前，乙方须将其申请的各该项专利以及意欲向哪些国家申请等决定通知甲方。

3.preclude v.阻止，排除，妨碍

Litigation may be instituted by a governmental agency，which，if successful，would preclude such transaction.

政府机构可以提出诉讼，如果诉讼成功，则可阻止这种交易。

Nothing contained in this article shall be deemed to conflict with or preclude termination of this Agreement.

本条所列的内容不应被认为同终止本协议的事宜有所冲突或有所妨碍。

4.addendum n.附录，附件；补遗；附加物

All other terms and conditions of the Agreement shall remain in full force and effect，except to the extent that any such terms and conditions is inconsistent with the terms of this Addendum.

本协议的所有其他条款将保持完全有效，除非有任一条款与本协议的附录条款不一致。

5.entitlement n.权利；津贴

security entitlement 证券权益；证券权利

6.proceedings n.进行；程序；诉讼程序；事项

We should settle the dispute through negotiations without resorting to legal proceedings.

我们应通过协商来解决争议，而不应通过法律程序来解决。

7.in reliance upon 依赖

The Commissioner expressly disclaims any liability in respect to anything done or not done to any person in reliance upon any of the contents of this publication.

本委员会明确声明，不负责因依据本出版物之任何内容而对任何人采取或未采取的措施。

● Exercises

I.Translate the following sentences in to English:

1.本合同所有附件都是本合同不可分割的一部分。

2.根据第2.1款，要求雇主给予承包人进入现场的权利，以便承包商有权前往工地。

3.如果雇主选择对分包商直接付款，他应确保遵守本款规定的程序。

4.根据第一段，合同价格要考虑任何此类改变进行调整。

5.本指南在第三条解释末尾的表格中简要总结了承包商的权利。

6.承包商还应提交所有关于此类事件或情况的合同要求的任何其他通知，以及支持索赔的详细资料。

7.收到索赔方的书面委托后，要求乙方遵循程序规则。

8.在2018年期间，集团公司开始准备争端裁决员的名单，其中许多人也可认

为适宜担当调解员。

9.成员应适中保持他/她的公正性和独立性，每当发生任何能使成员的公正性和独立性受到怀疑的事宜时，应通知其他成员和当事各方。

10.第8.9款第一句授予承包商有权获得有关这些"复工"方面的延长期和付款。

II.Translate the following sentences into Chinese:

1.The Recipient acknowledges that the Confidential Information is confidential and undertakes hereby to use the Confidential Information solely for the purpose set out in Annex II.

2.If Buyer is in breach of this presentation and warrants in Clause 2.1 herein, Seller shall have the right to terminate this Purchase Agreement by a mere notice of termination and claim any loss and/or damage thus incurred.

3.Contractor's Equipment, which includes Subcontractor's equipment, is deemed to be intended for the execution of the Works, and not for use elsewhere.Consent is required before each major item leaves the Site, except in respect of transport vehicles, which typically leave the Site daily.

4.In this Sub-Clause, "table of adjustment data" means the completed table of adjustment data included in the Appendix to Tender.If there is no such table of adjustment data, this Sub-Clause shall not apply.

5.Unless and until the Employer receives this guarantee, or if the total advance payment is not stated in this Addendum to the Tender, this Sub-Clause shall not apply.

6.If the Contract includes a Schedule of Payments specifying the installments in which the Contract Price will be paid, then unless otherwise stated in this Schedule.

7.In the various Sub-Clauses, the Contractor's entitlements to claim are expressed using similar wording, typically as follows.

8.Unless the Parties agree otherwise, no Member should participate in a future arbitration, either as arbitrator or as witness.

9.The Contractor shall not interfere unnecessarily or improperly with the convenience of the public, or the access to and use and occupation of all roads and footpaths, irrespective of whether they are public or in the possession of the Employer or of others.

10.If the Employer's Requirements describe the Contractor's Documents which are to be submitted to the Engineer for review and/or for approval, they shall be submitted accordingly, together with a notice as described below.

# Unit Fourteen /国际借贷合同

## Agreement for International Loan

This Loan Agreement is made on⋯, 20⋯ between:

(1) A Company Ltd. (the Borrower) and

(2) C Bank (the Lender)

Whereas the Borrower applied to the Lender for, and the Lender agreed to make available to the Borrower, a foreign exchange loan Facility in the maximum (aggregate amount) of Euro⋯ plus USD⋯the two parties, after negotiations, agree as follows:

1.Definitions

In this Loan Agreement, unless where expressly provided for otherwise, the following terms shall have the following meanings:

"Availability Period" means the period stipulated in Clause 3.2 of this Loan Agreement during which the Borrower may draw the Facility;

"Banking Day" means a day on which:

(1) C Bank in Beijing

(2) French Banks in Paris

(3) C Bank in New York and

(4) C Bank in London

are all open for business;

"Construction Contract" means the Construction Contract of the Project (No. ⋯) made between the Borrower and the Contractor;

"Construction Expenditure" means the costs and expenses of construction, installation, purchase of equipment, maritime freight and other expenses relevant to the Project Construction;

"Construction Period" means a period commencing from the effective date of Construction Contract to the "Preliminary Handing Over Date";

"Contractor" means N whose head office is located in Paris, France, and China NCC Corporation whose head office is located in Beijing, China;

"Dollar (US Dollar)" means the legal currency of the United States of America;

"Events of Default" means any one of the events or circumstances specified in

Clause 16.1 of this Loan Agreement;

"Facility" means the amount of money stipulated in Clause 2.1 of this Loan Agreement which may be drawn and / or has been drawn by the Borrower, including Tranche A Facility, Tranche B Facility and Tranche C Facility;

"Final Mechanical Completion Date" means the last day of the twenty-six（26）months commencing from the effective date of the Construction Contract;

"Euro" refers to the currencies of 19 European Union countries;

"Interest Deposit Account" means the US Dollars account opened specifically for payment of interest, the commitment fee and the administration fee during the Construction Period of the Project;

"Interest Payment Date" means the last day of each Interest Period;

"Interest Period" means the period of each six months, starting from the date of initial drawdown and ending on the date on which the total principal, interest and all expenses and fees under this Loan Agreement have been fully repaid;

"Joint Venture Agreement" means the Joint Venture Agreement signed in Beijing, the People's Republic of China, on_____, 20_____among

（1）NC

（2）S and

（3）P

for the purpose of jointly establishing and managing the A Co.Ltd.;

"Mortgage" means mortgage, pledge or other security arrangement of any kind;

"Net Cash Flow" means the cash flow of the Borrower which is available for repayment of this loan, and the calculation of which is provided for in Clause 6.2 of this Loan Agreement;

"Notice of Drawing" means a notice to the Lender in the form set out in Exhibit 1 affixed hereto;

"Person（s）" means natural person, legal entity, partnership and the like;

"Preliminary Handing Over Date" means the last day of the four（4）months commencing from the Final Mechanical Completion Date;

"Project" means the F plant owned by the Borrower, which is to be built in Q, China;

"Retention Account" means the foreign exchange account and RMB account opened in the name of the Borrower with the Lender for the purpose of repayment;

"Surveyor" means the Project Engineer appointed by the Borrower with qualification certificate to the satisfaction of the Lender, responsible for reporting to the Lender the progress, quality, the budget and the final accounts of the Project Construction;

"Tranche A Facility" means the loan provided under the Agreement in the total amount of Euro···;

"Tranche B Facility" means the export credit provided in the amount of Euro···;

"Tranche C Facility" means the foreign exchange loan provided by the C Bank, in the amount of US $···

2.Facility a nd its Purpose

2.1   In accordance with this Loan Agreement, the maximum aggregate amount of this loan (the Facility) in foreign exchange available to the Borrower shall not exceed Euro ··· plus US Dollar···

2.2   The Facility shall only be used for the Construction Expenditure.

3.Lending Period and Availability Period

3.1   The length of the period of this loan shall be as follows:

(1) For Tranche A Facility, the lending period shall be twenty - six (26) years including eleven (11) years of grace period, commencing from the date on which the initial drawdown is made to the date on which the total principal, interest and expenses have been fully repaid;

(2) For Tranche B Facility, the lending period shall be thirteen (13) years, including three (3) years of grace period, commencing from the date on which the export credit agreement becomes effective to the date on which the total principal, interest and expenses have been fully repaid;

(3) For Tranche C Facility, the lending period shall be ten (10) years, including thirty-three (33) months of grace period, commencing from the date on which this Loan Agreement becomes effective to the date on which the total principal, interest and expenses have been fully repaid.

3.2   The Availability Period shall commence from the effective date of this Loan Agreement and shall end on the earliest date of the following dates:

(1) The last day of the fortieth (40th) month after the effective date of this Loan Agreement; or

(2) _____, 20_____; or

(3) The date on which the Facility has been fully drawn; or

(4) The date on which the Lender's commitment to make further advance to the Borrower is terminated due to the Borrower's fault.

4.Conditions Precedent (Omitted)

5.Drawdown (Omitted)

6.Retention Accounts and Application of Net Cash Flow

6.1   The Borrower shall open separately the interest-bearing Retention Account of US Dollar as well as the deposit accounts of US Dollar and RMB.The interest rate of US Dollar Retention Account (s) shall be three month or six month LIBOR (determined by the Lender) minus seven eighths of one percent (0.875%).

6.2　For the purpose of this Clause, the Borrower shall determine the Borrower's Net Cash Flow for each successive half-year based on the unaudited financial statements for the relevant half-year. The first half-year shall end on December 31st, 20_____ and each successive half-year shall end either on June 30th or December 31st of the relevant year. The Borrower shall, within fifteen (15) days after the end of each relevant half-year, submit to the Lender the figures of the Net Cash Flow determined. The Net Cash Flow of each half-year shall be determined according to the following formula:

Net Cash Flow = net profit + depreciation + amortization-current principal repayments

In depreciating, ten percent (10%) of the scrap value shall first be deducted from the estimated total value of the fixed assets, and then, the depreciation shall be made under the straight line method approved by the Fiscal Authorities.

Amortization shall be made on a straight line basis over the first five (5) years of operation of the Project on the estimated total value of the intangible property and other expenses pertinent to the Project construction.

6.3　All revenues of the Borrower must be deposited separately into its deposit accounts of US Dollar and RMB. The Net Cash Flow is to be calculated by the Borrower and confirmed by the Lender and the confirmed Net Cash Flow shall be transferred by the Lender to the Retention Accounts of the Borrower.

6.4　The Borrower's Net Cash Flow shall be used in the following way:

(1) First to retain an amount equal to the instalment of principal, interest and expenses due at the end of present half-year period as well as an amount equal to the instalment of principal, interest and expenses for the next half-year period;

(2) After retaining the amount stipulated in the preceding paragraph (1) the Borrower may determine the use of remainder of the Net Cash Flow by itself.

6.5　If the audited Net Cash Flow of a full year is different from the aggregate of the Net Cash Flow determined on the basis of the unaudited financial statements for each half of that year, appropriate adjustments of the margin and corresponding transfer shall be made.

7. Interest Deposit Account

The Borrower shall open the Interest Deposit Account with the Lender, the deposit of which shall be used specifically to pay the interest, commitment fee and administration fee during the Construction Period of the Project. The Borrower shall, for this purpose and in accordance with the Drawdown Schedule (Exhibit 6), deposit in advance into the said account the interest, commitment fee and administration fee for the next half-year.

8.Interest Rates and the Calculation of Interests（Omitted）

9.Commitment Fees

The Borrower shall pay to the Lender the commitment fees on undrawn balances of Tranche B Facility and Tranche C Facility. The rate of commitment fees of Tranche B Facility and Tranche C Facility shall be 0.3% per annum on the basis of 360 days a year. The Commitment fees shall be calculated from the first day of the Availability Period until the whole Facility has been drawn up or the last day of the Availability Period（whichever is earlier）in terms of the undrawn balances multiply the number of days elapsed, to be paid every six（6）months. The first date of the payment of the commitment fees shall be the first Interest Payment Date.

10.Repayment, Prepayment and Postpayment

10.1　The Borrower shall repay the principal and interest of the loan Facility by semi-annual instalments. The Borrower shall have noticed the Lender fifteen（15）days before the date of each actual repayment. The date of repayment（excluding the interest during the construction period）shall be as follows：

（1）For Tranche A Facility

The Tranche A Facility shall be repaid by the Borrower by thirty（30）consecutive equal semi-annual instalments commencing from the last day of one hundred thirty second（132th）month after the date on which the Availability Period commences.

（2）For Tranche B Facility

The Tranche B Facility shall be repaid by the Borrower by 20 consecutive equal semi-annual instalments commencing from the last day of thirty-sixth（36th）month after the date on which the Availability Period commences.

（3）For Tranche C Facility

The Tranche C Facility shall be repaid consecutively by the Borrower by 15 equal semi-annual instalments（except for the last instalment）commencing from the last day of thirty-third（33rd）month after the date on which the Availability Period commences.

10.2　The Borrower may, on any Interest Payment Date, prepay all or any part of the loan Facility, provided that：

（1）The Lender shall have received, no later than 35 days prior to the actual prepayment, irrevocable written notice of prepayment, specifying the amount thereof and the date on which the prepayment is to be made；

（2）The amount of any partial prepayment shall be at least Euro⋯ and an integral multiple of Euro⋯ or US Dollar⋯, and an integral multiple of US Dollar⋯；

（3）Any prepayment shall be made together with all accrued interest on the loan to the date of prepayment and all other sums then payable pursuant to this Loan Agreement；

（4）Prepayment shall be made in reverse order and any part of the prepayment can not be drawn again;

(5) The Borrower shall at the time of prepayment day pay to the Lender prepayment interest equal to 0.5% of the amount prepaid.

10.3　If the Borrower fails to repay any part of the loan as scheduled, the Borrower shall pay to the Lender therefor postpayment interest, the interest rate shall be the rate stipulated in Clause 8.1 plus an additional interest rate of 2.5% per annum. In the event that the Borrower fails to repay the principal or the interest of the Tranche C Facility as scheduled, the postpayment interest shall be calculated from the twenty-first (21st) day after the date due, to the date on which the repayment is actually effected; in the event of postpayment of interest of Tranche A Facility and/or Tranche B Facility, the postpayment interest shall be calculated from the Three Hundred Fifty-First (351st) day after the date due, to the date on which the repayment is actually effected.

11.Insurance

11.1　The Borrower shall secure the Contractor, for the period commencing from the beginning of the construction of the Project to the Preliminary Handing Over Date, to effect Contractor's All Risks Insurance and Erection All Risks Insurance with the People's Insurance Company of China and specify the Lender to be the sole first beneficiary thereunder; the Borrower shall, for the period commencing from the Preliminary Handing Over Date to the date when this loan Facility has been fully repaid, effect Property All Risks Insurance with the People's Insurance Company of China and specify the Lender to be the sole first beneficiary thereunder.

11.2　Prior to the Preliminary Handing Over Date of the Project, if the Borrower assumes that the Project can be completed and handed over as scheduled, the Borrower and the Contractor may, subject to the consent of the Lender, use the insurance compensation paid by the insurance company to repair or replace equipment damaged.

11.3　The Borrower shall deliver the insurance policies effected by the Contractor as provided for in Clause 11.1 to the Lender within three (3) days following the signature of such insurance policies, provided that the Borrower shall secure the Contractor to effect such insurance policies before the actual commencement of the execution of the works at site according to Article 10.1 of the Construction Contract. The Borrower shall further assign the insurance policies effected by the Borrower itself to the Lender within five (5) days following the Preliminary Handing Over Date.

12.Taxes

All withholding taxes on the interest of the loan occurred in China shall be borne by the Borrower. In the event the Borrower should be required by the law to make any deduction or withholding from any payment to the Lender, the Borrower shall, on withholding the same, pay to the Lender such additional amounts as equivalent to the sum withheld.

13.Expenses and Fees

13.1    The Borrower shall pay to the Lender an administration fee at the rate of 0.4%. The administration fee shall be payable each six （6） months on the loan Facility outstanding.The date of the first payment of the fee shall be the last Banking Day of the six （6） months commencing from the date of the initial drawdown.

13.2    The Borrower shall pay to the Lender a management fee equal to 0.2% for Tranche A Facility， 0.4% for Tranche B Facility and 0.2% for Tranche C Facility， all of which shall be paid in full amount within five （5） Banking Days after the effective date of this Loan Agreement.

13.3    The Borrower shall bear the attorney's fee incurred by the Lender for the loan of the Project， in particular， the attorney's fee in the sum of RMB… for drafting this Loan Agreement shall be paid within five （5） Banking Days after the signature of this Loan Agreement. Travel and accommodation fee， the documentation fee， the post communication fee， the loan insurance fee as well as any other fees and expenses charged by _____shall be reimbursed by the Borrower.

14.Representations and Warranties

The Borrower represents and warrants to the Lender that：

（1） It has obtained all governmental approval and authorization required to permit the Borrower to execute and perform this Loan Agreement at the time this Loan Agreement is executed；

（2） It has no indebtedness to any person；

（3） All the documents and information it has delivered or will deliver to the Lender are real， accurate， complete， valid， and up-to-date；

（4） It is not involved in any litigations or arbitrations；

（5） It has not and will not violate any laws involved in its existence and business operation；

（6） It shall secure a long-term and stable supply of raw materials under favourable conditions；

（7） It shall secure a long-term stable foreign exchange revenue during the repayment period；

（8） It shall undertake to pay in the Registered Capital to the Borrower's account opened with the C Bank in accordance with the Registered Capital Undertaking.

15.Covenants

Prior to the full repayment of this loan：

（1） Any modifications of， or amendments to the Joint Venture Agreement shall receive the prior written consent of the Lender；

(2) Resolutions relevant to the loan by the board of directors shall be made to the satisfaction of the Lender;

(3) Without the prior written consent of the Lender, the Borrower shall not modify any clauses of the Construction Contract;

(4) Without the prior written consent of the Lender, the Borrower shall not reduce its registered capital;

(5) The Borrower shall not expand the scope of business, specified in the Business License of the Borrower before the signing of this Loan Agreement, or sell or assign all or any part of its assets or business without the prior written consent of the Lender;

(6) Without the prior written consent of the Lender, the Borrower shall not enter into any guarantee or mortgage on any part of its property or benefits;

(7) The Borrower shall not borrow from any person without the prior written consent of the Lender;

(8) The Borrower shall not establish any branches or subsidiaries without the prior written consent of the Lender;

(9) The Borrower can only open accounts with the C Bank or subject to consent of the Lender, with other banks;

(10) Any other indebtedness shall be subordinated to this Loan Agreement;

(11) The Borrower shall, according to schedule or at the request of the Lender at any time, furnish the Lender with the operating and financial reports and other relating materials, and provide the necessary assistance to enable the Lender to examine the use of the loan;

(12) The Borrower shall promptly advise the Lender of any adverse change in the process of repayment of the loan and/or in the Borrower's ability to repay the loan;

(13) The Lender has the right to examine the production and operation of the Borrower, the Borrower shall provide the necessary assistance therefor.

16.Events of Default

16.1　Events of Default mean:

(1) The Borrower fails to repay the principal, interest and expenses on dates as specified in this Loan Agreement;

(2) The Borrower violates or fails to perform any of its obligations under this Loan Agreement;

(3) The Project is not completed or accepted in compliance with the Construction Contract;

(4) The Borrower ceases to carry on its business or is declared bankrupt;

(5) Any of the contracts or documents relating to this Loan Agreement is suspended;

(6) Any of the Borrower's indebtedness is declared or deemed to be declared

payable prior to its stated maturity by reason of a default of the Borrower, or the Borrower fails to pay any debt immediately which should be paid on demand;

（7）The Borrower is involved in any major suit or arbitration proceedings sufficient to have any materially adverse effect on the performance of this Loan Agreement;

（8）Any representation or warranty made by the Borrower in this Loan Agreement or in any notice or other document, certificate or statement delivered or made hereunder is incorrect or inaccurate in any material respect.

16.2  Upon the occurrence of an Event of Default, the Lender at its discretion may, by written notice to the Borrower, take any of the following actions:

（1）Declare the principal of, and accrued interest on the loan and all other sums payable thereunder to be immediately due and payable;

（2）Declare the Facility outstanding all due and thereupon the obligation of the Lender to make any further advance thereunder shall immediately terminate.

16.3  The actions taken by the Lender under Clause 16.2 shall not affect any rights or remedies the Lender has under this Loan Agreement or under the laws.

17.Modification

In the event of any difference in dates, amounts, figures and material specifications among this Loan Agreement, the Export Credit Agreement and the ···Agreement, the Lender is entitled at its discretion to make relevant modifications in this Loan Agreement.

18.Governing Law and Jurisdiction

18.1  This Loan Agreement shall be governed by the laws of the People's Republic of China.

18.2  Any dispute arising in the performance of this Loan Agreement shall be submitted to the competent court of the People's Republic of China.

19.Other Clauses

19.1  The Exhibits of this Loan Agreement constitute the integral parts of this Loan Agreement Clauses.

19.2  This Loan Agreement shall be made in Chinese and English and both are equally authentic.In case any discrepancy occurs between the two texts, the competent court will select one as the prevailing text.

19.3  This Loan Agreement shall be effective on the date both the ···Agreement and the Export Credit Agreement enter into force.

Signed for and on behalf of          Signed for and on behalf of

A COMPANY Ltd.  C BANK

（THE BORROWER）    （THE LENDER）

by···        by···

Exhibit 1

## Notice of Drawing

From： A Company Ltd.（the Borrower）

To： C Bank（the Lender）

_____, 20_____

Dear Sirs，

RE： Loan Agreement dated_____, 20_____

We refer to the above Loan Agreement， and hereby give notice that we intend to make a drawdown under the Facility Tranche…on_____, 20_____ in the following amount（s）：

Amount：（specify amount in Euro and/or Dollars）

The proceeds of the drawdown should be paid to the account of…bank account No.….

We confirm that：

（1）The representations and warranties set out in Clause 14 of the Loan Agreement, repeated with reference to the facts and circumstances subsisting at the date of this notice, remain true and correct； and

（2）No Event of Default or prospective Event of Default has occurred which remains unwaived or unremedied.

Terms defined in the Loan Agreement have the same meanings when used in this notice.

_____

For and on behalf of

A COMPANY LTD.

Exhibit 2

## Repayment Guarantee

Beneficiary： C Bank.

Whereas it is a condition precedent for the drawdown as stipulated in the Loan Agreement（hereinafter referred to as the Loan Agreement）signed between the A Co.Ltd.（hereinafter referred to as the Borrower）and the C Bank（hereinafter referred to as the Lender）that D and H（hereinafter referred to jointly as the Guarantors）agree to sign this Repayment Guarantee.

The Guarantors execute and deliver this Repayment Guarantee on_____, 20 ____.

The Facility provided by the Lender is Euro…plus US Dollars…The Guarantors hereby jointly and severally， unconditionally and irrevocably guarantee to the Lender all the repayment of principal， interest and expenses（the Guaranteed Sums）under the Loan Agreement. In case the Borrower fails to pay， or is unable to pay any part of the

Guaranteed Sums on the date of its maturity in time pursuant to the Loan Agreement, the Guarantors are obliged to pay the unpaid Guaranteed Sums in full within fifteen (15) days (Performance Period) after the receipt of the written notice of performance (Notice of Performance) delivered by the Lender.

The Guarantors agree to perform their obligations according to the following provisions:

(1) The obligations of the Guarantors shall be continuous and remain in full force and effect until all the Guaranteed Sums have been paid in full by the Borrower or by the Guarantors.

(2) The Guaranteed Sums shall be paid in Euro for Tranche A Facility and Tranche B Facility, and in US Dollars for Tranche C Facility.

(3) Before the full repayment of the Guaranteed Sums, the Guarantors shall not subrogate the claim of the Lender against the Borrower and exercise any rights under the Mortgage (the agreement under which the Borrower mortgages all its properties to the Guarantors). The debts owed by the Borrower to the Guarantors shall be subordinated to the debts owed by the Borrower to the Lender.

(4) Any successor (including the successor as a result of reorganization and / or merger) of the Guarantors shall be bound by this Guarantee and continue to undertake the obligations thereunder. The Guarantors shall not assign their obligations under this Guarantee without the prior written consent of the Lender.

(5) The obligations of the Guarantors under this Guarantee shall not be affected by the granting of time or other indulgence to the Borrower by the Lender, or by any modification of or amendment to the Loan Agreement or the Exhibits attached hereto.

(6) Once the Notice of Performance has been served to D by the Lender, it is deemed to have been served to the Guarantors, and D shall notice H to perform its Guarantor's obligation in proportion to its agreed ratio. D must pay all the Guaranteed Sums due as specified in the Notice of Performance to the Lender within the Performance Period regardless of the failure to pay the Guaranteed Sums payable by H for any reason within the Performance Period.

The Guarantors represent and warrant as follows:

(1) All necessary approval required for the execution and delivery of the Guarantee by the Guarantors has been duly obtained, and the Guarantors agree to ensure the full effectiveness of this Guarantee until all the Guaranteed Sums have been paid.

(2) The obligations of the Guarantors hereunder shall not be affected by any change in the reorganization, position or financial situation of the Guarantors.

(3) Any modification of, or supplementation to this Guarantee shall be made with the prior written consent of the Lender.

（4）In case the Guarantors fail to perform or are unable to perform their obligations hereunder within （15） days （including the fifteenth day）, after the receipt of the Notice of Performance from the Lender, the Guarantors' rights under the Mortgage shall be automatically and unconditionally assigned to the Lender. This assignment shall not discharge the Guarantors of their obligations under this Guarantee.The Lender is entitled to continue to claim against the Guarantors for the payment of the Guaranteed Sums pursuant to the Clause 6 of the Guarantors' obligations hereunder.

This Guarantee shall come into force on the effective day of the Loan Agreement.

| | |
|---|---|
| For and on behalf of D | For and on behalf of H |

**参考译文：**

## 借款合同

本借款合同于20_____年_____月_____日由下列双方签订：

一方：A有限公司（以下称"借款人"）

另一方：C银行（以下称"贷款人"）

鉴于借款人向贷款人申请贷款，贷款人同意向借款人提供最高限额（总金额）为_____欧元和_____美元的外汇贷款，经借贷双方协商，议定如下条款：

第1条　定义

在本借款合同中，除另有明确规定外，下列词语应具有下列含义：

"有效提款期"是指本借款合同第3条2款中规定的借款人可以提取本"借款额度"的期限；

"银行工作日"是指

（1）北京C银行

（2）巴黎的法国银行

（3）纽约C银行

（4）伦敦C银行

都营业的一天；

"承包合同"是指由借款人与"承包商"签订的关于"本项目"的承包合同（No._____）；

"建设费用"是指建筑安装工程费用、设备购置费、海运费以及其他与"本项目"建设有关的费用；

"建设期"是指从"承包合同"生效之日起至"初步交付日"为止的一段时间；

"承包商"是指法国N公司（其总部设在法国巴黎）和中国北京NCC总公司；

"美元（USD）"是指美利坚合众国的法定货币；

"违约事件"是指本借款合同第16条1款中规定的任何一个事件或事实；

"借款额度"是指本借款合同第2条1款中规定的可以由借款人提取的和/或已经提取的借款金额，包括"借款额度甲部分"、"借款额度乙部分"和"借款额度丙部分"；

"最终机械竣工日"是指自"承包合同"生效之日起26个月的最后一天；

"欧元"是指欧盟中19个国家的货币；

"利息存款账户"是指专门用于支付"本项目"建设期内银行利息、承担费和手续费的美元账户；

"付息日"是指每一个"利息期"的最后一天；

"利息期"是指自首次提款日至本借款合同项下全部本金、利息和一切费用全部偿清日止，每6个月为一期；

"合营协议"是指于20_____年_____月_____日在中华人民共和国北京由

（1）NC公司

（2）S公司

（3）P公司

三方签订的合资经营A有限公司的协议；

"抵押"是指抵押、质押或其他任何形式的担保安排；

"净现金收入"是指借款人用于偿还本借款的现金收入，其计算方法见本借款合同第6条第2款的规定；

"提款通知书"是指借款人按照本合同附件1格式，向贷款人出具的通知书；

"人"是指自然人、法人、合伙人及其类似的组织；

"初步交付日"是指自"最终机械竣工日"起4个月的最后一天；

"本项目"是指由借款人所有的、在中国Q地建设的F工厂；

"保管账户"是指借款人为偿还本借款而在贷款人处开立的外汇和人民币账户；

"测量师"是指借款人指派的、其资格证明为贷款人满意的、负责向贷款人报告工程进度、质量、预算和决算的项目工程师；

"借款额度甲部分"是指根据协议提供的贷款的部分，总额为_____欧元；

"借款额度乙部分"是指出口信贷部分，金额为_____欧元；

"借款额度丙部分"是指C银行提供的外汇贷款部分，金额为_____美元。

第2条　借款额度及用途

2.1　根据本借款合同，贷款人向借款人提供总金额不超过_____欧元和_____美元的外汇借款金额。

2.2　本借款只限用于"建设费用"。

第3条　借款期限及有效提款期

3.1　本借款的借款期限如下：

（1）借款额度甲部分，自首次提款之日起，至偿清全部借款本金、利息和费用为止，为期26年，其中包括宽限期11年；

（2）借款额度乙部分，自出口信贷协议生效之日起，至偿清全部借款本金、利息和费用为止，为期13年，其中包括宽限期3年；

（3）借款额度丙部分，自本合同生效之日起，至偿清全部借款本金、利息和费用为止，为期10年，其中包括宽限期33个月。

3.2　从本借款合同生效之日起，至下列日期中最早日期止，为本借款的有效提款期：

（1）本借款合同生效之日起第40个月的最后一天；

（2）20_____年_____月_____日；或

（3）借款额度已完全提取之日；

（4）因借款人的原因而使贷款人继续贷款的责任终止之日。

第4条　先决条件（略）

第5条　提款（略）

第6条　保管账户及净现金收入的使用

6.1　借款人应在贷款人处分别开立美元的有息保管账户以及美元和人民币的存款账户。美元保管账户利率为3个月或6个月（由贷款人决定）伦敦同业拆放利率（LIBOR）减0.875%。

6.2　为了本款的目的，借款人按未经审核的半年财务报表计算借款人每个半年期的净现金收入。第一个半年期在20____年12月31日终止，以后每个半年期均应在有关年度的6月30日或12月31日截止。借款人应在每个半年期结束后15天内，向贷款人提交计算出的净现金流量数额。每一半年期的"净现金流量"按下面公式计算：

净现金流量=纯利+折旧+摊销-当期已偿还之本金金额

折旧应按预计固定资产总值减去残值10%，然后按财政部门批准的直线折旧法进行。

摊销指按直线法将预计无形资产的总值和与本项目建设有关的其他费用在"本项目"开工后的头5年中摊销。

6.3　借款人的全部收入必须分别存入其美元和人民币的存款账户。净现金收入由借款人计算，贷款人确认，由贷款人将确认的净现金流量转入借款人的保管账户。

6.4　借款人的净现金流量须按下列方式使用：

（1）首先保管一笔相当于本期和下一期应予偿还的本金、利息和费用的金额；

（2）在保留了第（1）项中规定的金额之后，借款人可以自行决定净现金流量其余部分的用途。

6.5　如果一个完整年度经审核的净现金流量与根据该年度两个半年期未经审计的财务报表所决定的净现金流量总额有所不同，应作出适当差额调整及相应的转入。

第7条　利息存款账户

借款人应在贷款人处开立利息存款账户，其中存款只能用于支付本项目建设期内的利息、承担费和手续费。借款人应为此目的于本合同生效后的每半年按提款计划附件6提前向该账户存入下半年的利息、承担费和手续费。

第8条　借款利率及利息计算方法（略）

第9条　承诺费

借款人应就借款额度乙部分和借款额度丙部分的未用余额向贷款人支付承担费。借款额度乙部分和借款额度丙部分的承担费（按360天计算）年率为0.3%。承担费从有效提款期首日起，按未用余额乘以过去的天数计算，每6个月支付一次，直至提完本借款额度或有效提款期的最后一天为止（以其中较早者为准）。首次支付承担费的日期为第一个付息日。

第10条　还款、提前还款及迟延还款

10.1　借款人应以半年分期付款方式还清借款额度的本金和利息。借款人须在每一还款日前15天通知贷款人。还款日期（建设期内的利息除外）如下：

（1）借款额度甲部分，借款人应从有效提款期开始之日后的第132个月的最后一天起，以每半年等额分期付款方式，分30期连续还清；

（2）借款额度乙部分，借款人应从有效提款期开始之后的第36个月的最后一天起，以每半年等额分期付款方式，分20期连续还清；

（3）借款额度丙部分，借款人应从有效提款期开始之后的第33个月的最后一天起，以每半年（最后一期除外）等额付款方式，分15期连续还清。

10.2　借款人可以在上述还款期间提前偿还部分或全部借款，但须符合下列条件：

（1）贷款人应在预计提前还款日前35天收到借款人发出的不可撤销的提前还款通知书，详述拟提前还款的金额及日期；

（2）每次提前还款的金额至少应为……欧元和……欧元的整数倍数，或……美元和……美元的整数倍数；

（3）任何提前偿还的款项，应连同截止该提前还款日的全部应付借款利息及本借款合同规定的其他款项一并交付；

（4）提前还款应按到期日倒序偿还，提前偿还部分不得再提取；

（5）提前还款时，借款人应向贷款人就提前还款额加付0.5%利息。

10.3　借款人如不能按时偿还本息，应为此向贷款人支付迟付款利息，利率按8条1款规定的利率另加年率2.5%。如借款本金或借款额度丙部分的利息逾期未付，则从到期日后第21天起直至实际付款日按迟付款利率计息；如借款额度甲部分和/或借款额度乙部分的利息逾期未付，则从到期日后第351天起直至实际付款日按迟付款利率计息。

第11条　保险

11.1　借款人应确保承包商就本项目开工至初步交付日这段期间，向中国人民保险公司投保建筑工程一切险和安装工程一切险，并以贷款人作为唯一的第一受益人；借款人应就初步交付日直到本借款合同所规定的借款偿清之日这段期间，向中国人民保险公司投保财产—切险，并以贷款人作为唯一的第一受益人。

11.2 本项目初步交付日之前，借款人如果认为本项目能按期竣工和交付使用，经贷款人书面同意，借款人和承包商可以使用保险公司支付的赔偿费修理或更换损坏的设备。

11.3 借款人应将第11条1款中由承包商投保的保险单于该保险单签署之后3天内递交给贷款人。但借款人应确保承包商根据承包合同第10条1款的规定，在现场工程施工实际开始之前，投保该保险。借款人应将自己投保的保险单于初步交付日后5日之内转让给贷款人。

第12条 税款

在中国发生的贷款利息预提税等所有税款均由借款人承担。如果法律规定，借款人应该从它付给贷款人的任何款项中扣除任何税款，则借款人应在扣除款项的同时，向贷款人支付一笔相当于被扣除税款的款项。

第13条 费用

13.1 借款人向贷款人支付的手续费为0.4%，按贷款余额每6个月付一次。首次支付手续费日期为首次提款日起6个月的最后一个银行工作日。

13.2 借款人应向贷款人支付管理费，其中，借款额度甲部分为0.2%，借款额度乙部分为0.4%，借款额度丙部分为0.2%，并于本借款合同生效后的5个银行工作日内一次交清。

13.3 借款人须负担贷款人为本项目贷款而支付的律师费，特别是为起草本借款合同而应支付的律师费人民币……元应在本借款合同签字后5个银行工作日内支付给贷款人。贷款人为本项目贷款而支付的差旅费、文件费、邮电通信费、贷款保险费和……（银行）收取的任何其他费用和开支，均向借款人实报实销。

第14条 声明及保证

借款人向贷款人声明并保证：

（1）在签订本借款合同时，它已获得签订和执行本借款合同所需的一切有关的政府批准和确认；

（2）它对任何人皆无负债；

（3）它已向或将向贷款人提供的一切文件和信息都是真实的、准确的、完整的、有效的和最新的；

（4）它没有受到任何诉讼或仲裁的牵连；

（5）它现在没有，将来也不违反任何与它的存在和经营有关的法律；

（6）它保证按优惠条件获得长期、稳定的原料供应；

（7）它确保在还款期间获得长期、稳定的外汇销售收入；

（8）它保证按注册资本承诺书将注册资本汇入借款人在C银行开立的借款人账户。

第15条 约定事项

在本贷款全部还清之前，必须：

（1）"合营协议"的任何修改应得到贷款人的事先书面同意；

（2）董事会作出的与本借款有关的决议应使贷款人满意；

（3）未经贷款人事先书面同意，借款人不得修改承包合同的任何条款；

（4）未经贷款人事先书面同意，借款人不得减少其注册资本；

（5）未经贷款人事先书面同意，借款人不得扩大在本借款合同签署前其营业执照规定的经营范围，不得出售、转让其任何资产或业务；

（6）未经贷款人事先书面同意，借款人不得将其任何财产权益进行担保或抵押；

（7）未经贷款人事先书面同意，借款人不得向任何人借款；

（8）未经贷款人事先书面同意，借款人不得设立分支或附属机构；

（9）借款人只限于在C银行或其他经贷款人同意的银行开户；

（10）借款人的任何其他债务均应从属于本借款合同；

（11）借款人按时或随时按贷款人的要求，向贷款人提供其经营和财务报告及有关资料，为贷款人检查借款使用情况提供必要的方便；

（12）借款人应及时通知贷款人任何影响借款人偿还贷款的情况和/或借款人还款能力的任何不利变化；

（13）贷款人有权审查借款人生产经营状况，借款人应为此提供必要的协助。

第16条　违约事件

16.1　违约事件是指：

（1）借款人未能按本借款合同规定的日期偿还本金、利息和费用；

（2）借款人违反或不履行本借款合同的任何义务；

（3）本项目建设未能按照承包合同规定竣工或验收；

（4）借款人停止经营或宣告破产；

（5）任何与本借款合同有关的合同或文件被停止执行；

（6）由于借款人违约，借款人的任何债务在原定到期日之前应予支付或可能被宣布应予支付，或借款人未能立即支付任何需要立即支付的债务；

（7）借款人卷入足以在实质上影响本借款合同执行的任何重大诉讼或仲裁程序；

（8）借款人在本借款合同中的声明及保证以及据此作出或递交的通知、其他文件、证明或声明有实质性失实或不准确。

16.2　在发生违约事件后，贷款人可以自行采取下列措施，并书面通知借款人：

（1）宣布本借款的本金、利息以及借款人应付的一切其他款项全部到期，必须立即支付；

（2）宣布尚未执行的借款额度全部到期，贷款人继续提供借款的责任也因此而立刻终止。

16.3 贷款人采取第16条2款中规定的措施，并不影响它根据本借款合同或法律的规定所享有的任何其他权利或补救措施。

第17条 修改

如果本借款合同在日期、金额、数字和实质性规定方面与出口信贷协议和/或协议有不同之处，贷款人有权自行对本借款合同进行相应的修改。

第18条 适用的法律及诉讼管辖

18.1 本借款合同适用于中华人民共和国的法律。

18.2 双方在执行本借款合同中如有争议，应在中华人民共和国法院进行诉讼。

第19条 其他条款

19.1 本借款合同的各个附件是本合同条款的不可分割的部分。

19.2 本借款合同用中、英两种文字写成，具有同等效力。如果两种文字有出入，法院将选择以其中一种为准。

19.3 本借款合同自_____协议和出口信贷协议均于_____年___月___日日起生效。

借款人　　　　　　　　　　　贷款人

A有限公司　　　　　　　　　　C银行

代表：　　　　　　　　　　　代表：

附件1　　　　　　　　　　　**提款通知书**

由：A有限公司（借款人）

致：C银行（贷款人）

　　　　　　　　　　　　　　　　　　　20____年____月____日

敬启者：

　　关于：20_____年_____月_____日签订的借款合同

根据上述借款合同，我公司谨此通知贵行，我公司拟于20_____年____月_____日提取借款额度_____部分中的一笔提款：

款额为_____欧元或美元。

请将此次提款之款额付入_____（银行账户）账号。

我公司确认：

（1）借款合同第14条所载的声明及保证，按照今日存在的事实和环境予以重申，仍是真实和正确的；

（2）至今并未发生尚未获得纠正或贷款人并未放弃追究的任何"违约事件"或可能的违约事件。

在借款合同中所阐明定义的词语，在本通知中仍然含有相同的意义。

　　　　　　　　　　　　　　　　　　　　　　　　A有限公司

　　　　　　　　　　　　　　　　　　　　　　　代表：_____

附件2　　　　　　　　　　　　**还款担保书**

受益人：C银行

鉴于还款担保书是 A 有限公司（以下简称"借款人"）和 C 银行（以下简称"贷款人"）签订的借款合同（以下简称"借款合同"）所规定的提款先决条件之一，D 和 H（以下简称"担保人"）同意签署本还款担保书。

担保人于20_____年_____月_____日签署和递交本担保书。

贷款人向借款人提供的贷款额度为_____欧元和_____美元，担保人在此共同地、分别地、无条件地和不可撤销地向贷款人担保偿还上述借款合同项下全部本金、利息和费用（以下简称担保金额）。在借款人到期应付之日没有或不能根据借款合同之规定按时支付担保金额任何部分时，担保人保证在接到贷款人出具的履约书面通知（履约通知）后的15天（履约期限）内如数支付该未付的担保金额。

担保人同意按照以下规定履行担保义务：

（1）担保人的义务是持续地并将保持有效直至所有担保金额已由借款人或担保人全部偿还为止。

（2）应以欧元支付借款额度甲部分和借款额度乙部分的担保金额，以美元支付"借款额度丙部分"的担保金额。

（3）在担保金额没有全部偿还之前，担保人不得取代贷款人对借款人的债权人的地位；不得行使担保人在抵押书（借款人将全部房地产抵押给担保人的协议）项下的权利。借款人对担保人的债务须从属于借款人对贷款人的债务。

（4）担保人的继承人（包括因改组和/或合并而继承）将受本担保书的约束，并继续承担本担保责任。未得到贷款人事先书面同意，担保人不得转让其担保义务。

（5）贷款人给予借款人的任何宽限或特惠，或者借款合同及其附件的任何修改补充，都不影响担保人在本担保书项下的义务。

（6）贷款人将履约通知送达 D，即被视为已送达所有担保人，由 D 通知 H 按其约定比例履行担保义务。不论 H 由于任何原因在履约期限内不能支付其应支付的担保金额，D 则必须在履约期限内将履约通知上注明的全部应付担保金额支付给贷款人。

担保人在此声明并保证：

（1）担保人已为签署和递交本担保书办妥一切必需的批准，并同意在担保金额全部偿还之前确保本担保书的充分有效性。

（2）担保人的改组、地位改变和财务状况的变化都不影响担保人履行其担保义务。

（3）本担保书的任何修改或补充都须事先征得贷款人的书面同意。

（4）如果担保人在接到履约通知后15天内（包括第15天）未能或没有履行其担保义务，则担保人应立即自动地、无条件地将担保人对借款人全部房地产的抵押权转让给贷款人。该转让并不因此解除担保人在本担保书项下的义务，贷款人有权继续按上述担保人义务第（6）条的规定，向担保人追索其应付的担保金额。

本担保书与借款合同同时生效。

D代表：＿＿＿＿＿＿　　　　　　　H代表：＿＿＿＿＿＿

# Notes

1.loan n.用作可数名词，表示贷款；用作不可数名词，表示借的动作。v.在美国英语中作及物动词，表示借给，并可带双宾语；在英国英语中，表示借给的，动词要用lend

The rest can be obtained through bank loans.

其余的可通过银行贷款解决。

He said he had applied for fresh loan to save them from bankruptcy.

他说，为了免于破产，他已经再借了一笔债。

| | |
|---|---|
| day-to-day loan | 日拆 |
| demand loan | 活期放款 |
| industrial loan | 工业放款 |
| long-term loan | 长期放款，长期贷款 |
| non-interest bearing/interest-free loan | 无息贷款 |
| secured loan | 抵押放款 |
| domestic loan | 内债 |
| government/public loan | 公债 |

loan作名词时与之搭配的动词有：want（想要），solicit（请求），negotiate（洽商），raise（筹集），float（招募），arrange（安排），conclude（达成），contract（约定），give/make/provide/grant（给予），have/get/obtain/receive（得到），secure（担保），under-write（承保贷款风险），repay/pay off/liquidate（清还），renew（按原来条件展期）

The house had been loaned to the Yales by its owner, who used it during summers.

房子的主人只有夏天才在这里住，现在把它借给耶尔家暂用。

辨析：loan，facility，advance，credit

这组词均指贷款。

loan是贷款的总称，是正式用语，多用于政府和国际金融组织的正式贷款。

facility是资金便利方面的特殊安排，多用于国际银团和私人银行对其客户的便利贷款。

advance指银行为客户垫款、预付、透支等给予金额不大、为期不长的贷款。

credit强调"信用"两字，多用于商人间的出口信贷、买方信贷、卖方信贷；credit与facility连用，则指银行的信用贷款（credit facility）。

The bank also extends export credit insurance facilities to cover risks undertaken by US exporters.

银行扩大出口信贷保险业务，为美国出口商承担风险。

The bank advanced me ￡2,000.

银行借给我2,000英镑。

A revolving credit of \$125m has been signed between the World Bank and Turkey's Agricultural Bank.

世界银行与土耳其农业银行签订了1.25亿美元的循环信贷（协议）。

2.availability period 有效提款期

3.expenditure n.较正规的词，表示"政府和机构的开支花销"

表示"支出"和"花费"的词还有：costs, spending, expenses, overhead 和 outlay。

costs 指成本；

spending 尤指（政府、机构或个人的）开支和花销；

expenses （个人或机构的）开支，花费；（由雇主报销的）费用，开支；

overheads （企业或机构的）经常性开支，运营费用（如租金、电费、人工等）；

outlay （启动新项目或为减省日后资金或时间的）开支，费用。

A monthly summary of all sum expenditures shall be furnished to Owner and shall compare actual to projected expenditures.

所有这些费用必须按月给业主提供一份月度汇总报表，列明实际支出与预计支出相对比的情况。

The money they are making is barely enough to cover costs.

他们赚的钱勉强能弥补他们的成本。

This government wants to keep a tight rein on public spending.

这个政府想严格控制公共支出。

If the Project is suspended, the Engineer shall be paid his compensation together with all terminal expenses resulting from such suspension.

如工程项目中途停止，则须付给工程师赔偿费，连同一切由于工程终止而造成的结尾费用。

The Buyer agrees to pay the Seller's reasonable costs plus...percent for overhead.

买方同意向卖方支付合理的费用，再加上百分之……的运营费用。

The increase in sales quickly repaid the outlay on advertising.

销售量的增加很快弥补了广告费支出。

4.affix vt.附加，附录，签署，使附于

The notary's seal or stamp must be affixed.

公证人的印戳或图章必须签署。

The box is reserved for Vendor to affix legal stipulation of contents or terms of sale, or other indicative information.

这一栏是为卖主保留的，由他附上可含内容的法律规定，或销售条件，或其他指示性的信息。

5.retention n.保留，保持，保留额，留成

On completion and acceptance of each separate building, payment may be made therefore without retention of a percentage.

每一幢建筑物竣工接收后，可以付款，此种款项不得留成。

6.satisfaction n.偿还，补偿，满意

After the satisfaction of any claim by the buyer, the buyer shall pay the balance of shares to such record holders.

在买方对任何要求给予补偿之后，买方应把股份的余额付给此类记录的所有人。

All indebtedness to AAA shall be settled to the satisfaction of AAA.

应偿清对甲方的全部债务，使甲方感到满意。

satisfy v.使满意，使确信，赔偿

The purchaser shall have the right out of the said purchase price to pay and satisfy any portion of any such indebtedness.

买方应有权以上述购置价格支付和赔偿债务的任何部分。

The buyer may satisfy itself as to the corporate authority and structure of the seller.

买方确信卖方法人组织的权威性及结构。

satisfactory adj.令人满意的

The operator will maintain the interior and exterior of the buildings and sanitary condition satisfactory to the Company.

经营者愿保护建筑物的内外和卫生环境，以使公司满意。

The bond shall, in manner and form satisfactory to the First Party, guarantee to it the faithful performance of this contract by the Second Party.

保证人应以使甲方感到满意的态度和方式保证乙方忠实地履行合同。

7.credit n.信用，信贷，赊购；（银行、金融业用语）存款，存入（款项）。v.记入贷方（账）

credit inquiry　资信调查

credit rating　资信评价，资信分类

credit standing/status　资信状况

credit restriction　信贷限制

export credit　出口信贷

swap credit　互惠信贷

credit interest　存息

The seller shall credit to the buyer such amount as soon as possible.

卖方须尽快地退给买方（记入买主贷方）这笔金额。

ZZZ shall be requested to check the credit risk and standing of the purchaser prior to the Contract.

在签订合同以前，应要求乙方先对买主将承担的信贷风险及其声望加以审查

（一番）。

We have entered this amount to your credit.

我方已将这笔款项贷记你方账。

Does this item go among credits or debits?

这笔账记贷方还是借方？

The consignee shall sell such goods only to such person or persons as the consignor shall judge to be of good credit.

承销人将这些物品只销售给那些委托人认为信誉良好的人。

You have $56 standing to your credit.

您的存款尚余56美元。

8.depreciate vi.贬值，跌价，折旧；vt.使（货币）贬值

Franchisor shall assume the responsibility of purchasing the assets and inventory of terminated franchise for their depreciated value.

特许权者应承担责任以折余价值购买特许权已告终止的资产和存货。

The price of sugar has greatly depreciated.

糖价大跌。

The dollar has depreciated by fifteen percent in the recent twenty months.

美元在最近20个月中贬值了15%。

depreciation n.贬值，减值，折旧

depreciation base 折旧基数

depreciation-arbitrary method 任意折旧法

depreciation-composite life method 平均年限折旧法

The depreciation of the dollar can be directly linked to the deterioration of the current account of the US balance of payment.

美元的贬值与美国国际收支中经常项目的恶化有直接联系。

9.retain vt.保有，保留

The Buyer shall retain the goods in his possession after delivery to the Buyer's warehouse.

货物送抵买方的仓库以后，货物的所有权应归买方保有。

The licensee shall have the right to retain a perpetual nonexclusive royalty-free right.

许可证持有者应有权保留一种永久的免收专利权使用费的非独占性权利。

The Committee decided that American Selling Price must be treated like other non-tariff barriers, which means Congress retains a veto over any move to eliminate it.

委员会决定，美国售价必须当作非关税壁垒那样对待，这意味着国会对任何排除它的行动保有否决权。

10.amortization n.摊销，摊还，分期偿付，折旧；分期偿还

amortization of government bond 政府公债的分期偿还

amortization period 摊销期

Consolidated income for the seller shall exclude any amortization of capitalized royalty rights.

卖方的固定收入将不包括资本化提成权利的摊还。

amortize vt. 分期偿还，摊提

The cost shall be amortized out of royalties.

成本将从利润提成中分期摊还。

The taxes will be due and payable by the operator during the current tax year, amortized on a weekly basis.

本税务年度的税款行将到期，将由经营者（业主）按周分期缴纳。

11. preceding adj. 先前的，此前的

We agree to pay you USD…for each square inch of such space used by us during the preceding calendar month.

对在前一个日历月度期间我方使用的场地，我方同意按每一平方英寸向贵方支付……美元的使用费。

The Agent shall furnish by 10th day of every month the Company with the report of the preceding month.

代理商应在每月10日向公司提供上一月度的报告。

12. audit n. 审计，查账，集合，决算；vt. 查（账）；vi. 审计，查账

audit diary      查账日记

audit programme      查账程序

The franchisee agrees that all books and records shall be audited by the franchisor.

特许证持有人同意所有账册和记录均由特许人来查账。

Any adjustments shall be made on the basis of the quarterly audited statements.

任何调整须按季度决算报表进行。

General services, such as auditing, tax, legal, etc., provided or paid for by the buyer for the seller will be charged to the seller.

买方为卖方提供或支付一般劳务费，如审计费、税费、律师费等应记在卖方账上。

auditor n. 查账员，审计员，稽核员

The Auditors shall be appointed at the annual meeting.

审计员在年会上选定。

Joint Venture Company shall have four directors and two auditors.

合营公司应有四名董事和两名审计员。

13. installment n. 分期摊付的一期（款项）；分期装运的一期（货物）

monthly installments      按月摊付

installment payment/payment by installments      分期付款

The goods will be shipped in two equal installments 货物分两期（批）平均装运

If the Second Party shall elect to exercise either of the options granted to him, then the purchase price shall be paid in the following installments…

如第二方选择行使所授予他的两种优先购买权中的一种，则其购货款将按下列方式分期付款……

If shipment by installments within given periods is stipulated and any installment is not shipped within the period allowed for that installment, the credit ceases to be available for that or any subsequent installment, unless otherwise specified in the credit.

如果规定在一定时期内分期装运，而其中一批未能按期装运，应认为对于这一货物和以后的各批货物都不能再利用信用证，除非信用证另有规定。

14.consecutive adj.连续的，顺序的

Each subsequent contract year shall consist of the period of twelve consecutive calendar months.

每一后续合同年将包括连续12个日历月度的时期。

（Amount） of such purchase price shall be paid in consecutive installments of （amount） each on the first day of each month following the payment of the sum of （amount）.

此购买价格（金额）将于付讫这笔（金额）后在每月的第一天，连续分批、每批（金额），予以支付。

consecutively adv.连续地，顺序地

All certificates of shares shall be consecutively numbered or otherwise indicated.

所有股票（证）均须按顺序编号或另作说明。

15.integral adj.完整的，整体的；n.整体

Such specifications shall be incorporated in this agreement as an integral.

各项技术规定构成本方案的一个组成部分。

Technical specifications which are attached hereto constitute an integral part of this proposal.

此处随附的各项技术规格应构成本建议的一个组成部分。

16.pursuant adj.追踪的，依照的，与……一致的

All goods shall be manufactured and sold by him under or pursuant to the provisions and the conditions of this agreement.

根据或按照本协议的条款和条件，一切货物均应由他制造和销售。

Contractor shall arrange Subcontracts in such a way that any amount due pursuant to Article （…） will be separately identifiable.

承包商必须用这样的方式安排转包合同：按照第……款规定的一切款项均需分别予以验证。

17.beneficiary n.受惠者，受益人，收款人

beneficiary of an L/C 　　信用证受益人

beneficiary of remittance 　　汇款收款人

The Board of Directors shall have full authority to take such action to officers and their survivors and beneficiaries.

董事会有充分权力对职员们及其遗属和受益人采取（必要）行动。

Please advise the credit to the beneficiary without adding your confirmation.

请向受益人通知信用证，不加保兑。

18.withhold vt.使停止，拒给，保留，抑制；vi.忍住

withhold offers for one week 　　暂停报盘一周

withhold payment 　　不（予）支付，拒绝付款

All taxes, other assessments and levies which the Seller is required by law to withhold and collect shall be duly withheld and collected.

按照法律需要向卖方扣留和征收的一切税款、其他资产和征用物，必须按时予以扣留和征收。

19.attorney（美）律师，（业务或法律事务的）代理人

letter of attorney 　　委任状，授权书

power of attorney 　　委托书，代理权

The Arbitration Tribunal may require the parties or their attorneys, witnesses or other persons to sign on the records.

仲裁庭可以令当事人或者他们的代理人、证人或者其他人员在开庭记录上签字。

Each party shall submit to the attorney a full showing of the evidence.

每一当事人应向律师提供一份充分的证据。

20.indebtedness n.受恩惠，亏欠，债务，负债

The Company shall have the right to treat any payment against such delinquent amount or other indebtedness of the Operator.

公司有权处理任何用于抵付经营者拖欠金额或其他债务的款项。

indebted adj.负债的，受惠的

Whereas the Second Party is now justly indebted to the First Party in the sum of （amount）…

有鉴于此，第二方目前正好结欠第一方债款……元。

21.expand vt.使膨胀，详述，扩张，扩大；vi.张开，发展，推广

The Licensor and the Licensee agree that the Territory of the License may be expanded from time to time as necessity arises, during the validity of this License Agreement.

发证人和受证人均同意，在此许可证协议的有效期间，此许可证（适用）的地区范围可根据需要随时予以扩充。

We hope you will exert your efforts to expand the sales of this article.

希望你方努力扩大这一商品的销售。

China's foreign trade has greatly expanded during recent years.

中国的对外贸易近年来有很大发展。

expansion n.扩大，扩充，发展，扩张

The study concludes that western shipowners can expect only limited benefit from the Chinese trading expansion.

该研究报告得出结论称，西方的船东们从中国航运业的扩展中只能指望有限的好处。

22.subordinate adj.从属的，次要的

The attached sub-clauses shall be subordinated to the provisions of this Clause.

随附的各项附属条款必须从属于本条的各款。

23.adverse  adj.不利的，敌对的，相反的

adverse balance of trade/adverse trade balance 贸易逆差，入超

The demand for arbitration shall be delivered in writing to the adverse party.

提出仲裁的要求须用书面（形式）递交给对立面的当事人。

24.occurrence n.出现，发生

The Assignor shall notify the other party to this Agreement of each of the following matters within（…）days after the occurrence thereof.

在下列事项发生以后的……天以内，转让人必须将每一事项通知本协议的另一方。

occur vi.出现

As new developments in the methods occur, the Company may require that the operator attends additional courses of training by the Company.

采用的方法如出现了新的发展，公司可以要求经营者参加公司举办的额外培训课程。

25.authentic  adj.        可信的，权威的

an authentic deed        手续完备的契约

an authentic document    真实的文件

A contract executed by an attorney or agent on behalf of the contractor shall be accompanied by two authenticated copies of his power of attorney or other evidence of his authority of act on behalf of the contractor.

由代表承包商的律师或代理人签署的合同应附有两份经认证的授权书副本或代表承包商的其他授权证据。

authenticate vt.证实，鉴证，使生效

authenticated protest（公证人对汇票等）经鉴证的拒付证书

26.maturity n.成熟，完备，（票据）到期，到期日

We do not think the time of sole agency negotiation has come to maturity.

我方认为商谈独家代理的时机尚未成熟。

We are pleased to inform you that your draft No. 123 has been duly honoured on maturity.

兹乐于奉告，你方第123号汇票已于到期日全数兑付。

mature vt. 使成熟，使到期；vi. （票据等）到期

matured check/cheque　到期支票

matured notes 到期票据

You may rest assured that we will discuss the question of exclusive distribution with you when opportunity matures.

你方可放心，时机成熟时我方定与你方商讨独家经销问题。

Upon the failure to comply with any such demand, then the principal of this note shall mature.

遇有不能遵守这种要求的情况时，则本票据的本金即告到期。

27. successor n. 继承人，继任人

Each officer will hold office until his successor shall have been duly elected.

每一名高级职员必须继续留任，直到选出他的继任人为止。

This Agreement shall not be assignable by ZZZ except to the successors of ZZZ.

乙方不得转让本协议，但转让给乙方的继承人不在此列。

28. regardless adv. 不论

Deviations, regardless of reason, are not permissible, unless the franchisor consents thereto in writing.

不论出于何种原因，不容许有任何偏差，但特许证签发人业已用书面同意者不在此列。

All export business regardless of origin shall be excluded from this Agreement.

一切出口业务，不论其来源如何，都应排除在本协议之外。

29. duly adv. 按时地，正式地，适当地

Buyer is a corporation duly organized and validity existing under the laws of the （country）.

买方是按照（某国）的法律正式组成而合法存在的一家公司。

The draft will be duly honoured when it falls due.

汇票到期时定予全数兑付。

While reimbursing, the negotiating bank is required to certify that all the credit terms have been duly complied with.

议付行在索偿时须证明信用证所有条款业已完全照办。

We believe that the goods will duly arrive at your end.

相信货物将会按时到达你方。

## ●Exercises

I.Translate the following into English：

1.一般来说，出口信贷只能用于从贷款国家购买资本商品、半资本商品或与其有关的劳务。

2.今年年底，中国银行与12家英国银行签订了总额为120亿美元的买方信贷，即存款便利。

3.使用卖方信贷时，买方需支付15%的现款（5%在贸易合同签订时向卖方支付，10%在交货前支付），其余的85%货款则用延期付款的方式分期偿还。

4.买方信贷通常是指出口方的银行直接向进口商或其银行提供的信贷。

5.银团贷款通常提供金额较大的贷款，它是由几家银行筹集资金而由一家银行作为牵头银行。

6.为了扶植本国的出口，有些国家也用外国货币向国内出口商或国外进口商提供出口信贷。

7.由于有些国家对出口信贷的利息实行政府补贴，所以贷款利率低于市场利率。

8.在买方信贷方式下，可由出口方银行直接向进口商提供信贷，进口商与出口商之间的商品买卖以现汇方式结算，或由出口方银行向进口方银行提供信贷，然后由进口商从他的银行得到这笔贷款，以现汇支付给出口商。

9.买方信贷的归还，一般做法是以交货完毕日起或建设安装妥善日起或工程建成日起，由进口商或进口银行按约定的期限分期归还贷款，约定的还款期一般每半年一次，同时支付利息。

10.出口信贷的贷款额一般是合同金额的80%~85%，其余资金须由进口商自筹。

II.Translate the following into Chinese：

1.A loan contract refers to a contract whereby the borrower raises a loan from the lender，and repay the loan with interest thereof when it becomes due.

2.The contents of a loan contract shall contain such clauses as the category of loans，the kind of currency，the purpose of use，the amount，the interest rate，the term and the method of returning the loan.

3.A floating rate is quoted according to the London Interbank Offered Rate of the Euro-currency market while a fixed rate according to the purpose，term，anticipated economic and social benefit of the loan.

4.After a formal loan agreement is reached，the lending bank will commit itself to provide the borrower with funds. The borrower may make several drawings but the aggregate amount should not exceed the maximum amount which the lending bank has committed.

5. After the bank advances money to the borrower, it will also have to supervise how the money is used and whether there are any progress of the construction and the execution of the plan of the relative project.

6. A government supported export credit is a credit provided by a western capitalist country at a preferential interest rate lower than the market rate through guarantee or interest make-up subsidy for the purpose of expanding its export.

7. By "payment on receipt of documents" we mean payment will not be made until our receipt of the export shipping documents.

8. Where the lender fails to extend the loan in accordance with the agreed date and amount and causes losses to the borrower, the lender shall compensate for the losses.

9. Where the borrower fails to return the loan in accordance with the agreed time limit, the borrower shall pay overdue interest according to the terms of the contract or the relevant provisions of the State.

10. Export credit is one of the principal measures for the promotion of international trade.

# Unit Fifteen /第三方监管账户协议

## Escrow Account Agreement

1.This Escrow Account Agreement is made on 14 April，2018 between:

本监管账户协议于2018年4月1日由以下各方签订：

2.Malaysia（the "ABC"），acting through the Ministry of Finance

马来西亚政府（以下简称"ABC"）通过财政部来行使职能

3. BCD-P.O. Box 188，Kuala Lumpur，Malaysia

BCD——马来西亚吉隆坡邮箱188号

4. XYZ，No.222 Fu Cheng Men Street，Beijing，China；and

XYZ——中国北京阜城门大街222号

5. China Bank UUU，No. 10 Financial Street，Xicheng Distrrict，Beijing，China（the "Escrow Bank"）.

中国银行UUU——中国北京市西城区金融大街10号（以下简称"监管银行"）

## WHEREAS

Article 1.The ABC as borrower and Escrow Bank as arranger（the "Arranger"，when referred to in relation to the Loan Facility Framework Agreement as defined below）have entered on or about the date of this Agreement into a loan facility framework agreement（the "Loan Facility Framework Agreement"，including any amendments thereto from time to time）.

Article 2.BCD as supplier and XYZ as purchaser have entered on or before the date of this Agreement into a coal sales contract（the "Coal Sales Contract"，including any amendments thereto from time to time）.

Article 3.Both XYZ and BCD under the Coal Sales Contract and the ABC and the Arranger under the Loan Facility Framework Agreement have agreed that entering into this Escrow Account Agreement is a condition precedent for the effectiveness of the Coal Sales Contract and the Loan Facility Framework Agreement.

Article 4.The ABC，BCD and XYZ wish to appoint the Escrow Bank，and the Escrow Bank agrees to accept such appointment，to act as the escrow bank for the Escrow Account（as defined below）.

IT IS AGREED as follows：

## 1.Scope and Definitions

1.1　Pursuant to the Agreement，the ABC，BCD and XYZ hereby appoint the Escrow Bank，and the Escrow Bank hereby accepts and acts as the escrow bank in relation to an account （the "Escrow Account"） which opened and maintained in the name of ABC with the Escrow Bank within the People's Republic of China （for the purpose of this Agreement only，excluding Hong Kong，Macau and Taiwan，referred to as the "PRC"） in accordance with the terms and conditions of this Agreement.

1.2　The Escrow Account will be used to collect and deposit the proceeds payable by XYZ to BCD under the Coal Sales Contract so as to ensure that the ABC has sufficient cash reserve to pay any amount due and payable under the Specific Loan Agreements in accordance with Clause 3 of this Agreement.

1.3　Terms defined in the Loan Facility Framework Agreement shall have the same meaning when used herein.

## 2. Escrow Account—General Provisions

2.1　Opening of the Escrow Account

2.1.1　The Escrow Bank shall open the Escrow Account in accordance with Clause 1.1 as soon as practicable after this Agreement becomes effective，and maintain and operate the Escrow Account pursuant to this Agreement. The ABC shall，promptly upon the request of the Escrow Bank，provide the Escrow Bank with such necessary assistance and documents as required under the applicable laws and regulations of the PRC in relation to the opening，maintenance and operation of the Escrow Account.

2.1.2　The ABC shall be liable for the payment of all fees and taxes in relation to the operation and maintenance of the Escrow Account.

2.1.3　The ABC shall，within ten （10） Business Days after the date of signature of this Agreement，provide the Escrow Bank with a list of the specimen signatures of its authorized signatories and the specimen of its corporate or financial stamps，together with the details of their account bank （s） or correspondence bank （s） （including its/their name （s），address （es） and SWIFT code （s） ） which shall be authorized to send SWIFT payment instructions on their behalf to the Escrow Bank. The ABC shall furthermore promptly provide the Escrow Bank with written updates in the event of any changes to the above information and data. The Escrow Bank shall not be liable for any loss or damage caused by the failure of the ABC to timely provide such updated information.

2.2　Currency of the Escrow Account

The currency of the Escrow Account shall be US Dollar （USD）.

2.3　Management fee of the Escrow Account

The management fee of the Escrow Account shall amount to one hundred thousand US dollars flat per annum （USD 100，000 p.a.），starting from the date of signature of the first Specific Loan Agreement， payable each year in one single installment upon collection in the Escrow Account of the proceeds of the first cargo to be delivered during such year under the Coal sales contract. The Escrow Account Bank may deduct such management fee directly from the Escrow Account.

2.4　Interest on the Escrow Account

Interest on deposits in the Escrow Account shall be calculated semi-annually on the basis of the prevailing interest rate for US dollar deposits as published by the People's Bank of China.

## 3.Escrow Account—Operation

3.1　Deposits into the Escrow Account

3.1.1　BCD hereby instructs XYZ， and XYZ hereby accepts such instruction， to deposit into the Escrow Account any purchase price payable by XYZ to BCD in accordance with the Coal sales contract，at the time and in the manner as prescribed under the Coal sales contract.

3.1.2　The ABC hereby acknowledges that，in each Specific Loan Agreement， one condition precedent for each utilization of the facility thereunder is and shall be that the amount standing to the credit of the Escrow Account shall not be less than the aggregate amount of the next two （2） repayment installments payable by the ABC as borrower under each Specific Loan Agreement （comprising the amount of interest accrued thereon， the amount of principal to be repaid and/or the commitment fee payable thereunder， as the case may be） （the "Minimum Amount"） . Should the amount standing to the credit of the Escrow Account be or become lower than the Minimum Amount， the Escrow Bank shall request in writing the ABC to promptly deposit such additional funds into the Escrow Account to allow balance of the Escrow Account to be at least equal to the Minimum Amount.

3.2　Withdrawals from the Escrow Account

3.2.1　Unless otherwise foreseen in this Agreement，the ABC may withdraw funds from the Escrow Account provided that；

（i）the ABC has given to the Escrow Bank written notice， signed by its authorized signatories， no less than five （5） Business Days prior to the proposed withdrawal date， together with the SWIFT payment instruction from its designated account bank or correspondence bank， indicating such withdrawal date， the amount to be withdrawn from the Escrow Account and the remittance route （including the name of the beneficiary， the account bank's name， address and SWIFT code and the correspondence bank's name， address and SWIFT code）；

（ii）for outgoing transfers in Euros （EUR），the ABC has authorized under the written notice referred to in sub - paragraph (i) above the Escrow Bank to convert US dollars in the Escrow Account into Euros at the prevailing market exchange rate then applied by the Escrow Bank and to remit such Euros to the designated account; the Escrow Bank shall after each such transfer inform the ABC in writing of the exchange rate applied;

(iii) no default by the ABC as borrower under each Specific Loan Agreement or by BCD under the Coal sales contract is continuing on the proposed withdrawal date; and

(iv) the amount standing to the credit of the Escrow Account after such proposed withdrawal is not less than the Minimum Amount.

3.2.2　Upon receipt of the written notice from the ABC as referred to in Clause 3.2.1 (i) above, the Escrow Bank shall promptly calculate the Minimum Amount and notify to the ABC whether and to what extent the request of such withdrawal can be satisfied. Should the proposed requested withdrawal result in the balance of the Escrow Account falling below the Minimum Amount, the Escrow Bank shall inform the ABC that the requested withdrawal can not be processed and ask whether the ABC wishes to issue new instructions to the Escrow Bank for the withdrawal of a lesser amount not resulting in the Minimum Amount to be affected. For the avoidance of doubt, no withdrawals shall be allowed from the Escrow Account: (i) if the amount standing to the credit of the Escrow Account is already below the Minimum Amount at the time of the corresponding written notice from the ABC or, as the case may be, (ii) until the ABC issues new instructions to the Escrow Bank for the withdrawal of an amount not resulting in the Minimum Amount to be affected.

3.2.3　Subject to Clauses 3.2.1 and 3.2.2, the Escrow Bank shall transfer to such account designated by the ABC the applicable amount of funds from the Escrow Account by wire transfer on the proposed withdrawal date.

3.3　Application of the Minimum Amount

3.3.1　The ABC hereby instructs the Escrow Bank to apply up to all the Minimum Amount to discharge any amount due and payable by the ABC under any Specific Loan Agreement, provided and to the extent that;

(i) the ABC confirms in writing to the agent bank under such Specific Loan Agreement, no later than ten (10) Business Days prior to the scheduled payment date, that its payment obligations under said Specific Loan Agreement shall be discharged by applying those funds standing to the credit of the Escrow Account, and such agent bank sends a copy of such notice and the relevant payment instruction to the Escrow Bank no later than five (5) Business Days prior to the scheduled payment date, indicating in particular whether the Escrow Bank shall pay such amount from the Escrow Account to the agent bank or to each lender directly; or （ii）the ABC fails to discharge on the scheduled payment date any amount due and payable under such Specific Loan Agreement, and the relevant agent bank sends a written notice of such event the Escrow Bank requesting the Escrow Bank to discharge the ABC's due and outstanding payment obligation under such Specific Loan Agreement by applying those funds standing to the credit of the Escrow Account, together with the relevant payment instructions.

3.3.2　The Escrow Bank shall transfer to such agent bank or, upon such agent bank's instruction, to the relevant lenders under such Specific Loan Agreement, only such amount from the Escrow Account which is required and sufficient to discharge ABC's relevant payment obligation thereunder or, as the case may be and if the amount standing to the credit of the Escrow Account is not sufficient to discharge such payment obligation, the balance standing to the credit of the Escrow Account.

3.4　Except as provided under Clauses 2.1.2, 3.2 and 3.3, the Escrow Bank shall not apply the deposits in the Escrow Account for any other purposes or transfer, pledge or otherwise dispose of such deposits.

## 4.Change of the Escrow bank

The Escrow Bank may at any time resign from its position as escrow bank under this Agreement, provided that such resignation will become effective only thirty （30） days after the date on which: (i) all parties have been informed thereof in writing ; and （ii） a new escrow bank operating in the PRC and acceptable to ABC has formally accepted to act as successor to the Escrow Bank in accordance with the terms and conditions of the Agreement, whichever date is later. All information and date relating to the change of escrow bank shall be delivered exclusively by registered air mail, e-mail or telex with return receipt and/or confirmation.

## 5. Representations and Warranties of the ABC and of BCD

5.1　The ABC hereby represents and warrant to the Escrow Bank that;

5.1.1　it is a Ministry of the government of Malaysia, and has the power, and has been duly authorized, to act on behalf of Malaysia to enter into and perform this Agreement;

5.1.2　by entering into and performing this Agreement, it will not violate any applicable laws in Malaysia, or treaties or arrangements of Malaysia with the World Bank and/or the International Monetary Fund, and this Agreement will not be affected by an agreement signed by the Malaysia government and any third party （including, Without limitation, any agreement in relation to the Paris Club of creditor countries）.

5.2　Each of the ABC and BCD hereby represents and warrant to the Escrow Bank that:

5.2.1　this Agreement constitutes legal, binding, valid and enforceable obligations on it;

5.2.2  this Agreement is signed in due form and recognised by Malaysian courts notwithstanding the fact that it is government by the laws of the PRC;

5.2.3  an arbitral award by a Chinese arbitration tribunal will be recognised and enforced by Malaysian courts;

5.2.4  so far as it is aware, all information it has provided to the Escrow Bank under or in connection with this Agreement is true, accurate, complete and updated; and

5.2.5  it understands that the Escrow Banks enters into this Agreement on the basis of the above representations and warranties.

## 6. Liability of the Escrow Bank

The Escrow Bank shall be responsible only for the proper management of the Escrow Account, in conformity with this Agreement during its term and applicable laws and regulations in the PRC from time to time.Save for the above, the Escrow Bank shall not be responsible or any losses of the ABC, BCD or XYZ as result of actions or omissions in relation to this Agreement.

## 7. Communications and Notices

7.1  Save as otherwise agreed herein, notices and communications in relation to this Agreement shall be sent by registered air mail with a return receipt.Email shall require a return receipt to be deemed sent and telex messages shall be confirmed by a transmission receipt. All notices and communications shall be deemed as received on the date of receipt by signature, e-mail confirmation or transmission receipt.

7.2  Notices and communications under this Agreement shall be sent:

7.2.1  If to ABC:

Address: ×××××××

Tel. No.: ×××××××

Fax No.: ×××××××

Attention: ×××××××

7.2.2  If to BCD:

Address: ×××××××

Tel. No.: ×××××××

Fax No.: ×××××××

Attention: ×××××××

7.2.3  If to XYZ:

Address: ×××××××

Tel. No.: ×××××××

Fax No.: ×××××××

Attention: ×××××××

7.2.4 If to the Escrow Bank:

Address: ×××××××

Tel. No.: ×××××××

Fax No.: ×××××××

Attention: ×××××××

## 8.Effectiveness of this Agreement

This Contract shall come into effect subject to and upon satisfaction of each of the following cumulative conditions precedent:

(i) signature of the Loan Facility Framework Agreement;

(ii) signature of the Coal Contract;

(iii) (if applicable) issuance by the State Administration of Foreign Exchange of the People's Republic of China-or by a designated branch thereof of a written authorization to the Escrow Bank to open and maintain the Escrow Account in accordance with this Agreement.

The Escrow Bank shall inform the other parties in writing of the date upon which all above conditions precedent are satisfied (the "Effective Date").

## 9. Miscellaneous

9.1 Term. This Agreement shall come into force on the Effective Date and remain valid for fifteen (15) years, subject to an automatic extension to the later of the expiry date of the Coal sales contract or when the ABC has discharged all its payment obligations under any Specific Loan Agreement.

9.2 Amendments. Amendments to this Agreement shall require the written form.

9.3 Confidentiality. Each party hereby undertakes to keep all information contained in this Agreement confidential except for the purpose of necessary disclosure to appropriate governmental authorities, regulatory bodies or courts as required by applicable laws and regulations or to their directors, senior management, staff or advisors on a "need to know" basis, the parties hereby undertake not to disclose to any third party any information in relation to this Agreement, the transactions described in this Agreement or such related documents, without prior authorization of each other party to that effect.

9.4 Severability. If at any time any provision of this Agreement is or becomes illegal, invalid or unenforceable in any respect under any law of any jurisdiction, neither the legality, validity or enforceability of the remaining provisions nor the legality, validity or enforceability of such provision under the law of any other jurisdiction will in any way be affected or impaired.

9.5 Prior agreements. This Agreement supersedes any previous written or oral agreement between the parties in relation to the matters dealt with in this Agreement and contains the whole agreement between the parties relating to the subject matter of this Agreement at the date hereof.

9.6　Number of copies. This Agreement is made in four　(4) original copies, and each party will hold one　(1) original copy.

9.7　Language. This Agreement is entered into the English, Chinese and French versions. In the event of any conflict between these versions, the English version shall prevail.

## 10. Waiver of Immunities

Each of the ABC and BCD irrevocably and unconditionally agrees and represents that:

irrevocably waives, to the fullest extent permitted by applicable law, all immunity to which it or its property may be or become entitled, whether on the basis of sovereignty or otherwise, from jurisdiction, attachment or execution in any action or proceeding arising out of or relating to this Agreement.

## 11. Governing Law and Dispute Resolution

11.1　This Agreement is governed by and construed in accordance with the laws of the PRC.

11.2　In the event of any dispute arising under or in connection with this Agreement, the parties shall use their best endeavors to resolve such dispute by an amicable negotiation. If such dispute cannot be so solved within two　(2) months from the date of a Party's request for such negotiation, any party shall be entitled to submit such dispute to the China International Economic and Trade Arbitration Commission　(the "Commission"　) for arbitration in Beijing. The language to be used in the arbitration shall be English. The arbitral tribunal shall comprise three arbitrators. Each of the ABC and BCD　(acting as a whole) and the Escrow Bank shall appoint one arbitrator, and the third arbitrator　(acting as the chairman of the arbitration tribunal) shall be appointed by the Commission. The arbitration award shall be final and binding on the parties.

In witness whereof this Agreement has been entered into in Beijing, China on the date stated at the beginning.

[Signature Page]


**The Ministry of Finance, Malaysia**

———————————

Authorised Representative

Name:

Title:

(Stamp)

**BCD**

_____

Authorised Representative

Name：

Title：

（Stamp）

**XYZ**

_____

Authorised Representative

Name：

Title：

（Stamp）

**China Bank UUU**

_____

Authorised Representative

Name：

Title：

（Stamp）

**参考译文：**

鉴于

A.作为借款人的ABC和作为安排方的监管银行（在以下涉及的贷款框架协议中简称"安排方"）在本协议的签署之日已经签署了贷款的框架协议（以下简称"贷款框架协议"，其包括所有相关的补充协议）。

B.作为供货方的BCD与作为购买方的XYZ在本协议的签署之日或者签署之前已经签署了煤炭销售合同（以下简称"煤炭销售合同"，包括所有的补充协议）。

C.煤炭销售合同下的XYZ和BCD，贷款框架协议项下的ABC和安排方都同意签署此第三方监管账户协议，并以此协议作为煤炭销售合同和贷款框架协议的生效条件。

D.ABC，BCD和XYZ共同指定监管银行，监管银行同意此安排，并设置监管账户。

以上各方同意如下条款：

### 1.合同范围和定义

1.1　根据此协议，ABC，BCD 和 XYZ 指定监管银行，监管银行同意此安排，并按照此合同的约定在中华人民共和国境内（不含中国香港、澳门和中国台湾地区）以 ABC 的名义开户并维护账户（以下称为"监管账户"）。

1.2　煤炭销售合同由 XYZ 支付给 BCD 的款项将存放在监管账户中。根据本协议条款 3 的约定，ABC 要确保拥有足够的现金储备来支付项目贷款协议项下的应付账款。

1.3　贷款框架协议中的术语在本协议中具有相同的意义。

### 2.监管账户——总则

2.1　监管账户的开立

2.1.1　依据本合同的约定，监管银行在本协议生效后，应按照条款 1.1 的约定尽快开立、维护和管理监管账户。在监管银行的要求下，ABC 应尽快提供必要的协助和文件以满足中华人民共和国对监管账户开立、维护和管理的法律要求。

2.1.2　ABC 负责支付监管账户维护和管理的所有费用和相关税费。

2.1.3　ABC 应在本协议签署 10 个工作日后提供给监管银行授权签字的样本、企业或者财务的印章样本，提供其开户银行或者往来银行的详细信息，包括银行名称、地址和 SWIFT 编码，并确保这些银行能够通过 SWIFT 电文发布付款指令给监管银行。ABC 应在以上信息发生变更时，及时将变更信息通知监管银行。监管银行不负责由于 ABC 信息更新不及时所造成的任何损失。

2.2　监管账户的币种

监管账户的币种为美元。

2.3　监管账户的管理费

监管账户的管理费为每年固定 10 万美元，计费起始日为项目贷款协议的签署日。在煤炭采购协议项下本年内第一笔销售款支付到监管账户时，管理费一次性支付。监管银行可以直接从监管账户里扣除管理费。

2.4　监管账户的利息

监管账户中监管资金的利息每半年计算一次，基于中国人民银行公布的美元存款的现行利率确定。

### 3.监管账户——操作

3.1　监管账户的存入资金

3.1.1　BCD 指示 XYZ，XYZ 接受此指示，按照煤炭销售协议中的时间和支付方式，将 XYZ 支付给 BCD 的购买款项存入监管账户。

3.1.2　ABC 确认在每一个项目的贷款协议中，提款的前提条件为监管账户中的余额（以下简称"最低余额"）不低于借款人 ABC 接下来两次提款的总额（包括相关的利息，将要支付的本金和/或承担费）。如果监管账户中剩余的金额低于最低余额，监管银行会书面要求 ABC 储存相应的金额以满足最低余额的要求。

3.2　监管账户的资金提取

3.2.1　除了本协议中的其他约定，ABC可以在满足以下情况的前提下从监管账户中支取资金：

（i）ABC在计划支取的5个工作日前，经授权签字后，以书面形式通知监管银行，并由其指定的开户银行或者往来银行开出SWIFT支付电文，明确资金提取日、提取金额和汇款路径（包括受益人的名称、开户行名称、地址和SWIFT编码，往来银行名称、地址和SWIFT编码）；

（ii）如果提取的币种为欧元，ABC应在（i）段的书面通知中授权监管银行在监管账户中按照当时的市场汇率将美元转换为欧元，并将欧元汇到指定的账户中。监管银行在每次汇款后要将所采用的汇率书面通知给ABC；

（iii）在预计的提款日，ABC作为借款人在项目贷款协议项下没有违约或者BCD在煤炭销售协议中没有违约；并且

（iv）提取资金后监管账户的余额不低于最低余额的要求。

3.2.2　按照3.2.1（i）的规定，在收到ABC的书面申请之后，监管银行应尽快计算最低余额，并通知ABC其提取申请是否可以满足或者在多大程度上可以满足。如果提请的金额导致账户余额低于最低余额，监管银行应通知ABC其申请的金额无法处理，并问询ABC是否需要重新发出指令，降低提取金额，以满足账户最低余额的要求。为了避免任何可能的争议，以下情况下不能从监管账户中提取资金（i）如果在收到ABC书面通知时，监管账户余额已经低于最低余额或者视其他具体情况；（ii）直到ABC开出新的指令给监管银行更改提取金额，保证账户余额不低于最低余额的要求。

3.2.3　基于条款3.2.1和3.2.2的约定，监管银行要在指定的提取日期以电汇的方式将申请的金额汇到ABC指定的账户。

3.3　最低余额的申请使用

3.3.1　在项目贷款协议下，如果能够满足如下条件，ABC可以指示监管银行申请使用最低余额的金额来支付其余的贷款：

（i）在项目贷款协议项下，ABC应在计划还款日期的10个工作日之前书面通知代理银行其将使用监管账户的资金来偿还项目贷款协议项下的借款，代理银行应在计划还款日期的5个工作日之前将通知副本和付款指令发给监管银行，并请监管银行答复是否可以将申请款项支付给代理银行或者直接支付给借款人；或者

（ii）ABC在应付款日无法清偿项目贷款协议项下的债务，相关代理银行以书面形式通知监管银行并提出申请，申请使用监管账户的资金来清偿项目贷款协议项下的债务，并将付款指令一并提交给监管银行。

3.3.2　监管银行在最低余额足够偿付ABC的付款金额时，应直接支付给代理银行或者在代理银行指示下支付给项目贷款协议中的借款人。如果最低余额无法满足其付款义务的要求，则仅支付剩余的金额。

3.4　除了条款2.1.2、3.2和3.3的约定，监管银行不得使用账户的资金用于其

他任何目的，包括转移支付、抵押或者处置资金。

## 4.监管银行的变更

在本协议下，监管银行要充分履行监管银行的职责，监管银行只有在以下事项发生 30 天之后可以免除责任：（i）所有方都接到书面通知更换监管银行；并且（ii）经由 ABC 同意，中华人民共和国境内的银行正式声明接受本协议的条款，履行监管银行的责任。所有关于监管银行变更的信息和日期都应该以附带回执或者收到确认的挂号航空信、邮件或者电报的形式发送。

## 5.ABC 和 BCD 的陈述和保证

5.1　ABC 在此向监管银行做出如下陈述和保证：

5.1.1　其作为马来西亚政府的部委，已经被充分授权，有权代表马来西亚政府达成并履行此协议；

5.1.2　签署和履行此协议不会违反马来西亚的法律，也不会违反马来西亚政府同世界银行和/或国际货币基金组织签署的条约或者资金安排，且此协议也不会受马来西亚政府同任何第三方签署协议的影响（包括但不限于同债权国所组成的巴黎债权国俱乐部所签署的任何协议）。

5.2　ABC 和 BCD 的每一方都向监管银行做出如下陈述和保证：

5.2.1　本协议的签署意味着其具有法律遵从的、有约束力的、有效的和可执行的义务；

5.2.2　尽管本协议法律适用为中华人民共和国的法律，本协议的签署格式已经获得马来西亚法院的认可；

5.2.3　中国仲裁机构的仲裁决议在马来西亚是被认可且可执行的；

5.2.4　其提给监管银行的所有与本协议有关的信息都是真实的、准确的、完整的和及时的；并且

5.2.5　双方都明确监管银行签署此协议完全是基于以上的陈述和保证。

## 6.监管银行的义务

监管银行只负责按照中华人民共和国的法律法规规定，在协议有效期之内管理监管账户。除了以上义务之外，由于 ABC、BCD 或者 XYZ 执行此协议的行为或者过失导致的损失，监管银行不负任何责任。

## 7.沟通信息和通知

7.1　除了本协议其他条款的约定，所有的通知和沟通信息应以带有回执的挂号航空信的形式进行。收到回执的电子邮件和发送确认收据的电报亦被认可为发送成功。所有的通知和沟通信息收到的时间以签收、电子邮件回执或者收到发送确认收据为准。

7.2　本协议的通知和沟通信息应发送给如下联系方式：

7.2.1　如果给 ABC：

地址：××××××××

电话号码：××××××××

传真号码：×××××××

联系人：×××××××

7.2.2 如果给 BCD：

地址：×××××××

电话号码：×××××××

传真号码：×××××××

联系人：×××××××

7.2.3 如果给 XYZ：

地址：×××××××

电话号码：×××××××

传真号码：×××××××

联系人：×××××××

7.2.4 如果给监管银行：

地址：×××××××

电话号码：×××××××

传真号码：×××××××

联系人：×××××××

## 8.协议生效

本协议的生效前提为满足以下的要求：

（i）贷款框架协议的签署；

（ii）煤炭采购协议的签署；

（iii）（如果适用）由中华人民共和国外汇管理局或者其分支机构签发，允许监管银行按照此协议的要求开立并维护监管账号。

监管银行应该以书面的形式通知其他各方以上条件都达到满足的日期（即"协议生效日期"）。

## 9.其他约定

9.1 期限。本协议从协议生效日起生效，有效期限15年，并基于以下两个日期的晚者自动延期：煤炭销售合同的终止日期或者 ABC 在项目贷款协议中清偿完毕的日期。

9.2 协议的修改。本协议的修改需要以书面形式进行。

9.3 保密。合同中每一方承诺本协议涉及的任何信息都将为保密信息，除非由于法律规定要求披露给政府主管部门、监管主体或者法院，或者基于需要了解的基础上披露给主管、高级管理层、职员或者顾问。各方承诺在未获得其他各方同意的前提下，不将协议相关信息、交易信息或者其他文件披露给任何第三方。

9.4 条款可分割性。如果在任何时间，协议中的某些条款不符合法律要求、条款失效或无法执行，协议中的其他条款不受这些条款的影响。

9.5 之前达成的协议。在本协议签署之日，本协议取代以往涉及本协议交易或者标的物的任何书面或者口头达成的协议。

9.6 协议的数量。本协议一式四份，每一方保留一份原件。

9.7 语言。本协议有英文、中文和法语三个版本。如果各个版本之间有所不同，以英文版本为准。

## 10.豁免权的放弃

ABC 和 BCD 的每一方都不可撤销且无条件地同意并作出如下承诺：

在适用法律允许的最大范围内，以上各方不可撤销地放弃所有财产的豁免权，无论是根据主权或管辖权、附件或因本协议引起或与本协议有关的任何行动或程序的执行。

## 11.适用法律和争端解决

11.1 本协议的适用法律为中华人民共和国法律。

11.2 所有关于本协议和本协议执行过程中的纠纷都应本着友好协商的方式解决。如果在两个月之内通过协商无法解决纠纷，任何一方有权将案件提交北京中国国际贸易仲裁委员会仲裁。仲裁地在北京，仲裁语言为英语。仲裁员由三人组成，ABC 和 BCD 指定一名仲裁员，监管银行指定一名仲裁员，另外一名仲裁员作为仲裁庭主席，由委员会指定。仲裁效力为终局的，对双方都具有约束力。

本协议于中国北京，在协议首页列明的日期签署，特此为证。

［签字页］

**马来西亚财政部**

_____

授权签字人

名称：

职位：

公章：

**BCD**

_____

授权签字人

名称：

职位：

公章：

XYZ

——————————

授权签字人
名称：
职位：
公章：

**中国银行 UUU**

——————————

授权签字人
名称：
职位：
公章：

## Notes

1. "escrow" 第三方支付/履约保证，指一种代管契约，由买卖双方的第三方保管某特定文件、契约、金钱、证券或其他财产，当特定条件成就或法律事件发生时，该第三人即将其保管物交给特定之人。

2.condition（s）precedent 先决条件

相当于中国附条件合同制度中的"所附生效条件"。只有该条件发生，合同才生效。

在涉外商务活动中经常会涉及合同的登记审批、项目批准等问题。合同双方为开展实质性合同，很可能约定由一方当事人向政府相关部门申请报批工作是合同的先决条件。再比如在重大设备采购合同时，甲方资金不足以全额支付乙方的价款，从而需要甲方首先向银行方面融资，而双方就完全可能将此融资问题规定于买卖合同中的先决条件之一，并约定违反该条件的法律后果。

Completion of the sale and purchase of the Shares shall be conditioned upon the following conditions having been fulfilled: The written consent in due form of X BANK must be obtained by the Vendor and produced for inspection by the Purchaser.

股份交易的完成应当以下列事项的履行完毕为条件：卖方必须得到 X 银行出具的格式适当的书面同意，供买方审验。

Payment of Registered Capital; Conditions Precedent

（a）Subject to Article 2.1, each Party shall make its contribution to the registered capital of the Company in accordance with the schedule set forth in Schedule C.

（b）Subject to Article 2.1, in the event that one Party fails to make its capital contribution, in whole or in part, in accordance with the provisions of this Contract, such Party shall be liable to pay simple interests to the Company at rate equal to （…） per annum on the unpaid amount from the time due until the time the full outstanding amount including penalty interest is paid to and received by the Company.

注册资本的缴付；先决条件

（1）按照第2.1条的规定，每一方应按照附录三中规定的时间表缴付其认缴的注册资本。

（2）按照第2.1条的规定，如果一方未依照本合同的条款全额或部分缴纳出资额，则该方应就欠缴的出资额按年利率（……）的单利向合营公司支付利息，计息期为该笔出资应缴日起至该笔出资及罚金全额支付，并由合营公司收到之日。

3.Commitment Fee 承担费，承诺费

除了利息支出之外，使用国际银团贷款时，借款人不仅需要支付利息，还需要支付一些其他的费用，包括承担费或承诺费。

承担费是借款人对未提用的贷款部分支付的费用，其比率大约为0.25%~0.75%。

4.amount standing to the credit of somebody's account

amount standing to the credit of somebody

某人银行账户中的余额

● Exercises

I. Translate the following into English：

1.本协议的修改需要以书面形式进行。

2.在本协议签署之日，本协议取代以往涉及本协议交易或者标的物的任何书面或者口头达成的协议。

3.本协议的签署意味着其具有法律遵从的、有约束力的、有效的和可执行的义务。

4.ABC负责支付监管账户维护和管理的所有费用和相关税费。

5.本合同不得以口头方式修改，而须经双方签署书面文件后方可修改。

6.当乙方向甲方提供已存款的证明文件后，甲方将提供给乙方相应的收据。

7.乙方已向母公司交付所有乙方合同及其修订的准确和完整的附件。

8.法律顾问参与了本协议的谈判、签署和交付过程。

9.就第2条而言，"土地"并不包括继承财产。

10.如果不存在相反的合同规定，通常不得向赔偿方要求补偿间接损失。

II. Translate the following sentences into Chinese：

1. Subject to Clauses 3.2.1 and 3.2.2, the Escrow Bank shall transfer to such account designated by the ABC the applicable amount of funds from the Escrow Account by wire transfer on the proposed withdrawal date.

2. The ABC hereby instructs the Escrow Bank to apply up to all the Minimum Amount to discharge any amount due and payable by the ABC under any Specific Loan Agreement, provided and to the extent that.

3. This Agreement shall come into force on the Effective Date and remain valid for fifteen (15) years, subject to an automatic extension to the later of the expiry date of the Coal sales contract or when the ABC has discharged all its payment obligations under any Specific Loan Agreement.

4. No terms or provisions of this Agreement shall be varied or modified by any prior or subsequent statement, conduct or act of either of the Parties, except that the Parties may amend this Agreement by written instruments referring to and executed in the same manner as this Agreement.

5. The Parties hereby warrant that they are not engaged in and will not engage either directly or through subsidiaries or associated companies, in activities included in the business of the Joint Venture unless agreed upon by the Parties in writing.

6. If the country of either arty restricts the remittance of funds to the other party's country, the Party A may instruct the Party B to deposit sums due into an account in the Party B's country but in the Party A's name.

7. Except as expressly set forth in the Party B Closing Certificate, each of the representations and warranties made by the Party B in this Agreement is accurate in all material respects as of the Closing Date as if made on the Closing Date.

8. Except for the stay of the Party B Pending Litigation and the Parent Pending Litigation pursuant to the Stay Order, the Party B Corporations do not commence or settle any Proceeding.

9. In case of default of the Applicant, the Society must first notify the Applicant it is in default and allows the Applicant a thirty business day remedy period.

10. Where the Contract provided for payment in whole or in part to be made to the Contractor in foreign currency or currencies, such payment shall not be subject to variations in the rate or rates of exchange between such specified foreign currency or currencies and the currency of the country in which the Works are to be executed.

# Unit Sixteen /保密协议

## Nondisclosure Agreement

This Nondisclosure Agreement（hereinafter called "Agreement"）is entered into by and between Andrew Inc.（ "Disclosing Party"）and James Smith, with the nationality of…, located at…（ "Receiving Party"）for the purpose of preventing the authorized disclosure of confidential information as defined below. The Parties agree to enter into a confidential relationship with respect to the following disclosure of certain proprietary and confidential information（hereinafter called "Confidential Information"）:

### 1.Confidential Information

Confidential Information means all information that has or could have commercial value or other utility in the business in which Disclosing Party is engaged.

### 2.Exclusions from Confidential Information

Receiving Party's obligations under this Agreement do not extend to information that is:

a）publicly known at the time of disclosure or subsequently becomes publicly known through no fault of the Receiving Party;

b）discovered or created by the Receiving Party before disclosure by Disclosing Party;

c）learned by the Receiving Party's through legitimate means other than from the Disclosing Party or Disclosing Party's representatives;

d）or is disclosed by Receiving Party with Disclosing Party's prior written approval.

### 3.Obligations of Receiving Party

Receiving Party shall hold and maintain the Confidential Information in strictest confidence for the sole and exclusive benefit of the Disclosing Party. Receiving Party shall carefully restrict access to Confidential Information to employees, contractors, and third parties as is reasonably required and shall require those persons to sign nondisclosure restrictions at least as protective as those in this Agreement. Receiving Party shall not, without prior written approval of Disclosing Party, use for Receiving Party's own benefit, publish, copy, or otherwise disclose to others, or permit the use by others for their benefit or to the detriment of Disclosing Party, and Confidential Information. Receiving Party shall return to Disclosing Party any and all records, and other written, printed, or tangible materials in its possession pertaining to Confidential information immediately if Disclosing Party requests it in writing.

### 4. Time Periods

The nondisclosure provisions of this Agreement shall survive the termination of this Agreement and Receiving Party's duty to hold Confidential Information in confidence shall remain in effect until the Confidential Information no longer qualifies as a trade secret or until Disclosing Party sends Receiving Party written notice releasing Receiving Party from this Agreement, whichever occurs first.

### 5. Relationship

Nothing contained in this Agreement shall be deemed to constitute either Party a partner, joint venture or employee of the other party for any purpose.

### 6. Severability

If a court finds any provisions of this Agreement invalid or unenforceable, the remainder of this Agreement shall be interpreted so as best to effect the intent of the parties.

### 7. Integration

This Agreement expresses the complete understanding of the parties with respect to the subject matter and supersedes all prior proposals agreements, representation, and understandings. This Agreement may not be amended except in a writing signed by both parties.

### 8. Waiver

The failure to exercise any right provided in this Agreement shall not be a waiver of prior or subsequent rights.

This Agreement and each Party's obligations shall be binding on the representatives, assigns, and successors of such party. Each party has signed this Agreement through its authorized representative.

| Disclosing Party | Receiving Party |
|---|---|
| By: | By: |
| Printed Name: | Printed Name: |
| Title: | Title: |
| Dated: | Dated: |

**参考译文：**

本保密协议（以下简称"协议"）是由安德鲁公司（信息提供方）与詹姆斯·斯密斯，国籍……住址……（信息接收方）就防止以下定义的保密信息的泄露所订立。签约双方同意就以下所有权和保密信息（以下简称保密信息）建立一种保密关系：

1. 保密信息

保密信息是指信息提供方所拥有的以及可能拥有的具有商业价值或其他商业用途的信息。

2. 保密信息除外条款

本合同项下的信息接受方保密义务不包含如下内容：

1）在信息披露时，已被外界知晓，或随后不是信息接收方的过失而使外界获悉；

2）在信息提供方发布之前就已被信息接收方所发现或获得；

3）由信息接收方通过合法手段而不是通过信息提供方或其代表的渠道获得；

4）经信息提供方的事先书面同意，由信息接收方披露的信息。

3. 信息接收方义务

信息接收方应为了信息提供方的独家利益对于"保密信息"予以最严格的保密。如工作需要，信息接收方要有限度地向其雇员、承包商和第三方披露"保密信息"并要求他们签署保密协议，其协议的保密程度等同于本协议。没有信息提供方的书面同意，信息接收方不能为了自身利益使用、出版、复制或把信息披露给其他方，或允许其他方为了自身的利益或对信息提供方有危害的"保密信息"。如信息接收方有书面要求，信息接收方应立即把与"保密信息"相关的任何和全部的录制、书面、印刷或实物材料归还信息提供方。

4. 保密期限

本协议的保密条款在本协议终止后应继续有效。信息接收方的保密义务也将持续到"保密信息"不再是商业秘密或信息提供方向信息接收方发出书面解除通告，先发生者为准。

5. 关系

任何目的都将不构成本合同任何一方为合伙人、合营公司或另一方的雇员的关系。

6. 可分性条款

若法院发现本协议的任何条款无效，余下的部分应被视为与约各方的意图。

7. 合并条款

本协议完全表达了与约各方对合同标的物的理解并替代了先前的书面意向书、陈述和协议。本协议除非有双方的书面签署，否则不得修改。

8. 弃权

没能够行使本协议所赋予的权利不意味着对先前或此后权利的放弃。

本协议及各方的义务对各方的代表，责任人和继承人均有约束力。各方指派授权代表签署本协议。

| 信息提供方 | 信息接收方 |
| --- | --- |
| 印刷体名字 | 印刷体名字 |
| 职位 | 职位 |
| 日期 | 日期 |

# Notes

1.保密条款

在英美国家，通常为了保护有价值的信息，人们会依靠普通法或者商业秘密法令的救济。但是，如果一方向另一方提供信息是基于合同约定的义务或者与契约上的安排有关，就需要在合同上列明"保密条款（confidentiality）"。在所有订立的"保密条款"和"保密协议"中，签约方的唯一目的就是保护一方向另一方提供的信息的机密性。

完整的保密条款内容大致如下：

机密信息的范围或定义（Definition/Scope）、保密义务（Obligation to Maintain Confidentiality）、未经授权的使用（Unauthorized Use）、允许获得披露的人（Permitted Disclose）、终止（Termination）、强制披露（Compelled Disclosure）、禁止令救济（Injunctive Relief）、赔偿（Indemnity）和继续效力（Survival）等。

"Confidential Information" means any and all data, reports, records, notes, compilation, studies and other information disclosed directly or indirectly by one Party to the other Party relating to or in any way connected with the Work, whether such information is disclosed orally, in writing, or by any other means.

"保密信息"指一方直接或间接向另一方披露的与工作有关的所有数据、报告、记录、笔记、汇编、研究或其他信息，不管口头披露，还是书面披露，还是以其他任何方式披露概不例外。

2.效力持续（条款）

英文合同中，survive 的用法比较特别，表示效力持续条款。在英文合同中，两个概念上的效力进行比较时，存续期间一个比另一个长的，惯用 A survive B.

The nondisclosure provisions of this Agreement shall survive the termination of this Agreement and Receiving Party's duty to hold Confidential Information in confidence shall remain in effect until the Confidential Information no longer qualifies as a trade secret or until Disclosing Party sends Receiving Party written notice releasing Receiving Party from this Agreement, whichever occurs first.

本协议的保密条款在本协议终止后应继续有效。信息接收方的保密义务也将持续到"保密信息"不再是商业秘密或信息提供方向信息接收方发出书面解除通告，先发生者为准。

The confidential obligation shall survive termination of this Contract.

本合同终止时，本保密义务应继续有效。

The representations, warranties and covenants contained herein shall survive the closing of any transaction pursuant to the terms of this Contract.

本合同声明、保证、承诺依据本合同进行的某交易完成后继续有效。

3.severable adj. 可分开的

This Contract shall be construed to be severable as to each installment of goods shipped.

对于分批发货的每批货物，本合同应予分别作出相应的解释。

severally adv. 各自地

The president and the vice-president shall severally represent the Company.

总裁和副总裁均可各自代表本公司。

The Creditors hereby severally agree with the Debtor…

债权人特此各自与债务人商定……

severally and jointly liable 个别及连带责任

The new partner who has been admitted to the partnership shall be jointly and the liabilities incurred by the partnership prior to his admission.

入伙的新合伙人对入伙前合伙企业的债务承担连带责任。

4.不弃权条款 Waiver of Right/Disclaimer，Non-waiver Provision

弃权条款有时候也用Non-waiver（不/非弃权）作为本条款的标题，但该条款的目的只有一个，表明合同在什么情况下弃权或者不视为弃权。

Waiver

Clause 1.1    No delay or omission by either Party in exercising any right，power or remedy provide by law or under this Agreement shall：

（a）affect that right，power or remedy；or

（b）operate as a waiver of it.

Clause 1.2    The single or partial exercise of any right，power or remedy provided by law or under this Agreement shall not preclude any further exercise of it or the exercise of any other right，power or remedy.

Clause 1.3    No waiver of any right，power or remedy provided by law or under this Agreement shall take effect unless it is in writing and signed by authorized representatives of the Party giving the waiver.

弃权

第一条第一款    任何一方延迟或没有行使任何法律或本协议规定的权利、权力或进行补救并不

（1）影响该权利、权力或补救权利；或

（2）构成弃权。

第一条第二款    单独进行或部分行使任何法律或本协议规定的权利、权力或进行补救并不阻碍进一步行使这些权利或行使其他的权利、权力或进行补救。

第一条第三款    放弃任何法律或本协议规定的权利、权力或进行补救必须采用书面形式并经弃权方授权代表签字后方才有效。

5.assigns n. （法律）受让人，接受财产等转让的人，受托者

This Agreement and each Party's obligations shall be binding on the representatives, assigns, and successors of such party. Each party has signed this Agreement through its authorized representative.

本协议及各方的义务对各方的代表，受让人和继承人均有约束力。各方指派授权代表签署本协议。

## ● Exercises

I.Translate the following sentences into English：

1. 承包商都应是在他们各自工种或职业内，具有相当资质、技能和经验的人员。

2. 本协议任何一方都可以在任何时候将其在本协议项下的全部或部分利益或权利进行转让。

3. 本合同终止时，本保密义务应继续有效。

4. 本合同条款中一部分或全部被法院判决无效，不影响其他有效部分条款的执行效力。

5. 鉴于公司需要为已经正式取得申请权的发明人的创造发明和所有权寻求转让，因此……

6. 任何目的都将不构成本合同任何一方为合伙人、合营公司或另一方的雇员的关系。

7. 货物所有权的转移并不影响货物与合同规定不符时甲方拒收货物的权利。

8. 本协议作为盖印文书，盖章后生效。

9. 本协议一方因违反本协议约定未能行使本协议规定的权利的，不得视为放弃了该权利。

10. 本协议可由当事人订立，副本不限。

II. Translate the following sentences into Chinese：

1. The Party B agrees that it will not at any time after the signature of this Agreement disclose any information in relation to the Company's method of manufacture or design or the Party B's method of distribution in relation to the Products.

2. The Recipient undertakes to disclose the Confidential Information furnished to it only to its employees who have a legitimate and absolute need to know the Confidential Information in order to perform their duties relating to the purpose set out herein.

3.The Recipient shall not disclose the Confidential Information to anyone other than its own employees without a prior consent from the Disclosing Party.

4.Failure of any Party to exercise its right or take any action against the other Party for any breach of Contract shall not be deemed as a waiver of such breach. No waiver of any Party to any right shall be deemed as a waiver to any other rights. Waiver of any Party to any of its right shall be sent to the other Party in writing.

5. Save and except expressly set out in this Agreement, each party acknowledge that no representation, warranty, or other promises not expressly contained herein have been made to the party by the other party.

6. The nondisclosure provisions of this Agreement shall survive the termination of this Agreement and Receiving Party's duty to hold Confidential Information in confidence shall remain in effect until the Confidential Information no longer qualifies as a trade secret or until Disclosing Party sends Receiving Party written notice releasing Receiving Party from this Agreement, whichever occurs first.

7. The Architect represents and guarantees that the work is free from defects and contains no matter that infringes any proprietary right at country laws.

8. "Confidential Information" means any and all data, reports, records, notes, compilation, studies and other information disclosed directly or indirectly by one Party to the other Party relating to or in any way connected with the Work, whether such information is disclosed orally, in writing, or by any other means.

9. Nothing contained in this Agreement shall be deemed to constitute either Party a partner, joint venture or employee of the other party for any purpose.

10.The invalidity, or what is not to be achieved as per the terms hereof, in whole or in part, of any term of this Agreement does not affect the validity of the remainder of the Agreement.

# 参考文献
# Bibliography

［1］许邦兴，等. 经济合同常用词汇［M］. 北京：外文出版社，1989.

［2］高同福，等. 英汉财贸词典［M］. 大连：东北财经大学出版社，1990.

［3］王仆，等. 英汉国际贸易合同术语词典［M］. 北京：中国商业出版社，1990.

［4］胡庚申，等. 国际商务合同起草与翻译［M］. 北京：外文出版社，2001.

［5］傅伟良. 对外经济合同英文写作［M］. 北京：石油工业出版社，2003.

［6］韦箫. 对外贸易最新合同范本［M］. 北京：经济管理出版社，2005.

［7］吴敏，等. 国际经贸英语合同写作［M］. 广州：暨南大学出版社，2005.

［8］罗进德. 法律文本与法律翻译［M］. 北京：中国对外翻译出版公司，2006.

［9］Calamari J C.The Law of Contracts ［M］. 3rd，ed.St.Paul：West Publishing Co.，1987.

［10］乔焕然. 英文合同阅读指南［M］. 北京：中国法制出版社，2008.

［11］葛亚军. 英文合同［M］. 天津：天津科技翻译出版公司，2008.

［12］范文祥. 英文合同阅读与分析技巧［M］. 北京：法律出版社，2007.

［13］刘川，王菲. 英文合同阅读与翻译［M］. 北京：国防工业出版社，2010.

# 单词索引
# Vocabulary Index